The Protection of Cultural Property in the Event of Armed Conflict

THE PROTECTION OF CULTURAL PROPERTY IN THE EVENT OF ARMED CONFLICT

Commentary on the Convention for the Protection of Cultural Property in the Event of Armed Conflict and its Protocol, signed on 14 May 1954 in The Hague, and on other instruments of international law concerning such protection

JIŘÍ TOMAN

Dartmouth

UNESCO
Publishing

Published by
Dartmouth Publishing Company Limited
Gower House
Croft Road
Aldershot
Hants GU11 3HR
England

Dartmouth Publishing Company
Old Post Road
Brookfield
Vermont 05036
USA

Published jointly with the United Nations
Educational, Scientific and Cultural Organization
7, place de Fontenoy, 75352, Paris 07 SP

British Library Cataloguing in Publication Data
Toman, Jiří ,
   Protection of cultural property in the event of armed
   conflict
   1. Cultural property, Protection of (International law)
   2. Art treasures in war
   I. Title   II. Unesco
   341.6'3

Library of Congress Cataloging-in-Publication Data
Toman, Jiří.
      The protection of cultural property in the event of armed conflict:
   commentary on the Convention for the Protection of Cultural
   Property in the event of Armed Conflict and its protocol, signed on
   14 May, 1954 in the Hague, and on other instruments of international
   law concerning such protection / Jiří Toman.
         p.   cm.
      Includes bibliographical references and index.
      ISBN 1-85521-793-7 (hardcover). — ISBN 1-85521-800-3 (pbk.)
      1. Convention for the Protection of Cultural Property in the Event
   of Armed Conflict (1954) 2. Cultural property, Protection of
   (International law)   I. Unesco.   II. Title.
   K3791.A4154A38   1996
   341.7'677—dc20   95–46953
                                                                                         CIP

Dartmouth ISBN 1 85521 793 7 Hbk
Dartmouth ISBN 1 85521 800 3 Pbk
UNESCO ISBN 92–3–102862–6

Typeset by Manton Typesetters, 5–7 Eastfield Road, Louth, Lincolnshire LN11 7AJ, UK.
Printed and bound in Great Britain by Biddles Limited, Guildford and King's Lynn.

Contents

Preface

War is the enemy of man. It is also the enemy of the best that man has made – art, culture, monuments and the whole cultural and historic heritage. Many works of art have been destroyed over the centuries, works that we have never known and that we shall never see again. In the course of 5000 years of history, some 14 000 wars have afflicted humanity, causing close on 5000 million deaths. In the twentieth century, two great world wars exceeded in volume and extent all the destruction that humanity had hitherto experienced. The conflicts that have followed these two wars have continued this work of destruction, and we have only to think of the Iran–Iraq War, the Gulf War, the destruction of the national library in Bucharest during the civil war in Romania and, on top of that, the devastation of the historic towns of Dubrovnik, Sarajevo and many others besides in the former Yugoslavia.

Confronted by the horrors of war, people have not stayed silent. Countless efforts have been made to do something about them. During the twentieth century, restrictions on recourse to warfare were introduced mainly by the Covenant of the League of Nations and Kellogg–Briand Pact, before war was outlawed by the Charter of the United Nations. Unhappily, prohibiting wars has not prevented them from breaking out in the world. Being unable to eliminate wars, people have thus attempted, throughout history, to mitigate their most destructive effects. This is how international humanitarian law came into being. Humanitarian law is part of international law and seeks to protect victims of war and regulate hostilities. Legal provisions thus came into being which were designed first of all to protect the life of individuals. Shaken by the experience of the Second World War, the international community adopted the 1949 Geneva Conventions to protect the victims of war such as the wounded, the sick, the shipwrecked, prisoners of war and the civilian population.

Codification of the protection of the cultural heritage, begun under the auspices of the League of Nations, fell after 1945 to UNESCO. From its very beginnings, UNESCO was given a special mandate in the application of standards relating to the protection of cultural property. This mandate was conferred on it by its Constitution, signed in London on 16 November 1945. Following the example of the Geneva Conventions, UNESCO took the initiative of convening the Intergovernmental Conference which adopted the Hague Convention in 1954. Adopting a convention is nevertheless not enough. It has to be applied. On the thirtieth anniversary of the Convention, UNESCO introduced a programme of action whose aim, among other things, was to produce a commentary on the 1954 Hague Convention, the Regulations for its execution and the related Protocol. This was also something that the States themselves wanted, as in the case of Switzerland when it presented its report on the application of the Convention in 1967 (*Information on the application of the Convention*, Paris, UNESCO, 1967, p.36). Those in charge of cultural property also called for it. Experts like Mr V. Elisseeff and Mr A. Noblecourt hoped that it could be used in order to smooth out a number of difficulties of interpretation and enlarge the number of States Parties to the Convention.

International organizations have sometimes been criticized for not being able to provide governments with information that could help in interpreting the provisions of treaties. In this connection, mention should be made of a study by UNITAR (*Towards Wider Acceptance of UN Treaties*, New York, ARNO Press, 1971, p.17) which emphasizes the importance of providing a suitable structure in order to make available to governments the instruments summarizing the work done preparatory to the drafting of the Convention, and the results of its application, in terms that non-specialists can understand, and providing an explanation of the content and aims of the treaties already concluded, particularly within the United Nations system. This Commentary attempts to provide a response to these requirements.

The general aim of this Commentary is to explain the provisions of the Convention signed in The Hague on 14 May 1954 concerning the protection of cultural property in the event of armed conflict, and those of the Regulations for its execution and the related Protocol. Implementation of the Convention by the High Contracting Parties should be made easier by a description of the historical development and origin of these texts, with examples of their application and suggestions as to practical steps which could be taken to put the provisions of these instruments into practice. The Commentary should also help to encourage States, which have not yet done so, to ratify or accede to these instruments.

The Commentary follows the arrangement of the Convention, article by article. It includes, as it goes along, the provisions of the Regulations for the Convention's execution in order to avoid repetition and to make clear, as quickly as possible, the way in which the

Convention can be applied. It is preceded by a short historical outline of the development of the protection of cultural property and by a description of the way in which the Convention was prepared (preparatory work).

To give substance to the explanation of the texts of the Convention, the Regulations for its execution and the Protocol, the author has made considerable use of the materials that emerged from the preparatory work for the 1954 Conference and from work done previously. He has also taken into account what has been written by legal and other experts in this field. Very special attention has also been devoted to the practical experience that has been accumulated during the 40 years for which the Convention has been in existence. The Commentary also makes use of the experience and development of legislation to be found in domains close to that of the Convention, such as the application of international humanitarian law. In addition, this book has been written in language which is easy to understand so that it can be read by everyone.

This work is the first of its kind where cultural property is concerned. As with anything new, it will certainly have its inadequacies. Anyone who has comments to make should communicate them to us and account will be taken of them if a revised edition is brought out at a later date.

We dedicate this Commentary to all those who, throughout the world, in peace as in war, and sometimes in peril of their lives, are unsparing in their efforts to safeguard the monuments of the past for future generations.

Acknowledgements

We would like to express our warm gratitude to UNESCO and particularly to Ms Lyndel V. Prott, Ms Anne Raidl, Ms Margaret Van Vliet, Ms Monique Couratier and Mr Etienne Clément, who encouraged us with their advice and their suggestions to write this voluminous work and to make it more readable. We are also grateful to Ms Sylvie Pierre who helped us to finalize the manuscript.

We should like, in addition, to thank the following for their patient work in connection with the translation of the text from French to English: Mr T.E. Burton, Mr Philip Cockle, Mr John Hargreaves and Mr Louis Janssens; also Ms Marilyn Farge (reviser), Mr Malachy Quinn (editor) and Ms Haydée Colmenares-Szepesi (documentalist and referencer).

The ideas and opinions expressed in this book are those of the author and do not necessarily represent the views of UNESCO or of any other institution with which the author is associated.

Editor's note
References in the present text to Byelorussian SSR, Czechoslovakia, Federal Republic of Germany, German Democratic Republic, Ukrainian SSR, USSR and Yugoslavia refer to those states prior to the changes of recent years.

Abbreviations

AJIL	*American Journal of International Law* (Washington, D.C.)
BYIL	*British Yearbook of International Law* (Oxford)
CDDH	Diplomatic Conference on the Reaffirmation and Development of International Humanitarian Law Applicable in Armed Conflicts, 1974–1977
Commentary	Refers to the present Commentary on the 1954 Hague Convention
Commentary to additional Protocols	Yves Sandoz, Christophe Swinarski, Bruno Zimmermann (eds), *Commentary on the Additional Protocols of 8 June 1977 to the Geneva Conventions of 12 August 1949*, Geneva, Martinus Nijhoff Publishers, 1987, 1625pp.
Conference	Conference convened by the United Nations Educational, Scientific and Cultural Organization and held at The Hague from 21 April to 14 May 1954
Convention	Convention for the Protection of Cultural Property in the Event of Armed Conflict, adopted at The Hague on 14 May 1954
ICCROM	International Centre for the Study of the Preservation and Restoration of Cultural Property
ICOM	International Council of Museums
ICOMOS	International Council on Monuments and Sites
ICRC	International Committee of the Red Cross
IRRC	*International Review of the Red Cross* (Geneva)
IUCN	International Union for Conservation of Nature and Natural Resources
PCIJ	Permanent Court of International Justice
Preliminary Draft Convention of 1938	Preliminary Draft of the International Convention for the Protection of Historic Buildings and Works of Art in Time of War. International Museum Office, 1938 (League of

	Nations, *Official Journal*, XIXth year, No. 11, November 1938)
Records	Intergovernmental Conference on the Protection of Cultural Property in the Event of Armed Conflict, *Records of the Conference convened by the United Nations Educational, Scientific and Cultural Organization and held at The Hague from 21 April to 14 May 1954*, published by the Government of the Netherlands, The Hague, Staatsdrukkerij en Uitgeverijbedrijf, 1961, 464 pp.
Regulations for execution	Regulations for the execution of the Convention for the Protection of Cultural Property in the Event of Armed Conflict, annexed to the Convention, adopted at The Hague on 14 May 1954
The Hague Convention	Convention for the Protection of Cultural Property in the Event of Armed Conflict, adopted at The Hague on 14 May 1954
UNDP	United Nations Development Programme
UNESCO Draft	CBC/3 – Text of the Draft Convention, the Regulations for its Execution and the Protocol which formed the basis of the discussions at the Hague Conference. See the *Records of the Conference convened by the United Nations Educational, Scientific and Cultural Organization and held at The Hague from 21 April to 14 May 1954*, published by the Government of the Netherlands
UNFICYP	United Nations Force in Cyprus

PART I
GENERAL INTRODUCTION

*'Manches Herrliche der Welt ist
in Krieg und Streit zerronnen;
wer beschützt und erhält,
hat das schönste Los gewonnen.''*
(Goethe)

Armed conflict, whether international or not, destroys people and property. Humanity has struggled against war and has made great efforts to reduce its most destructive effects, of which the loss of cultural property constitutes but an infinitesimal part.

We have no statistics about how many works of art were destroyed in centuries past. It scarcely needs recalling that these belonged to a heritage shared by all mankind. No military necessity ought to warrant their destruction, just as there can be no justification for attacking the civilian population.

Professor Stanislaw Nahlik, an eminent specialist in the protection of cultural property, described the relationships between the protection of individuals and cultural and historical property in the following way: 'The human individual is mortal and generations follow one upon the other. It is nevertheless possible for every generation, however fleeting its existence, to leave here below an immortal trace of its genius, embodied in a work of art here, an historical monument there or cultural property in another case. We should never forget the relationship between what is fleeting and what, alone, can endow people and their works with perennial qualities. *Vita brevis – Ars longa....*'[1]

HISTORICAL DEVELOPMENT OF THE RULES OF INTERNATIONAL LAW CONCERNING THE PROTECTION OF CULTURAL PROPERTY

Throughout history, war has gone hand in hand with widespread destruction and the 'right to booty'. War feeds on war. In antiquity, no rule prevented armed forces from devastating a country or from seizing the enemy's goods, the destruction of cultural property being then considered an inevitable consequence of war. The aim of war was booty. The general law had it that the property of the vanquished belonged to the conqueror: 'It is a universal and eternal law that, in a city captured by enemies in a state of war, everything, both persons and goods, shall belong to the conquerors.'[2]

3

Any opposition to practices of this kind was unusual. Respect for religious property and places was linked to their sacred nature and not to the artistic value of the temples and the property inside them. The Greek historian Polybius (202–120 BC) wrote: 'The city should not owe its beauty to embellishments brought from elsewhere but to the virtue of its inhabitants. ... Future conquerors should learn not to strip the towns that they subjugate and not to inflict misfortune on other peoples, the embellishment of their native land.' Elsewhere he says: 'The laws and the right of war oblige the victor to ruin and destroy fortresses, forts, towns, people, ships, resources and all other such like things belonging to the enemy in order to undermine his strength while increasing the victor's own. But although some advantage may be derived from that, no one can deny that to abandon oneself to the pointless destruction of temples, statues and other sacred objects is the action of a madman.'

The aim of warfare for the Romans was conquest, and conquest was accompanied by massacres, destruction and pillage. Regard was nevertheless often shown for sacred things out of respect of their hallowed nature. In addition, as pillage hindered the smooth conduct of military operations, voices were raised against pointless destruction: 'Ars servat patrum perpetuat populum'.[3] Cicero did not condemn war but tried to allot to it aims and rules in accordance with the law. He thus recommended moderation and selflessness in pillage, saying that it was not right for people to pillage for themselves but only to enrich or embellish their motherland.[4]

The situation in the Middle Ages was not very different. Towns, villages, castles and even churches were destroyed. How many of these would today be considered as artistic or cultural property! The Germanic armies and the Crusaders laid everything waste as they went. There was little consistency in the way the rules of chivalry were applied. The Church attempted to mitigate the consequences of war but did not forbid it, even though Saint Augustine had preached that the taking of booty was a sin. The Synod of Charroux (989) proclaimed that places of worship and property were protected but this was due to their sacred nature and not to their quality as works of art. To protect churches, the Germanic emperor, Frederick I (1152–94) promulgated an edict in 1158 by which he forbade pillage. This edict and other prohibitions issued at the same time were little heeded. On the contrary, rules and customs concerning the division of booty multiplied.

The first stirrings of a wish to protect works of art were to be seen at the Renaissance. In the sixteenth and seventeenth centuries, the first references to the protection of cultural property appeared among the writers on international law. Jacob Przyluski, for example, put forward the idea that every belligerent should show regard for a

work of art, but not solely because of its religious nature.[5] Alberic
and Justin Gentilis held similar ideas.[6] Hugo Grotius, the 'father of
international law', remained faithful to the old ideas: 'It is permitted
to harm an enemy both in his person and in his property; that is, it is
permissible not merely for him who wages war for a just cause, but
for either side indiscriminately.'[7] In this way, the burning of corn, the
destruction of houses and the plunder of men and cattle were licit:
'the law of nations in itself does not exempt things that are sacred,
that is, things dedicated to God or to the gods.[8] By the law of nations
... in a public war anyone at all becomes owner, without limit or
restriction, of what he has taken from the enemy.'[9]

Beginning with the Peace of Westphalia (1648), we find more and
more clauses providing for the restoration of things to their places of
origin, first of archives alone and then of works of art, displaced in
the course of the fighting.[10] In his famous work entitled *The Law of
Nations or the Principles of Natural Law*, Emmerich de Vattel writes
that 'for whatever cause a country be devastated, these buildings
should be spared which are an honour to the human race and which
do not add to the strength of the enemy, such as temples, tombs,
public buildings and all edifices of remarkable beauty. What is gained
by destroying them? It is the act of a declared enemy of the human
race thus wantonly to deprive men of these monuments of art and
models of architecture....'[11]

Influenced by the concept developed by Jean-Jacques Rousseau,[12]
there were possibly the beginnings of a distinction being made between public and private property. Public property belonging to the
enemy State – particularly property which could assist the conduct of
a war, such as arms, munitions, stores and public treasuries – could
be sequestrated, seized and destroyed. 'The military authority may,
within the limits of its power, seize the movable public property of
the enemy to the extent that it may serve for the operations of war.'[13]
A measure of protection was thus accorded to public property which
did not directly serve military interests. Regard was accordingly
shown for temples and churches, schools, libraries, collections and
laboratories. Again, in 1815, the allies provided for the restitution of
works of art taken to France by Napoleon because, in the words of a
memorandum circulated by Lord Castlereagh, the removal of works
of art was 'contrary to every principle of justice and to the usages of
modern warfare'.[14]

Such an approach was not foreign to other religions and civilizations in the world. The protection of cultural property is in fact
universal in nature. It is not the product of one single civilization;
quite the reverse. We find striking examples in all cultures, all religions and all political systems. In traditional and pre-colonial Africa,
there were innumerable sacred places (trees, ancestral huts, shrines

in which fetishes were kept, places where initiation ceremonies were held, and so on) that were all protected. There was therefore respect for places of a religious nature, of culture and art.[15] The peoples of Tallensi strictly forbade any kind of pillage which would confer personal advantage. (There are also opposite examples, since the Fulani of northern Nigeria destroyed ancient buildings on the grounds that they belonged to non-believers.) In Japan, Emperor Go-Daigo, in 1339, sent his army to put down a rebellion but he strictly forbade setting fire to shrines and temples.[16]

Under Islamic law, 'the obligation to distinguish between civilian and military objects is clearly imperative and permits no exception. Caliph Abu Bakr gave orders never to destroy palm trees, burn dwellings or cornfields, cut down fruit trees, kill livestock unless constrained by hunger, and never to lay hands on monasteries. Attacks should therefore be strictly confined to military targets, that is to objects which by their nature or use are intended for the pursuit of hostilities. The nature, use and intended purpose of the objects are the criteria for distinguishing between military and civilian objects. The Islamic concept presumes all objects to be civilian unless proved otherwise. This is obvious from the instructions and orders given by Abu Bakr. It is worth adding that under this concept all destruction is "ugly and blameworthy" and can be tolerated only in exceptional circumstances. The scope of application of the protection of civilian goods is wider under the Islamic concept than in the provisions of Chapters III *et seq.* of Part IV of the First Additional Protocol to the Geneva Conventions of 1949, for it is more precise, more general and more humanitarian; however, the stipulations, criteria and details enunciated in the provisions of Articles 52–60 and 62–65 of the First Additional Protocol are, of course, in perfect harmony with the very essence of the Islamic concept and can therefore be regarded as forming an integral part of it.'[17] This long quotation from a famous Egyptian lawyer shows that the protection of cultural property, as expressed in the Hague Convention of 1954, also corresponds to the Islamic tradition.

During the wars at the time of the French Revolution, the booty of war included *objets d'art* and scientific objects. There was thus, during that period, a return to the old customs of the sixteenth and seventeenth centuries, and those of the eighteenth century were abandoned. This was explained by the superiority of one of the belligerents, France, which, thanks to the Revolution, had reached a higher level of civilization and had thus become in some degree the intellectual centre of the human race. In the peace treaties that Bonaparte concluded with the Italian princes, it was stipulated that war reparations were payable partly in coin and partly in *objets d'art*. Care was therefore taken, at least sometimes, to legalize the operation by an ad hoc agreement and not in application of the right of warfare. Restitution was made in 1815 of some of the items received as booty, when the Duke of Wellington declared that these annexations had been contrary to the practice of war between civilized nations.

The Lieber Instructions (1863)

The 1863 instructions for the government of armies of the United States of America in the field, known after their author as the Lieber Instructions for the Government of Armies, had a great influence on the shaping and codification of the laws of war. They also provided an example for the codification, at the international level, of the law concerning cultural property. While recognizing, in Article 31, the appropriation of public money, Article 34 specifies that 'as a general rule, the property belonging to churches, to hospitals or other establishments of an exclusively charitable nature, to establishments of education, or foundations for the promotion of knowledge, whether public schools, universities, academies of learning or observatories, museums of the fine arts, or of a scientific character – such property is not to be considered public property in the sense of Article 31; but it may be taxed or used when the public service may require it.'[18] According to Article 35, 'classical works of art, libraries, scientific collections or precious instruments, such as astronomical telescopes, as well as hospitals, must be secured against all avoidable injury, even when they are contained in fortified places whilst besieged or bombarded'. Article 36 indicates: 'If such works of art, libraries, collections, or instruments belonging to a hostile nation or government, can be removed without injury, the ruler of the conquering state or nation may order them to be seized and removed for the benefit of the said nation. The ultimate ownership is to be settled by the ensuing treaty of peace. In no case shall they be sold or given away, if captured by the armies of the United States, nor shall they ever be privately appropriated, or wantonly destroyed or injured.' The Lieber Instructions also had repercussions on the development of military law in other countries, particularly on the service regulations for the field armies of France, Germany, Great Britain, Italy, Japan, Russia and Spain.[19]

The work by Jean-Gaspar Bluntschli entitled *Das moderne Völkerrecht der civilisierten Staaten als Rechtbuch dargestellt*, first published in 1868, summarizes this step-by-step evolution of the legal awareness of the need to protect cultural property.[20] In particular, Bluntschli states that 'the removal of items or documents of artistic value, although it was still the custom during the revolutionary wars at the start of this century, is already considered by public opinion to be an act of vandalism because *objets d'art* have no direct connection with the aims pursued by the State when it wages war but are the eternal monuments of the peaceful development of nations'.[21] Referring to the articles in the Lieber Instructions, Bluntschli says that 'it is the duty of a chief to forbid these acts of brutality and to prevent the pointless destruction of the noblest products of the human spirit. Pointless devastation is never excusable. Our century blushes at having witnessed, scarcely fifty years ago, soldiers hammering nails into frescoes, cutting pictures into shreds, mutilating statues and damaging monuments. Some people may have thought this principle too abstract and lacking in juridical force to be included in laws or regulations for armies. We can easily override that objection, however, since in seeking to spread this idea, we have the hope of perhaps preventing the destruction of some works of art. Despite all their logic, the jurisconsults would not be able to replace one single example of the masterpieces whose annihilation they have permitted.'[22]

At the same time, it was realized that, if certain property belonging to the public domain were safeguarded, protection was also quite naturally accorded to private property: 'The victor is no longer recognized as having the right to appropriate buildings belonging to the nationals of the enemy State. The equipment of enemy soldiers, their weapons and their horses may still be seized today because these objects can be considered as the means of waging war and their nature as private property here remains in the background. These things are used for waging war and are the victor's prize. To take from a conquered enemy his money or other objects of value, however, is considered an unworthy act, contrary to the laws of warfare of civilized nations.'[23] The Franco-Prussian War (1870–71) also roused public opinion, particularly when the cathedral and library in Strasbourg were destroyed.

Henry Dunant, the initiator and one of the founders of the Red Cross, was not unconcerned by the dangers threatening cultural property. In his manuscript, written towards the end of the last century, he gave a warning to future generations: 'Outdo each other in destroying the most beautiful masterpieces of which civilization is proud: palaces, castles, ports, docks, aqueducts, bridges, buildings and monuments of all kinds. But remember that this civilization which is now your pride will inevitably become, through your militarism, the prey to military blockheads, that very inferior part of the warrior caste, or, in other words, prey to omnipotent and tyrannical absolutism which will crush you in its turn, you and your national liberties, and with you your prosperity, your trade, your industry, your agriculture, your free institutions and your domestic happiness. This is where we are heading, slowly but inevitably, without wishing it, but inexorably. And we should add that, given just a little more time, man, thanks to science, will have such prodigious means of doing evil that it will not be possible to save him from himself, amidst frightful disasters, other than by divine intervention.'[24]

The Brussels Declaration (1874)

On the initiative of Henry Dunant, and with the assistance of the Emperor of Russia, the Brussels Conference, held from 27 July to 27 August 1874, adopted a project of an international Declaration concerning the laws and customs of war. The Declaration was not ratified but it nevertheless influenced the future codification of laws.

In Article 8, the Russian draft submitted to the 1874 Brussels Conference[25] contained the stipulation that: 'the property of municipalities, that of institutions dedicated to religion, charity and education, the arts and sciences, even when State property, shall be treated as private property. All seizure or destruction of, or wilful damage to, institutions of this character, historic monuments, works of art and science, should be made the subject of legal proceedings by the competent authorities.' This is the provision concerning occupied territories. Regarding the means of injuring the enemy, the draft permitted the seizure or destruction of everything needed by the enemy in order to wage war or of anything which could reinforce the enemy (Article 13 (g)). With regard to sieges and bombardments, it stated that 'if a town or fortress, agglomeration of dwellings, or village, is defended, the officer in command of an attacking force must, before commencing a bombardment' take all necessary steps 'to spare, as far as possible, buildings dedicated to art, science, or charitable purposes' (Articles 16 and 17).

The Brussels Conference expanded on this draft by adding to Article 16 (which became Article 17 in the final text of the Draft Declaration) 'the duty of the besieged to indicate the presence of such buildings by distinctive and visible signs to be communicated to the enemy beforehand'.[26] In the same article, the definition of protected property was modified by making reference to buildings dedicated to religion, art, science or charitable purposes. The aim of this was to meet the request of the Turkish delegate to cover non-Christian religious buildings (mosques, Islamic establishments, synagogues). A similar modification was made to Article 8.

The Oxford Manual of the Institute of International Law (1880)

As part of the process of the development of rules concerning the protection of cultural property in time of war, mention must also be made of the Manual of the Institute of International Law, entitled *The Laws and Customs of War on Land*, adopted at the session held in Oxford in 1880, which repeated almost word for word the relevant standards laid down in this area by the Brussels Declaration.[27] The Oxford Manual laid down that offenders against the rules contained in it were liable to the punishments specified in the penal law (Article 84).

The International Peace Conferences (1899 and 1907)

The two international peace conferences held in 1899 and 1907 nevertheless played a particularly pioneering role in the development of the protection of cultural property in time of war. This was especially true of Conventions Nos IV and IX of 1907. The protection of cultural property is covered by these Conventions first of all by provisions relating to the protection of civilian property in general (especially by Articles 23(g), 25, 28 and 47 of the Hague Regulations) as well as by special provisions concerning cultural property.

The Regulations of 1907, annexed to Convention No. IV, and in particular Articles 27 and 56, deal with cultural property. The importance of these rules was reinforced still further by the assertion of the Nuremberg International Military Tribunal that, by 1939, they were rules 'recognized by all civilized nations and were regarded as being declaratory of the laws and customs of war'.[28] Article 27, in the Section on Hostilities (Chapter 1 on Means of Injuring the Enemy, Sieges and Bombardments), states:

> In sieges and bombardments all necessary steps must be taken to spare, as afar as possible, buildings dedicated to religion, art, science, or charitable purposes, historic monuments, hospitals, and places where the sick and wounded are collected, provided they are not being used at the same time for military purposes.
>
> It is the duty of the besieged to indicate the presence of such buildings or places by distinctive and visible signs, which shall be notified to the enemy beforehand.

In this article the protection accorded is not absolute but limited by a reservation of military necessity expressed by the words 'as far as possible'. The same reservation is to be found in Article 5 of Convention No. IX but not in Article 56 of the Hague Regulations. Such protection, moreover, is territorially restricted to the immediate zone of combat. The commanders of the besieging forces are required to take such protective measures only if the besieged comply with the following two prescriptions: (1) not to use such buildings for military purposes; and (2) to indicate them by distinctive and visible signs. To ensure the effectiveness of this measure, the signs must be notified to the besieging forces beforehand. The expression 'buildings dedicated to religions' covers the buildings of all religious persuasions, both Christian and non-Christian, churches, places of worship, mosques, synagogues and so forth. It was introduced at the request of the Turkish delegate (to replace the word 'churches') at the Brussels Conference.

Article 56, under Section III on occupied territories, entitled 'Military authority over the territory of the hostile State', reads:

> The property of municipalities, that of institutions dedicated to religion, charity and education, the arts and sciences, even when State property, shall be treated as private property.
>
> All seizure of, destruction or wilful damage done to institutions of this character, historic monuments, works of art and science, is forbidden, and should be made the subject of legal proceedings.

This article rounds off Articles 53 and 55 by limiting, with respect to certain property and in the public interest, the authority of the occupying power. Article 53 deals with property and objects seized by the army of occupation. It has two parts, one concerning the State and the other concerning companies and private individuals. The first paragraph of Article 53 allows the seizure of movable property belonging to the occupied State. The second paragraph recognizes the right of the occupying force to seize objects that may be used for hostile purposes. Article 55 deals with the immovable property of the occupied State.

Article 56 applies to the following categories of property: (a) the property of municipalities; (b) institutions dedicated to religion, charity and education, the arts and sciences; (c) historic monuments; and (d) works of art and science. In the provisions applicable to property in categories (b), (c) and (d), no distinction is made between that belonging to private individuals, public administrations or even the State. The property referred to in the first paragraph is treated as private property and is therefore liable to requisition. Categories (b), (c) and (d) are given greater protection by the prohibition of 'all seizure of, destruction or wilful damage' and the provision that the authors of such acts should be made the subject of legal proceedings. The term 'institutions dedicated to religion' applies, as in the case of Article 27, to the buildings of all religions without exception – churches, places of worship, mosques, synagogues and so forth. This protection is absolute, without any reservations on the grounds of military or other necessity.

Mention should also be made of Article 5 of the Hague Convention of 1907 (No. IX) respecting bombardment by naval forces. The article in the chapter devoted to general provisions states that:

In bombardments by naval forces all the necessary measures must be taken by the commander to spare as far as possible sacred edifices, buildings used for artistic, scientific, or charitable purposes, historic

Emblem marking protected sites in case of naval bombardment

The Hague Convention No. IX of 18 October 1907 respecting bombardment by naval forces in time of war protects places where the sick and wounded are collected, hospitals, buildings devoted to religion, charitable purposes, art and science, and historic monuments. Under the Convention, it is the duty of the inhabitants to indicate such protected places by visible signs in the form of large, stiff rectangular panels divided diagonally into two coloured triangular portions, the upper one black and the lower one white.

To ensure visibility from a distance the panels must be very large; their effectiveness depends on the conditions of visibility and on the possibility of identifying them from positions at sea (Article 5 of the Hague Convention No. IX of 1907).

monuments, hospitals, and places where the sick and wounded are collected, on the understanding that they are not used at the same time for military purposes.

It is the duty of the inhabitants to indicate such monuments, edifices, or places by visible signs, which shall consist of large, stiff rectangular panels divided diagonally into two coloured triangular portions, the upper portion black, the lower portion white.

In this article, again, the protection is not absolute. It is limited by a reservation of military necessity – 'as far as possible'. The same reservation is to be found in Article 27 of the Hague Regulations but not in Article 56. The provisions of the Hague Conventions are not detailed and do not give a precise definition of the objects to be protected. Protected property is listed by its nature or its purpose. Article 27 of the Regulations affords protection against hostile acts solely to immovable property. Article 56, relating to seizure and destruction, extends the protection to movable property.

The system of protection thus established was based on the distinction between defended and non-defended places, and more particularly on the protection of certain buildings not used for military purposes. In Convention No. IX one exception was made with respect to naval bombardment but not for land or air bombardment. The provisions of the Hague Convention are still in force and are generally considered part of customary international law. The 1954 Convention, moreover, explicitly refers to earlier rules. Lastly, despite the highly specific protection of cultural property formulated in the Hague Convention of 1954, not all the problems were overcome. In such cases other international conventions and customary law remain applicable. These rules form part of international law and the Hague Convention must, when being applied, take account of such earlier rules. Taken together with those rules, therefore, the Hague Convention of 1954 forms a comprehensive code for the international protection of the cultural heritage of mankind.[29]

The Oxford Manual of the Institute of International Law (1913)

On 9 August 1913, the Institute of International Law gave its approval to a manual similar to the one brought out in 1880 but concerning naval warfare. Article 28 of this manual reproduces the exact wording of Article 5 of the Hague Convention No. IX of 1907 respecting the bombardment of terrestrial objectives by naval forces.

The First World War

At the time of the First World War the provisions were too succinct to afford effective protection. Moreover, the extent of the theatre of operations made real protection impossible because firing techniques were not sufficiently accurate at the time to guarantee the protection of specific buildings.

During that war, especially after the destruction of Rheims, Louvain and Arras, increasing efforts were made to strengthen the protection of cultural property. Mr Vetter of Berne and Mr Mauriaud of Geneva suggested, during a public gathering in Geneva in April 1915, the setting up of an international body called 'La Croix d'Or' (the 'Gold Cross'). The idea, clearly inspired by the Red Cross, took root. A conference convened in Brussels in August 1915, which was attended by representatives of Germany, Austria–Hungary and Switzerland, drew up the broad lines of a convention. The failure of this conference led the Dutch Archaeological Society (Nederlandsche Oudleidhundige Bond) to propose to the Queen of the Netherlands, in April 1918, the convening of an international conference on the protection of historic and artistic monuments and objects against the dangers of war. On 31 October 1918, Mr Van Eysinga submitted a report to the Ministry for Foreign Affairs which, in 1919, was forwarded to foreign cultural organizations.

The project of the Dutch society had no more success than the preceding plan but it had undeniable influence on two other proposals put forward at the end of the First World War. A Preliminary Conference to the Treaty of Versailles had considered punishing those responsible for violations of Hague Conventions. The Commission on Responsibility for War and Guarantees, set up in January 1919, collected evidence concerning attacks against cultural property.

The Hague Rules Concerning the Control of Radio in Time of War and Air Warfare (1922)

The Washington Conference of 1922 on the Limitation of Armaments adopted a resolution (4 February 1922) recommending the appointment of a Commission of Jurists charged with the preparation of rules relating to the use of radio in time of war and to air warfare. The Commission was to examine whether the existing principles of international law were still sufficient, having regard to the methods of attack or defence introduced and developed since the second International Peace Conference in 1907. The Commission, presided over by John Bassett Moore, was composed of representatives of France, Italy, Japan, the Netherlands, the United Kingdom and the United

States of America. It was to report its conclusions to each of the governments of the six countries. It met from December 1922 to February 1923 at The Hague, and prepared rules for the control of radio in time of war (Part I of the Commission's report) and rules of air warfare (Part II). Although these rules were never adopted in legally binding form, they were of importance 'as an authoritative attempt to clarify and formulate rules of law governing the use of aircraft in war'.[30] The rules drawn up by this Commission were simply recommendations, but they corresponded to a large extent to the customary rules and general principles derived from conventions on the law of war on land and at sea. Although they never came into force they exerted a great influence on future developments.[31]

In fact, these rules made a distinction for the first time between *general protection* (identical to that contained in Article 27 of the Hague Regulations) and *special protection*. What is more, they abandoned the criterion of 'defence' and replaced it with a new approach concerning the military objective. Articles 25 and 26 added certain principles according to which more effective protection must be given to monuments of great historic value.

Article 25

In bombardment by aircraft, all necessary steps must be taken by the commander to spare as far as possible buildings dedicated to public worship, art, science, or charitable purposes, historic monuments, hospital ships, hospitals and other places where the sick and wounded are collected, provided such buildings, objects or places are not at the time used for military purposes. Such buildings, objects and places must by day be indicated by marks visible to aircraft. The use of marks to indicate other buildings, objects, or places than those specified above is to be deemed an act of perfidy. The marks used as aforesaid shall be in the case of buildings protected under the Geneva Convention the red cross on a white ground, and in the case of other protected buildings a large rectangular panel divided diagonally into two pointed triangular portions, one black and the other white.

A belligerent who desires to secure by night the protection for the hospitals and other privileged buildings above mentioned must take the necessary measures to render the special signs referred to sufficiently visible.

Article 26

The following special rules are adopted for the purpose of enabling states to obtain more efficient protection for important historic monuments situated within their territory, provided that they are willing to refrain from the use of such monuments and a surrounding zone for military purposes, and to accept a special regime for their inspection.

1   A state shall be entitled, if it sees fit, to establish a zone of protection round such monuments situated in its territory. Such zones shall in time of war enjoy immunity from bombardment.
2   The monuments round which a zone is to be established shall be notified to other Powers in peace time through the diplomatic channel; the notification shall also indicate the limits of the zones. The notification may not be withdrawn in time of war.
3   The zone of protection may include, in addition to the area actually occupied by the monument or group of monuments, an outer zone, not exceeding 500 metres in width, measured from the circumference of the said area.
4   Marks clearly visible from aircraft either by day or by night will be employed for the purpose of ensuring the identification by belligerent airmen of the limits of the zones.
5   The marks on the monuments themselves will be those defined in Article 25. The marks employed for indicating the surrounding zones will be fixed by each state adopting the provisions of this article, and will be notified to other Powers at the same time as the monuments and zones are notified.
6   Any abusive use of the marks indicating the zones referred to in paragraph 5 will be regarded as an act of perfidy.
7   A state adopting the provisions of this article must abstain from using the monument and the surrounding zone for military purposes, or for the benefit in any way whatever of its military organization, or from committing within such monument or zone any act with a military purpose in view.
8   An inspection committee consisting of three neutral representatives accredited to the state adopting the provisions of this article, or their delegates, shall be appointed for the purpose of ensuring that no violation is committed of the provisions of paragraph 7. One of the members of the committee of inspection shall be the representative (or his delegate) of the state to which has been entrusted the interests of the opposing belligerent.

The Roerich Pact (1935)

Following the suggestion of Professor Nicholas Roerich, the Roerich Museum of New York asked Mr Georges Chklaver of the Institut des Hautes Etudes Internationales, University of Paris, to prepare a draft convention. This draft was discussed by the International Museums Office of the League of Nations. Private conferences held at Bruges in 1931 and 1932 and at Washington in 1933 recommended its adoption by governments. In 1933, the seventh International Conference of American States also recommended the signature of the Roerich Pact.

The final text of the Treaty was then drawn up by the Governing Board of the Pan-American Union and signed on 15 April 1935.[32] It

Emblem of the Roerich Pact of 1935 for the protection of cultural property

This Pact, signed in Washington on 15 April 1935, has been ratified by numerous States in North and South America and is still in force.
The flag – a red circle enclosing three small red spheres on a white background – has the same meaning as the blue and white emblem of the 1954 Hague Convention. The effectiveness of this flag at great distances depends on the conditions of visibility and on the possibility of perceiving its red surfaces.

came into force on 26 August 1935 and is now binding on 11 States of the Western hemisphere, including the United States of America. Under the Treaty of Washington, which applies both in time of war and in peacetime:

> the following immovable objects must be respected and protected: historic monuments, museums, scientific, artistic, educational and cultural institutions, which are considered as 'neutral';[33] movable objects are protected only when they are located in protected buildings;
>
> the same protection is accorded to the personnel of such institutions;
>
> the principle of territoriality applies throughout the territory subject to the sovereignty of each Signatory State;
>
> measures of internal legislation should be adopted;
>
> a distinctive flag (red circle with triple red spheres in the circle) may be displayed;
>
> a list of monuments and institutions for which the Signatory States desire protection must be registered with the Pan-American Union;
>
> cultural property will not be protected if use is made of it for military purposes.

It is important to stress that no other condition is mentioned in this treaty, not even the condition of military necessity.

Codification Under the Auspices of the League of Nations

During this period a little progress was made at the international level. The Conference of Athens, convened in 1931 at the initiative of the International Museums Office, recommended that the public be educated in their duty to respect cultural property in time of war. But the Directors' Committee of the Office, meeting on 6 and 7 December 1933 and basing itself on the opinion expressed by the League of Nations, asserted that 'it could in no circumstances give its support to an action of this kind, which it deems both impossible to apply and undesirable in principle'.

It was the Spanish Civil War[34] that made the Office realize the ambiguous nature of its measures. The Sixth Committee of the Assembly of the League of Nations re-examined the problem. The Directors' Committee of the International Museums Office called in Professor Charles de Visscher to prepare a preliminary report. A

Committee of Experts (composed of Mr Gouffre de Lapradelle, Mr N. Politis, Mr Charles de Visscher, Mr F. Moineville and Mr G.J. Sas), convened by the Office in Paris, produced a Preliminary Draft International Convention for the Protection of Historic Buildings and Works of Art in Time of War,[35] which proved extremely useful when the draft of the 1954 Convention was being prepared.

The 'Preliminary Draft' sought to reconcile the exigencies of war with the maximum degree of safety for threatened monuments and works of art. This shows that account was taken both of military necessity and of the requirements of protection. The Committee even stated that it had 'carefully refrained from proposing any rules or measures which would prove inoperative or inapplicable when the time came. It preferred to confine itself to what seemed feasible in practice, rather than aim at a higher mark and a more complete programme which would inevitably involve breaches of the projected international convention.'[36] The draft was based on several fundamental principles: organization and preparation of defence in time of peace; education of troops; the undertaking to introduce into military regulations and instructions recommendations to ensure respect; the undertaking to take steps to punish looting or depredation. With respect to movable property the draft introduced the idea of establishing refuges.

In this connection, it will be recalled that in this draft monuments and works of art were not protected as the national heritage but as the universal heritage to be safeguarded for the benefit of mankind as a whole. The Committee also incorporated a new idea by demonstrating, from the military standpoint, that no purpose was served by the destruction of cultural property. As regards the structure of the Convention, it should be noted that the text was accompanied by Regulations for its Execution. This idea was retained for the 1954 Convention. The draft Convention prepared by the International Museums Office was submitted to the Council and Assembly of the League of Nations during the autumn 1938 session. The Assembly accepted the offer of the Government of the Netherlands to convene a diplomatic conference.[37] But it was too late. War broke out in 1939.

The International Museums Office tried to cope with the new situation by suggesting that the States adopt a declaration of principle. A Project of a Declaration consisting of ten articles was therefore prepared.[38] After making a few changes to the text of the Declaration, the governments of Belgium and the Netherlands had decided to adopt the project when the military events of May 1940 occurred, which were to bring the two countries into the war.

The Second World War

The Second World War was an absolute shock since, as confirmed in a great many works, a vast amount of cultural property was utterly destroyed. Only the provisions of the Hague Conventions of 1907 on the subject were applicable, but they were scarcely applied.

At the beginning of the war, on 3 September 1939, the British and French governments made a solemn and public declaration that in case of war they would conduct hostilities while safeguarding the civilian population and protecting by all possible means the monuments which bore witness to human genius.[39] The studies that had been conducted after the First World War had an influence on governments, which adopted certain protective measures. The United States of America set up the 'American Commission for the protection and salvation of artistic and historic monuments in war areas' and a special corps of officers known as the 'Monuments, Fine Arts and Archives Officers'. Two Orders issued by the Commander-in-Chief of the Allied Forces, General Eisenhower, contain specific instructions for the safeguarding of cultural property. These instructions develop the doctrine according to which it is the duty of each commander to respect and spare, as far as possible and taking account of the supreme necessity to spare the lives of combatants, the cultural heritage of the countries in which the fighting takes place since that heritage symbolizes the civilization in defence of which the allies had taken up their arms.[40]

The Inter-Allied Declaration of London of 5 January 1943, signed by 18 powers, condemned the plundering committed in occupied territories and 'reserved all their rights to declare invalid any transfers of, or dealings with, property, rights and interests of any description whatsoever which are, or have been, situated in the territories which have come under the occupation or control, direct or indirect, of the governments with which they are at war, or which belong, or have belonged, to persons (including juridicial persons) resident in such territories. This warning applies whether such transfers or dealings have taken the form of open looting or plunder, or of transactions apparently legal in form, even when they purport to be voluntarily effected .'

The Armistice Agreements following the First World War provided for the restitution 'within the periods indicated by the Allied High Command ... and in complete good order of all valuables and materials removed ... during the war, belonging to State, public and co-operative organizations, enterprises, institutions or individual citizens such as: ... historic monuments, museum valuables ...'.[41] The peace treaties concluded after the Second World War contained clauses of the same kind. The International Military Tribunal at Nuremberg took account in its judgement of the massive seizure of works of art, furniture, textiles and other objects of a similar nature: 'During the period from March 1941 to July 1944 the special staff for Pictorial Art brought into the Reich 29 large shipments, including 137 freight cars with 4,174 cases of art works.' All this was done for the 'strengthening of Germanism'.[42]

The atrocities committed during the war prompted a firm resolve to avoid this type of horror in future. The fact that war had been outlawed by the Charter of the United Nations, the adoption of the Universal Declaration of Human Rights and the adoption of the Genocide Convention and of the Geneva Conventions of 12 August 1949 show how the international community reacted to the great worldwide conflict of 1939–45. The 1954 Hague Convention is set against this historical background and can be seen to illustrate this broad humanitarian movement.

The Geneva Conventions of 1949, and in particular the IVth Geneva Convention relative to the protection of civilian persons in time of war, have no specific provision for the protection of cultural property, but reinforced already existing provisions of customary international law and The Hague Conventions of 1899 and 1907 on civilian population and civilian property. Article 53 of the Fourth Geneva Convention says:

Any destruction by the Occupying Power of real and personal property belonging individually or collectively to private persons, or to the State, or to other public authorities, or to social or co-operative organizations, is prohibited, except where such destruction is rendered absolutely necessary by military operations.

As we shall see in all this text of the Commentary of the 1954 Hague Convention, the 1949 Geneva Conventions exercised fundamental influence in the drafting of the Hague Convention, which many called the 'Red Cross Charter for cultural property'.

INTERGOVERNMENTAL CONFERENCE ON THE PROTECTION OF CULTURAL PROPERTY IN THE EVENT OF ARMED CONFLICT, HELD IN THE HAGUE FROM 21 APRIL TO 14 MAY 1954

Preparation of the Conference of The Hague

The destruction of numerous historic monuments during the Second World War and the weakness of legal procedures for the protection of cultural property were the reasons for the initiative taken to improve such protection immediately after 1945. UNESCO, which, under its Constitution, was given responsibility for the preservation of the cultural heritage of humanity, was the most appropriate forum for the accomplishment of this task.

On the initiative of the Netherlands, the General Conference of UNESCO, at its fourth session (Paris 1949), adopted resolution 6.42, which drew attention to the protection of 'all objects of cultural value'. To follow up this resolution the Secretariat undertook a new study of the problem in cooperation with technical and legal experts and in consultation with the International Council of Museums (ICOM). The findings of this study were submitted in a report[43] which was discussed at the fifth session of the General Conference held in Florence in 1950. There the Italian delegation presented the draft version of an international convention based on the 1938 project of the International Museums Office. The Director-General was authorized by resolution 4.44 to prepare and submit to Member States a draft for an international convention. This draft was sent to Member States (CL/484, March 1951) and the replies received from governments were submitted to the General Conference at its sixth session in Paris in 1951 (6C/PRG/22). The International Committee on Monuments, Artistic and Historical Sites and Archaeological Excavations revised the draft and added the Regulations for its Execution (ODG/2, pp.12 *et seq.*).

Once again the draft was submitted to governments (CL/561/An.1) and revised by the UNESCO Secretariat in the light of their comments and suggestions (CL/656/Annex). The new version was examined by a Committee of Governmental Experts representing 23 Member States, whose work led to the preparation of three separate documents: a commentary, a draft Convention and draft Regulations for its Execution. On 10 September 1952, these three documents were submitted to the General Conference of UNESCO at its seventh session (7C/PRG/7).

The Programme Commission of the General Conference set up a working group, which prepared two reports. The working group proposed certain amendments to the drafts, in particular the deletion from the text of the Convention of the provisions concerning the restitution of cultural property having changed hands during an occupation, which would form the subject of an appended protocol.

In accordance with the decision taken at the General Conference, the Director-General of UNESCO communicated the text of the draft international convention to Member States in a circular letter (CL/717). The replies received up to 15 January 1954 were reproduced in document CBC/4 and analysed in document CBC/5.

UNESCO accepted the offer of the Dutch government to host an Intergovernmental Conference, which was convened at The Hague in April–May 1954.[44]

1954 Conference of The Hague: Procedure and Decisions, Proceedings of the Conference

The Conference of The Hague met from 21 April to 14 May 1954 and was attended by the representatives of 56 States. The proceedings began with a solemn meeting at the Peace Palace in the audience chamber of the International Court of Justice. After the opening addresses, the President of the Conference was elected in the person of Mr Schurmann, Head of the Netherlands Delegation and Chief of the Permanent Mission of the Netherlands to the United Nations.

Following adoption of the report of the Credentials Committee and the Rules of Procedure of the Conference[45] and after a general discussion of the drafts, the Conference proceeded to examine the draft Convention. This was done within the framework of the Main Commission, which made a detailed examination of the preliminary draft of the Convention and its appended instruments. It prepared a final draft, which was submitted to a plenary meeting of the Conference. The President and Rapporteur-General of the Conference served respectively as President and Rapporteur-General of the Main Commission. The proceedings were directed by the Bureau of the Conference. A Drafting Committee was given the task of putting the final touches to the Convention and its appended instruments. Numerous questions were resolved in two committees, the working group and the legal committee.

The final meeting of the Conference took place on 14 May 1954 in Ridderzaal. Thirty-seven States signed the Final Act of the Intergovernmental Conference on the Protection of Cultural Property in the Event of Armed Conflict and the Convention for the Protection of Cultural Property in the Event of Armed Conflict.

As in all instances of codification in the area of international humanitarian law, the aim was to maintain a balance between humanitarian and military requirements. In the Convention adopted at the Conference in The Hague numerous concessions were made to exigencies of a military nature. The Netherlands Minister of Public Instruction, Arts and Science even considered that the law, supported by the views of the various High Commands and military experts, had been more conservative than 'prudent moderation' demanded.[46]

It is as well to emphasize that the Convention applied only to situations in which conventional weapons could be used.[47] Both the Conference and the Convention accordingly followed the same approach as the other conferences on international humanitarian law in which the issue of weapons of mass destruction, such as nuclear weapons, was left on one side. There can be no doubt that The Hague Convention of 14 May 1954 for the Protection of Cultural Property in the Event of Armed Conflict, the Regulations for its Execution, which form an integral part of it, and the Protocol of The Hague of 14 May 1954 for the Protection of Cultural Property in the Event of Armed Conflict[48] constitute the most important instruments for the protection of cultural property in contemporary international law. They form a true code for cultural property.

The Convention is based on the idea that the preservation of the cultural heritage is not only a matter for the State on whose territory it is located but 'is of great importance for all peoples of the world and that it is important that this heritage should receive international protection'. The concern for such protection thus transcends the borders of a single State and becomes a matter of international importance. To be effective, such protection must be organized in time of peace by means of both national and international measures.

The adoption of the Convention is also important because it concentrates all the provisions relating to the protection of cultural property in a single instrument, or rather two instruments, whereas in the past such provisions had been scattered among several legal instruments. The Hague Convention is also based on the equitable balance of commitments between all the parties to a conflict. It is not limited to wartime but commits all the High Contracting Parties to take action in time of peace.

DEVELOPMENTS IN THE PROTECTION OF CULTURAL PROPERTY SINCE THE HAGUE CONVENTION

The codification of rules concerning the protection of cultural property in time of war did not come to a halt with the adoption of The Hague Convention and Protocol. We have already mentioned certain gaps in the previous codification and the fact that the Convention remained limited to a relatively small number of States. During the period following the adoption of the 1954 Convention and Protocol the codification of rules for the protection of cultural property in time of armed conflict involved two different courses of action. The first concerned the codification of rules relating to culture, a task carried out chiefly by UNESCO; in the other, the process became linked with the reaffirmation and development of international humanitarian law, initiated chiefly by the International Committee of the Red Cross.

Codification Within the Framework of UNESCO

The Constitution of the United Nations Educational, Scientific and Cultural Organization, signed in London on 16 November 1945,[49] defined one of its purposes as 'assuring the conservation and protection of the world's inheritance of books, works of art and monuments of history and science, and recommending to the nations concerned the necessary international conventions'.

UNESCO has adopted numerous recommendations in carrying out this task, some of which are of great importance in the case of situations of conflict. It has also adopted two conventions which have had a considerable impact on the protection of cultural property in a time of armed conflict:

1   The first such instrument is the Convention on the Means of Prohibiting and Preventing the Illicit Import, Export and Transfer of Ownership of Cultural Property, adopted by the General Conference at its sixteenth session in Paris on 14 November 1970.[50] This Convention represented a decisive advance in the international campaign against illicit traffic in cultural property. Even though the idea of a convention of this kind had long existed, work on its preparation began only in the 1960s. The Convention seeks to protect movable cultural property chiefly in time of peace but it also contains some important provisions in the event of armed conflict.[51]

2   The second instrument is the Convention for the Protection of the World Cultural and Natural Heritage, adopted by the General Conference at its seventeenth session in Paris on 16 November 1972.[52] Although this Convention is not primarily intended for the protection of the cultural heritage in time of war, such protection is included. In the Preamble to the Convention, the General Conference of UNESCO notes that 'the cultural heritage and the natural heritage are increasingly threatened with destruction not only by the traditional causes of decay [which – in our view – probably include international and non-international armed conflicts] but also by changing social and economic conditions which aggravate the situation with even more formidable phenomena of damage or destruction'.[53]

UNESCO has also made noteworthy efforts to implement the 1954 Convention and Protocol to which we shall refer in the body of this Commentary. Among other things, it has published periodical reports, the most recent of which was issued in 1989. In 1983, it convened a meeting of legal experts to consider the role of UNESCO in the implementation of the Convention (CLT-83/CONF.641/1). A programme of action was also prepared which included a recommendation for the publication of a commentary on the Convention. The publication of this present Commentary forms part of UNESCO's efforts to improve the protection of cultural property in the event of armed conflict.

Additional Protocols of 1977

The international humanitarian law applicable in armed conflicts was defined by the International Committee of the Red Cross as the set of 'international rules, established by treaties or custom, which are specifically intended to solve humanitarian problems directly arising from international or non-international armed conflicts and which, for humanitarian reasons, limit the right of parties to a conflict to use the methods and means of warfare of their choice or protect persons and property that are, or may be, affected by conflict'. Cultural property is, then, also covered by this protection.

Since The Hague Conventions of 1899 and 1907, the protection of cultural property was not included in the Geneva Conventions of 1864, 1906, 1929 and 1949. However, the situation changed with the reaffirmation and development of international humanitarian law that began at the end of the 1960s. The development of humanitarian law resulted from the activities of the International Committee of the Red Cross which had been the originator and mainspring of the Geneva Conventions ever since its foundation.

The Diplomatic Conference on the Reaffirmation and Development of International Humanitarian Law Applicable in Armed Conflicts (Geneva, 1974–77) adopted two Additional Protocols, each of which contained an article relating to the protection of cultural property. These articles were proposed by the Greek delegate and included in the text of the Protocols.[54] The Diplomatic Conference also adopted a resolution 'urging' States which had not yet done so to become Parties to the 1954 Convention.[55]

The 1980 Convention on Conventional Weapons

The present Commentary would be incomplete if it did not take account of events since the reaffirmation and development of international humanitarian law. Mention should be made in particular of new measures concerning the use of certain conventional weapons, considering that prohibitions or restrictions on the use of certain conventional weapons may be deemed to be excessively injurious or to have indiscriminate effects. The need to prepare further international conventions of a humanitarian nature or other appropriate legal instruments to prohibit or restrict the use of certain methods and means of warfare was stressed in the resolutions of the XXth International Red Cross Conference in 1965[56] and by the International Conference on Human Rights of 1968[57] as well as by resolution 2444/XXIII of the United Nations General Assembly in 1968.[58] At the conferences of governmental experts convened by the International Committee of the Red Cross in 1971 and 1972 with a view to preparing the 1977 Protocols Additional to the Geneva Conventions and at the Diplomatic Conference of 1974–77, the prevailing opinion was that an attempt should be made to work towards an agreement on conventional weapons, leaving to one side the weapons of mass destruction. The ICRC, encouraged by the Diplomatic Conference on the Reaffirmation and Development of International Humanitarian Law Applicable in Armed Conflicts, convened two conferences of governmental experts on the use of certain conventional weapons, which were held at Lucerne in 1974 and at Lugano in 1976. On 9 June 1977, the Diplomatic Conference adopted resolution 22(IV)[59] which recommended the convening of a conference of governments not later than 1979 with a view to reaching agreements on the prohibition or restriction of the use of specific conventional weapons. The United Nations General Assembly took note of this recommendation and the Conference was held in Geneva from 10 to 28 September 1979 and from 15 September to 10 October 1980. On 10 October 1980, the Conference adopted the Convention and the three Protocols appended thereto.[60] The Convention on Prohibitions or Restrictions on the Use of Certain Conventional Weapons Which May be Deemed to be Excessively Injurious or to have Indiscriminate Effects was opened for signature on 10 April 1981.

This Convention is simply a general introductory document which rounds off the whole: that is, the three Protocols; it contains only general provisions and no provisions that directly prohibit the use of certain specific weapons. The provisions on the prohibitions or restrictions on the use of particular weapons are to be found in the Protocols appended to the Convention, namely Protocol on Non-Detectable Fragments (Protocol I), Protocol on Prohibitions or Restrictions on the Use of Mines, Booby-Traps and Other Devices (Protocol II), Protocol on Prohibitions or Restrictions on the Use of Incendiary Weapons (Protocol III).

Under the Convention, expressions of consent to be bound by any of the Protocols annexed to it are optional for each State, provided that, at the time of the deposit of its instrument of ratification, acceptance or approval of the Convention or of accession thereto, that State notifies the Depository of its consent to be bound by any two or more of these Protocols (Article 4, paragraph 3, of the Convention). Where the protection of cultural property is concerned, particular note should be taken of Protocols II and III.

Protocol II on Prohibitions or Restrictions on the Use of Mines, Booby-traps and Other Devices (subparagraph to the 1980 Convention)

Article 1 of this Protocol defines its practical area of application, namely, that it relates to the use on land of mines, booby-traps and other devices defined later in the text, including mines laid to inter-dict beaches, waterway crossings or river crossings, but does not apply to the use of anti-ship mines at sea or in inland waterways.

The principal concepts, such as 'mine', 'booby-trap' and 'other devices' are defined in Article 2.[61] Article 3 lays down some general restrictions on the use of mines, booby-traps and other devices; in particular, it prohibits in all circumstances the directing of such weap-ons against the civilian population in general or against individual civilians in offence, defence or by way of reprisals, and their indis-criminate use.

Under Article 4, it is prohibited to use mines other than remotely delivered mines, booby-traps and other devices in populated areas, particularly in any city, village or other area containing a similar concentration of civilians in which combat between ground forces is not taking place or does not appear to be imminent, unless they are placed on or in the close vicinity of a military objective belonging to or under the control of an adverse party, or measures are taken to protect civilians from their effects, for example, the posting of warn-ing signs, the posting of sentries, the issue of warnings or the provi-sion of fences.

As concerns the remotely delivered mines, their use is prohibited by Article 5 of the Protocol, unless such mines are only used within an area which is itself a military objective or which contains military objectives, and unless their location can be accurately recorded or an effective neutralizing mechanism is used on each such mine. This article requires effective advance warning of any delivery or drop-ping of remotely delivered mines which may affect the civilian popu-lation, unless circumstances do not permit.

The protection of cultural property and places of worship is spe-cifically referred to in Article 6 of the Protocol covering prohibition on the use of certain booby-traps:[62]

1. Without prejudice to the rules of international law applicable in armed conflict relating to treachery and perfidy, it is prohibited in all circumstances to use:
    (a) any booby-trap in the form of an apparently harmless port-able object which is specifically designed and constructed to

contain explosive material and to detonate when it is disturbed or approached, or

(b) booby-traps which are in any way attached to or associated with:
    - internationally recognized protective emblems, signs or signals;
    - sick, wounded or dead persons;
    - burial or cremation sites or graves
    - medical facilities, medical equipment, medical supplies or medical transportation;
    - children's toys or other portable objects or products specially designed for the feeding, health, hygiene, clothing or education of children;
    - food or drink;
    - kitchen utensils or appliances except in military establishments, military locations or military supply depots;
    - objects clearly of a religious nature;
    - historic monuments, works of art or places of worship which constitute the cultural or spiritual heritage of peoples;
    - animals or their carcasses.

2. It is prohibited in all circumstances to use any booby-trap which is designed to cause superfluous injury or unnecessary suffering.

The other articles of Protocol II deal with the recording and publication of the location of minefields, mines and booby-traps (Article 7), the protection of United Nations forces and missions from the effects of minefields, mines and booby-traps (Article 8) and international cooperation in the removal of minefields, mines and booby-traps (Article 9).

Protocol III on Prohibitions or Restrictions on the Use of Incendiary Weapons (subparagraph to the 1990 Convention)

Incendiary weapons also constitute a great danger for cultural property, which is protected against them by the 1954 Hague Convention but also, incidentally, by the provisions of this Protocol as being civilian objects.[63] Article 2 of Protocol III on the protection of civilians and civilian objects states:

1. It is prohibited in all circumstances to make the civilian population as such, individual civilians or civilian objects the object of attack by incendiary weapons.
2. It is prohibited in all circumstances to make any military objective located within a concentration of civilians the object of attack by air-delivered incendiary weapons.

3.   It is further prohibited to make any military objective located within a concentration of civilians the object of attack by means of incendiary weapons other than air-delivered incendiary weapons, except when such military objective is clearly separated from the concentration of civilians and all feasible precautions are taken with a view to limiting the incendiary effects to the military objective and to avoiding, and in any event to minimizing, incidental loss of civilian life, injury to civilians and damage to civilian objects.
4.   It is prohibited to make forests or other kinds of plant cover the object of attack by incendiary weapons except when such natural elements are used to cover, conceal or camouflage combatants or other military objectives, or are themselves military objectives.

The International Conference for the Protection of War Victims, 30 August to 1 September 1993

We consider it essential, as we come to the end of this Introduction, to reiterate that the provisions of international humanitarian law must be applied and complied with. Article 1 of the 1949 Geneva Conventions makes this clear by requesting the States Parties to respect and ensure respect for this law in all circumstances. To bring these obligations to the attention of States, the Swiss Federal Council convened an International Conference for the Protection of War Victims which was held in Geneva from 30 August to 1 September 1993 and attended by delegations from 160 States, who adopted a Declaration.

The protection of cultural property was mentioned by several delegations, including those of Brazil, Bulgaria, the Russian Federation[64] the Republic of Slovenia[65] and the Sovereign Order of Malta. During the work of the Contact Group and the Drafting Committee, the Russian Federation submitted an amendment to the text of the Declaration.[66]

The Declaration adopted by consensus reminds States of their commitment to respect and ensure respect for international humanitarian law and of the need to disseminate this law, to organize the teaching of it and to adopt other practical measures. In the second part of the Declaration, the Conference urges

all States to make every effort to:

4.   Consider or reconsider, in order to enhance the universal character of international humanitarian law, becoming party or confirming their succession, where appropriate, to the relevant treaties concluded since the adoption of the 1949 Geneva Conventions.'

Among these instruments, the Declaration mentions the two Protocols Additional to the Geneva Conventions (1977), the 1980 Convention on Prohibitions or Restrictions on the Use of Certain Conventional Weapons and its three Protocols, and, in addition, the 1954 Convention for the Protection of Cultural Property in the Event of Armed Conflict.

9. Increase respect for the emblems of the Red Cross and Red Crescent as well as for the other emblems provided for by international humanitarian law and protecting medical personnel, objects, installations and means of transport, religious personnel and places of worship and relief personnel, goods and convoys as defined in international humanitarian law.
10. Reaffirm and ensure respect for the rules of international humanitarian law applicable during armed conflicts protecting cultural property, places of worship and the natural environment, either against attacks on the environment as such or against wanton destruction causing serious environmental damage; and continue to examine the opportunity of strengthening them.

The Declaration concludes as follows:

> With this Declaration in mind, we reaffirm the necessity to make the implementation of international humanitarian law more effective. In this spirit, we call upon the Swiss Government to convene an open-ended intergovernmental group of experts to study practical means of promoting full respect for and compliance with that law, and to prepare a report for submission to the States and to the next session of the International Conference of the Red Cross and the Red Crescent.
>
> In conclusion we affirm our conviction that, by preserving a spirit of humanity in the midst of armed conflicts, international humanitarian law keeps open the road to reconciliation, facilitates the restoration of peace between the belligerents, and fosters harmony between all peoples.

NOTES

1   Stanislaw E. Nahlik, 'La protection internationale des biens culturels en cas de conflit armé', in *Recueil des cours de l'Académie de droit international*, Vol. 120, II, 1967, p.159.
2   Xenophon, 'Cyropaedia (The education of Cyrus)' (VII, 5, 73), cited by Pierre Ducrey in *Guerre et Guerriers dans la Grèce Antique*, Paris, Payot, 1985, p.243.
3   Cicero, for example. See Marcus Tullius Cicero, *Actionis in C. Verrem secundae liber quartus* (De signis); *De officiis ad Marcum filium*, I (11 and 24) and III (6); *De republica*, III (23 and 35), cited by S.E. Nahlik, 'Des crimes contre les biens culturels', in *Annuaire de l'Association des auditeurs et anciens auditeurs de l'Académie de droit international de La Haye*, Vol. 29, The Hague, 1959, p.14. See

also Pietro Verri, 'The condition of cultural property in armed conflicts (I)', in *International Review of the Red Cross* (Geneva), No. 245, March–April 1985, pp.67 *et seq.*

4   Jean-Paul Brisson, *Problèmes de la Guerre à Rome*, Paris, Mouton & Co., 1969, pp.174–5.

5   Jacob Przyluski (Jacobus Prilusius), *Leges seu statuta ac privilegia Regni Poloniae*, Cracow, 1553, pp.875ff.: 'Item (miles) sacra, literarum et artificium nobilium monumenta conservabit integra, cunctis ab iniuriis defensa. Viris item et virtutibus et eruditione conspicuis parci iubebit.'

6   Justin Gentilis, *Dissertatio de eo quod in bello licet*, p.21 *et seq.*, Argentorati, 1690.

7   Hugo Grotius, *De Jure Belli Ac Pacis Libri Treos* (*The Law of War and Peace*), Book III, pp.643–4 (III/IV/III), translated by F.W. Kelse, Oxford, at the Clarendon Press, 1925.

8   Ibid., p.658 (III/V/(II/1).

9   Ibid., p.664 (III/VI/II/1).

10   Stanislaw E. Nahlik, 'Protection of Cultural Property', in *International Dimensions of Humanitarian Law*, Paris/Geneva, Henry Dunant Institute/UNESCO/ Martinus Nijhoff Publishers, 1988, pp.203–4. See also Comte de Garden, *Histoire générale des traités de paix et autres transactions principales entre toutes les puissances de l'Europe depuis la Paix de Westphalie*, Paris, Amyot (n.d.), 14 volumes.

11   Emerich de Vattel, *The Law of Nations or the Principles of Natural Law, applied to the Conduct and to the Affairs of Nations and of Sovereigns*, Vol. 3, Chapter IX, p.293, para. 168, Washington, D.C., Carnegie Institution of Washington, 1916 (reproduction of the 1758 edition).

12   'War, then, is not a relation between men, but between States; in war individuals are enemies wholly by chance, not as men, not even as citizens, but only as soldiers, not as members of their country, but only as its defenders' (Jean-Jacques Rousseau, *The Social Contract*, Book I, Chapter IV, p.56, translated by Maurice Cranston, Harmondsworth, Penguin Books, 1968).

13   Jean-Gaspar Bluntschli, 'Code de droit international, article 644', in *Le droit international codifié*, fifth edition revised with additions, Paris, Félix Alcan, 1895, p.362. See also Articles 645 to 663.

14   Stanislaw E. Nahlik, 'Protection of Cultural Property', p.204, who cites G.F. Martens, *Nouveau receuil de traités d'alliance, de paix, de trève, de neutralité, de commerce, de limites, d'échange, etc. et de plusieurs autres actes servant à la connaissance des relations étrangères des puissances et Etats de l'Europe tant dans leur rapport mutuel que dans celui envers les puissances et Etats dans d'autres parties du globe, depuis 1808 jusqu'à présent*, Vol. II, Göttingen, Dieterich, 1817, p.632 *et seq.*

15   Adamou Ndam Njoya, 'The African Concept', in *International Dimensions of Humanitarian Law*, p.8.

161 Sumio Adachi, 'The Asian Concept', in Nahlik, *International Dimensions of Humanitarian Law*, p.16.

17   Hamed Sultan, 'The Islamic Concept', in Nahlik, *International Dimensions of Humanitarian Law*, p.38.

18   Instructions for the Government of Armies of the United States in the Field, prepared by Francis Lieber and promulgated as General Order No. 100 by President Lincoln on 24 April 1863. See Dietrich Schindler and Jiří Toman (eds), *The Laws of Armed Conflicts. A collection of conventions, resolutions and other documents*, third edition, Dordrecht, Martinus Nijhoff Publishers, 1988, p.8.

19   Pietro Verri, 'The condition of cultural property in armed conflicts (II)', in *International Review of the Red Cross* (Geneva), No. 246, May–June 1985, p.127.

20   Jean-Gaspar Bluntschli, *Das moderne Völkerrecht der civilisierten Staaten als Rechtbuch dargestellt*, published in German in 1868, 1872, 1878 and in French in

1869, 1881 and 1895. We refer here to the last French edition, *Le droit interna-*
   tional codifié, p.602.

21   Jean-Gaspar Bluntschli, *Le droit international codifié*, pp.42–3.

22   Jean-Gaspar Bluntschli, Article 649, in *Le droit international codifié*, p.365.

23   Jean-Gaspar Bluntschli, *Le droit international codifié*, pp.43 and 45.

24   Henry Dunant, 'Trahison de la science', in *Un souvenir de Solferino suivi de*
     l'Avenir sanglant, Geneva/Lausanne, Henry Dunant Institute/Editions de L'Age
     d'Homme, 1969, p.188.

25   Brussels Conference, 1874, Project of an International Declaration concerning
     the Laws and Customs of War, in D. Schindler and J. Topman (eds), *The Laws of*
     Armed Conflicts (a collection of conventions, resolutions and other documents),
     second revised and completed edition, Alpher aan der Rijn/Rockville, Sijthoff
     & Noordheff/Henry Dunant Institute, 1981, pp.27 *et seq.*

26   Ibid., p.29.

27   *General Collection of the Laws and Customs of War*, collected and commented on
     by Marcel Deltenre, Brussels, F. Wellens-Pay, 1943, p.634 *et seq.* Mention should
     also be made of the Manual of the Institute, *The Laws of Naval War governing the*
     relations between belligerents, adopted at the session held at Oxford in 1913. This
     Manual was based mainly on The Hague Conventions of 1907. See the *General*
     Collection, pp.666 *et seq.* A Russian author, de Soncevo, had already formulated
     a number of the future convention's principles in an article published in *Trib-*
     une des arts, No. 27, Paris, 1904: respect for and protection of works of art,
     liability of governments if it is proved that the destruction was caused by
     malevolence or negligence, procedure for establishing the causes of destruc-
     tion and list of monuments and works of art placed under international protec-
     tion.

28   See 'Trial of the Major War Criminals before the International Military Tribu-
     nal, Nuremberg, 14 November 1945–1 October 1946', Vol. I, Nuremberg, Secre-
     tariat of the Tribunal, under the jurisdiction of the Allied Control Authority for
     Germany, 1947, p.254; reprinted in *The American Journal of International Law*,
     Vol. 41, 1947, pp.248–9.

29   Stanislaw E. Nahlik, 'Des crimes contre les biens culturels', pp.17–18.

30   L. Oppenheim and H. Lauterpacht, *International Law*, Vol. II, seventh edition,
     London, Longmans, 1952, p.519.

31   Under the influence of these rules, the Italian government won acceptance for
     the possibility of establishing a 'protective area' around monuments with his-
     toric value. This area, delimited beforehand, would enjoy neutral status and be
     subject to monitoring during the conflict.

32   League of Nations, *Treaty Series*, Vol. CLVII, 1936, pp.290–49; M. Deltenre,
     General Collection, pp. 760–65; D. Schindler and J. Toman (eds), *Laws of Armed*
     Conflicts, pp.653–5. See Annex I.

33   This terminology is reminiscent of the first Geneva Convention of 1864, on
     which the authors of the Pact probably based their work.

34   Regarding the scale of destruction see, for example, Hugh Thomas, *The Spanish*
     Civil War, revised and enlarged edition, New York, Harper & Row, 1977, pp.59,
     244, 269–70, 928; but see especially the letter from E. Foundoukidis, dated 25
     November 1937, to José Renau, Director-General for Fine Arts, Ministry of
     Public Instruction and the Arts in Barcelona, in which he forwarded the resolu-
     tion of the Committee of Experts for study of the protection of monuments and
     works of art in time of war or civil disturbances. The Committee noted that the
     documents concerning the civil war in Spain 'had been extremely useful to the
     Committee for establishing the principles on which the preparation of the
     planned convention should be based' (Archives of the League of Nations,
     Geneva).

35   See 'Report by the Directors' Committee of the International Museums Office
      to the International Committee on Intellectual Co-operation for the year 1937/
      38, together with a Preliminary Draft International Convention on the Protec-
      tion of Historic Buildings and Works of Art in Time of War', *League of Nations
      Official Journal*, 19th year, No. 11, November 1938. Minutes of the Council,
      Hundred-and-Second Session, held at Geneva from Friday 9 September to
      Monday 19 September 1938. Hundred-and-Third Session, held at Geneva from
      Monday 26 September to Friday 30 September 1938, pp.936–41. See also P.J.
      Boylan, *Review of the Convention for the Protection of Cultural Property in the Event
      of Armed Conflict* (The Hague Convention of 1954), Paris, UNESCO, 1993, pp.181–
      8. For French text see also *Revue de droit international et de législation comparée*
      (Bruxelles), 1939, pp.614 *et seq.*
36   League of Nations, *Official Journal*, 19th Year, No. 11, November 1938, p.937.
      See Annex II. It is also worth recalling that the second International Congress
      of History from 5 to 16 July 1937 offered some practical suggestions for protec-
      tion, including the establishment of an inventory of the historic and artistic
      heritage, sanctions, the setting up of institutes and art laboratories, and so on.
      See José de J. Núñez y Domínguez, 'La protection des monuments historiques
      et artistiques en temps de guerre et le droit international', in *Premier Congrès
      d'Etudes Internationales organisé par l'Association des Etudes Internationales. Publi-
      cation de l'Institut de Hautes Etudes Internationales de l'Université de Paris*, Paris,
      Les Editions Internationales, 1938, pp.80–82.
37   The Government of the Netherlands sent the preliminary draft of the Conven-
      tion to 62 governments in January 1939; according to the summary of replies
      received, issued on 3 October 1939, 30 States declared themselves willing to
      take part in a conference. Some other States made no statement in regard to
      participation but in general rallied to the principles laid down in the prelimi-
      nary draft.
38   Project of a Declaration concerning the Protection of Monuments and Works of
      Art in case of Armed Conflicts. See *General Collection*, pp.755–9.
39   'The Governments of the United Kingdom and France solemnly and publicly
      affirm their intention should a war be forced upon them to conduct hostilities
      with a firm desire to spare the civilian population and to preserve in every way
      possible those monuments of human achievement which are treasured in all
      civilized countries' (M.M. Whiteman, *Digest of International Law*, Vol. 10, Wash-
      ington, D.C., Government Printing Office, 1968, pp.329–30). For more details,
      see Boylan, *Review of the Convention*, pp.32–4.
40   Instructions of 29 December 1943 and 26 May 1944. For more details, see
      Boylan, *Review of the Convention*, paras 2, 43–2, 45, pp.36–7.
41   Similar clauses are to be found, for example, in Article 12 of the Armistice
      Agreement with Romania of 12 September 1944, Article 14 of the Agreement
      with Finland of 19 October 1944, Article 11 of the Agreement with Bulgaria of
      28 October 1944 and Article 6 of the Agreement with Hungary of 20 January
      1945.
42   See 'Trial of the Major War Criminals before the International Military Tribu-
      nal, Nuremberg, 14 November 1945–1 October 1946', pp.241–2; cited in *The
      American Journal of International Law*, Vol. 41, 1947, pp.237–8.
43   UNESCO document 5C/PRG/6. This report was based on the principle of
      direct protection, on the adoption of preventive measures and on the sanctions
      that should be incorporated into any international penal law.
44   Intergovernmental Conference on the Protection of Cultural Property in the
      Event of Armed Conflict, *Records of the Conference convened by the United Nations
      Educational, Scientific and Cultural Organization, held at The Hague from 21 April to*

14 May 1954, published by the Government of the Netherlands, The Hague, Staatsdrukkerijen Uitgevrijbedrijf, 1961 (hereafter referred to as *Records*).
45 CBC/2, *Records*, p.304 *et seq.*
46 CBC/INF/3, p.2.
47 Observation by Sir Gerald Fitzmaurice in *Annuaire de l'Institut de Droit International*, Vol. 47, 1957, I, p.553.
48 United Nations, *Treaty Series*, Vol. 249, pp.240 *et seq.*; *Records*, pp.5–75; *International Red Cross Handbook*, twelfth edition, Geneva, ICRC, League of Red Cross Societies, 1983, p.340; D. Schindler and J. Toman (eds), *Laws of Armed Conflicts*, p.661 *et seq.*
49 United Nations, *Treaty Series*, Vol. 4, pp.275 *et seq.*
50 The Convention came into force on 24 April 1972. Its text is set out in *UNESCO's Standard-Setting Instruments*, Paris, UNESCO, 1980, No. IV.A.4.
51 For further details, see Part V.
52 The Convention came into force on 17 December 1975. On 31 March 1994, 137 States were bound by the Convention. Its text may be found in *UNESCO's Standard-Setting Instruments*, Paris, UNESCO, 1980, No. IV.A.5.
53 For further details, see Part VI.
54 For the articles of the Additional Protocols of 1977, see Part VII.
55 See *Official Records of the Diplomatic Conference on the Reaffirmation and Development of International Humanitarian Law Applicable in Armed Conflicts, Geneva (1974–1977)*, Federal Political Department, Berne, 1978, Vol. I, p.213; *International Red Cross Handbook*, League of Red Cross Societies, 1983, pp.226–7.
56 XXth International Red Cross Conference, *Report*, Vienna, 2–9 October 1965, Neue Hofburg, pp.108–9; *International Red Cross Handbook*, 1983, pp.626–7.
57 *Final Act of the International Conference on Human Rights*, Tehran, 22 April–13 May 1968, New York, United Nations, 1968 (United Nations document A/CONF.32/41, Sales No. E.68.XIV.2), pp.17–18.
58 *Resolutions adopted by the General Assembly during its twenty-third session, 24 September–21 December 1968. General Assembly, Official Records: Twenty-Third Session*, Supplement No. 18 (A/7218), New York, United Nations, 1969, pp.50–51; *International Red Cross Handbook*, 1983, pp.396–7.
59 *Official Records of the Diplomatic Conference on the Reaffirmation and Development of International Humanitarian Law Applicable in Armed Conflicts*, Geneva (1974–77), Vol. 1, pt. 1, Federal Political Department, Berne, 1978, pp.215–16.
60 On 31 December 1993, there were 43 States Parties to this Convention, the text of which may be found in United Nations document A/CONF.95/15 and Corr. 3, Annex I, pp.1 *et seq.*; *International Red Cross Handbook*, Final Act, Convention, Protocols, Resolution, 1983, pp.380–94.
61 Article 2 of Protocol II includes for the purpose of this Protocol the following definitions:

> 1. 'Mine' means any munition placed under, on or near the ground or other surface area and designed to be detonated or exploded by the presence, proximity or contact of a person or vehicle, and 'remotely delivered mine' means any mine so defined delivered by artillery, rocket, mortar or similar means or dropped from an aircraft.
> 2. 'Booby-trap' means any device or material which is designed, constructed or adapted to kill or injure and which functions unexpectedly when a person disturbs or approaches an apparently harmless object or performs an apparently safe act.
> 3. 'Other devices' means manually-emplaced munitions and devices designed to kill, injure or damage and which are actuated by remote control or automatically after a lapse of time.

4. 'Military objective' means, so far as objects are concerned, any object which by its nature, location, purpose or use makes an effective contribution to military action and whose total or partial destruction, capture or neutralization, in the circumstances ruling at the time, offers a definite military advantage.

5. 'Civilian objects' are all objects which are not military objectives as defined in paragraph 4.

6. 'Recording' means a physical, administrative and technical operation designed to obtain, for the purpose of registration in the official records, all available information facilitating the location of minefields, mines and booby-traps.

62 Proposals submitted by Bulgaria, Italy and Morocco; working documents Nos 2, 5 and 6 of the Preparatory Conference of 1979. See also A/CONF.95/PREP.CONF./L.9, p.4.
63 For the definition of civilian objects, see note 61 above.
64 Statement by the Minister for Foreign Affairs of the Russian Federation, pp.4–5.
65 Statement by the Minister for Foreign Affairs of the Russian Federation on 31 August 1993, raising in particular the question of the protection of cultural property in non-international armed conflicts (p.2).
66 The amendment proposed by the Russian Federation to the Drafting Committee was as follows: 'In connection with the protection of the cultural heritage, it would seem useful to include a new paragraph containing an appeal to States and parties to a conflict to use, in internal armed conflicts, the protection mechanisms provided for in the 1954 Hague Convention, e.g. by setting up particular areas for the protection of cultural goods or by establishing, under the auspices of UNESCO, the Institute of the High Commissioner for Cultural Goods, or by permitting monitoring or enquiries. Mention should also be made of the necessity to take national measures to implement the 1954 Convention: broad application of the distinctive signs, inclusion of additional data in the international register of cultural goods, appointment in the armed forces of the persons responsible for the preservation of cultural goods, etc.' (proposed amendments, p.10).

PART II
CONVENTION FOR THE PROTECTION OF CULTURAL PROPERTY IN THE EVENT OF ARMED CONFLICT, SIGNED AT THE HAGUE ON 14 MAY 1954 (INCLUDING THE REGULATIONS FOR ITS EXECUTION)

Preamble

The High Contracting Parties,

1. *Recognizing that cultural property has suffered grave damage during recent armed conflicts and that, by reason of the developments in the technique of warfare, it is in increasing danger of destruction;*
2. *Being convinced that damage to cultural property belonging to any people whatsoever means damage to the cultural heritage of all mankind, since each people makes its contribution to the culture of the world;*
3. *Considering that the preservation of the cultural heritage is of great importance for all peoples of the world and that it is important that this heritage should receive international protection;*
4. *Guided by the principles concerning the protection of cultural property during armed conflict, as established in the Conventions of The Hague of 1899 and of 1907 and in the Washington Pact of 15 April 1935;*
5. *Being of the opinion that such protection cannot be effective unless both national and international measures have been taken to organize it in time of peace;*
6. *Being determined to take all possible steps to protect cultural property;*

Have agreed upon the following provisions:

> *Records*: Text: p.6.
> Minutes: paras 137, 143, 153, 159, 225, 265, 274, 293, 344, 448, 453, 454, 849–67, 1555, 1897, 1898, 2147.
> Working documents: pp. 307,343, 370–2;
> CBC/DR/3/6/10/15/21/30/37/100.
> *Bibliography*: Eustathiades, T., 'La réserve des nécessités militaires et la Convention de La Haye pour la protection des biens culturels en cas de conflit

armé', in *Hommage d'une génération de juristes au Président Basdevant*, Paris, Editions A. Pedone, 1960, pp.202–3.

PARAGRAPH 1

The first paragraph of the Preamble contains two main ideas: it first reminds us of the experience of the Second World War, during which cultural property suffered grave damage, and then points out that, with the development of the technique of warfare, cultural property is increasingly threatened with destruction.

This paragraph was included in the UNESCO draft but it has been moved from third to first position, thus showing the impact of the Second World War experiences on the authors of the Convention.

PARAGRAPH 2

This paragraph was added to the Preamble by the Working Group of the Conference, which probably remembered that this new concept had been introduced by the International Museums Office into its 1938 draft convention. But it is also based on the Constitution of UNESCO which states that, among the purposes of the Organization, it is to maintain, increase and diffuse knowledge 'By assuring the conservation and protection of the world's inheritance of books, works of art and monuments of history and science, and recommending to the nations concerned the necessary international conventions' (Article 1, para. 2(c)).

The second paragraph of the Preamble refers to the cultural heritage of all mankind and stresses the contribution of each people to the formation of that heritage. The last phrase was added on the proposal of the USSR delegation.

The concepts of 'culture' and 'cultural heritage of mankind' are not easy to define. The heritage includes movable property (artistic works) as well as immovable property (monuments, buildings, sites), works of expression (music, dance, theatre), intangible cultural property (folklore, talents, rituals, religious beliefs, intellectual traditions) and so on. It implies respect for and a resolve to protect the values that form part of that heritage.

In UNESCO's standard-setting instruments (conventions and recommendations), the concept has gradually evolved. There is no single concept of 'cultural heritage': each UNESCO instrument gives a different definition. UNESCO took up the concept of the 'cultural heritage' in a series of recommendations, especially the Declaration of the Principles of International Cultural Co-operation adopted by the General Conference of UNESCO at its fourteenth session in 1966.[1] Among other things, these texts affirm that all cultures form part of the cultural heritage of mankind. The 1970 Convention appears to be concerned more especially with the national heritage while recalling in its Preamble that 'cultural property constitutes one of the basic elements of civilization and national culture'.[2] A more precise definition was adopted in the context of the Convention for the Protection of the World Cultural and Natural Heritage of 1972.[3] This Convention established an effective system of collective protection for this heritage that was organized on a permanent basis and in accordance with modern scientific methods. In it the cultural heritage is defined as monuments, groups of buildings and sites of outstanding universal value from the point of view of history, art or science. Article 1 of the 1972 Convention defines the cultural heritage as follows:

...shall be considered as 'cultural heritage':

monuments: architectural works, works of monumental sculpture and painting, elements or structures of an archaeological nature, inscriptions, cave dwellings and combinations of features, which are of outstanding universal value from the point of view of history, art or science;

groups of buildings: groups of separate or connected buildings which, because of their architecture, their homogeneity or their place in the landscape, are of outstanding universal value from the point of view of history, art or science;

sites: works of man or the combined works of nature and of man, and areas including archaeological sites which are of outstanding universal vale from the historical, aesthetic, ethnological or anthropological points of view.

The concept of cultural heritage has also been developed in a regional context by the European Cultural Convention of 19 December 1954[4] and the European Convention for the Protection of the Archaeological Heritage of 6 May 1969,[5] which both stressed more especially the responsibility of all European States. In the Western hemisphere, a similar responsibility has been incorporated into the Convention on the Protection of the Archaeological, Historical and Artistic Heritage of the American Nations, signed in San Salvador on 16 June 1976.[6]

PARAGRAPH 3

The third paragraph, which follows up the second, stresses the importance of the preservation of the cultural heritage for all peoples of the world and the need to ensure that it receives international protection.

The wording of this paragraph was taken with very slight changes by the Working Group of The Hague Conference from the text of the UNESCO draft, to which it corresponds in substance and whose original version was as follows: 'Considering that the preservation of the cultural heritage is the concern of the community of States and that it is important that this heritage should receive international protection...'. Instead of employing the usual term 'international community of States', the authors placed emphasis on the importance for people to protect cultural property without this necessarily having to be done through the traditional governmental networks.

PARAGRAPH 4

Here the authors of the Convention establish a direct link with previous treaties and in so doing refer to the principles concerning the protection of cultural property in the event of armed conflict as set out in the Conventions of The Hague of 1899 and 1907 and in the Washington Pact of 15 April 1935. This general reference should be seen in close conjunction with Article 36 of the Convention.

However, it is interesting to note that at no point do the Preamble or the text of the Convention mention the Geneva Conventions of 12 August 1949 for the protection of war victims, even though the latter served as models for the numerous provisions of the 1954 Hague Convention. We shall have frequent occasion to refer to these provisions, many of which have been taken word for word from the Geneva Conventions.

PARAGRAPH 5

This paragraph conforms with the text of the UNESCO daft. In the commentary on Article 3 we shall see that the idea of dealing with the protection of cultural property in time of peace had already been introduced into the preliminary draft of the 1938 Convention. The authors of the Convention stress that it is not enough to provide limited protection in the event of armed conflict. To be effective, the protection of cultural property must be organized in time of peace by measures of both national and international scope.

The text of Article 3 of the Convention provides, in fact, that the High Contracting Parties undertake to prepare in time of peace for the safeguarding of cultural property situated within their own territory against the foreseeable effects of an armed conflict, by taking such measures as they consider appropriate. Moreover, the fact that a Party has not taken such measures – for example, for economic reasons – does not absolve the other Party from its responsibility to ensure respect for the cultural property of the High Contracting Party which did not take the necessary measures in time of peace. Article 4, paragraph 5 provides that 'No High Contracting Party may evade the obligations incumbent upon it under the present article, in respect of another High Contracting Party, by reason of the fact that the latter has not applied the measures of safeguard referred to in Article 3.'

PARAGRAPH 6

The sixth paragraph expresses the resolve and determination of the High Contracting Parties to take all possible steps and measures to protect cultural property. The paragraph has been taken from the UNESCO draft but the word 'appropriate' in the original text was replaced at the request of the United Kingdom delegate by the word 'possible'.[7] This change restricts the meaning of the paragraph and makes it more subjective than the original text.

This final paragraph of the Preamble signifies that the importance of all the possible steps to protect cultural property outweighs any other consideration.

Supplementary Remark Concerning Military Necessity

The Preamble to the UNESCO Draft contained a reference to military necessity worded as follows: 'Being determined, having regard to the exigencies of imperative military necessity, to take all appropriate steps to protect cultural property'. T. Eustathiades, the Greek delegate to the Conference, rightly observed that endorsement of the reservation concerning military necessity as a guiding motive of the Convention would help to endorse a retrograde step rather than progress in the field of international law.[8] This proposal was supported by numerous other delegations despite the insistence of Turkey and the United Kingdom on the need to retain this reservation in the Preamble.

According to Mr Eustathiades, the wording of the Preamble should indicate only the reasons giving rise to the conclusion of the Convention; the refusal to insert therein the concept of military necessity in no way infringed the independence of States. The discussion and the decision concerning the reservation in regard to military necessity under Article 4 was decisive.[9] Inasmuch as the reservation in that article had been deleted as a guiding principle of the Convention, it was all the more necessary to delete it from the Preamble. The paragraph concerning military necessity was accordingly deleted from the Preamble by 26 votes to four, with seven abstentions.

NOTES

1   *UNESCO's Standard-Setting Instruments*, Paris, UNESCO, 1980, IV.C.1.
2   Ibid., I.A.4.
3   Ibid., IV.A.5.
4   United Nations, *Treaty Series*, Vol. 218, p.139.
5   United Nations, *Treaty Series*, Vol. 788, p.227.
6   *International Legal Materials*, Washington, D.C., Vol. XV, No.6, p.1350.
7   *Records*, para. 852, p.199.
8   *Records*, para. 153, pp.123–4.
9   See commentary on Article 4.

Chapter I
General Provisions
Regarding Protection

The first chapter of the Convention contains general provisions that apply both to cultural property receiving the special protection to which Chapter II is devoted and to cultural property not enjoying such protection. In this chapter, the protection concerns cultural property as defined in Article 1 of the Convention. Some of this property, as defined in Article 8 of the Convention, enjoys special protection (Chapter II of the Convention).

Article 1
Definition of Cultural Property

For the purposes of the present Convention, the term 'cultural property' shall cover, irrespective of origin or ownership:
(a)   movable or immovable property of great importance to the cultural heritage of every people, such as monuments of architecture, art or history, whether religious or secular; archaeological sites; groups of buildings which, as a whole, are of historical or artistic interest; works of art; manuscripts, books and other objects of artistic, historical or archaeological interest; as well as scientific collections and important collections of books or archives or of reproductions of the property defined above;
(b)   buildings whose main and effective purpose is to preserve or exhibit the movable cultural property defined in subparagraph (a) such as museums, large libraries and depositories of archives, and refuges intended to shelter, in the event of armed conflict, the movable cultural property defined in subparagraph (a);
(c)   centres containing a large amount of cultural property as defined in subparagraphs (a) and (b), to be known as 'centres containing monuments'.

Records: Text: pp.7, 9.
          Minutes: paras 128, 129, 135, 151, 152, 159–224, 233,
          234, 266, 271, 279, 341, 388, 392, 411, 448, 470, 571, 764,
          868–74, 1902.
          Working documents: pp.318, 333, 334, 336, 346, 354,
          357, 383, 384;
          CBC/DR/1/2/4/11/16/19/22/31/36/41/42/100.
Bibliography: Bolan, P.J. *Review of the Convention for the Protec-*
          tion of Cultural Property in the Event of Armed Con-
          flict (The Hague Convention of 1954), Paris,
          UNESCO, 1993, paras 3.1–3.11, pp.49–51; Appen-
          dix VI, pp.189–97.

HISTORICAL BACKGROUND AND PREPARATORY WORK

The authors of this provision and of the UNESCO draft that preceded the 1954 Conference felt it necessary to provide a definition of
the property protected. Bearing in mind the realities of conflict, they
considered it unreasonable to expect to obtain general protection for
every building or object devoted to science and culture. In wanting
too much, too little might be obtained.

When the Conference of The Hague tackled the question of defining cultural property it decided to abandon the general concepts
used hitherto by The Hague Conventions or the Roerich Pact. But
what definitions did those treaties offer?

Definitions in The Hague Conventions of 1907

In The Hague Conventions of 1907, the protection of cultural property is, as was mentioned in the Introduction, associated with the
general protection of civilian objects. The Hague Regulations of 1907
contained only a very general definition. Their Article 27 referred
simply to the need, in sieges and bombardments, to spare, *as far as
possible*, buildings dedicated to religion, art, science, or charitable
purposes, historic monuments, hospitals, and places where the sick
and wounded were collected, provided they were not being used at
the time for military purposes.

Article 56 of the Regulations referred to the property of municipalities and to that of institutions dedicated to religion, charity and
education, the arts and science, even when State property. It forbade
all seizure of, and destruction or wilful damage done to, institutions
of this character, historic monuments and works of art and science.

This protection was absolute, without the reservation of military, or any other, necessity.

It should also be mentioned that Article 5 of The Hague Convention No. IX of 1907 respecting bombardment by armed forces stated that, in the case of bombardment by naval forces, all the necessary measures must be taken by the commander to spare *as far as possible* sacred edifices, buildings used for artistic, scientific, or charitable purposes, historic monuments, hospitals, and places where the sick or wounded are collected, on the understanding that they are not used at the same time for military purposes.

As we see, the provisions of The Hague Conventions are not detailed and give no precise definition of the objects protected, which are sacred edifices (including those used for charitable works and religious instruction), buildings used for artistic, scientific or charitable purposes and historic monuments. The protected property tends to be listed in terms of its nature or purpose.

The term 'sacred edifices' includes the buildings of all religions, both Christian and non-Christian, churches, mosques, synagogues and so on.[1] It was the Hague Conference of 1907 which added historic monuments, not mentioned in the text of 1899. This proposal was 'greeted with applause and unanimously approved by the Assembly'.[2] The Conference did not cite archives and it has been concluded that the occupying power had the right to seize archives and military plans.[3]

Definitions in the Roerich Pact of 1935

The Roerich Pact of 1935 contains no more than a very general definition based on the purpose of the property. It covers only immovable property, so that movable property is protected only if it is located in the immovable property. Article I of the Pact provides that 'historic monuments, museums, scientific, artistic, educational and cultural institutions... shall be respected and protected'. Under Article IV, 'the signatory Governments...shall send to the Pan American Union... a list of the monuments and institutions for which they desire the protection agreed to in this treaty'.

Definition of Cultural Property Chosen by the Hague Conference of 1954

The 1954 Conference of The Hague also took account of the definitions adopted in national regulations but sought to arrive, by comparison, at an average standard that would be acceptable to and applicable by the majority of States.

During the Conference, certain States continued to favour a more general definition. This was so more especially in the case of the delegate of France, who defended the idea of a general definition of cultural property that could be made specific by the various countries which could subsequently take legal steps to elucidate the sense of the definition.[4] Other delegations advocated a list. For the delegate of the United States of America, experts in international law as well as military experts 'would find it useful to have not an inclusive, but an illustrative list, indicating certain classes and items of cultural property which the conference believed should be protected. An inclusive and complete enumeration would mean the opposite extreme to the French proposal for a general definition. The United States wanted an intermediate solution, a clear general statement, with "such as" clauses as a psychological aid to those who had not made a preliminary study of the subject, and which would make the Convention fulfil its principal purpose, namely, to be useful.'[5]

The withdrawal by the French delegation of its amendment enabled the Working Group to proceed along these lines and arrive at an intermediate solution. The British delegate wanted the list of examples to be short and to indicate only the principal categories. On the basis of the discussion which took place in the Main Commission, a Working Group (composed of Denmark, France, Greece, Israel, Italy, Japan, Norway, Spain, Sweden, Switzerland, the United Kingdom, the United States of America, the USSR and Yugoslavia) prepared the draft of Article 1. In its definition the Convention makes no distinction regarding either the origin (the country concerned or another country), or the ownership (State, company, municipality or private individual) of the property. It is the value – and the value alone – of the property that counts.

During the preparatory work for the Hague Conference it was also proposed to classify as cultural property all religious buildings, whether they were works of art or of historic interest. This idea was abandoned in the UNESCO draft, as there was no wish to broaden the framework of protection to include other elements such as schools and laboratories (Viet Nam proposed adding the protection of scientific research centres.[6] Religious buildings are also protected by the Regulations annexed to Convention No. IV of The Hague. On the other hand it should be recalled that the Additional Protocols of 1977 included that protection among the provisions relating to the protection of cultural property.

The UNESCO draft classified the property to be protected according to its quality: art, religion, charity, education, and so forth. Nine amendments to the draft of Article 1 were tabled and the Chairman of the Conference summed them up according to their main tendencies:

1. to consider only objects of high cultural value or importance as cultural property (amendments by the United Kingdom CBC/DR/31 and by the United States of America CB/DR/22);
2. to include places of natural beauty in the definition (Spain CBC/DR/4, Yugoslavia CBC/DR/16, Japan CBC/DR/19 and the United States of America);
3   to include archaeological sites (Israel CBC/DR/1, Spain, United Kingdom);
4. to make specific mention of archives and libraries (Israel, Spain, United States of America);
5. to include not only collections of manuscripts and books, but individual manuscripts and books as well (Switzerland CBC/DR/2, Spain, Japan, United States of America, United Kingdom).

Finally, the delegate of Greece had proposed omitting 'collections of reproductions' from the definition (CBC/DR/11).[7]

In principle, all cultural property referred to in this article is capable of being protected within the framework of general protection. The decision depends entirely on the authorities of the country on whose territory the property is located and is signalled by the decision to place on it the distinctive emblem ▼ in accordance with Articles 6, 16 and 17 of the Convention. States are not very generous, and practical experience shows that the placing under general – or even special – protection is treated in a highly restrictive fashion.

COMMENTARY ON SUBPARAGRAPHS (A), (B) AND (C)

Subparagraph (A)

The first subparagraph of the article refers to movable and immovable property which is of great importance to the cultural heritage of peoples. This restriction was adopted by the Main Commission of the Conference by 17 votes to eight, with ten abstentions. The definition is thus restricted to property of great importance only. The UNECSO draft was more comprehensive on this point since it spoke of movable or immovable, public or private property which was of cultural value through its intrinsic nature.[8] In introducing the UNESCO draft, Mr Saba expressed doubts regarding the concept of 'intrinsic nature': 'A large number of objects were of cultural value because of their historic background and not because of their intrinsic nature. For example, a papyrus reporting a marriage that took place three thousand years ago, although it was of no intrinsic cultural value, was of very great cultural importance because of the fact that it enabled an institution, on which no such ancient information existed, to be studied.'[9]

It must nevertheless be observed that the reference here is to importance and not to value. Certain objects, although of limited value, may be important for the national culture while others, even though of great value, can be replaced and are therefore less important. The concept of 'importance' enables the national authorities to draw up a list of property to be protected. Such a list should not be too extensive because, if protection is made too broad and thus lowers the threshold at which an object is considered important, the material possibility of protection will also be reduced. The enemy army which finds itself confronted with a multiplicity of buildings marked with the distinctive emblem of the Convention will be obliged – in order to conduct its military operations – to resort to the clause of military necessity and will not be able to take its decisions in the light of the importance of that property. And yet it is worth noting that even cultural property which is not considered as being of 'great importance' may be protected within the framework of international customary law, in particular the Hague Regulations of 1907.

The concept of 'great importance' is also a very subjective concept for which it is difficult, and even impossible, to fix criteria. The delegate of Switzerland cautioned the Conference against restricting too severely the property qualifying for general protection: 'The amount of cultural property liable to general protection should not be too small as otherwise the following absurdity would result, namely that – by virtue of Articles 3 and 4, which protect only property of great importance – pillage and theft would be implicitly permitted in regard to all other property.'[10]

The concept of 'artistic and historic monuments' varies in national legislations. The authors of the Convention sought to draw upon elements common to the various legal systems, and consideration was given to allowing the importance of cultural property to be assessed by each nation.[11] They were thinking above all of property of a certain age or design 'whatever [its] purpose, as well as monuments, in the more limited sense, erected to commemorate some event or person'.[12] By way of example, the Convention mentions several forms of such property:

Monuments of architecture, art or history, whether religious or secular: the monuments are defined as works of architecture, sculpture, specially designed to perpetuate the memory of a person, action, period, event or thing, or as buildings, structures, edifices remarkable for their archaeological, historical or aesthetic interest or intended to commemorate a notable person, action or event.[13] They include works irrespective of the importance of their purpose, secular or religious.

Archaeological sites: these were mentioned by the delegate of Israel, who considered that 'it was absurd to protect museums and allow their sources, which were the sources of history itself, to be exposed to the ravages of war'.[14] It was stated that such sites should also include huyuks or ancient tombs of the Hittites in Anatolia.[15] The inclusion of archaeological sites was adopted by 30 votes to one, with five abstentions. Tells or tumuli of archaeological interest were included among the immovable monuments of art or history.

Groups of buildings which, as a whole, are of historical or artistic interest: the Scandinavian countries proposed the protection of certain sites which, although not containing particularly remarkable monuments, were of undoubted value from a cultural point of view and for that reason had a right to be protected. It was explained that the Scandinavian countries had very little cultural property and that 'their gift to culture consisted mainly in distant mediaeval villages or lonely farms. There were surely other countries in the same position, whose cultural treasures would not be covered by the Convention without the special paragraph which the United Kingdom proposed to delete.'[16] (The British delegate, considering the term to be too vague, had asked for it to be deleted.)[17] The Scandinavian proposal was adopted by the Main Commission by 14 votes to ten, with 14 abstentions.

Works of art; these were defined broadly to include the decorative and graphic arts. The terms also covered exhibitions of works of art, galleries, art museums and all productions of a period or country in the arts.

Manuscripts, books and other objects of artistic, historical or archaeological interest: 'manuscripts' refers to original works written by hand by their authors as well as to works copied out by hand or to typed texts that are not printed, published or reproduced. Manuscripts in this 'modern' form would also be protected when of artistic or historical interest. 'Books' comprise 'a written or printed treatise or series of treatises, occupying several sheets of paper or other substance fastened together so as to compose a material whole' (*Oxford English Dictionary*, Vol. I)[18] – and may take manuscript, printed, ancient (roll of handwritten sheets) or modern (folded sheets) form. In the present case we are above all concerned with collections of manuscripts and with 'rare', that is ancient, libraries. Movable objects are also included, though these are always manuscripts, books or other objects which represent 'an artistic, historical or archaeological interest'.

Scientific collections: these collections are made up of scientific books but also cover other objects such as Boissier's herbarium in Geneva or the collections of important laboratories. The delegate of Japan mentioned national monuments that were objects of valuable scientific research, such as rare animals or plants that were becoming extinct.[19] In referring to 'scientific collections', objects belonging to private individuals in the sense specified by the British delegate had been excluded. In this particular connection the latter was 'not prepared to agree to afford protection to individual scientific objects which could be used for warlike purposes'.[20]

Important collections of books or archives or of reproductions of the property defined above: protection is accorded to important collections of books without their necessarily having to be of artistic, historical or archaeological interest. Any important library is thus protected, probably in the spirit of protecting human knowledge. Archives, as a living memory containing documents offering irrefutable evidence of the past, are also protected. As the concept of archives varies widely from country to country, the clearer concepts of 'collections – of documents or objects – of scientific interest', which includes historical archives and the major libraries, was preferred. Indeed, the aim was to cover also any other collection of documents or objects of scientific interest.[22] A proposal was made to mention valuable libraries,[23] thus amending the text in favour not only of 'collections of documents of scientific interest' but also of 'important collections of books, archives or reproductions'.

According to the experts who met at UNESCO in March 1976, 'Archives are an essential part of the heritage of any national community. They not only document the historical, cultural and economic development of a country and provide a basis for a national identity, they are also a basic source of evidence needed to assert the rights of individual citizens.'[24] When the International Law Commission examined the draft version of articles on the succession of States in matters of property, archives and national debts, it also drew attention to the destructive effects of wars on the integrity of archival collections. Almost all annexation treaties in Europe since the Middle Ages have required the conquered to restore the archives belonging to or concerning the ceded territories. The draft of the Convention defined 'State archives' as 'all documents of whatever kind which, at the date of the succession of States, belonged to the predecessor State according to its internal law and had been kept by it as archives'.[25]

The question of reproductions also gave rise to a debate in the Main Commission of the Conference. Supported by the delegate of Switzerland, the delegate of France affirmed that 'it was more than ever necessary to preserve reproductions of essential works of art, whether in museums or other places, so that future generations would at least have the opportunity of seeing photographs of such works if the originals had been destroyed. At present, with that end in view, microfilms were being made in several countries, which ought to be protected for the same reason. It was particularly desirable that copies of the principal frescoes be made, as those were especially fragile and could be damaged even through fairly distant explosions.'[26] This proposal was also adopted, by 34 votes to one, with three abstentions.

The Conference also discussed the protection of 'natural sites of great beauty' (United States of America and Japan), but appears to have given up the idea for reasons mentioned by the delegate of France, who considered that 'it was probably difficult to define the protection of natural sites as their value was of a subjective nature. At best, only a diluted form of protection could result. Finally, it had been observed that natural sites could often be restored very quickly. Moreover, the first article of the Draft Convention covered the protection of a natural site when, for example, the site concerned was an interesting tree, which then fell under the heading of immovable property.'[27] The Main Commission of the Conference rejected the proposal to include sites of natural beauty by16 votes to ten, with 11 absentions. Thus natural sites, though mentioned and supported by several delegations,[28] are not protected by the Hague Convention of 1954 but by the Convention of 1972. This difference is probably due to the fact that there was not then as much concern for the environment as there is today.

Recent studies on the development of the law of naval warfare also refer to the fact that Article 1, subparagraph (a) also covers underwater sites of archaeological and historical interest, even though such sites are not explicitly mentioned in the present article. It has also been asserted that the protection accorded by the Hague Convention of 1954 extends to naval bombardment.[29]

Subparagraph (B)

This subparagraph concerns two types of buildings to be protected. Firstly, it includes buildings, that is to say, 'any structure (building, construction work) erected by assembling elements set in the ground'.[30] As examples, the subparagraph mentions museums, large libraries and depositories of archives. If such buildings have a cultural value they are protected under subparagraph (a). According to subparagraph (b), such buildings are protected not because of their own historical value but because of their purpose and their content. The purpose must be the primary one, the very aim and *raison d'être* of such a building; it must also be effectively true – the building must in fact contain, conserve or exhibit movable cultural property. Secondly, it includes refuges intended to shelter, in the event of armed conflict, the movable cultural property defined in subparagraph (a). In ordinary language, a refuge is a place to which a person withdraws to evade a danger or an unpleasant occurrence and to be safe; shelter or protection from danger or trouble; succour sought by, or rendered to, a person.[31] This article envisaged special constructions intended to shelter movable cultural property built in anticipation of possible armed conflict. But it would also be possible to include refuges constructed for situations resembling armed conflict – that is emergency situations, such as shelters for cultural property in the event of a natural disaster.

Subparagraph (C)

The term 'centres containing monuments' was preferred to the terms 'groups' or 'groups of buildings' when the reference was to larger areas containing a considerable amount of cultural property coming under subparagraphs (a) and (b). The term comprises a group of historical or artistic monuments situated in the same vicinity, such as the districts of certain cities or even entire cities.

Whereas subparagraph (a) includes movable and immovable cultural property on an individual basis, subparagraph (b) protects buildings and refuges, and hence small groups of buildings, that shelter movable property, and subparagraph (c) protects centres containing monuments, that is major groups of buildings which include both movable and immovable property. The definition of cultural property in this article is probably the broadest to be found in all the Conventions dealing with cultural property.

It is useful to recall – as we shall see later that the Convention for the Protection of the World Cultural and Natural Heritage, adopted by the General Conference of UNESCO on 16 November 1972, deals only with immovable property. The Protocols Additional to the Geneva Conventions of 1977 protect only the most important property that constitutes the cultural and spiritual heritage of peoples.

NOTES

1   Brussels Conference, 1874, Session of the Commission of 22 August 1874, Protocol No. XVIII. The Hague International Peace Conference of 1899, Second

Commission, Second Subcommission, Eleventh Meeting of 20 June 1899, in *The Proceedings of The Hague Peace Conferences, Translation of the Official Texts, prepared in the Division of International Law of the Carnegie Endowment for International Peace under the supervision of James Brown Scott, director. The Conference of 1899*, New York, Oxford University Press, 1920, p.546.

2   The Hague International Peace Conference of 1907, Second Commission, First Subcommission, Fourth Meeting of 31 July 1907, in *The Proceedings of The Hague Peace Conferences, Translation of the Official Texts, The Conference of 1907, Volume III – Meetings of the Second, Third and Fourth Commission*, New York, Oxford University Press, 1921, p.136.

3   Brussels Conference, 1874, Plenary Session of 26 August 1874, Protocol No. IV. See *Actes de la Conférence de Bruxelles, 1874*, Brussels, F. Hayez, 1874, pp.243–4.

4   *Records*, para. 164, p.126.

5   *Records* , para. 172, p.128.

6   *Records*, p.335.

7   *Records*, para. 161, pp.125–6.

8   The reference to the importance of the property or to its 'high cultural value' was introduced by the United Kingdom delegate (CBC/DR/31) who asserted that he requested its insertion in order to make protection a reality: *Records*, para. 151, p.122.

9   *Records*, para. 160, p.125.

10 *Records*, para. 407, pp.163–4.

11 *Records*, para. 188, p.131.

12 CBC/3, *Records*, p.308.

13 *The Oxford English Dictionary*, Vol. VI, Oxford, The Clarendon Press, 1933, p.636. Cf. also *Le Robert, Dictionnaire alphabétique et analogique de la langue française*, Vol. 4, Paris, Le Robert, 1983, p.89.

14 *Records*, para. 135, p.117.

15 *Records*, paras 871–3, p.201.

16 *Records*, para. 869, p.201.

17 *Records*, para. 868, p.200.

18 'To define a book is a difficult undertaking … Littré hesitates between a material definition, "the union of several printed pages or manuscript pages", and a half-intellectual one, "work of the mind, either in prose or in verse, large enough to make at least a volume". … The fault of all these definitions [is that] they consider the book to be a material object, not a means of cultural exchange … And if some of these definitions take into account the contents of a book, it is curious that none considers its use. But a book is a "thing to read" and reading itself defines it' (R. Escarpit, *Sociology of Literature*, second edition, London, Cass, 1971, pp.11–12.

19 *Records*, para. 162, p.126.

20 *Records*, para. 221, p.133.

21 In the Main Commission of the Conference the inclusion of archives, libraries and museums was adopted by 35 votes to none, with two abstentions.

22 CBC/3, *Records*, p.372.

23 Israel, *Records*, p.323.

24 UNESCO, *Final Report of the Consultation Group to prepare a report on the possibility of transferring documents from archives constituted within the territory of other countries* (document CC-76/WS/9), p.2.

25 Article 19 of the draft. See *Yearbook of the International Law Commission*, New York, United Nations, 1981, Vol. II, Part II, p.50.

26 *Records*, para. 215, p.133.

27 *Records*, para. 129, p.115.

28 *Records* , para. 137, p.118 (CBC/DR/22); para. 162, p.126, para. 173, p.129.

29 Lyndel V. Prott, 'Commentary: the 1954 Hague Convention for the protection of cultural property in the event of armed conflict', in N. Ronzitti (ed.), *The Law of Naval Warfare*, Dordrecht, Martinus Nijhoff Publishers, 1988, pp.582–3. In this connection, it must also be remembered that Article 149 of the United Nations Convention on the Law of the Sea, signed at Montego Bay on 10 December 1982, states: 'All objects of an archaeological or historical nature found in the Area shall be preserved or disposed of for the benefit of mankind as a whole, particular regard being paid to the preferential rights of the State or country of origin, or the State of cultural origin, or the State of historical and archaeological origin.' The 'Area' is defined by this Convention as 'the sea-bed and ocean floor and subsoil thereof, beyond the limits of national jurisdiction'. 'This Area and its resources are the common heritage of mankind' (Article 136) and 'no State shall claim or exercise sovereignty or sovereign rights over any part of the Area or its resources' (Article 137).

30 Gérard Cornu (ed.), *Vocabulaire Juridique*, second edition, revised and corrected, Paris, PUF, 1990, p.299; 'A fabric or edifice designed to stand more or less permanently', *Black's Law Dictionary*, fourth revised edition, St Paul, West Publishing Co., 1968, p.244.

31 *The Oxford English Dictionary*, Vol. III, Oxford, The Clarendon Press, 1933, p.856; cf. also: *Le Robert*, Vol. 5, p.732.

Article 2
Protection of Cultural Property

For the purposes of the present Convention, the protection of cultural property shall comprise the safeguarding of and respect for such property.

Records: Text: p.8.
        Minutes: paras 127–9, 137, 152, 225–32, 235–9, 241, 248, 358, 411, 569, 875, 878–9, 966, 1903.
        Working documents: pp.307, 337, 340, 343, 373; CBC/DR/20/23/32/100.

Article 2 sets out a general and comprehensive definition of protection and comprises two separate aspects: safeguarding and respect. The authors of the UNESCO Draft felt it appropriate, then, to define from the outset the construction placed on the term 'protection'.[1] 'Safeguarding' consists of all the positive measures (defining the action to be taken) which are designed to ensure the best possible material conditions for the protection of cultural property. 'Respect for such property' on the other hand has an *essentially negative* character: it represents an obligation not to commit a number of prohibited acts. 'Respect' therefore implies a requirement to refrain from certain acts, such as placing cultural property in peril or causing damage to it.

The authors of this provision preferred to give a general definition of protection which is set out in detail in Articles 3 and 4, despite the fact that some States would have preferred not to define protection at all. The latter criticized the draft for being vague and extremely broad; they wanted a version that was as simple as possible for practical reasons (United Kingdom). The authors of the amendment (Belgium, France, the Netherlands and Switzerland) simplified the proposal so as to provide a far more general foundation for the concept of 'respect' and to make it a duty towards all mankind. This interpretation which tends to provide cover extending beyond the cultural property situated on the territory of any one Contracting Party was supported by the Soviet representative. It was thought important to define the term 'protection' and to assert the principle of the universality of the concept of respect in relation both to the property itself and to the place where it is situated.

This general provision requires further clarification which is given by Articles 3 and 4. Article 2 is a kind of framework encompassing these two specific articles. That is why the heading 'Elements of protection' or 'Scope of protection' was proposed during the preparatory work.

Emphasis must be placed on the fact that the Convention imposes responsibility for the protection of cultural property on both Parties to a conflict and not simply on the opposing Party, as was often the case in the instruments which preceded the Convention.

NOTE

1   UNESCO Draft, Article 2: 'For the purposes of the present Convention the protection of cultural property consists: (a) in taking positive steps to safeguard such property; (b) in respecting it, by taking appropriate steps on the one hand to avoid the use of the property or the use of its immediate vicinity for purposes which might expose the property to destruction or damage in the event of armed conflict and, on the other, to spare such property in the course of operations, refraining from any act of hostility directed against such property'.

Article 3
Safeguarding of Cultural Property

The High Contracting Parties undertake to prepare in time of peace for the safeguarding of cultural property situated within their own territory against the foreseeable effects of an armed conflict, by taking such measures as they consider appropriate.

Records: Text: p.8.
             Minutes: paras 127, 129, 152, 225, 229–30, 232, 240–56, 257, 268, 271, 276, 294, 306, 341–2, 349, 351, 358–9, 361, 375–6, 388, 407, 411, 448, 569, 571, 764, 876, 881–93, 966, 1022, 1904.
             Working documents: pp.308–9, 322–3, 328–9, 333, 337–8, 340, 345–6, 374;
             CBC/DR/20/24/33/46/100.
Bibliography: Boyland, P.J., *Review of the Convention for the Protection of Cultural Property in the Event of Armed Conflict* (The Hague Convention of 1954), Paris, UNESCO, 1993, paras 3.1–3.11, pp.49–51.

In its draft of 15 May 1919, the Netherlands Archaeological Society had drawn attention to the omission in the 1899 and 1907 Hague Conventions inasmuch as they did not recommend any preparation for protection in peacetime and refrained altogether from any reference to the matter. However, the 1938 Preliminary Draft International Convention for the Protection of Historic Buildings and Works of Art in Time of War pointed out in its preamble that 'defensive action cannot be effectual unless it has already been prepared in time of peace'. A similar reference is made in Article 1, which does not speak of safeguarding but uses the synonym 'defence'. Article 1 of the preliminary draft stated that 'the High Contracting Parties deem it to be incumbent upon every government to organize the defence of historic buildings and works of art against the foreseeable effects of war, and undertake, each for its own part, to prepare that defence in time of peace'. Article 2 of the preliminary draft provided for the mutual exchange of information for the purpose of implementation of Article 1 and also stated that the administrations of the Contracting States might request technical collaboration from the International Museums Office in organizing such protection.[1]

PREPARATORY WORK

It is well to define the term 'safeguarding' as used in this particular context. As indicated earlier, safeguarding consists of a series of positive measures for ensuring the best possible material arrangements for the protection of cultural property. The UNESCO Draft set out some examples of safeguarding:

(a) Special measures of an architectonic nature designed to ensure the protection, particularly against the dangers of fire and collapse, of a certain number of buildings of great value and of *buildings containing collections of cultural property* (museums, archives, libraries, etc.).

(b) Special measures designed to ensure the protection of *movable property* of cultural value in the building where it is generally to be found or in the immediate neighbourhood of the latter (organization, stocking of packing material, etc.).

(c) The establishment of *refuges* for the shelter, in case of armed conflict, of the most important and most seriously endangered movable cultural property, and organization of the necessary transport to these refuges.

(d) The institution of a *civilian service* which in case of war or threat of war would put into execution the measures taken or prepared under paragraphs (a), (b) and (c) above.[2]

The final version of this provision was whittled down. That was the object, in particular, of the amendments tabled by the United States of America and the United Kingdom and of the draft proposed by four powers: Belgium, France, the Netherlands and Switzerland.

The United States delegate to the Hague Conference, Mr Crosby, expressed the hope that the article on safeguarding would go beyond the original draft by requiring the armed forces to take action during a conflict not only to ensure the respect for cultural property but also its safeguarding. The French delegate added that 'all positive measures of safeguard are the affair of the government of the territory in which the monument is situated'.[3]

Mention must be made of the fact that the safeguarding measures concern not only the direct effects of war, but also its indirect and secondary effects. While direct damage is caused by the military operations as such (for example, explosions of heat, fire, flood, pillage and vandalism), the indirect effects take many different forms which are often hard to predict and avert: excessive humidity, extreme temperatures, variable climatic conditions, and so forth.[4]

COMMENTARY

By virtue of the article which was adopted by the Conference, each of the High Contracting Parties undertakes to prepare safeguarding measures which are both geographical – that is, on its own territory[5] – and of a preventive nature: prepared in time of peace. This undertaking is based on the fundamental concept that the cultural heritage and its safeguarding are a matter of concern to the entire international community and that the country which holds this cultural property *remains accountable* (or even responsible) to that community for the safeguarding of such property.

When an enemy army is asked to respect the cultural property of a particular country, it can also reasonably be required to take care of the property situated on its own soil. This self-evident fact is summarized as follows in the commentary on the UNESCO Draft: 'The greatest measure of security will always be provided primarily by the measures taken by the country itself'.[6] This provision leaves each of the Parties a broad measure of freedom to evaluate the measures which it wishes to take. Each High Contracting Party must in fact define the foreseeable effects of an armed conflict. And irrespective of that definition, the Party remains free to take and to choose the measures which it holds to be appropriate. The article accordingly leaves great freedom of adaptation and imagination to the High Contracting Parties.

The replacement of the word 'ensure' by 'prepare' reduced the impact of the article by comparison with the original draft. Moreover, the United Kingdom delegation tabled an amendment requiring each of the High Contracting Parties to take 'such measures as it considers appropriate'.[7] This latitude permits each government to organize the safeguarding of the cultural property to be protected on the basis of its financial, material and technical resources by drawing up a list of priorities and deciding which measures to take in each particular instance. The authors of the article evidently took account of the financial aspect of the problem of safeguarding.[8]

This principle of internal freedom of action is also to be found in the other provisions of the Convention. For example, responsibility for determining the forms of protection and control rests with the High Contracting Parties. However, it is essential to designate a government agency which will be responsible both for safeguarding measures and for other measures seeking to ensure that the Convention is widely known and applied. The text itself refers to the national authorities without specifying which agency has responsibility for cultural property. The States themselves therefore have exclusive responsibility here. The 1954 Conference did, however, fix certain lines of conduct in the form of recommendations. Resolution II adopted by the Conference suggested that each of the High Contracting Parties should set up a national advisory committee and define, if possible, its composition and main functions.[9] This Committee would be authorized to perform the tasks required under the Convention and also to take part in the appointment of the representative for cultural property (see Article 18).

The suggestion was also made that a private national association for the protection of cultural property be created alongside the government committee, similar to the one proposed later in Article 17 of the 1972 Convention. Its aim would be to support the action of the government while having the resources necessary to take initiatives, present recommendations and cooperate with other organizations and institutions. The example of national societies of this kind, such as the Red Cross, shows the extent to which such associations are useful in the area of protection and assistance. Associations of this kind already exist in Austria and Switzerland.[10]

While the Convention entrusts safeguarding responsibility to the High Contracting Parties, it will also be noted that, pursuant to Article 23 of the instrument, part of this responsibility lies with UNESCO as 'the High Contracting Parties may call upon the United Nations Educational, Scientific and Cultural Organization for technical assistance in organizing the protection of their cultural property'. UNESCO has given invaluable assistance to the High Contracting Parties, notably in regard to the placing of distinctive emblems on the main monuments, the compilation of lists, inventories and maps of protected property,[11] the construction of refuges and other technical forms of protection, the preparation of packaging for safeguarding purposes and protection against fire or the consequences of bombardments. For this purpose, UNESCO calls upon experts and other technical teams and cooperates with other international organizations or agencies such as the United Nations Development Programme (UNDP).

PRACTICAL APPLICATION

The reports of the High Contracting Parties are a source of abundant information on the safeguarding of cultural property. Some of these measures even predate the Convention, more particularly in Europe. They include the following.

Safeguarding/Protection Policy

Some countries have endeavoured to define their position on the protection of cultural property and have decided to draw up an action programme (for example, Belgium in 1962) and/or to establish certain priorities (for example, Czechoslovakia). Austria and Switzerland treat their policy for protection of their heritage as part of an overall national defence plan. The drawing up of a policy on safeguarding is also closely bound up with thinking on the nature of modern conflicts – in particular, the nuclear threat – and this link is for instance given clear expression in the report of the Netherlands in 1983 on the organization of shelters. Other countries make reference to it in connection with decentralization (for example, France and Switzerland), or with 'health care reception zones' (for example, Italy). Efforts to ensure the safeguarding of cultural property must not overlook situations in which the destruction of cultural property becomes a war objective and forms part of a deliberate resolve to destroy the culture and traditions of the enemy country so as to break the resistance of its population. The policy pursued by Hitler is a glaring illustration of this.

Legislative Measures

Information on decrees and orders governing the administrative and technical organization of protection ties in with the details provided by Article 34 (effective application). Italy indicated that it was preparing a reform of the town-planning law which will take account of the provisions of the Convention, particularly in regard to the need to keep cultural property at a safe distance from industrial plants and major military targets. A similar measure is also likely to be taken in other countries.

Creation of an Infrastructure of Protection

Some reports call attention to the sharing of responsibilities between different government agencies. Federated countries endeavour to define the respective responsibilities of the federation and of its Member States and provinces. Frequent mention is also made of the role of private associations.

Budgetary Provisions

In their reports, some countries refer to the method of financing the safeguarding measures and to the amount of the funds earmarked for this purpose (Germany – former German Democratic Republic and former Federal Republic of Germany – Italy and Switzerland).

The financial aspect inherent in safeguarding measures would no doubt constitute an obstacle for countries with limited resources, such as the developing countries. The creation of an international fund enabling aid to be provided to the countries which are exposed to the risk of conflicts or disasters is highly desirable.[12] The establishment of such a fund was proposed by Spain during the preparatory work on the Hague Convention, but its proposal was not adopted. The 1972 Convention provides for the existence of such a fund (Article 15) for the property which is protected by it. Perhaps this fund could be enlarged to include the financing of the safeguarding measures provided for in the present article.

Safeguarding Activities as Such

The information provided covers a whole range of activities and programmes whose detail has been worked out to a varying extent according to the level of development of the protection policies. Some measures can serve as an example for others,[13] such as:

1   archaeological diggings, sheltering the objects;
2   restoration work;
3   inventories: survey, identification, classification and registration of movable and immovable property, drawing up of lists, publication of maps, preparation of indexes;
4   documentation: scientific and technical studies designed to identify and describe the property and preserve a record of it in the event of damage or destruction (microfilming, microfiche records, photography, photogrammetry, cartography, constitution of scientific files, and so on). With a view to ensuring the preservation of the information and documentation compiled in this way, some measures might be taken at international or regional level;
5   storage of movable property: some reports contain information on schemes for the siting of refuges (decentralization, intermediate stores) and for the security of these refuges;
6   special measures: these relate to the arrangements made to ensure protection against theft, pillage (alarm device), fire, natural disasters and special measures to be applied in the event of armed conflict (packaging, evacuation and transport of the property, special shelters);
7   studies, drawing up of standards and technical directives which may also be of use to other countries. A documentation centre should be set up in which all the technical and legal documentation would be available. That centre might also answer inquiries[14] and serve as an advisory centre with experts available to it.

Some countries, such as Austria and Switzerland, have presented detailed reports on the measures already taken by them. It would no doubt be useful to publish dossiers on certain countries which have made particularly good progress with the preparation of safeguard measures with a view to assisting the other States which are less advanced in this area.[15] The Member States of UNESCO might also make sufficient resources available to the Organization to develop its services in the area of the safeguarding of cultural property with a view to its protection in the event of armed conflict: it could send experts to countries on request and organize seminars and training courses in cooperation with the countries which have made significant progress with their safeguarding measures. It would also be desirable to encourage the publication of technical manuals,[16] the circulation of national works on this matter and the dissemination of an information bulletin to those responsible for the protection of cultural property in time of war.

NOTES

1 Preliminary Draft International Convention for the Protection of Historic Buildings and Works of Art in Time of War, *League of Nations Official Journal* (Geneva), 19th year, No. 11, November 1938, pp.937–8.
2 *Records*, p.308.
3 *Records*, paras. 253 and 255, p.138.
4 A recent document raised the subject of the measures to be taken in different circumstances such as disasters and other major calamities. In April 1983, the Director-General of UNESCO submitted to the Organization's Executive Board a 'Preliminary study on the technical and legal aspects of the preservation of the cultural heritage against disasters and other major calamities'. That study was prepared on the basis of information obtained from governments and international organizations and discussed at an international meeting of experts, organized from 31 January to 2 February 1983 by the Yugoslav authorities at the Institute of Earthquake Engineering and Engineering Seismology, Skopje (116 EX/21 of 25 April 1983). Even if that study focuses entirely on protection against disasters caused by natural phenomena over which man has no control, the safeguard measures envisaged in it would often be identical to those which the States would have to take in the context of safeguards against the dangers of war. The study refers to a number of measures of a preventive nature and the need to plan technical, organizational, legal, administrative and financial measures. The technical aspects such as risk evaluation, the exhaustive inventory of the risk maps, the classification of monuments, complete documentation, inspection, use of a distinctive emblem, the siting of refuges and so on, also apply in the event of armed conflict and can serve both purposes. This also includes the need to educate and inform the threatened population and to take urgent action following the conflict or disaster (restoration).
5 The principle of territoriality was criticized by a number of delegations at the Hague Conference which maintained that cultural property should be respected by all States, regardless of its particular site, having regard to the fact that in wartime military vicissitudes might lead a State to advance beyond its fron-

tiers (*Records*, para. 247). Despite the discussion which surrounded the territoriality principle, it was nevertheless maintained by the Working Party.

6 *Records*, p.308.
7 Doc. CBC/DR/33, *Records*, p.374; the United Kingdom delegate stressed that 'measures taken in peace-time would then be decided entirely by the country concerned' (*Records*, para. 881, p.201).
8 The Greek government pointed out that it was difficult to judge precisely what was meant by the term 'organize' in the UNESCO Draft (*Records*, p.323).
9 See text of the resolution, pp.414–15.
10 Österreichische Gesellschaft für Kulturgüterschutz; Société suisse pour la protection des biens culturels.
11 See also Second Medium-Term Plan (1984–89), UNESCO, 4 XC/4, pp.227–8, 238–9.
12 See J. Toman, *La protection des biens culturels en cas de conflit armé. Projet d'un Programme d'Action (Etude et commentaire)*, Paris, UNESCO, 1984, p.85.
13 For further details, see J. Toman, *La protection des biens culturels*, p.86 et seq.
14 Some States asked in their reports for more details to be given of the technical aspects of safeguarding; for example, Saudi Arabia wanted to know more about the packaging and storage of property.
15 For Austria, see J. Toman, *La protection des biens culturels*, pp.88–90.
16 Such as the manual by A. Noblecourt, *Protection of Cultural Property in the Event of Armed Conflict*, Museums and Monuments, VIII, Paris, UNESCO, 1958.

Article 4
Respect for Cultural Property

1. The High Contracting Parties undertake to respect cultural property situated within their own territory as well as within the territory of other High Contracting Parties by refraining from any use of the property and its immediate surroundings or of the appliances in use for its protection for purposes which are likely to expose it to destruction or damage in the event of armed conflict, and by refraining from any act of hostility directed against such property.
2. The obligations mentioned in paragraph 1 of the present article may be waived only in cases where military necessity imperatively requires such a waiver.
3. The High Contracting Parties further undertake to prohibit, prevent and, if necessary, put a stop to any form of theft, pillage or misappropriation of, and any acts of vandalism directed against, cultural property. They shall refrain from requisitioning movable cultural property situated in the territory of another High Contracting Party.
4. They shall refrain from any act directed by way of reprisals against cultural property.
5. No High Contracting Party may evade the obligations incumbent upon it under the present article in respect of another High Contracting Party, by reason of the fact that the latter has not applied the measures of safeguard referred to in Article 3.

Records: Text: pp.8–10.
           Minutes: paras 127–9, 137, 151–2, 189, 225, 227, 229–33, 240–41, 245–339, 341, 344–66, 375–6, 388, 407, 448, 570–71, 575, 764, 894–926, 966, 1022–33, 1048, 1054–8, 1093–7, 1167–70, 1413, 1905–9, 1966, 2183.
           Working documents: pp.308–11, 318–19, 322, 324–5, 328–30, 333, 337–8, 340, 343, 345–7, 374–6;
           CBC/DR/8/12/17/20/25/29/34/38/43/80/100/125.
Bibliography: Breucker, Jean de, 'La réserve des nécessités militaires dans la Convention de La Haye du 14 mai 1954 sur la protection des biens culturels', Revue de droit pénal militaire et de droit de la guerre

(Brussels), XIV-3-4, 1975, pp.225–69; Dinstein, Y., 'Military necessity', in Rudolf Bernhardt (ed.), *Encyclopaedia of Public International Law*, Vol. 3, Amsterdam, North-Holland Publishing Company, 1982, pp.274–6; Dunbar, N.C.H., 'Military necessity in war crimes trials', in *The British Yearbook of International Law*, Oxford, Oxford University Press, 1952, pp.442–52; Eustathiades, T., 'La réserve des nécessités militaires et la Convention de La Haye pour la protection des biens culturels en cas de conflit armé', in *Hommage d'une génération de juristes au Président Basdevant*, pp.183–209.

The safeguarding measures set out in Article 3 constitute a set of positive acts which remind the States of their duties in respect of the property held by them. On the other hand, respect for cultural property, which is the subject of the present article, has a negative aspect to the extent that it makes reference only to the conduct of the adversary of the State which holds this property. As Mr Saba pointed out during the Conference at The Hague, respect is also a duty of the territorial State and of its armed forces in regard to the cultural property situated on its soil.

The most important aspect of the present article is the question of military necessity which, by the same token, is the most controversial issue, although it appears in the various provisions of the Convention. However, we felt it appropriate to analyse the aspect of military necessity primarily in our commentary on the present provision, after examining and commenting on the paragraphs of Article 4.

COMMENTARY ON THE TEXT OF PARAGRAPHS 1 TO 5

Paragraph 1

Under the terms of this paragraph, the High Contracting Parties undertake to respect cultural property situated within their own territory as well as within the territory of other High Contracting Parties by refraining from any use of the property and its immediate surroundings, or of the appliances in use for its protection, for purposes which are likely to expose it to destruction or damage in the event of armed conflict, and by refraining from any act of hostility directed against such property.

This paragraph expresses recognition of the *principle of respect* as one which already exists in international conventions and in customary law and represents a dictate of the universal conscience. This respect extends to both movable and immovable cultural property as defined in Article 1 of the Convention. The cultural property defined in that article may benefit from special protection, but the decision to provide such protection depends solely on the authorities of the country on whose territory the property is situated. It is, in fact, the authorities of that country which decide to put the distinctive emblem in place and so to assume responsibility for safeguarding and respecting this property with all the resulting obligations.

The High Contracting Parties undertake to respect cultural property situated within their own territory and within that of the other Contracting Parties. This provision therefore differs from the UNESCO Draft which had confined this respect to the territory of a High Contracting Party. This new approach was introduced by an amendment tabled by four powers – Belgium, France, the Netherlands and Switzerland – with the twofold objective of enhancing the importance of respect and waiving the territoriality principle: 'The basic principle of the convention is to define the steps with respect to protection that all governments will undertake. Our amendment has been designed to break with the territorial concept and to affirm the principle that cultural property, wherever situated, must be respected by all States. It is important to break away from the notion of frontiers as, in time of war, military vicissitudes may lead to a State's overflowing its fontiers.'[1]

Neither is any reference made to occupied territories since the intention was also to cover circumstances other than occupation, such as the stationing of troops on the territory of an allied power in peacetime or in time of war.

The authors of this provision also defined the notion of 'respect' for cultural property and, by reason of the 'imperative military necessity' waiver, this definition was divided into two parts: the first which appears in the first and second paragraphs states that respect may be waived in cases where military necessity imperatively requires such a waiver (second paragraph). It involves firstly a ban on the use of this property, the appliances in use for its protection and its immediate surroundings for purposes that are likely to expose it to destruction or damage in the event of armed conflict; and secondly an undertaking to refrain from any act of hostility directed against such property. The second is set out in paragraph 3 of Article 4: this is the undertaking to prohibit, prevent and, if necessary, put a stop to any form of theft, pillage or misappropriation and any acts of vandalism. It goes without saying that no waiver whatever applies to such acts, as explained earlier.

Paragraph 2

The Contracting Parties adopted this important exception at the Hague Conference in order to enable the Parties to waive the obligations mentioned in paragraph 1 in cases where military necessity imperatively requires this. Of course, this waiver guarantees the relative freedom of the Parties. But it also considerably weakens the undertaking to refrain from exposing property to destruction or deterioration and to refrain from any act of hostility directed against such property.

Before looking at the application of the military necessity reservation in the second part of the commentary on this article, brief reference may be made to some of the observations formulated during the Conference.

On the initiative of Mr Saba, UNESCO's Legal Adviser, the Legal Committee examined the possibility of adding to this paragraph a provision which would introduce into Article 4 a clause similar to that appearing in Article 11: 'However, if one of the Parties to the conflict violates the obligation laid down in the preceding paragraph and as long as this violation persists, the opposing Party shall be released from the obligation to respect the cultural property against which the violation has been committed.'[2] However, a majority of members of the Legal Committee opposed this proposal since they held that 'Paragraph 2 of Article 4 already referred to the possibility of the Parties being freed from their obligation to respect cultural property in the event of imperative military necessity and that it was therefore preferable to make no further provision freeing the Parties from their obligation to respect. That rule would remain applicable except in the case of military necessity, even if the opposing Party did not adhere to its undertaking'.[3] At the request of Mr Saba, the minutes included an observation to the effect that Article 4 was to be interpreted as follows: 'The obligation to respect an item of cultural property remains even if that item is used by the opposing Party for military purposes. The obligation of respect is therefore only withdrawn in the event of imperative military necessity'.[4]

Paragraph 3

The notion of 'respect for cultural property' also includes a requirement to prohibit, prevent and, if necessary, put a stop to any form of theft, pillage or misappropriation of cultural property and any acts of vandalism directed against it. As we have seen, this limitation cannot be waived, not even for reasons of imperative military necessity.

The Contracting Parties undertake to refrain from requisitioning movable cultural property situated in the territory of another High Contracting Party. The UNESCO Draft also referred to the 'removal of property' but that wording was not adopted. According to Mr Saba, the notion of 'removal' was to be understood as a prelude to pillage, theft or misappropriation but not within the meaning of the protection and safeguarding measures referred to in Articles 3 and 5. Some representatives felt that, under certain circumstances, it would on the contrary be necessary to transfer the property to safer refuges. The initial expression was replaced by the term 'misappropriation' of property which is used in the first sentence and better reflects the intention of the authors of this provision.

The application of this provision posed a problem during the Suez conflict in 1956, when Egypt requisitioned the French Institute of Oriental Archaeology in Cairo. It would seem that the prohibition of requisitioning should also apply to property existing on the territory of a High Contracting Party but belonging to the nationals of another High Contracting Party, as in the case of the collections of the historical or scientific institutes in Athens, Cairo, Paris and Rome. The same guarantee should also apply in respect of movable cultural property made available on loan for an exhibition. To achieve that protection in conformity with the spirit of the Convention, it would be desirable to clarify the text by adding the following words to paragraph 3: 'or on their own territory when it belongs to another Contracting Party or to one of its citizens'.

Paragraph 4

The prohibition of reprisals was already embodied in the Preliminary Draft Convention of 1938 in respect of monuments and works of art.

In contrast with the provisions of the UNESCO Draft which prohibited reprisals only in the form of an attack or seizure, the Conference came out in favour of an absolute ban on reprisals, with no exceptions whatsoever.[5] The ban on reprisals in any case followed from the general obligation of respect. By virtue of this paragraph, the High Contracting Parties accordingly undertake to refrain from any act directed by way of reprisals against cultural property.

Paragraph 5

Pursuant to paragraph 5, no High Contracting Party may evade the obligations incumbent upon it under the present article in respect of another High Contracting Party by reason of the fact that the latter has not applied the measures of safeguard referred to in Article 3. This paragraph refers to a situation in which, by reason of internal circumstances or because a conflict broke out shortly after the adoption of the Convention, the organization of the safeguard of cultural property in a particular country has not been completed. The opponent cannot use that fact as a pretext to refrain from according the cultural property of this country the respect which he has undertaken to ensure, save of course in the event of imperative military necessity.

In this regard, S. Nahlik draws attention to another difficulty of interpretation: while the present paragraph states that a High Contracting Party cannot evade the obligations stipulated in the present article in respect of another High Contracting Party by invoking the fact that the latter has not applied the measures of safeguard referred to in Article 3, the text remains silent on 'respect'. 'As "respect" has not been mentioned in this context, one can wonder: does it mean that, in case of a Party evading its duties covered by that latter notion, for instance using some cultural property for military purposes, the adverse Party is released from its counter-obligation consisting in not directing against such property any act of hostility? Some such argument could be devised by way of *a contrario* reasoning. On the other hand, it could be argued that such an act of hostility would be in such a case, even if specifically not so named, tantamount to a measure of reprisals which have been explicitly prohibited.'[6]

Working on the basis of the first paragraph, we are of the opinion that the answer to this question must be negative. The prohibition on the use of cultural property for military purposes is a parallel to the measures dictated by respect, and the reciprocity principle would no doubt lead the Parties to the conflict to envisage the possibility of taking hostile action against this property which has become a military target. Hostilities may, however, only be launched against this property in cases where 'a military necessity imperatively requires such a waiver'. It would certainly be very hard for an offending Party to the conflict to contest the right of the other party to invoke military necessity.

MILITARY NECESSITY

The subject of military necessity in the context of the Convention was discussed on three occasions at the Hague Conference: in connection with the Preamble, Article 4 and Article 8. As the discussion first arose at the Conference in connection with Article 4, we consider it appropriate to set out here a number of general observations on military necessity in international law; this subject will also be dealt with as and when reference is made to it in the different articles of the Convention.

Military Necessity in International Law

International law embodies no general reservation of military necessity which might justify failure to observe a rule of international law. The theory advanced by the old military manual of the German Supreme Headquarters (*Kriegsbrauch im Landkriege*, 1902) at the beginning of this century of the primacy of *Kriegsraison* over *Kriegsmanier* has been rejected and is regarded as destructive to the entire body of the law of war. Moreover, it is incompatible with the principle of the law of war embodied in Article 22 of the Hague Regulations according to which the belligerents do not have an unlimited choice as to the means that they may deploy in order to harm the enemy. Case-law on war crimes and legal theory both confirm this point of view.[7] It is therefore widely conceded that no general clause of necessity exists either in the law of conventions or in customary law. It follows that military necessity may only be invoked when an express provision so allows.

In regard to the law of conventions, military necessity may only be invoked in two specific cases. Firstly, it may be invoked when the text of a rule of international law is drafted. In that case, the legislators strike a balance between humanitarian requirements on the one hand and military necessity and demands on the other. The Convention of The Hague and other conventions of humanitarian law provide examples. When the text has been adopted and becomes a rule of law no further military necessity can be invoked in the application or interpretation of this rule. The Preamble to the Fourth Hague Convention confirms this fact when it states that the wording 'has been inspired by the desire to diminish the evils of war, as far as military requirements permit'. The law of war is thus situated halfway between military necessity and the principles of humanity and chivalry which both determine the formation and application of the law. The Declaration of Saint Petersburg of 1868 already made reference to the reconciliation of the necessities of war with the principles of humanity. Secondly, it may be invoked when the reservation of military necessity figures *expressis verbis* in the text of the rule of international law[8] either by making reference to military necessity or by using equivalent expression.[9]

The reservation of military necessity is not admitted in other circumstances and conventions must be respected in all circumstances, as is also pointed out in Article 1 common to the Geneva Conventions of 1949. This clause is never implicit but must be expressly stipulated. The concept of 'military necessity' in current international law signifies the fact that the law must be respected under all circumstances. In the application of the law, military necessity is admissible only within the limits expressed, for example, by the Military Tribunal of the United States of America in the hostages case, to the effect that 'military necessity permits a belligerent, subject to the laws of war, to apply any amount and kind of force to compel the complete submission of the enemy with the least possible expenditure of time, life and money'.[10] Military necessity cannot disregard the law of war and military operations must proceed within the limits laid down in that law.

Except in the cases where specific mention is made of military necessity, general international law does not indicate in precise terms the acts or situations in which the exception of military necessity is applied. To determine such a situation, reference must be made to the principle that no violence beyond that which is *absolutely necessary* may be used.

Military necessity applies not only at the level of the Parties to the conflict but also in relation to the individual members of the armed forces,[11] save where the law expressly grants them a degree of latitude in their conduct.

Military Necessity at the Hague Conference

As was pointed out earlier, the question of military necessities arose during the discussion of the Preamble and of Articles 4 and 8. It was referred to somewhat less during the examination of Articles 5, 13 and 15 in which this point is nevertheless dealt with.

The commentary on the UNESCO Draft[12] expressed the hope that a compromise might be struck between military necessity and concern to protect cultural property. To illustrate this compromise, it quoted the words of General Eisenhower which appear in his Order of the Day of 24 December 1943: 'Nothing can stand against the argument of military necessity. This is an accepted principle. The phrase "military necessity" is sometimes used where it would be more truthful to speak of military convenience or even of personal convenience. I do not want it to cloak slackness or indifference.' In his Order of the Day of 26 May 1944, General Eisenhower summed up the problem by saying that it was the duty of every commander to respect and to spare, in so far as compatible with the supreme necessity of sparing the lives of combatants, the cultural heritage of those countries where his troops were fighting, as that heritage was the symbol of the civilization for the defence of which the Allies had taken up arms.[13]

It must be pointed out that military necessity is the only exception to the general rule of protection. The Main Commission of the Hague Conference also examined the possibility of including another exception similar to that contained in Article 11, paragraph 1, to the effect that 'if one of the Parties to the conflict violates the obligation laid down in paragraph 1 and as long as this violation persists, the opposing Party shall be released from the obligation to respect the cultural property against which the violation has been committed'.[14] This clause was not included in the text of the provision and Article 4 must therefore be construed as follows: the obligation to respect the cultural property subsists for a Party when this property is used by the opposing Party for military purposes. It is therefore only in case of imperative military necessity that the obligation of respect may be waived.

The history of law and of the codification of humanitarian rules, including the protection of cultural property, shows humanitarian law to be the result of a compromise between military necessity and the principles of chivalry and humanity. The development of this law tends towards greater humanity in the conduct of military operations, but it must not curtail military operations to such an extent that they become impossible. Were that limit crossed, it would be detrimental to humanitarian law itself as this would lead to the violation of these rules and even to the violation of norms which would be applicable and applied in a situation where a balance is struck between these two principles.

When the Conference began to discuss the subject of military necessity, Colonel Perham from the US Defense Department presented three schools of thought: 'Firstly, the extreme view, according to which every rule of law might be violated where the necessity arose; secondly, the middle view which stated that when applied on legal grounds, military necessity was paramount in every case, while when it was applied on moral grounds, there were laws which should never be violated; and thirdly, the conservative view, which was the only one applicable to the Convention, namely that the principle was never implied, and should be applied only when specifically provided for in legislation.'[15] He drew attention in this way to the quandary of the military authorities faced with such divergences of opinion.

Clear opposition accordingly arose at the Hague Conference of 1954 between the 'realists' who favoured the inclusion of the clause of military necessity and the 'idealists' who wanted to eliminate, or at least curtail, its use. The 'realistic' delegations insisted on the retention of a waiver of military necessity which would make the

Convention militarily applicable. The delegates of Belgium, Israel and the Netherlands spoke out against a utopian approach and in favour of a text which would be acceptable to the military authorities of every country. One important argument was the desire to make the Convention acceptable to everybody.

Other reputedly 'idealistic' countries (as in the case of the delegate of the USSR) asked for the words 'military necessity' to be deleted or at least restricted. It was asserted that the 1907 Hague Regulations prohibited any confiscation, destruction or deliberate damage to historic monuments without this ban being determined by military necessities. The introduction of a waiver was regarded as a retrograde step in relation to previous international law. The delegate of Greece expressed the fear that the Conference might attach too great importance to military necessities and concluded that, 'if the law of war makes the use of force on land, at sea and in the air legitimate, it is not the aim of a conference convened for the protection of cultural property to establish as a principle the rule of force in the cultural sphere which it is its task to protect'.[16]

The delegate of Spain felt that, if the Convention was to be widely applied and to receive the real and effective support of the largest possible number of countries, including the great powers, it was preferable to work out a compromise formula which would avoid radical positions and recognize, but only by way of exception, military necessity in the text of Article 4. Most of the delegations accepted, then, the opinion of the delegate of France that 'only cultural property of high value should be protected, and that everything should be done to ensure its safeguard but that in some rare cases – an extremely limited number – there should be a possibility of sacrificing it'. This waiver was applicable solely to the obligations expressed in the first paragraph and under no circumstances to the prohibitions set out in paragraphs 3 and 4 of the present article, namely theft, pillage of misappropriation and, in particular, reprisals. In these instances, the ban remained absolute and unconditional. This waiver also stipulated that the military necessity must be 'imperative'. But from what point does a military necessity become imperative in qualitative terms? And who is to decide and assess this necessity? The answer must be sought in the concept of military necessity embodied in international law.[17]

We also find the expression 'imperative military necessity' once again in Articles 54(5) and 62(1) of Additional Protocol I of 1977. The commentary on this Protocol concluded that 'the "scorched earth" policies exercised by an Occupying Power withdrawing from occupied territory were judged legitimate if required by imperative military necessity'.[18] The commentary points out that Article 54 did not change this situation, except in regard to objects indispensable to the survival of the civilian population, as this reservation did not apply to the Occupying Power who may not destroy property situated in occupied territories. The 'scorched earth' policy pursued by an Occupying Power, even when withdrawing from the occupied territory, should not affect such property. On the other hand, a belligerent power may, if imperative military necessities so require, destroy – in an extreme case – objects which are indispensable to the survival of the population in the part of its national territory which it controls. However, it may not effect such destruction in the part of its territory which is under enemy control.

Military Necessity in the Present Article 4

The Draft Convention proposed by UNESCO contained the reservation of military necessity in paragraphs 1 and 2. It read as follows:

1. Each High Contracting Party undertakes to respect cultural property situated within the territory of another High Contracting Party, except in cases of imperative military necessity.
2. In particular, each Party undertakes not to use movable cultural property for purposes which might expose it to destruction or damage. It further undertakes not to remove or requisition movable cultural property or the material for its protection and to take the necessary measures to prevent or put a stop to any form of theft and any acts of damage or destruction not justified by imperative military necessity.
3. Cultural property shall not by way of reprisals be singled out for attack nor seized.
4. No High Contracting Party may take as a pretext for evading the obligations incumbent upon it under the present article the fact that another High Contracting Party has been unable to apply the measures of safeguard referred to in Article 3.

Two tendencies became apparent during the discussion at the Conference which took up several meetings: one viewed the reservation of military necessity as a regulatory principle, while the other sought to eliminate or at least reduce it. Examples include amendments seeking to delete the reservation of imperative military necessity from paragraphs 1 and 2 (Ecuador and the USSR) and the amendment by Greece which proposed its deletion only in the first paragraph of Article 4. It was the delegation from San Marino, the world's smallest republic, which not only insisted on the deletion of the reference to military necessity in this article but also asked for military necessity to be excluded from the scope of application of this provision. The delegations which were opposed to the reservation felt that involuntary destruction might occur and that it was therefore preferable not to include the notion of deliberate destruction in the text: 'Would it be any consolation to think that ... destruction has been carried out legally in accordance with the Hague Convention?'[19]

The UNESCO Draft contained in its first paragraph a general derogation which, if it had been adopted, would have been a retrograde step in comparison with existing international law. Article 27 of the Hague Regulations of 1907 concedes the exception of military necessity ('as far as possible') in the context of respect during sieges and bombardments, while Article 56 which prohibits appropriation, seizure, destruction or intentional damage provides for no limitation. The Nuremberg Tribunal held that these rules were no longer simply provisions of a convention but also extended to customary law.

The proposal by Greece seeking the deletion of the reservation from Article 4(1) of the UNESCO Draft was adopted by the Working Party and by the Conference. Military necessity was therefore rejected as a guiding principle or general reservation. This rejection also applied to the text of the Preamble where the deletion had to be made *a fortiori*. A compromise solution was therefore sought, one which would avoid radical attitudes and admit military necessity in exceptional cases, while making its abusive application impossible.

The French delegate gave the Conference the view of the French General Staff that the adoption of the reservation 'would considerably diminish the scope of the Convention'.[20] A few years later, the Commission on Cultural Property, meeting on the occasion of the second International Conference on Civil Defence (Florence, January 1957), noted that the waiver provided for under Article 4(2) of the Hague Convention 'would render any convention null and void in the event of war'.[21]

Contrary to this trend of opinion, many delegations at the Conference favoured maintenance of the reservation, first and foremost to make adoption of the Convention more probable and also for humanitarian reasons. During a combat, military necessity might require the destruction of cultural property because 'the lives of thousands of soldiers might depend on it, and in such an event no military leader would hesitate'.[22] Some delegations preferred direct mention to be made of the reservation in the text; they felt this to be a condition for application of the Convention. They also made reference to the Geneva Conventions of 1949 which conceded military necessity, in particular in Article 50 of the first Convention on grave breaches, where reference is made to the 'destruction and appropriation of property not justified by military necessity and carried out unlawfully and wantonly'.

The United Kingdom representative preferred mention to be made of military necessity so as to give the text greater clarity: it could be invoked in imperative cases (which would not be so if the measured terms 'desirable' or 'convenient' were used). If such acts were committed 'and there were no reference to military necessity in the Convention, the High Contracting Parties would fall back on the discredited and dangerous doctrine that any violation was allowable in cases of extreme necessity'.[23]

Attention was also drawn to the fact that the concept of 'military necessity' was not clear. The Swiss representative felt that this was of no great importance 'as the Convention was above all an affair of good faith. Honesty alone compelled reservations to be made but provisions could be made for brochures which, distributed by UNESCO, would be designed to explain the meaning of the Convention to soldiers.'[24] Mention must also be made of the example of practical application cited by the Italian delegate. He spoke of the requisition of a historic castle by a commander who in mid-winter could find no shelter for his unit and could not let his soldiers die of cold. He would then have recourse to military necessity.[25]

Some also felt that the 'judgement on the existence and extent of military necessity must necessarily be subjective and open the door to arbitrary action and to a situation in which the military, who have no qualifications in this matter, might set themselves up as judges of cultural values'.[26] The representative of Belarus raised the following problem: 'Who will decide on this imperative military necessity: a colonel, a captain or a mere lieutenant?'[27] The representative of Spain felt that this decision must rest with General Staffs[28] and the delegate of Israel proposed that 'decisions in case of really imperative military necessity would have to be taken by high military authorities'.[29]

Contrary to Article 8 of the Convention on special protection, the assessment of military necessity is left to the military with no stipulation of special conditions. That opens the door to arbitrary action. S. Nahlik pointed out in 1986 that the decision could be taken by 'any officer of the adverse party, acting merely upon his subjective judgement, perhaps on the spur of the moment, who is competent enough to decide that such or such other property is to be pulled down'.[30]

The proposal to delete any reference to military necessity was rejected by 22 votes to eight with eight abstentions, eight members being absent.

Pursuant to Article 4, as adopted by the Conference, the reservation of imperative military necessity no longer referred to all the obligations concerning respect for cultural property. This reservation was not adopted in respect of the prohibition of acts of theft, pillage, misappropriation, vandalism and requisition. In those cases the ban remains absolute.

PRACTICAL APPLICATION

The information provided in the country reports on this article coincides to some extent with the details concerning Article 7 (Military measures), Article 34 (Effective application) and even Article 28 (Sanctions).

Laws and decrees adopted during the socialist regime by the countries of Central and Eastern Europe and the former Soviet Union make explicit reference to the notion of the use of property. In general, these same countries tended to lay emphasis on the efforts made to inculcate respect for the cultural heritage not only within the armed forces but among the population at large. Such was the case in Bulgaria, Hungary, the Ukrainian Soviet Socialist Republic and Czechoslovakia. It also applies to the Islamic Republic of Iran.

In its 1962 report, Spain mentions the restoration to the civil authorities of a number of historic monuments which were in the hands of the army. That was a fundamental decision to ensure respect for this property in wartime. France developed the concept of 'open towns' as a means of ensuring respect for sites. San Marino advances the argument of its neutrality as a guarantee of the respect for cultural property. Switzerland, on the other hand, points out that absolute respect for cultural values by the armed forces cannot be regarded as an established fact.

To avoid possible confusion, it is recommended in the report by A. Noblecourt on his mission to Cambodia that the custodians of cultural property should not wear military or paramilitary uniform and that their clothing should be readily distinguishable from clothes which suggest a military presence. Another idea has also been put forward in Cambodia: the possibility of creating neutral zones in order to protect cultural property. That proposal was formulated by the Director-General of UNESCO in 1981 in connection with the area of Angkor. A zone of this kind was intended to protect the temples of Angkor against military operations, the entire zone being placed under the protection of UNESCO.[31]

The Italian Consultative Committee proposed that localities benefiting from special protection should also accommodate centres to receive the sick. If the health authorities accept that proposal, the existence, in a zone containing monuments, of health care centres and shelters for works of art would enhance the safety of these areas and respect for them by the belligerent powers. This measure was applied in Cambodia where 3000 civilians found shelter in the temples of Angkor. V. Elisseeff refers to this in his report on his mission to Cambodia in 1970: he believed that it was possible to combine the protection of civilians and cultural property when the civilians were accommodated in cultural buildings, as was the case in Angkor.

Protection is then assured both by the Geneva Conventions of 1949 and by the Hague Convention of 1954.

NOTES

1 *Records*, para. 247, p.136.
2 CBC/DR/125, *Records*, para. 1167, p.221.
3 *Records*, para. 1167, p.221.
4 Ibid.
5 *Records*, para. 344, p.155.
6 Stanislaw E. Nahlik, 'Convention for the protection of cultural property in the event of armed conflict, The Hague, 1954: General and Special Protection', in *Istituto internazionale di diritto umanitario/La Protezione internazionale dei beni culturali/The international protection of cultural property/La protection internationale des biens culturels*, Rome, Fondazione Europea Dragan, 1986, pp.92–3.
7 See the trials after the Second World War: trial of Krupp (in two separate publications) and others, *Annual Digest and Reports of Public International Law Cases* (1948, Vol. XV, I I. Lauterpacht (ed.), London, Butterworth and Co., 1953, pp.620 *et seq.*; *War Crimes Reports*, 10, 1949, pp.69 *et seq.*, *The Law of War, A Documentary History*, Volume II, edited by Leon Friedman, New York, Random House, pp.1344–72; trial of W. List and others (Hostages Trial), *Annual Digest and Reports of Public International Law Cases*, 1948, Vol. XV, H. Lauterpacht (ed.), London, Butterworth and Co., 1953, pp.632 *et seq.*; *War Crimes Reports*, 8, 1949, p.34 *et seq.*, *The Law of War*, Volume II, edited by Leon Friedman, pp.1303–43 (and on page 1325: 'the rules of international law must be followed even if it results in the loss of a battle or even a war. Expediency or necessity cannot warrant their violation'); Trial of Wilhelm von Leeb and others, *War Crimes Reports*, 12, 1949, pp.1–95, *The Law of War*, Volume II, edited by Leon Friedman, pp.1421–70. For the doctrine, see in particular Paul Weidenbaum, 'Necessity in international law', in *Transactions of Grotius Society*, London, Vol. 24, 1939, pp.105–32.
8 By way of example, mention may be made of the specific clauses in the Regulations for the Execution of the Hague Convention (Art. 23(g)), Hague Convention No. X of 1907 (Art. 7(2)), Hague Convention No. XI of 1907 (Art. 2(3) and Art. 6), Geneva Conventions of 1949 (Art. 33 of the First and Art. 49(2) of the Fourth Convention), Protocol I of 1977 (Art. 54(5), 62(1), 67(4)); Protocol II of 1977 (Art. 17(1)).
9 For example, the following expressions: 'as far as possible' (Arts 27, 43, 48 and 51 of the Hague Regulations); 'the officer in command ... must ... do all in his power' (idem, Art. 26); 'absolute necessity' (Art. 4(6), Arts 13 and 17 of Convention X of The Hague, Art. 11 of Convention XI of The Hague, Art. 19(2) of Geneva Convention I of 1949); 'except where and to the extent that it is absolutely necessary' (Art. 19 of Convention V of The Hague, 1907); 'if important circumstances require it' (Art. 4(5) of Convention X of The Hague, 1907); 'as far as possible' or 'so far as military interests permit' (Arts 7(1) and 16, respectively, of Convention X of The Hague, 1907); 'as far as circumstances permit' (Art. 17 of Geneva Convention I of 1949); 'to the fullest extent practicable' (Article 71(3) of Protocol I, 1977).
10 Trial of W. List and others (Hostages Trial, *Annual Digest and Reports of Public International Law Cases*, 1948, Vol. XV, H. Lauterpacht (ed.), London, Butterworth and Co., 1953, p.646.

11 Trial of Thiele and Steinert, *Annual Digest*, 1946, Vol. XIII, H. Lauterpacht (ed.), 1951, pp. 305 *et seq.*; *War Crimes Reports*, 3, 1948, p.56.
12 CBC/3, *Records*, p.309.
13 Statement by the delegate of Lebanon to the Conference, *Records*, para. 131.
14 CBC/DR/125, *Records*, pp.374–6.
15 *Records*, para. 264, pp.140–41.
16 CBC/SR/6, p.9; T. Eustathiades, 'La réserve des nécessités militaires et la Convention de La Haye pour la protection des biens culturels en cas de conflit armé', in *Hommage d'une génération de juristes au Président Basdevant*, p.192.
17 The Hague Conference brought no solution towards an analysis of this term. Its ambiguity led the French representative to seek a different expression, being of the opinion that 'imperative military necessity' was too vast. He proposed that a vote be taken on the possibility of finding an acceptable formula such as 'should the safety of the country demand it', which would eliminate the risk of dangerous interpretation that the term 'imperative military necessity' might engender (*Records*, para. 296, p.149). The delegate of Israel felt that such an expression 'was open to misunderstanding' and preferred to retain the traditional terminology.
18 Yves Sandoz, Christophe Swinarski and Bruno Zimmermann (eds), *Commentary on the Additional Protocols of 8 June 1977 to the Geneva Conventions of 12 August 1949*, Geneva, ICRC, Martinus Nijhoff Publishers, 1987, p.659. The text of the Commentary refers in particular to Volume 8 of the *Law Reports Trials of War Criminals, selected and prepared by the United Nations War Crimes Commission*, 15 vols, London, HMSO, 1948–9, pp.67–9.
19 *Records*, para. 299, p.150.
20 *Records*, para. 176, p.145.
21 Civil Defence, *International Bulletin* (Geneva), 4th year, No. 25–26, July–August 1957, (Editor: 'Lieux de Genève', International Civil Defence Organization), p.3.
22 *Records*, para. 277, p.145 (Roeling), CBC/SR/10, p.8.
23 *Records*, para. 302, p.152.
24 *Records*, para. 281, pp.146–7.
25 *Records*, para. 270, pp.142–3.
26 CBC/SR/10, p.12.
27 CBC/SR/10, p.4.
28 *Records*, para. 293, p.148.
29 *Records*, para. 300, pp.150–1.
30 Stanislaw E. Nahlik, 'Convention', p.90.
31 *Revue de la presse*, No. 96 of 22 May 1981, p.1; *Rapport annuel (1970) du Comité national pour la protection des biens culturels en cas de conflit armé au Cambodge*, p.43.

Article 5
Occupation

1. *Any High Contracting Party in occupation of the whole or part of the territory of another High Contracting Party shall as far as possible support the competent national authorities of the occupied country in safeguarding and preserving its cultural property.*
2. *Should it prove necessary to take measures to preserve cultural property situated in occupied territory and damaged by military operations, and should the competent national authorities be unable to take such measures, the Occupying Power shall, as far as possible, and in close co-operation with such authorities, take the most necessary measures of preservation.*
3. *Any High Contracting Party whose government is considered their legitimate government by members of a resistance movement shall, if possible, draw their attention to the obligation to comply with those provisions of the Convention dealing with respect for cultural property.*

Records: Text: p.10.
Minutes: paras 127, 152, 225, 229, 232–3, 240–41, 253, 255, 257, 306, 341, 349, 357, 360, 361–81, 387–8, 415, 432, 436, 448, 571, 764, 922–3, 927–66, 1247–8, 1911–16.
Working documents: pp.309, 329, 330–31, 344, 347, 376–7;
CBC/DR/18/20/26/35/45/54/100/135.

The preliminary draft text of the 1938 Convention contained one single provision on cultural property in occupied territories. This was Article 8(4), according to which 'in occupied territories, any other exceptional measures that may be dictated by unforeseeable circumstances and by the necessity of preserving monuments and works of art must be taken with the agreement of the International Commission of Inspection' whose establishment was provided for in Article 11 of the Preliminary Draft Convention and Article 7 of the Regulations for its Execution.

COMMENTARY ON THE TEXT OF PARAGRAPHS 1 TO 3

Paragraph 1

During the preparatory work, it was the view that, while the Occupying Power was obliged to respect the cultural property of the opposing Party, it could not reasonably be expected to assume responsibility also for measures to safeguard and preserve this property. Contrary to the UNESCO Draft, the reference to safeguarding was added to prevent an Occupying Power from taking action prejudicial to the national character of the monuments.

In the spirit of the Convention, since responsibility for safeguarding and preservation measures rests with the national authorities, they accordingly have the duty to take the necessary action even if their territory is occupied. However, the possibility of the efforts of the responsible national authorities being hampered by the occupant was not conceded. Quite the contrary: the first paragraph of Article 5 stipulates that the Occupying Power shall, as far as possible, support the national authorities. This of course means that they cannot be divested of their responsibility. The article is therefore based on the close cooperation which must be established between the Occupying Power and the national authorities.

The aid granted by the Occupying Power is nonetheless weakened and limited by the expression 'as far as possible'. In the circumstances of a military occupation and an imbalance of forces, it will be the Occupying Power which will decide what is possible.[1] This provision introduces the reservation of military considerations and necessities into the present article. The introduction of that reservation did not give rise to any objections since it involved a commitment *in faciendo* in the context of international cooperation and not acts directed against cultural property.

Emphasis was also placed on the fact that the term 'occupation' had an exact legal meaning and that this article did not cover the case of allied troops occupying a territory which the national authorities had been able to evacuate.[2] Article 42 of the Hague Regulations of 1907, which also sets out the customary rules of international law, gave the following definition of the term 'occupation': 'Territory is considered occupied when it is actually placed under the authority of the hostile army. The occupation extends only to the territory where such authority has been established and can be exercised.'

It is apparent from the spirit of this paragraph that, during a military occupation, the civilian authorities of the occupied State or territory may and should establish contact with the authorities of the Occupying Power in order to remind them of the provisions of the Convention for the protection of cultural property and to discuss specific measures of protection. When Czechoslovakia was occupied by the troops of the Warsaw Pact in 1968, the Director of Monuments of the city of Bratislava (the capital of Slovakia) sent the commanders of the armies of the five Member States of the Warsaw Pact a memorandum reminding them of the provisions of the Convention and of their responsibilities.[3]

The concept of 'occupation' was widened by the adoption of the Geneva Conventions of 1949 which stipulate in Article 2(2) – which is common to the texts of the four Conventions – that they 'also apply to all cases of partial or total occupation of the territory of a High Contracting Party even if the said occupation meets with no armed resistance'. We shall see later on in our analysis of Article 18 that the same formula was to be adopted in the Hague Convention of 1954. The common Article 2(2) relates to situations in which the occupation takes place without a declaration of war and without hostilities. The present paragraph is applicable in the same cases.

Paragraph 2

This paragraph makes provision for situations in which the national authorities are unable to take the necessary urgent action to preserve damaged cultural property. It will then be the responsibility of the Occupying Power to take action itself.[4]

Such action may be necessary while military operations are still in progress. The appropriate measures which the Occupying Power is required to take must therefore fall within the realm of what is possible: it is in effect asked to take the most necessary measures of preservation in close cooperation with the national authorities, but only *as far as is possible*. The notion of military necessity which, for the reasons referred to previously, elicited no objections, therefore appears once again.

The text of this paragraph states that the measures involved are simply those of preservation designed to safeguard cultural property. Such measures will be taken, as far as possible, in cooperation with the national authorities; this will, in particular, enable suitable preservation techniques to be chosen. It will also ensure that the measures and methods of restoration are not contrary to national traditions. As the Polish representative rightly pointed out, it is impossible to count on the good faith of all the occupying authorities; he cited the example of the deliberate alteration of the style of Wawel Castle (Cracow) during the Second World War.[5]

What does the expression 'should it prove necessary to take measures' mean here? No doubt the Convention seeks to cover a situation which threatens the very existence of cultural property or its deterioration. The delegate of the United States of America stressed the need to ensure not only respect for, but also the safeguarding of, cultural property (in particular protecting damaged bridges), by making sure more especially that further deterioration was prohibited.[6] This wider concept was not adopted, as many delegations felt that the safeguarding measures fell within the sole responsibility of the national authorities and that it was only in exceptional cases and with the agreement of the latter that an Occupying Power might take the necessary measures.[7]

Paragraph 3

This paragraph was not included in the UNESCO Draft but added to the text during the Conference. Its origin can be traced to the amendment tabled by Denmark, Norway and Sweden requiring the national authorities of the occupied country to draw the attention of any resistance movement to its duty to respect the provisions of the Convention. This provision was introduced after the Second World War as 'nearly all the damage to cultural property had been done during the period of occupation, in the course of the fighting between the Occupying Power and the forces of the resistance movement'. Experience had therefore proved that unfamiliarity, or inadequate knowledge, in this area was liable to prove highly prejudicial.[8]

Although some delegations felt that Article 25 concerning the dissemination of the Convention was sufficient, this provision was nevertheless maintained. It was considered appropriate to make fresh reference to this text and ensure its respect by private individuals, particularly as 'in some countries it would be legally impossible to insist on the inclusion of study of the Convention in educational curricula'.[9] It was also pointed out that resistance movements did not form part of the military forces of a country and could not therefore be given training in the provisions of the Convention. Reference was made to the Danish resistance, which used the museums in Copenhagen as weapons storerooms.

The Conference clarified this provision but also reduced its significance. It pointed out that the reference was to the Contracting Party whose government was regarded by the members of a resistance movement as their legitimate government. It nevertheless introduced the words 'if possible', and asked for the attention of the members of resistance movements to be drawn to the obligation to comply with the provisions of the Convention relating to respect for cultural property. It was indicated that the words 'if possible' implied that not all sovereign governments would necessarily be in a position to communicate with resistance movements.[10] Stressing the declaratory value of paragraph 3, the Swiss delegate pointed out that, when a government was unable to notify the resistance movements, the latter were not by that token released from their obligation to respect cultural property.

ARCHAEOLOGICAL EXCAVATIONS IN OCCUPIED TERRITORY

During the plenary session of the 1954 Conference, the representative of Greece proposed the following provision: 'The Occupying Power shall refrain from excavations or other action for the discovery of unknown cultural property save with the consent and participation of the competent national authorities of the occupied country.' Partly because of the fact that it was formulated orally in the closing phase of the Conference, this amendment (supported by the Federal Republic of Germany, France, Iraq and Yugoslavia) was finally rejected by a narrow majority of nine votes to eight, with 22 abstentions.[11]

At its ninth session, the General Conference of UNESCO adopted, on 5 December 1956, a Recommendation defining the fundamental principles applicable to archaeological excavations. In Chapter VI, entitled 'Excavations in occupied territory', Article 32 states: 'In the event of an armed conflict, any Member State occupying the territory of another State should refrain from carrying out archaeological excavations in the occupied territory. In the event of chance finds being made, particularly during military works, the Occupying Power should take all possible measures to protect these finds, which should be handed over, on the termination of hostilities, to the competent authorities of the territory previously occupied, together with all documentation relating thereto.' These principles were drafted by the Committee of Governmental Experts which met in Palermo from 4 to 19 May 1956. It was the experts' unanimous wish that the principle concerning archaeological excavations in occupied territory 'and the necessary implementing regulations, be embodied in an addendum to the International Convention for the Protection of Cultural Property in the Event of Armed Conflict which should be revised accordingly'. The report of the Committee noted that 'it was clear from the discussion that this question raised complex problems which should be given the most careful study and which could be finally settled only by the adoption of provisions having the force of a convention'.[12]

The report by Jordan on the implementation of the Convention refers to the problems posed by archaeological excavations conducted by Israel in the occupied territories. Having regard to the character of the conflict, Jordan felt that the purpose of these excavations was to conceal and misrepresent the facts for political ends. A problem of interpretation therefore arose as to the entitlement of the Occupying Power to make reference (in its report pursuant to Article 26(2)) to measures taken in the occupied territory.

Neither the UNESCO Recommendation of 1956 nor the national legislation contain any provisions on the philosophy to be adopted in the area of archaeological research. The few provisions existing on this subject include the Bulgarian directives of 19 July 1956 specifying the purpose of the excavations.[13]

NOTES

1   It should be noted here that Additional Protocol I of 1977 – Article 69 (and Article 55 of the Fourth Geneva Convention of 1949) – uses a more precise and limited restrictive formula with the wording 'to the fullest extent of the means available'. It is stated, in particular, that there was 'an obligation upon the Occupying Power to arrange for other steps to be taken if it could not supply the requirements in question from its own resources or those of the occupied territory' (*Records*, CDDH, XII, p.335 – CDDH/II/SR.87, para. 15).

2   *Records*, para. 240, p.135.

3   Letter from the Director of Monuments in Bratislava dated 23 August 1968 to the Director-General of UNESCO.

4   The delegate of the Federal Republic of Germany cited examples of measures taken by the German military authorities to prevent damage to cultural property: during fighting in Rouen in 1940, property situated between the Seine and the Cathedral was set on fire and the Cathedral was endangered. No French authorities were available to deal with the emergency and the German military commander took it upon himself to order the blowing up of the intervening property to prevent the fire spreading to the Cathedral. That was a measure taken to safeguard cultural property. Secondly, in the autumn of 1943, the unexpected Allied landings in Italy endangered the treasures from Roman museums and galleries, which had previously been moved from Rome to areas safe from air attack. The Italian units in the vicinity were incapable of taking any action to protect those treasures. The German cultural officer, in liaison with the Italian authorities, agreed to return the treasures to Rome. The German headquarters had provided transport and soldiers for the purpose, and the treasures were handed over to the Italian authorities in Rome. A refuge was found for them as close as possible to the Vatican, as it was considered that that place was safest from attack (see *Records*, para. 365). It should be pointed out that, in this context, the term 'preservation' does not imply reconstruction but only 'safeguarding'.

5   *Records*, para. 368, p.159.

6   *Records*, para. 253. p.138.

7   *Records*, para. 255, pp.138–9.

8   The Norwegian delegate explained that, if the Convention had been in force during the Second World War, the Norwegian government, then in Great Britain, would have been obliged to send instructions to the national resistance movement to respect cultural property. The very opposite occurred. It was, in

fact, the Norwegian resistance movement which furnished the SHAEF members in Britain with detailed lists and maps of refuges in Norway, many of which were old mediaeval churches or small district museums, used to shelter treasures from the large city museums. They asked the SHAEF members to respect such repositories in the event of military operations in the final stages of the war (*Records*, para. 367, p.159).

9 *Records*, para. 373, p.160 (United Kingdom delegate).

10 *Records*, paras 927, 959, pp.205–6.

11 See *Records*, paras 912–15.

12 Report by the Committee of Governmental Experts, doc. 9C/PRG/7, in particular paragraphs 62–3, p.16 – Annex II.

13 Directions on archaeological probes and excavations, 19 July 1956, cited by Lyndel V. Prott and P.J. O'Keefe, *Law and the Cultural Heritage*, Vol. I: *Discovery and Excavation*, Abingdon, Professional Books Ltd., 1984, p.232. According to these directives, 'the aim of excavations is to find and study the archaeological monuments underground so as to explain the basic questions of historical development, the history of the development of the production forces of a given society, the characteristics of the state and development of its economic basis, social relations, specific traits in the development of the culture of a given society, its interrelations with neighbouring peoples and many other questions related to the life and culture of the tribes and peoples who have created the material monuments excavated. In view of (1) the great scientific importance of the archaeological monuments unearthed as prime historical sources of given epochs, (2) the fact that the excavations of such monuments are frequently connected by necessity with their demolition, and (3) the fact that any mishandling of finds is irreparable, archaeological excavations should be carried out according to present-day methods of archaeological studies by trained persons only, employing all necessary scientific methods and observations which guarantee the further scientific utilization of the results of the excavations as fully valuable historical sources.'

Article 6
Distinctive Marking of Cultural Property

In accordance with the provisions of Article 16, cultural property may bear a distinctive emblem so as to facilitate its recognition.

Records: Text: p.10.
Minutes: paras 386, 388–413, 1465, 1469, 1471, 1474, 1917, 1921–6.
Working documents: pp. 309, 377;
CBC/DR/47/55/143.

This article, which appears in the section concerning general protection, makes reference to Article 16 of the Convention and to the distinctive emblem described therein. The distinctive marking of property under general protection must not be confused with specific provisions relating to the special protection of cultural property.

Article 6 of the UNESCO Draft stated that 'cultural property shall, as far as possible, be so designated as to facilitate its recognition' and accordingly referred to the publication of lists and to the affixing of posters or other indications such as would facilitate the identification of cultural property under general protection. The Italian delegation to the Conference wanted to go further by proposing that 'cultural property to be accorded protection shall be listed in the "International Register of Cultural Property" in accordance with the procedure laid down in the Regulations for the Execution of the Convention. In the even of armed conflict, such property shall be so designated as to facilitate its recognition.' The Conference did not approve this proposal.

As the distinctive marking of property is not compulsory, it is not a condition for the respect of cultural property. The absence of distinctive marking which permits the identification of such property might lessen the responsibility of the adverse party in the event of bombardment since the act of destruction might be excused on the grounds of ignorance of the presence of a cultural property.

This provision rounds off Article 4 since, by the distinctive marking, the State signifies its decision on the property which it considers to be of great importance and therefore covered by the scheme of general protection.

Article 7
Military Measures

1. *The High Contracting Parties undertake to introduce in time of peace into their military regulations or instructions such provisions as may ensure observance of the present Convention and to foster in the members of their armed forces a spirit of respect for the culture and cultural property of all peoples.*
2. *The High Contracting Parties undertake to plan or establish in peacetime within their armed forces, services or specialist personnel whose purpose will be to secure respect for cultural property and to co-operate with the civilian authorities responsible for safeguarding it.*

Records: Text: pp.10, 12.
            Minutes: paras 137, 415–47, 953, 1927.
            Working documents: pp.310, 338, 341, 377–8;
            CBC/DR/13/27/39.

As its title indicates, this provision concerns military measures. It follows the example of the provisions in the Fourth Hague Convention of 1907 and the Geneva Conventions of 1949. Article 1 of the Hague Convention states that the Contracting Powers shall give instructions in conformity with the Regulations to their land forces. The Geneva Conventions provide that the study of these conventions shall form an integral part of military, and if possible, of civil instruction programmes so that the principles may become known to the entire population (in particular to the armed fighting forces, the medical personnel and the chaplains) (Art. 47/48/127/144).

Similarly, the 1938 Preliminary Draft International Convention for the Protection of Historic Monuments and Works of Art in Time of War stated, in its Article 3, that the High Contracting Parties would undertake to include in their military regulations and instructions such recommendations as might ensure that historic monuments and works of art were respected.[1]

Unlike the Geneva Conventions, the Hague Convention refers only to military measures and entrusts their implementation to the military authorities. The Contracting Party is required to give precise instructions to these authorities.

This provision must be read in conjunction with Article 24 dealing with the dissemination of the Convention, in which, moreover, its inclusion had been proposed. Nevertheless, it has been retained in the present chapter which deals with military measures so as to make sure that the armed forces fully understand the value of cultural property.

PARAGRAPH 1

During the debates at the Hague Conference in 1954, emphasis was placed on the need to take such measures in peacetime. An amendment by Greece led to the replacement of the notion of 'at an appropriate moment' by that of 'in time of peace' which is far more precise since it does not leave the authorities the latitude to await the occurrence of a conflict before providing the necessary training.

The amendment proposed by the USSR broadened the scope of the instruction by stipulating that the aim was not simply to provide training in the convention but also to develop 'a spirit of respect for the cultures and cultural property of all peoples'. As in the case of humanitarian conventions, the spirit of the traditions of the peoples must take precedence and that fact is highlighted in the 1954 Convention. It was hoped that UNESCO might supply substantial aid towards the accomplishment of that task. The reference to 'culture' is a reaction to the unfortunate experience of the Second World War when the right of a people to its own specific culture was denied.

Practical Application

The reports by the High Contracting Parties on the implementation of the Convention give a number of indications which coincide to a varying extent with the provisions set out in Article 25 of the Convention (dissemination). Information, whose detail varies according to the country, is available on:

1 the articles of laws and decrees which define the obligations of military personnel of all ranks;
2 the instructions and notices distributed to the different corps of the armed forces;
3 military exercises: headquarters maps showing protected sites and monuments;
4 the means used to make the military forces more keenly aware of the provisions of the Convention (courses, instruction methods, and so on);

5   the appointment, training and responsibilities of the personnel whose task is the protection of property;
6   the procedures for cooperation between the civilian and military authorities.[2]

To implement international humanitarian law applicable in the event of armed conflicts, a number of States placed emphasis on manuals as training tools. These manuals contain the provisions on the protection of cultural property.[3]

Regulations for the United Nations Emergency Force of 20 February 1957 include only one short provision in Article 44 according to which 'the Force shall observe the principles and spirit of the general international conventions applicable to the conduct of military personnel'.[4] We have already pointed out that it was the wish of the 1954 Conference that the 'competent organs of the United Nations should decide, in the event of military action being taken in implementation of the Charter, to ensure application of the provisions of the convention by the armed forces taking part in such action'. The Institute of International Law had adopted two resolutions on the subject of the application of humanitarian conventions by the United Nations, one dated 3 September 1971 and the other 13 August 1975. It will also be noted that the draft military handbook published by the International Committee of the Red Cross attaches great importance to the protection of cultural property.[5]

PARAGRAPH 2

This paragraph goes further than the provisions of the Geneva Conventions as it provides for the preparation and establishment in peacetime of the services or specialist personnel within the armed forces whose purpose will be to secure respect for cultural property and to cooperate with the civilian authorities responsible for safeguarding it.

The commentary on the UNESCO Draft calls attention to the experience acquired during the Second World War which 'has shown that effective protection of cultural property can only be achieved if there exists in each army a special service, however small, whose members are expert in the protection of monuments, museum objects, historic documents and rare books ... [so that] when operations are being prepared, account can be taken of the interests which the Convention is designed to protect. Secondly, in time of war, the military authorities possess means of communication which civilians cannot use. In the area round a theatre of military operations, all civilian organization is paralysed. In order to take the appropriate measures and to get the troops to respect cultural property, the commanding officers need advisers who will give them an expert opinion and act as the "conscience of the army" on the subject. The armies thus set up special corps of officers whose task was not only to secure the "respect" of cultural property, but often also to provide for its "safeguarding". It is indispensable that the nucleus of such a service should exist in peacetime, not only to provide for the necessary steps in the military sector, but to establish contact with the civilian protection authorities who will need to ask the opinion of the military authorities and to act in agreement with them in the preparation of certain measures they will have to take. From what has gone before it follows that this special service should form part of the army staff and that the officers belonging to it should have a fairly high rank.'[6] During the Conference, particular emphasis was placed on the importance of cooperation between the military and civilian authorities.

While the Geneva Conventions of 1949 exerted a distinct influence on the provisions of the Hague Convention of 1954, the latter also served as a source of inspiration to the authors of the Additional Protocols of 1977 whose aim was to reaffirm and develop international humanitarian law. Article 6 of Protocol I in particular states that 'the High Contracting Parties shall, also in peacetime, endeavour, with the assistance of the national Red Cross (Red Crescent, Red Lion and Sun) societies, to train qualified personnel to facilitate the application of the Conventions and of this Protocol and in particular the activities of the Protecting Powers'. Mention should also be made of Article 82 of the same Protocol by virtue of which 'the High Contracting Parties at all times, and the Parties to the conflict in time of armed conflict, shall ensure that legal advisers are available, when necessary, to advise the military commanders at the appropriate level on the application of the conventions and this Protocol and on the appropriate instruction to be given to the armed forces on this subject'.

N.B.: The amendment requested by Greece proposed the addition of a third paragraph providing that the High Contracting Parties shall submit annual reports on the measures taken in compliance with the obligations set out in Article 7. That provision would no doubt have substantially strengthened implementation of the Convention. However, the reports referred to in Article 26(2) contain this type of information, although they are four-yearly reports while the Greek proposal was for the submission of annual reports. Had it been adopted, this provision would have brought pressure to bear on the national authorities with a view to the adoption and constant review by them of implementation measures.

NOTES

1   Preliminary Draft International Convention for the Protection of Historic Build-
    ings and Works of Art in Time of War, *League of Nations Official Journal*, Geneva,
    League of Nations, 19th year, No. 11, November 1938, p.937.
2   Austria, Federal Republic of Germany, Hungary and Switzerland provide infor-
    mation on this subject. See also the reports by Bulgaria, Islamic Republic of Iran,
    Israel, Italy, Nigeria, Norway, Spain and Thailand. A considerable number of
    countries supply no information whatsoever on this subject.
3   Here are some examples of these provisions: *Manuel des lois et coutumes de la
    guerre de l'Armée suisse* – 51.7/11f – Articles 49–53 and 177 refer to cultural
    property. The British military manual entitled *The Law of War on Land*, 1956,
    paragraph 290 reads: 'churches and monuments duly marked by signs notified
    beforehand must not be deliberately attacked if they are not used for military
    purposes'; *The Law of Land Warfare, Department of the Army Field Manual FM 27–
    10* (July 1956) of the armies of the United States of America deals with cultural
    property in its Articles 45, 46, 57 and 405. The manual refers to the Hague
    Regulations of 1907 and the Roerich Pact of 1935. More recently, the air force
    manual (*Air Force Pamphlet AFP 110–31*, US Department of the Air Force, 19
    November 1976) also includes the provisions of the Hague Regulations of 1907
    as the expression of customary rules 'binding on all nations and all armed
    forces in international conflicts'. We find reference here to the Hague Conven-
    tion IX of 1907 and to international customary law. Section 5–5(c) states more
    especially: 'c. Religious, Cultural and Charitable Buildings and Monuments.
    Buildings devoted to religion, art, or charitable purposes as well as historical
    monuments may not be made the object of aerial bombardment. Protection is
    based on their not being used for military purposes. Combatants have a duty to
    indicate such places by distinctive and visible signs. When used by the enemy
    for military purposes, such buildings may be attacked if they are, under the
    circumstances, valid military objectives. Lawful military objectives located near
    protected buildings are not immune from aerial attack by reason of such loca-
    tion but, insofar as possible, necessary precautions must be taken to spare such
    protected buildings along with other civilian objects.' Section 10–4(b) reads:
    'reprisals against protected cultural property are not taken because of their
    questionable legality'. The note refers to Article 4(4) of the Hague Convention
    and points out that the United States has signed but not ratified this Conven-
    tion. For the authors of the manual, the prohibition ('questionable') of reprisals
    is based on international customary law and they refer to court rulings and
    legal theory. (See Trial of Franz Holstein and others, 8 *UN War Crimes Reports* 30
    (1949); Trial of Hanz Szabados, 9 *UN War Crimes Reports* (61 (1949); Albrecht,
    'War reprisals in the war crime trials and in the Geneva Conventions of 1949',
    American Journal of International Law (Washington, D.C.), Vol. 47, 1953, p.601; E.
    Stowell, 'Military reprisals and their sanctions of the law of war', ibid., Vol. 36,
    1942, pp.643, 647–8; 'Protection of art in transnational law', *Vanderbilt Journal of
    Transnational Law* (Nashville, TN), Vol. 7, 1974, p.690. The manual of naval
    operations of the United States, *Law of Naval Operations*, NWP 10–1, August
    1982, contains a chapter on cultural property. The general definition is as fol-
    lows: '3.12.1 Protection and loss of protection. During military operations rea-
    sonable measures should be taken to avoid damaging religious and cultural
    buildings such as churches, temples, mosques, synagogues, museums, charita-
    ble institutions, historic monuments, archaeological sites and works of art. These
    structures may lawfully be attacked if used for military purposes, although
    Rules of Engagement may restrict military operations.' This definition is wider

than that set out in the Hague Convention IX and in the Roerich Pact which, as the manual points out, are binding on the United States. The manual also makes reference to the 1954 Hague Convention by stating that several allies and potential adversaries of the United States are parties to this Convention: 'Although the United States is not a party to this Convention, we do recognize that all cultural property, including that property marked with the Hague emblem, should be protected unless used for military purposes.' The protection of cultural property and the reference to the Convention appear in the military instruction manual, although the United States of America is not a party to the Convention (US Department of the Army, *Training circular TC 27–10–1*), June 1979, Selected problems in the law of war, cases 34 and 35). An interesting application of customary law was also included in the American Rules of Engagement in Cambodia in 1973 which prohibited the use of B52s less than one kilometre from villages and also from monuments, temples, pagodas or holy places (Jean de Preux, 'La Convention de La Haye et le récent développement du droit des conflits armés', in Istituto internazionale de diritto umanitario (ed.), *La protezione internazionale dei beni culturali/The international protection of cultural property/La protection internationale des biens culturels*, Rome, Fondazione Europea Dragan, 1986, p.110, which quotes H. Kissinger, *Les années orageuses*, Paris, Fayard, 1982, p.712). The manual of the law of war of the former Federal Republic of Germany also contains all the texts relating to the protection of cultural property, including that of the 1954 Convention and Protocol (*Kriegsvölkerrecht*, Sammlung der Abkommenstexte (Sonderdruck), ZDv 15/3, Bonn, July 1959). The Military Service Regulations of June 1975 entitled 'Legal bases for the conduct of operations in the field' also sets out the fundamental provisions on protection. The recent German Military Manual published in August 1992 contains an important Chapter 9 on the protection of cultural property (ZDv 15/2 *Humanitäres Völkerrecht in bewaffneten Konflikten – Handbuch; Humanitarian law in armed conflicts – Manual*, The Federal Ministry of Defence of the Federal Republic of Germany VR II 3, August 1992, paras 901–36, pp.91–6). The Hungarian Law No. 1 of 1976 stipulates that the armed forces shall respect the rules of international humanitarian and military law, in particular the provisions of the 1954 Convention. The service regulations of the armed forces state that soldiers shall: '1) Refrain from abusing their powers by depriving the population of its property and by causing destruction which is "not justified by military necessity" in operational zones of occupied territories; 2) respect and treat as inviolable the medical institutions and units of the enemy and cultural property marked by a distinctive emblem.'

4   *UNTS*, Vol. 271, p.168. See also, for example, United Nations documents ST/SGB/ONUC/1 of 15 July 1963, ST/SGB/UNFICP/1 of 25 April 1964, and *UNTS*, Vol. 555, pp.149 *et seq*.

5   Frederic de Mulinen, *Handbook on the Law of War for Armed Forces*, Geneva, ICRC, 1987, 232 pages.

6   *Records*, pp.309–10.

Chapter II
Special Protection

The idea of special protection originated in the Preliminary Draft International Convention drawn up by the International Museums Office in 1938. This idea was taken up again in the draft presented by the Italian government to the General Conference of UNESCO in Florence in 1950.

The first chapter of the Convention defines minimum protection for all cultural property which is of great importance to the cultural heritage of every people. A broad definition is given of cultural property; on the other hand, the extent of actual protection is relatively narrow. The choice of protected property is left to the discretion of the States on whose territory the cultural property is situated.

This chapter adopts a different approach. Cultural property is defined here in a restrictive sense which also enables the level of material protection to be increased. The threshold of protection is high: the definition of property relates only to a limited range of cultural property in the form of movable and immovable items of 'very great importance'.

Article 8
Granting of Special Protection

1. *There may be placed under special protection a limited number of refuges intended to shelter movable cultural property in the event of armed conflict, of centres containing monuments and other immovable cultural property of very great importance, provided that they:*
   (a) *are situated at an adequate distance from any large industrial centre or from any important military objective constituting a vulnerable point, such as, for example, an aerodrome, broadcasting station, establishment engaged upon*

work of national defence, a port or railway station of relative importance or a main line of communication;
(b)   are not used for military purposes.

2.   A refuge for movable cultural property may also be placed under
special protection, whatever its location, if it is so constructed
that, in all probability, it will not be damaged by bombs.

3.   A centre containing monuments shall be deemed to be used for
military purposes whenever it is used for the movement of military personnel or material, even in transit. The same shall apply
whenever activities directly connected with military operations,
the stationing of military personnel, or the production of war
material are carried on within the centre.

4.   The guarding of cultural property mentioned in paragraph 1 above
by armed custodians specially empowered to do so, or the presence, in the vicinity of such cultural property, of police forces
normally responsible for the maintenance of public order shall
not be deemed to be used for military purposes.

5.   If any cultural property mentioned in paragraph 1 of the present
article is situated near an important military objective as defined in the said paragraph, it may nevertheless be placed under
special protection if the High Contracting Party asking for that
protection undertakes, in the event of armed conflict, to make no
use of the objective and particularly, in the case of a port, railway station or aerodrome, to divert all traffic therefrom. In that
event, such diversion shall be prepared in time of peace.

6.   Special protection is granted to cultural property by its entry in
the 'International Register of Cultural Property under Special
Protection'. This entry shall only be made in accordance with
the provisions of the present Convention and under the conditions provided for in the Regulations for the Execution of the
Convention.

Records: Text: pp.12, 14.
Minutes: paras 462–507, 519, 522, 532–7, 539, 550, 579,
653–75, 694, 772–91, 968, 1284, 1287, 1295–1307, 1327,
1335, 1451, 1928–49, 1952, 1954–60, 1961.
Working documents: pp.310, 316–17, 327, 331, 338, 344–
5, 349–50, 378–80;
CBC/DR/56/61/66/94/114/121.

Bibliography: Boylan, P.J., *Review of the Convention for the Protection of Cultural Property in the Event of Armed Con-
flict*, (The Hague Convention of 1954), Paris,
UNESCO, 1993, paras 6.1–6.28, pp.75–82;
Malintroppi, Antonio, 'La protezione "speciale"
della Città del Vaticano in caso di conflitto armato',

Rivista di Diritto Internazionale (Milan), Vol. 43, pp.607–29.

The 1938 Preliminary Draft Convention had already made provision for the prohibition of any act of hostility towards the refuges designated by a High Contracting Party on its territory to shelter works of art or of historic interest in time of armed conflict: 'The number of such refuges shall be limited; they may take the form either of buildings erected for the purpose or of existing buildings or groups of buildings' (Art. 4(2) of the Preliminary Draft). The refuges and monuments benefiting from special protection were to be designated immediately upon ratification of the Convention. The list of these refuges and monuments was to be sent to the Standing Committee of the Conference, together with the written approval of the International Verification Commission (Article 2 of the Regulations for the Execution of the Convention annexed to the 1938 Preliminary Draft).

PARAGRAPH 1

The choice of the cultural property to be entered in the International Register and, hence to be granted the special protection envisaged, depends entirely on the decision of the High Contracting Party on whose territory this property is situated. This first paragraph defines the property to which special protection is granted. This definition is in three parts: the first defines the property as such, the second points out that only cultural property of very great importance may benefit from special protection, while the third part lays down two conditions which preclude special protection it they are not met.

Definition of Property to Receive Special Protection

The definition indicates three categories of property to which special protection is to be given:

1   *A limited number of refuges intended to shelter movable cultural property in the event of armed conflict.* It was difficult, it was considered, to ensure protection which was more extensive than general protection for movable cultural property if such property was not sheltered in refuges fitted out by the State for this specific purpose. These shelters should be specially built to protect the property against bombardment and fire or against dryness and damp. For financial reasons, each country would only be able to build a limited number of shelters of this kind for property regarded as

the most important or the most threatened. The number of refuges was not fixed precisely, but it was felt preferable not to increase their number unduly as this would merely heighten the difficulty of providing protection. The number of refuges will depend on the size of territory, the quantity of property to be protected and also on transport problems, fire risks and so on. Governments will have to take account of two considerations which might at first sight seem contradictory: firstly, the desirability of dispersing the cultural property to be protected as widely as possible so as to reduce the risk factor, and secondly, the need to avoid setting up an excessive number of refuges if protection is to be effective and identification easy.

2   *Centres containing monuments.*
3   *Other immovable cultural property of very great importance.*

It was stated at the Conference that no difference was to be made in regard to the degree of protection accorded to these three categories of cultural property.

Property of Very Great Importance

The protected property – refuges, centres containing monuments and other property – benefits from special protection only when it is regarded as being of very great importance. By comparison with general protection, the standard of qualification for protection changes from property of 'great importance' (Article 1(a)) to property of 'very great importance' (Article 8(1)).

Conditions for Special Protection

These three categories of property 'of very great importance' may be placed under special protection, but only if the two following conditions are fulfilled and respected.

First Condition

The protected property must be situated at an adequate distance from any large industrial centre or from any important military objective constituting a vulnerable point, such as, for example, an aerodrome, broadcasting station, establishment engaged upon work of national defence, a port or railway station of relative importance or a main line of communication.

To explain this provision, we should first consider the notion of 'adequate distance' and the reference to the location which must be remote from 'any large industrial centre' or from 'any important military objective constituting a vulnerable point'. Neither the text of the Convention nor the preparatory work clarified the notion of an 'adequate distance'. It must be interpreted in the light of the specific situation and there is no general criterion that might enable us to say exactly what distance is involved. The notion of an 'adequate distance' must therefore be assessed on a case-by-case basis.[1] The meeting of the High Contracting Parties in 1962 asked for this notion to be clarified but the matter was referred to a consultative committee, which was never set up.

The vagueness of the notion of 'adequate distance' may explain why so few requests for entry in the Register have been made to date. The States which are Parties to the Convention are in fact experiencing difficulties in regard to the application of Article 8. 'In conformity with paragraph (a) of this article, special protection may be accorded to refuges or centres containing monuments which are situated at an adequate distance from any large industrial centre or from any important military objective constituting a vulnerable point, such as an aerodrome, broadcasting station, establishment engaged upon work of national defence, a port or railway station of relative importance or a main line of communication. However, taking into consideration the evolution of military technology, the definition of the distance which can be considered as "adequate" with respect to military objectives (such as those enumerated in Article 8) may well give rise to problems.'[2]

As to the location of the items of protected property, the first paragraph states that they must be situated away from any 'large industrial centre' or from any 'military objective constituting a vulnerable point'. The Conference maintained the reference to a 'large industrial centre',[3] although the observer from the International Committee of the Red Cross pointed out that this might imply that major industrial centres as such might be bombed in their entirety. He pointed out that the ICRC had always objected to the indiscriminate bombing of entire cities, whether they were industrial or not, bombing which was incompatible with Article 27 of the Hague Regulations and the provisions of the Geneva Conventions of 1949 referring to respect for hospitals. Most of the delegates accepted the observer's interpretation which was officially presented by the representative of France and adopted by the Main Commission of the Conference. However, no account was taken of this point in the final text.

The objection by the ICRC observer was all the more pertinent as Article 52 (2) of Protocol I of 1977 states that 'military objectives are limited to those objects which by their nature, location, purpose or use make an effective contribution to military action and whose total or partial destruction, capture or neutralization, in the circumstances ruling at the time, offers a definite military advantage'.

Article 8 (1) refers to the concept of 'any important military objective constituting a vulnerable point'. This expression was retained despite the opinion of the French delegate who felt that the term 'vulnerable point', recognized by all General Staffs, not only designated the military objective but covered and exceeded it.[4] The delegate of the United States of America felt that the Convention must be placed on a level higher than that of elementary tactics to which the notion of 'military objective' belonged. All military personnel responsible for application of the Convention required a higher strategic reference such as that defined by the notion of a 'military objective constituting a vulnerable point'. This was ultimately the opinion which prevailed in the mind of the authors of this provision. However, paragraph 5 of this article makes one exception: any of the cultural property listed in the first paragraph and situated near an important military objective may nevertheless be placed under special protection if the High Contracting Party asking for that protection undertakes, in the event of armed conflict, to make no use of the objective, by, for example, diverting traffic from a port, a railway station or an aerodrome. In that case, the diversion would have to be prepared in time of peace.

Second Condition

The authors of this provision took account of the objections of the military who cannot concede absolute immunity under certain circumstances. That is why exceptions are provided in Article 11.

The paragraph stipulates that the protected property must not be used for military purposes. Paragraphs 3 and 4 of Article 8 clarify to some extent the definition of what is to be regarded as 'use' or 'non-use' for military purposes (see below). This provision must be read in conjunction with Article 9 which ensures the immunity of cultural property under special protection and prohibits 'any use of such property or its surroundings for military purposes'. If that undertaking is infringed by any of the High Contracting Parties, the opposing Party shall be released from the obligation to ensure the immunity of the property in question 'so long as this violation persists' (Article 11(1) of the Convention).

A distinction must be drawn in this paragraph between use and purpose. The paragraph prohibits use for military purposes which naturally depend on a decision of the High Contracting Parties. As to their intended purpose or use, it is important to note that most of this cultural property could be used to accommodate troops, shelter military material or serve as the staff headquarters. It is for the High Contracting Parties to prevent such use of possible use.

This provision on 'use and non-use' for military purposes' therefore touches closely on the problem of the definition of what is to be regarded as a military objective. This definition became increasingly necessary as greater consideration came to be given to the protection of the population and of civilian property. Here the draft text drawn up by the Commission of Jurists which was convened at The Hague in 1922 should be recalled; its Article 24 contains a definition of property of a civilian nature and of military objectives:

1. Aerial bombardment is legitimate only when directed at a military objective, that is to say, an object of which the destruction or injury would constitute a distinct military advantage to the belligerent.
2. Such bombardment is legitimate only when directed exclusively at the following objectives: military forces; military works; military establishments or depots; factories constituting important and well-known centres engaged in the manufacture of arms, ammunition or distinctively military supplies; lines of communication or transportation used for military purposes.
3. The bombardment of cities, towns, villages, dwellings or buildings not in the immediate neighbourhood of the operations of land forces is prohibited ....
4. In the immediate neighbourhood of the operations of land forces, the bombardment of cities, towns, villages, dwellings or buildings is legitimate provided that there exists a reasonable presumption that the military concentration is sufficiently important to justify such bombardment, having regard to the danger thus caused to the civilian population ....

This attempt at a definition of military objectives was not taken up on the occasion of the codification of international humanitarian law in 1929 and 1949. However, it was generally recognized that attacks should be directed at military objectives alone, the interpretation of the term 'military objective' being left to the belligerents themselves.

Article 8 of the Convention sets out a first tentative definition which was continued in later draft codifications of international humanitarian law.[5] These efforts finally resulted in the definition set out in Article 52 of Protocol I of 1977:

1. Civilian objects shall not be the object of attack or of reprisals. Civilian objects are all objects which are not military objectives as defined in paragraph 2.
2. Attacks shall be limited strictly to military objectives. In so far as objects are concerned, military objectives are limited to those objects which by their nature, location, purpose or use make an

effective contribution to military action and whose total or partial destruction, capture or neutralization, in the circumstances ruling at the time, offers a definite military advantage.

3.   In case of doubt whether an object which is normally dedicated to civilian purposes, such as a place of worship, a house or other dwelling or a school, is being used to make an effective contribution to military action, it shall be presumed not to be so used.

The definition of military objectives naturally includes, indeed principally so, the armed forces, their members, installations, equipment and transport. The commentary on the 1977 Additional Protocols points out that 'the military character of an objective can sometimes be recognized visually, but most frequently those who give the order or take the decision to attack will do so on information provided by the competent services of the army. In the majority of cases they will not themselves have the opportunity to check the accuracy of such information; they should at least make sure that the information is precise and recent, and that the precautions and restrictions laid down in Article 57 (*Precautions in attack*) are observed. In case of doubt, additional information must be requested.'[6]

When combat takes place in a town which is defended house by house, there is a still greater risk that a civilian building which is a cultural property may more easily become a military objective (since such a building often makes an effective contribution to the military action). On the other hand, outside the combat zone, the character of the military objective must be clearly established and verified.[7]

PARAGRAPH 2

Contrary to the condition formulated in the first paragraph as to the existence of an adequate distance, the wording of the second paragraph which relates solely to refuges takes no account of their location provided that they are so constructed that, in all probability, they will not be damaged by bombs. The Swiss delegate to the Conference referred to the example of shelters built into mountainsides. In that case the distance between these shelters and a military objective may be relatively short.

PARAGRAPH 3

As was pointed out in connection with the first paragraph, the definition of use or non-use for military purposes is no easy matter. This is borne out by the many generations of legal experts who have turned their attention to the task of codifying international humanitarian law.

The present paragraph represents a partial endeavour to give a clear definition. It relates solely to centres containing monuments which are defined in Article 1 of the Convention and represent wider zones comprising a considerable number of cultural properties as designated in paragraphs (a) and (b) of this same article.

The paragraph states that a centre containing monuments shall be deemed to be used for military purposes whenever it is used for the movement of military personnel or equipment, even in transit. The same shall apply whenever activities directly connected with military operations, the stationing of military personnel or the production of war material are carried on within the centre. In that case, the centre containing monuments becomes a military objective and may be the target of attacks.

PARAGRAPH 4

Contrary to the previous paragraph, which defines the conditions under which a centre containing monuments may be regarded as being used for military purposes, paragraph 4 of Article 8 is couched in negative terms. It indicates the cases in which cultural property shall not be deemed to be used for military purposes.

This paragraph relates to all cultural property liable to be placed under special protection in conformity with paragraph 1. It therefore expressly precludes certain indications which might otherwise be deemed to provide evidence of military use. It states, for example, that the guarding of cultural property by armed custodians specially empowered to do so or the presence, in the vicinity of such cultural property, of police forces normally responsible for the maintenance of public order shall not be deemed to be used for military purposes.[8]

Even if the Hague Convention of 1954 does not refer to the use of arms, it seems quite natural that such personnel cannot be expected to become passive sacrificial victims. The commentary on the First Geneva Convention states in particular: 'Quite apart from the above extreme case, it is clearly necessary for medical personnel to be in a position to ensure the maintenance of order and discipline in the units under their charge. But such personnel may only resort to arms for purely defensive purposes, and in cases where it is obviously necessary. They must refrain from all aggressive action and may not use force to prevent the capture of their unit by the enemy (it is, on the other hand, perfectly legitimate for a medical unit to withdraw in the face of the enemy). Otherwise they would be violating the rules governing their status.'[9] It seems to us that this text is applicable *mutatis mutandis* in the case of the present paragraph.

This provision may also be interpreted in an extensive and non-limitative manner. As the Commentary on the 1949 Geneva Convention points out, 'cases can be imagined where the good faith of the unit remains beyond question in spite of certain appearances to the contrary. For each Party, the question will always be one of good faith.'[10]

PARAGRAPH 5

According to this paragraph, if any cultural property mentioned in paragraph 1 of the present article is situated near an important objective as defined in the said paragraph, it may be placed under special protection if the High Contracting Party asking for that protection undertakes, in the event of armed conflict, to make no use of the objective and particularly, in the case of a port, railway station or aerodrome, to divert all traffic therefrom. In that event, such diversion should be prepared in time of peace. Paragraph 5 accordingly offers some chance for property situated close to a military objective. This paragraph also relates to all cultural property eligible for special protection pursuant to paragraph 1.

Even if this property is situated in the vicinity of – and therefore not at an adequate distance from – an important military objective, it may, under the conditions set out, benefit from special protection. The conditions are as follows:

1   the High Contracting Party which asks for entry in the Register must undertake not to make use of the objective in question in the event of an armed conflict, for example by diverting all traffic from a port, railway station or aerodrome;
2   the diversion must be prepared in time of peace. A study of certain practical instances of special protection would enable lessons to be drawn for the future. For example, because of the presence of a radio broadcasting station in the Vatican City, a proposal was made that the text of the Convention should indicate that a radio station could be of some importance, by analogy with a railway station. As we saw earlier, Italy undertook on 18 September 1959 not to use the Via Aurelia for military purposes in the event of armed conflict. In that case, the military objective was situated on the territory of another country which was required to undertake not to use it in the event of conflict. A proposal was made for the words 'asking for' to be replaced by 'on whose territory the military objective is situated' (Article 8(5) of

the Convention). The situation which would arise in the event of registration of the Holy See would then also be covered. This same paragraph 5 also requires an undertaking, '*in the event of armed conflict, to make no use of the objective*' in question. Italy, in its declaration on the Via Aurelia speaks of the limitation 'to military purposes'. As no Party entered an objection, it was proposed to include this limitation in the article.

PARAGRAPH 6

This provision specifies, as was the case in the UNESCO Draft of Article 8, that special protection is granted to cultural property of the highest importance by its entry in the International Register. Entry in this Register is therefore the decisive consideration as it marks the start of special protection.

In this connection, fears were expressed concerning the danger of pillage or removal of movable cultural goods in view of the fact that the location of these refuges would be made public by their inclusion in the Register. On the other hand there was a risk that property abandoned in a secret refuge might be left to deteriorate. The authors of these provisions were also aware of the extreme fragility of the property to be protected and the need for it to be protected against excessive or insufficient humidity, with regular ventilation or other forms of technical protection. In the event of military occupation, the conservation of cultural objects in a secret refuge could not therefore be ensured either by the national authorities of the occupied country – perhaps unable to gain access to the refuge – or by the Occupying Powers which might not be aware of its location. For most cultural objects, their abandonment for a considerable length of time in this way would be disastrous. Moreover, account had to be taken of the fact that it seemed materially impossible for a substantial quantity of objects to be gathered together in a refuge without an occupying force being informed sooner or later. The (small) risk of removal was therefore considered preferable to that of deterioration and loss of this property. By deciding to adopt the solution of entry in the International Register, the authors of the provision opted for the lesser of two evils.

However, even when it adopts this provision, a State always has the possibility of assuming the risks of deterioration and of keeping the location of this property and of its refuges secret and, accordingly, of refraining from requesting special protection. In that case, the provisions governing general protection would be applicable.

The second sentence of this paragraph gave rise to an interpretation by the UNESCO representative at the Conference. In his view, this sentence meant that the task entrusted to the Director-General of UNESCO was confined to the keeping of the Register. The Director-General would make the entry in all cases when there was no opposition or if that opposition was not upheld. On the other hand, it would not be his responsibility to determine or establish whether a cultural property proposed for entry satisfied the basic conditions laid down in Article 8 of the Convention.

Entry in the Register accordingly replaced the proposals for international inspection and verification by the military authorities for which provision had been made in the 1938 preliminary draft text of the Convention (Arts 4(3)(d) and (4)).

PRACTICAL APPLICATION

The success of the arrangements for special protection has proved very limited. According to a UNESCO report, only five States – Austria, the Federal Republic of Germany, the Khmer Republic, the Netherlands and the Holy See – have, in the past, asked for such refuges or centres containing monuments to be entered in the Register.

In response to these requests, the following eight refuges and one centre containing monuments have been entered in the Register: the Vatican City (18 January 1960); a refuge at Alt-Aussee in Austria (17 November 1967); six refuges in the municipalities of Zandvoort, Heemskerk, Stlenwijkerwold and Maastricht in the Netherlands (12 May 1969); the central Oberrieder Stollen refuge in the Federal Republic of Germany (22 April 1978).

The application forwarded to the Director-General by the Khmer Republic on 31 March 1972 related to the entry of the centres containing the monuments of Angkor and Roluos and of the sanctuaries situated at Pnom-Bok and Pnom-Krom, together with a refuge situated at Angkor. As on the occasion of all the other requests for entry which were received, the Director-General informed the High Contracting Parties of the application from the Khmer Republic dated 25 April 1972 and referred to Article 14 of the Regulations for the Execution of the Convention which states that any of the High Contracting Parties may lodge an objection to the registration of a cultural property by addressing a letter to the Director-General of UNESCO.

Within the period stipulated for the receipt of communications, the Director-General received letters from four High Contracting Parties – Cuba, Egypt, Romania and Yugoslavia – which stated that the application for registration had not been presented by the authority which they considered to be the sole government entitled to represent the Khmer Republic. The Director-General of UNESCO accordingly did not proceed with the registration of these cultural properties. This case illustrates one of the situations which present an obstacle to the implementation of the Convention. The obstacles may derive, as we can see in the case of Cambodia, from exclusively political considerations which are hard to justify in terms of the need to protect property which undeniably forms part of the cultural heritage of all mankind.

The States which raise such obstacles should be aware of their responsibility for the deterioration of this property. They should in particular take account of the fact that short-term political interests have nothing to do with the fundamental objectives of the Convention. In connection with the opposition to an entry in the Register, it was pointed out at the meeting of experts in Vienna in 1983 that when opposition was lodged to the request for the registration of Angkor Vat, UNESCO may not have made full use of all the procedural means at its disposal to lift the objection. 'It was recalled that Article 14(4) of the Regulations for the Execution of the Convention provided that the Director-General could make whatever representations he deemed necessary to the Contracting Parties which lodged the objection, with a view to causing the objection to be withdrawn. The representative of the Director-General explained that, in the case of the request from the Khmer Republic, the Director-General had tried to implement the provisions of Article 14 but the objections had not been withdrawn and no further action could be taken by the Director-General, since the High Contracting Party applying for registration had not requested arbitration as foreseen in paragraphs 6 and 7 of Article 14.'[11]

The small number of applications for registration shows that the States are reluctant to register their cultural property because of the practical difficulties experienced by them with the application of Article 8. This concerns in particular the definition of the term 'adequate distance', to which we have already referred.

As few countries have made applications for special protection, the information contained in the reports by the High Contracting Parties on this subject is naturally very limited. According to reports prepared by a number of countries, the following applications are being examined: the Federal Republic of Germany (in addition to Oberried), Egypt (1970), Spain (1962), France (1983), Hungary (1970), Italy (1967), Liechtenstein (1983), Romania (1962), San Marino (1967), Czechoslovakia (1979) and Yugoslavia (1979). Some countries – Bulgaria, Poland and the USSR (1970) – seemed to have certain reservations over the provisions contained in Article 8 which constitute an obstacle to any application for special protection.

In its report, the Soviet Union noted that most of the monuments concerned by special protection were situated in the big cities (Moscow, Leningrad, Kiev, Riga, Tallin and so on) which were at one and the same time important urban, political, industrial and communication centres, as referred to in Article 8(1a) of the Convention. Only a few monuments among the tens of thousands placed under State protection could benefit from special protection under the conditions set out in the Convention. In the opinion of the competent Soviet authorities, it was impossible to envisage special protection for certain monuments since they were all of great value. The USSR report suggested that the subject of special protection should be examined again at the next meeting organized by UNESCO.

The first Italian report (1962) developed an original concept of zones of special protection having both cultural and health care functions (see our commentary on Article 4 of the Convention).

It will be noted that some confusion existed in a number of countries concerning the items of property entered in the Register of Special Protection (1954 Convention) and those included in the World Heritage List (Bulgaria, Jordan). It would be highly desirable to study the link between special protection and inclusion in the World Heritage List with a view to encouraging the states to enter property appearing in this List under the special protection arrangements covered by the 1954 Convention, or possibly to revise the 1954 Convention with that end in mind.

In general, it would seem that the interest in special protection is very limited. Only Liechtenstein claimed that there were no 'special reasons' for which it had not made use of this possibility. Some States, such as Albania, had created museum-cities which could form centres for which an application might be made for entry in the Register of Special Protection. Libya presented a list of 115 items of cultural property to be entered on the Register. This list was reduced to 47 but no undertaking was given by the government to divert means of communication or to refrain from using the ports in the vicinity of such property in the event of conflict. The application by Libya was not forwarded to the Parties as required by the Convention, but retained for discussion with the Libyan government.

In 1964, the Swiss authorities proposed to the Director-General of the United Nations Office in Geneva that an examination should be made of the possibility of entering the Palais des Nations in Geneva in the Register of Cultural Property under Special Protection. The Palais was regarded as an important building and also housed the archives of the League of Nations and a major library. Mr Stavropoulos, at the time Legal Adviser of the United Nations, believed that the United Nations Headquarters in Geneva and New York would both qualify for special protection. In his letter to the Director-General of UNESCO he raised the problem of the application as such: should it be made by UNESCO or by the States on whose territory the property was situated? Could such protection be granted within the framework of the Convention or must some other basis be sought for it? The Legal Adviser of UNESCO answered this letter by pointing out that this issue had not been raised during the preparatory work on the Convention but that such protection was not ruled out pursuant to Article 1 of the Convention. Since Switzerland had ratified the Convention, 'special protection' was applicable in that country including the possibility of placing the distinctive emblem on the building. In regard to special protection, Mr Saba felt that the question rested with the State on whose territory such property was situated. He considered that the formulation of the application by the Swiss authorities was the best solution, having regard to the circumstances prevailing at the time. He recommended that an agreement be concluded between the territorial State and the United Nations on the scope of the protection and the conditions for registration. No further action has been taken so far on these discussions.

In connection with the present article, reference should also be made to the proposal by Italy to stipulate in the Convention that all documentation regarding cultural property under special protection should be forwarded at regular intervals to the International Committee of the Red Cross (ICRC) in Geneva.[12]

NOTES

1   Stanislaw E. Nahlik, 'Protection of Cultural Property', in *International Dimensions of Humanitarian Law*, Geneva/Paris, Henry Dunant Institute/UNESCO, 1988, p.207. For the record it will be noted that the Preliminary Draft International Convention of 1938 did contain some stipulations on this distance. It made a distinction between protection granted to refuges and that accorded to monuments and centres containing monuments. The refuges should benefit from the prohibition of all acts of hostility. According to Article 4(3) of the Preliminary Draft Convention, the refuges must 'be situated at a distance of not less than 20 kilometres from the most likely theatres of military operations, from any military objective, from any main line of communication and from any large industrial centre (this distance may be reduced in certain cases in countries with a very dense population and small area)'. In this instance, the relevant factor is the distance in relation to ad hoc refuges whose siting might be determined in the light of this requirement. This is clearly not the case with the present article which ensures special protection not only for refuges but also for 'centres containing monuments and other immovable cultural property of very great importance' for which the distance cannot be chosen at will. In regard to these monuments and centres containing monuments (or groups of monuments), Article 5 of the 1938 Preliminary Draft Convention provided for respect and protection; in the case of protection similar to that stipulated in Article 4 of the 1954 Convention, a distance of 500 metres was proposed. Article 6 of the Preliminary Draft also provided for the conclusion of special agreements extending strengthened special protection – that is, the same immunity as is granted to refuges – to certain monuments or groups of monuments the preservation of which, although they do not satisfy the conditions

laid down in Article 4, is of fundamental importance to the international community.

2   *The Cultural Heritage of Mankind: a Shared Responsibility*, Paris, UNESCO, 1982, pp.21–2 (CLT-82/WS/27).

3   *Records*, paras 772–91, pp.194–6.

4   *Records*, para. 667, p.186.

5   See, in particular, the Draft Rules for the Limitation of the Dangers Incurred by the Civilian Population in Time of War (CRC, 1956). According to Article 7, 'only objectives belonging to the categories of objective which, in view of their essential characteristics, are generally acknowledged to be of military importance, may be considered as military objectives'. An annex drawn up with the assistance of military experts lists these categories. 'However, even if they belong to one of these categories, they cannot be considered as a military objective where their total or partial destruction, in the circumstances ruling at the time, offers no military advantage.' At its session in Edinburgh in 1969, the Institute of International Law adopted the following definition: 'There can be considered as military objectives only those which, by their very nature or purpose or use, make an effective contribution to military action, or exhibit a generally recognized military significance, such that their total or partial destruction in the actual circumstances gives a substantial, specific and immediate military advantage to those who are in a position to destroy them.'

6   This paragraph calls to mind Article 22 of the Geneva Convention for the Amelioration of the Condition of the Wounded and Sick in Armed Forces in the Field (Convention I) of 12 August 1949 which sets out the conditions which shall not be considered as depriving a medical unit or establishment of protection (Yves Sandoz, Christophe Swiniarski and Bruno Zimmermann (eds), *Commentary on the Additional Protocols of 8 June 1977 to the Geneva Conventions of 12 August 1949*, Geneva, ICRC/Martinus Nijhoff Publishers, 1986, p.620). The authors of this paragraph were no doubt guided by this provision even if it has been formulated differently since the protection concerned is also of a different kind. According to this paragraph the term 'use for military purposes' shall not include: (a) the guarding of cultural property by armed custodians specially empowered to do so, or (b) the presence, in the vicinity of such cultural property, of police forces normally responsible for the maintenance of public order. Article 22 of the First Geneva Convention of 1949 regarded the following as circumstances which do not deprive the unit or establishment concerned of protection: '1. That the personnel of the unit or establishment are armed and that they use the arms in their own defence, or in that of the wounded and sick in their charge. 2. That in the absence of armed orderlies, the unit or establishment is protected by a picket or by sentries or by an escort.'

7   Idem.

8   See also Article 35 of Convention II.

9   Jean S. Pictet (ed.), *The Geneva Conventions of 12 August 1949. Commentary*, Volume I – *Geneva Convention for the Amelioration of the Condition of the Wounded and Sick in Armed Forces in the Field*, Geneva, ICRC, 1952, p.203.

10 Ibid., p.203.

11 Final report of the Meeting of Legal Experts on the Convention for the Protection of Cultural Property in the Event of Armed Conflict (The Hague, 1954), held in Vienna from 17 to 19 October 1983, Paris, UNESCO, 1983, pp.8–9, para. 24 (CLT-83/CONF.641/1).

12 *Records*, p.350.

REGULATIONS FOR THE EXECUTION OF THE CONVENTION – CHAPTER II: SPECIAL PROTECTION

Article 11 of the Regulations for the Execution of the Convention: Improvised Refuges

1. *If, during an armed conflict, any High Contracting Party is induced by unforeseen circumstances to set up an improvised refuge and desires that it should be placed under special protection, it shall communicate this fact forthwith to the Commissioner-General accredited to that Party.*
2. *If the Commissioner-General considers that such a measure is justified by the circumstances and by the importance of the cultural property sheltered in this improvised refuge, he may authorize the High Contracting Party to display on such refuge the distinctive emblem defined in Article 16 of the Convention. He shall communicate his decision without delay to the delegates of the Protecting Powers who are concerned, each of whom may, within a time-limit of 30 days, order the immediate withdrawal of the emblem.*
3. *As soon as such delegates have signified their agreement or if the time-limit of 30 days has passed without any of the delegates concerned having made an objection and if, in the view of the Commissioner-General, the refuge fulfils the conditions laid down in Article 8 of the Convention, the Commissioner-General shall request the Director-General of the United Nations Educational, Scientific and Cultural Organization to enter the refuge in the Register of Cultural Property under Special Protection.*

Records: Text: pp.48–50.
Minutes: paras 1285–94, 1465, 1487–90, 2056–60.
Working documents: pp.317–18, 331, 345, 348–9, 402, 403;
CBC/DR/105/108/113/143/164.

Article 11 introduces a brief and simplified procedure to place cultural property under special temporary protection and expedite its entry in the Register of Cultural Property under Special Protection. This procedure is applicable only during an armed conflict.

The UNESCO Draft provided for a more complicated procedure: first it was necessary to consult the delegates of the Protecting Powers concerned and then, after their agreement or lack of objection, the Commissioner-General might request entry after 30 days.[1] According to the delegate of the Netherlands, this Draft had two shortcomings. First was the length of the period for making the entry even if no objection were formulated (the possibility of its being less than 30 days seems somewhat theoretical). Secondly, the article stipulated that if no objection was made the Commissioner-General should request entry of the refuge in the International Register. That meant that the refuge was placed under special protection even though it might not fulfil the conditions laid down in Article 12 of the Regulations.[2]

The Netherlands rightly preferred the Draft which was submitted to the meeting of governmental experts in 1952 (CL/656 Annex, Article 12 of the Regulations for Execution). According to this Draft, the Chairman of the International Control Commission (now the Commissioner-General) can authorize the affixing of a symbol to an improvised refuge (which can be done very quickly), after which the Parties concerned may submit their objections. If no objection is raised, the refuge may continue to bear the emblem without thereby acquiring the status of a monument placed under special protection. That would be possible only when the refuge, in the opinion of the Commissioner-General, fulfilled the conditions laid down in Article 12 of the Regulations for the Execution of the Convention.[3] This approach was received favourably by certain delegations at the Conference, as is indicated by the amendment proposed by the Netherlands and the USSR.[4]

Paragraph 1

Paragraph 1 provides for the application of this provision: solely during an armed conflict; when the High Contracting Party is induced by unforeseen circumstances to set up an improvised refuge; and if it wishes this refuge to be placed under special protection.[5] It is therefore this High Contracting Party which takes the initiative and immediately notifies or formulates a request to the Commissioner-General accredited to that Party.

Paragraph 2

From then on, the initiative rests with the Commissioner-General. It is his responsibility to consider and decide whether there are circumstances (for example a threat by the armed conflict to the cultural property concerned) which justify the application of this provision and also whether the cultural property sheltered in this improvised refuge is important enough for the application of this measure to be justified. At this stage the Commissioner-General does not examine whether the refuge satisfies the requirements of Article 8 of the Convention and his judgement is confined to the question of the importance of the property. If, under these circumstances, he decides to apply this measure, he may authorize the High Contracting Party to display the distinctive emblem as defined in Article 16 of the Convention on the improvised refuge. He shall notify his decision without delay to the delegates of the Protecting Powers concerned, each of whom may, within a time-limit of 30 days, order the immediate withdrawal of the emblem. This exceptional power is granted to the delegates of the Protecting Powers in order to bring about a rapid solution.

It will be noted that the Commissioner-General authorizes the display of the distinctive emblem but makes no pronouncement on the status of the refuge since, as indicated in the first sentence of this paragraph, he does not examine at this stage the question of whether the refuge satisfies the requirements of Article 8 of the Convention. In that sense, the final article differs from the proposal tabled by the USSR which wanted temporary protection to be granted to such refuges.[6]

Paragraph 3

Should the delegates of the Protecting Powers order the immediate withdrawal of the emblem within the time-limit of 30 days, it will not be possible to grant special protection to these improvised refuges. If, on the other hand, the delegates have signified their agreement or the time-limit of 30 days elapses without any objection by any of the delegates of the Protecting Powers, the procedure for entry may begin. In that case, the Commissioner-General must ascertain whether the improvised refuge fulfils the conditions laid down in Article 8 of the Convention. Once again, the Commissioner-General may take a positive or negative decision. If he is of the opinion that the improvised refuge satisfies the conditions stipulated in Article 8 of the Convention, and only in that case, he will ask the Director-General of UNESCO to enter the refuge in the Register of Cultural Property under Special Protection.

NOTES

1   *Records*, p.316.
2   *Records* , p.331.
3   Idem.
4   *Records*, pp.402–3, paras 1285–94, p.230.
5   The High Contracting Party must express a wish for this to be done. This requirement was added by the United Kingdom delegate in the final phase of the discussion of this article: *Records*, para. 2056, p.286.
6   *Records*, CBC/DR/113, p.402.

Article 12 of the Regulations for the Execution of the Convention: International Register of Cultural Property under Special Protection

1. *An International Register of Cultural Property under Special Protection shall be prepared.*
2. *The Director-General of the United Nations Educational, Scientific and Cultural Organization shall maintain this Register. He shall furnish copies to the Secretary-General of the United Nations and to the High Contracting Parties.*
3. *The Register shall be divided into sections, each in the name of a High Contracting Party. Each section shall be subdivided into three paragraphs headed: Refuges, Centres containing Monuments, Other Immovable Cultural Property. The Director-General shall determine what details each section shall contain.*

> *Records*:   Text: p.51.
> Minutes: paras 1296, 1308–20, 1370, 1773, 2060.
> Working documents: pp.317–18, 326–7, 349–50, 402–3; CBC/DR/115/164.

Pursuant to Article 8 of the Convention, special protection is granted to cultural property by its entry in the International Register of Cultural Property under Special Protection. Such entry shall only be made in accordance with the provisions of the present Convention and under the conditions provided for in the Regulations for the Execution of the Convention. That demonstrates the importance of the present article of the Regulations.

Paragraph 1

Paragraph 1 establishes the creation of an International Register of Cultural Property under Special Protection.

Paragraph 2

The UNESCO Draft document provided for the Register to be maintained by the Director-General of UNESCO, a copy being held by the Secretary-General of the United Nations. On a proposal from the Soviet Union,[1] this provision was modified since primary responsibility for keeping the Register was entrusted to the Director-General of UNESCO who was instructed to forward copies to the Secretary-General of the United Nations and to the High Contracting Parties.

Article 15 and 16 of the Regulations for the Execution of the Convention refer to the transmission of copies. Article 15(4) states that

'The Director-General shall send without delay to the Secretary-General of the United Nations, to the High Contracting Parties and, at the request of the Party applying for registration, to all other States referred to in Articles 30 and 32 of the Convention, a certified copy of each entry in the Register. Entries shall become effective 30 days after dispatch of such copies.' Article 16(2) states that 'the Director-General shall send without delay, to the Secretary-General of the United Nations and to all States which received a copy of the entry in the Register, a certified copy of its cancellation. Cancellation shall take effect 30 days after the dispatch of such copies.'

The Soviet delegate to the Conference rightly pointed out that it was not sufficient to forward copies of the entries and cancellations. 'Such copies must then be collected into a complete document. Every State should possess a copy of the Register.'[2]

Paragraph 3

This paragraph clarifies the form of the Register. In order to standardize practice in regard to the establishment of the Register, UNESCO prepared rules in 1956 designed to ensure implementation of the provisions of the Convention and of the Regulations; they contained a model of the pages of the Register and fictitious examples of entries.[3]

In our commentary on Article 8, we gave examples of the registration practice and explained why there had been little progress in this area. It will be recalled that the meeting of experts held in Vienna in 1983 noted the fact that few entries had been made. UNESCO can assist the High Contracting Parties to make an inventory of their cultural property which would qualify for entry in the Register and to encourage the States to apply for registration. In that regard, the World Heritage List drawn up under the 1972 Convention for the Protection of the World Cultural and Natural Heritage refers to the cultural property which warrants being taken into consideration and included in the Register. However, such cultural property must fulfil the conditions of Article 8; in particular it must be situated at an 'adequate distance' from any military objective, although, with the technical evolution of warfare, this criterion – which lacks precision – is becoming increasingly impossible to apply.

Links with the 1972 Convention

The provisions relating to the Register should be read in close conjunction with the article of the 1972 Convention concerning the World Heritage List. According to Article 11(2) of the 1972 Convention, the World Heritage Committee establishes, keeps up to date and publishes, on the basis of the inventories submitted by States, a list of properties forming part of the cultural heritage and natural heritage as defined in Articles 1 and 2 of the Convention and which it considers as having outstanding universal value in terms of such criteria as it shall have established. Paragraph 4 of this same Article 11 provides for the establishment, whenever circumstances shall so require, of a 'List of World Heritage in Danger' for the conservation of which major operations are necessary. This list may include only such property forming part of the cultural and natural heritage as is threatened by serious and specific dangers, such as the threat of disappearance caused by accelerated deterioration or, for example, the outbreak or the threat of an armed conflict.[4]

S.E. Nahlik suggested that a link should be established between the two Conventions; for that purpose an article should be adopted which would supplement Article 8 of the 1954 Convention and grant special protection to the property appearing on the World Heritage List.[5]

Annex CL/1136 (G) Rules established by the Director-General of the United Nations Educational, Scientific and Cultural Organization on 18 August 1956 concerning the International Register of Cultural Property under Special Protection　Whereas Article 8 of the Convention for the Protection of Cultural Property in the Event of Armed Conflict provides that, subject to certain conditions, a limited number of 'refuges intended to shelter movable cultural property in the event of armed conflict', 'centres containing monuments', and 'other immovable cultural property of very great importance' may be placed under special protection and that this special protection shall be granted by the entry of the said property in the 'International Register of Cultural Property under Special Protection';

Whereas Article 12 of the Regulations for the Execution of the Convention states that the Director-General of the United Nations Educational, Scientific and Cultural Organization shall maintain this Register and shall determine what details each section shall contain;

Considering Chapter II of the aforementioned Regulations for the Execution of the Convention.

The Director-General of UNESCO establishes the following rules:

Article 1

The International Register of Cultural Property under Special Protection shall be kept in French. Proper names and references to geographical features[6] and administrative units[7] shall, however, be given in the language of the country concerned in Latin characters, and shall be followed where applicable by a French translation in brackets.

Article 2

The Register shall take the form of a bound book, all the pages of which, consisting of lined paper, shall be numbered and initialled by the Director-General. Each page shall be marked 'Chapitre…' (Section…) and shall be divided into five columns headed as follows: (1) No.; (2) 'Indication du bien culturel' (Description of the cultural property); (3) 'Date d'inscription' (Date of registration); (4) 'Envoi des copies de l'inscription' (Dispatch of copies of the entry); (5) 'Radiation' (Cancellation).

Article 3

The Register shall be divided into sections, which shall not be numbered. Each section shall bear the name of the territory of a High Contracting Party, or the name of a territory for whose international relations a High Contracting Party is responsible, followed, in brackets, by the name of the High Contracting Party concerned.

Article 4

Each section shall be subdivided into three paragraphs headed: 'Refuges', 'Centres monumentaux' (Centres containing monuments), 'Autres biens culturels immeubles' (Other immovable cultural property).

Article 5

In column (1) shall be shown a serial number for each item of cultural property registered. In each paragraph, numbering shall begin with the figure 1.

Article 6

In column (2) shall be shown the following details, in order, for each item of cultural property accepted for entry in the Register:

1.   The name, underlined, of the place where the cultural property is situated [8] followed by the names of the series of administrative units to which it pertains.[9]
2.   The name, underlined, by which the cultural property is locally known;[10] in the case of 'other immovable cultural property', the character of that cultural property[11] shall be specified, after the name.
3.   The details necessary to enable the cultural property to be easily located; these to include:

(a) in the case of a 'centre containing monuments', precise indications of the boundaries of such centre, and details of the main cultural property contained therein, as defined in paragraphs (a) and (b) of Article 1 of the Convention; in the case of a 'refuge' or 'other movable cultural property', where appropriate, the name of the district, and the street in which it is situated, and the number in the street;

(b) the approximate surface area of the property, in square metres;

(c) its approximate distance, in metres, from the seat of the smallest administrative unit (town hall) and its situation in relation thereto; any other indications helpful for locating it may also be given;[12]

(d) the longitude and latitude, the former in relation to the Greenwich meridian, in seconds.

Article 7

In cases within the meaning of Article 8, paragraph 5, of the Convention, the entry in column (2) shall be followed by a mention of the important military objective near which the cultural property is situated, and a note that the High Contracting Party concerned has undertaken, in the event of armed conflict, to make no use of the objective; where a port, railway station or aerodrome is concerned, there shall, in addition, be a note to the effect that the High Contracting Party has undertaken to make preparations, in time of peace, to divert all traffic therefrom in the event of armed conflict.

Article 8

In cases within the meaning of paragraph 3 of Article 11 of the Regulations for the Execution of the Convention, it shall be noted, at the end of the entry in column (2), that the registration has been made at the request of the competent Commissioner-General for Cultural Property.

Article 9

In cases where the details entered in column (2) do not fill up the entire line, the blank space remaining shall be filled in by an unbroken stroke, in ink, so as to ensure that no subsequent addition can be made. The same shall be done if there is any blank space remaining at the foot of column (2).

Article 10

In column (3) shall be shown the date of entry in the Register, for each item of cultural property.

In the case mentioned in paragraph 5 of Article 14 of the Regulations for the Execution of the Convention, the word 'provisoire' (provisional) shall also be entered in column (3). If no objection has been lodged within the period stipulated in the Regulations, if an objection has been withdrawn of cancelled, or if it has failed to be confirmed following the procedure laid down in either paragraph 7 or paragraph 8 of Article 14, then the words 'inscription définitive' (final registration) shall be added under the word 'provisoire' together with the date.

Article 11

In column (4) shall be shown the dates of dispatch of a certified copy of the entry, in the Register, of an item of cultural property, or of a series of entries in the same section of the Register; and also, where applicable, the dates of dispatch of a certified copy of the declaration stating that a provisional registration has become final:

(a) to the Secretary-General of the United Nations and to the High Contracting Parties;

(b) where appropriate at the request of the High Contracting Party which applied for registration, to the other States mentioned in Articles 30 and 32 of the Convention;

(c) to all States which have become High Contracting Parties after the date of dispatch to the parties mentioned under (a).

Article 12

In column (5) shall be shown the dates:

(a) of any cancellation of an entry in the Register, or of a series of entries in the same section of the Register, with the reason therefor;

(b) of the dispatch by registered letter, of certified copies of the record of cancellation to the Secretary-General of the United Nations and to all States which received copies of the entry in the Register.

Article 13

For all entries, amendments or cancellations made in the Register, or for all series of entries, amendments or cancellations in the same section of the Register, a record shall be drawn up containing all relevant details of the procedure followed. These records shall be signed by the Director-General, and kept in the Secretariat of UNESCO.

Article 14

In the copies of the Register, furnished to the Secretary-General of the United Nations and to the High Contracting Parties in accordance with Article 12, paragraph 2, of the Regulations for the Execution of the Convention, the sections shall be published in alphabetical order by names of countries, regardless of the order of registration. Within each section, entries shall be published in the order of the paragraphs and shall follow the numbering of the entries.

The first copy of the complete register shall be furnished two years after the date of the first entry in the Register.

Paris, 18 August 1956
(signed)   Luther H. Evans
Director-General

NOTES

1   *Records*, para. 1309, p.231, CBC/DR/115, p.403.
2   *Records*, para. 1315, p.231.
3   Rules established by the Director-General of UNESCO, 18 August 1956, concerning the International Register of Cultural Property under Special Protection, doc. CL/1136. See annex to the commentary on this article.
4   See Part VI.
5   S.E. Nahlik, 'Convention for the Protection of Cultural Property in the Event of Armed Conflict, The Hague 1954: general and special protection', in *La protezione internazionale dei beni culturali*, Rome, Fondazione Europea Dragan, 1986, p.100, n.35.
6   For example: mountain, lake or forest.
7   For example: county, parish.
8   For example: the name of the town, village, hamlet, forest.
9   For example: in France, *canton* or *département*; in the United Kingdom, *county, city, borough, urban district or parish*; in Germany: *Gemeinde, Kreis, Regierungspräsidium*.
10 For example: *Refuge d'oeuvres d'art A.X.; Vieille ville, Quartier du Marché, Castel San'Angelo, Yeni Valide Cami, Nordisk Museet, Borobudur, Hôtel Sully*.
11 For example: *tell*, excavation site, old fortifications, castle, museum, town hall, public baths, temple, church, mosque, stupa, monastery, private house.

12   For example: in the western part of the forest of ...; at a height of 500 metres on the north slope of the mountain ...; in the centre of the only copse in the region.

Article 13 of the Regulations for the Execution of the Convention: Requests for Registration

1. *Any High Contracting Party may submit to the Director-General of the United Nations Educational, Scientific and Cultural Organization an application for the entry in the Register of certain refuges, centres containing monuments or other immovable cultural property situated within its territory. Such application shall contain a description of the location of such property and shall certify that the property complies with the provisions of Article 8 of the Convention.*
2. *In the event of occupation, the Occupying Power shall be competent to make such application.*
3. *The Director-General of the United Nations Educational, Scientific and Cultural Organization shall, without delay, send copies of applications for registration to each of the High Contracting Parties.*

    Records: Text: p.50.
                Minutes: paras 1321–33, 2061–8.
                Working documents: pp.317–18, 345, 403–4;
                CBC/DR/126/164.

Paragraph 1

The first sentence of this paragraph has been taken from the UNESCO Draft. On the other hand, the second sentence was formulated as follows in that Draft: 'Such application shall contain an exact description of the location of each item of such property and shall certify that the property complies with the conditions laid down in Article 11, 13 or 14 of the present Regulations' (these articles of the draft Regulations have been incorporated into Article 8 of the Convention).[1]

A discussion took place on the meaning of the words 'exact' description and 'of each item'. The delegate of the United States of America held that these words constituted a tedious and unwarrantable obligation which would be unacceptable to the military staffs of any State. He felt that information of this kind might prove particularly useful to an artillery man and proposed that less precise terms be used.[2] His proposal was accepted.

(The reference to Article 11, 13 and 14 of the Regulations was replaced by the reference to Article 8 of the Convention as these articles were embodied in Article 8 of the Convention.)

The first paragraph of the UNESCO Draft included the following sentence: 'In the cases foreseen in Articles 13(2) and 14(2), a summary of the scheme for diversion shall be annexed to the application.' Article 13(2) of the draft Regulations for the Execution of the Convention stipulated that 'when a centre containing monuments is situated near to such an objective [military objective – J.T.] it may nevertheless be placed under special protection if the High Contracting Party asking for that protection undertakes, in the event of armed conflict, to make no use of the objective, and particularly, in the case of a port, railway station or aerodrome, to divert all traffic therefrom. In that event such diversion shall be prepared in time of peace.' Article 14(2) concerning immovable cultural property states that Article 13(2) shall apply.

The reference to a 'summary of the scheme for diversion [which] shall be annexed to the application' was rejected on a proposal by Italy as being unacceptable for military security reasons.[3] The delegate of Israel on the other hand felt that the Italian proposal almost nullified the safeguards to be taken under Article 8 of the Convention.[4] According to this delegate, 'no one would believe facts unless there was proof that plans had been made for diversion'.[5]

The delegate of Italy put an important question: while affirming that UNESCO was not responsible for the entry in the Register he asked whether 'the Director-General, if certain certificates were lacking to back a request, or if further information were necessary, could use his initiative'.[6] The representative of the UNESCO Secretariat replied that the Director-General would have to verify if all the required documents arising out of Article 13 had been supplied, and that he could decide on their formal regularity and request any missing certificates.[7]

Paragraph 2

This paragraph states that, in the event of occupation, the Occupying Power shall be competent – in other words it has this possibility if it so wishes – to make applications for entry in the International Register. This optional task of the Occupying Power must be interpreted in the context of the general provision set out in Article 5 of the Convention. According to that provision, the Occupying Power shall, as far as possible, support the competent national authorities of the occupied territory in safeguarding and preserving its cultural property.

Paragraph 3

In order to keep the High Contracting Parties informed, but above all because of the possibility of lodging objections provided for in Article 14 of the Regulations, the Director-General of UNESCO is required to forward, without delay, copies of applications for registration to each of the High Contracting Parties.

This dispatch must be effected rapidly. The expression 'without delay' means that the dispatch shall be effected at once, instantly, immediately and without waiting, but also within the time allowed by law.[8]

NOTES

1   *Records*, Article 13, p.403.
2   *Records*, paras 1322, 1326, p.232.
3   *Records*, para. 1323, p.232.
4   *Records*, para. 1327, pp.232–3.
5   Idem.
6   *Records*, paras 2061–62, p.286.
7   *Records*, paras 2064–67, p.286.
8   *Black's Law Dictionary*, St Paul, Minn., West Publishing Co., 1968, p.1777; cf. also *Le Robert. Dictionnaire alphabétique et analogique de la langue française*, Vol. II, Paris, Société du nouveau Littré, Le Robert, 1974, p.85.

Article 14 of the Regulations for the Execution of the Convention: Objections

1.   *Any High Contracting Party may, by letter addressed to the Director-General of the United Nations Educational, Scientific and Cultural Organization, lodge an objection to the registration of cultural property. This letter must be received by him within four months of the day on which he sent a copy of the application for registration.*
2.   *Such objection shall state the reasons giving rise to it, the only valid grounds being that: (a) the property is not cultural property; (b) the property does not comply with the conditions mentioned in Article 8 of the Convention.*
3.   *The Director-General shall send a copy of the letter of objection to the High Contracting Parties without delay. He shall, if necessary, seek the advice of the International Committee on Monuments, Artistic and Historical Sites and Archaeological Excavations and also, if he thinks fit, of any other competent organization or person.*
4.   *The Director-General, or the High Contracting Party requesting registration, may make whatever representations they deem necessary to the High Contracting Parties which lodged the objection, with a view to causing the objection to be withdrawn.*
5.   *If a High Contracting Party which has made an application for registration in time of peace becomes involved in an armed conflict before*

the entry has been made, the cultural property concerned shall at once be provisionally entered in the Register, by the Director-General, pending the confirmation, withdrawal or cancellation of any objection that may be, or may have been, made.

6.   *If, within a period of six months from the date of receipt of the letter of objection, the Director-General has not received from the High Contracting Party lodging the objection a communication stating that it has been withdrawn, the High Contracting Party applying for registration may request arbitration in accordance with the procedure in the following paragraph.*

7.   *The request for arbitration shall not be made more than one year after the date of receipt by the Director-General of the letter of objection. Each of the two Parties to the dispute shall appoint an arbitrator. When more than one objection has been lodged against an application for registration, the High Contracting Parties which have lodged the objections shall, by common consent, appoint a single arbitrator. These two arbitrators shall select a chief arbitrator from the international list mentioned in Article 1 of the present Regulations. If such arbitrators cannot agree upon their choice, they shall ask the President of the International Court of Justice to appoint a chief arbitrator who need not necessarily be chosen from the international list. The arbitral tribunal thus constituted shall fix its own procedure. There shall be no appeal from its decisions.*

8.   *Each of the High Contracting Parties may declare, whenever a dispute to which it is a Party arises, that it does not wish to apply the arbitration procedure provided for in the preceding paragraph. In such cases, the objection to an application for registration shall be submitted by the Director-General to the High Contracting Parties. The objection will be confirmed only if the High Contracting Parties so decide by a two-thirds majority of the High Contracting Parties voting. The vote shall be taken by correspondence, unless the Director-General of the United Nations Educational, Scientific and Cultural Organization deems it essential to convene a meeting under the powers conferred upon him by Article 27 of the Convention. If the Director-General decides to proceed with the vote by correspondence, he shall invite the High Contracting Parties to transmit their votes by sealed letter within six months from the day on which they were invited to do so.*

Records: Text: pp.52, 54.
             Minutes: paras 1334–6, 1368–9, 1427–63, 1592–1607, 1702–15, 1764–72, 1778, 1780–1824, 2069–75, 2079–82.
             Working documents: pp.317–18, 324, 341–2, 349–50, 403–5;
             CBC/DR/116/122/127/131/140/147/149/150/156/160.

At the time of its drafting, this provision was already considered delicate and was no more than the outcome of a compromise. Nevertheless, the article was adopted, although with a number of amendments.

Some countries, in particular the United States of America, were against the arbitration procedure envisaged.

Paragraph 1

Any High Contracting Party may, by letter addressed to the Director-General of UNESCO, lodge an objection to the registration of cultural property. But this right of objection exists only for a period of four months so as not to leave it open indefinitely. The paragraph stipulates that this period is counted from the day on which the Director-General sends a copy of the application for registration. The day of dispatch is decisive.

Paragraph 2

The objection which any of the High Contracting Parties may send to the Director-General of UNESCO shall state the reasons, failing which it shall be invalid. The paragraph lists the only admissible reasons for an objection. This provision is very important as it excludes any reason other than those indicated in this paragraph, namely:

(a)   The nature of the property, that is, that 'it is not cultural property'. The nature of the property must be assessed in the light of Article 1 of the Convention which defines cultural property. Article 1 is the determining factor as it helps to decide whether the property is genuinely cultural. This provision does not require any judgement as to the value of the property concerned, that is, whether it is a property of 'great importance' (Article 1) or one of 'very great importance' (Article 8). We have already pointed out that the decision in this regard rests with the High Contracting Party on whose territory the property is situated.

(b)   The conditions mentioned in Article 8 of the Convention. We believe that this paragraph refers only to the two conditions (a) and (b) set out in paragraph 1 and to the indications given in paragraphs 2 and 6 of Article 8 of the Convention.

Paragraph 3

Paragraph 3 contains two main ideas. First, the Director-General of UNESCO is required to send without delay a copy of the letter of objection addressed to him by one or more Contracting States to the other High Contracting Parties. Secondly, he may arrange consultations in respect of the objection: he may (if necessary or appropriate) seek the opinion of the International Committee on Monuments, Artistic and Historical Sites and Archaeological Excavations. But, if he thinks fit, he may also consult any other competent organization or person.

Whereas the first provision sets out an unconditional duty of the Director-General, the second sentence provides that he may examine the content of the letter of objection in order to determine whether it effectively constitutes an objection and whether that objection satisfies the conditions set out in paragraph 2 of the present article. He may also do so in the situation referred to in paragraph 4 of the present article, that is, when he envisages making appropriate representations to the High Contracting Parties which have lodged the objection so as to cause it to be withdrawn.

The second sentence of this paragraph does not release the Director-General from the duty to send a copy of the letter of objection to the High Contracting Parties.

Paragraph 4

The Regulations give the Director-General or the High Contracting Party requesting registration the right to undertake – reflected in the words 'may make' – all appropriate representations to the High Contracting Parties which lodged the objection with a view to causing it to be withdrawn.

In this context the term 'withdrawal' has the sense of 'annulment', 'cancellation' or 'revocation'. The latter expression ('révoquer') is probably the closest equivalent in French to the English word 'withdrawn' used in the text.

In the formula envisaged originally by the Committee of Experts, in the event that these representations failed, the objection would have been upheld. That system would have given each State a veritable right of veto which might have nullified the Convention. For that reason, the first formula envisaged was finally rejected. The authors wondered whether it might not be appropriate to fix a quorum of objections necessary to prevent entry of the litigious cultural property in the Register.

To avert the danger of the collective veto, the arbitration system was adopted. It provided the best guarantee for the State making the application for entry that this would not fail without a valid reason.

Paragraph 5

This important paragraph did not appear in the UNESCO Draft. It was introduced in the form of an amendment by the delegate of Israel[1] and illustrated by the delegate of the United Kingdom who cited the example of an enemy State which might have 'submitted a malicious objection'. He felt that the purpose of the amendment was not only to cover 'that emergency but would apply also to the case of an enemy entering his objection shortly before planning an aggression'[2].

The delegate of Switzerland pointed out that the proposed procedure was too easy in relation to the guarantees required to ensure special protection. The delegate of Israel defended his amendment by stressing that 'many articles might be abused, but that the benefit of the doubt should always be on the side of the cultural property'.[3]

The purpose of this paragraph is to help to regulate the consequences of the outbreak of an armed conflict before the entry in the Register has been made. It accordingly covers the period between the application for such entry and the registration as such. This provision therefore exists for cases in which armed conflicts break out during this period, that is, before the registration procedure has been completed. Accordingly, if after requesting in time of peace the entry of a cultural property in the Register, a High Contracting Party finds itself engaged in an armed conflict before the entry has been effectively made, the cultural property will be immediately placed on the Register on a provisional basis by the Director-General of UNESCO pending the withdrawal, cancellation or confirmation of a possible objection pursuant to paragraphs 7 or 8 of the present article.

Paragraph 6

Paragraph 6 sets out the conditions under which the arbitration procedure will be initiated. If, within a period of six months from the date of receipt of the letter of objection, the Director-General of UNESCO has not received from the High Contracting Party lodging the objection a communication stating that it has been withdrawn, the High Contracting Party applying for registration may request arbitration in accordance with the procedure set out in paragraph 7.

Paragraph 7

If the objection is not withdrawn, the High Contracting Party which requested registration may resort to the arbitration procedure. The application must be made within one year of receipt of the letter of objection by the Director-General.

Some delegations to the Conference were opposed to the arbitration procedure. For example, legislation in the United States does not permit arbitration on a question of fact; the question as to the value of a cultural property or its distance from a military objective are questions of fact.

The deletion of this procedure was not accepted by the Main Commission of the Conference; the delegate of the United States therefore asked for the following reservation by the United States to be placed on record: 'That it was noted that any High Contracting Party might, at any time, withdraw its request for registration of a specific cultural object or might withdraw any objection which it had entered against the registration of a specific cultural object by another High Contracting Party.'[4]

The delegate of Italy sought a solution by proposing an expert judgement arrangement,[5] but it was Mr Saba (UNESCO Secretariat) who put forward an acceptable formula: 'If, when an objection to the registration of an item of cultural property had been made, arbitration might not be replaced by a decision taken by … a defined majority of a meeting of the High Contracting Parties themselves.'[6] The delegate of the United States accepted that proposal. The delegate of the United Kingdom submitted an amendment, drafted by a person who preferred to remain anonymous: the intention was to preserve the UNESCO text adopted by the Main Commission and to add an eighth paragraph to cover the particular case under discussion.[7] This proposal was adopted by 29 votes to seven with one abstention and accordingly appears in paragraph 8 of this article.

In the final version, responsibility for arbitration is entrusted to a college of three arbitrators. Each of the Parties to the dispute appoints an arbitrator and these two arbitrators then choose a chief arbitrator, selected from the international list established by the Director-General in conformity with Article 1 of the Regulations. If the two arbitrators are unable to reach agreement on the choice of a chief arbitrator, this paragraph provides that they shall request the President of the International Court of Justice to appoint a chief arbitrator who need not necessarily be chosen from the international list referred to in Article 1 of the Regulations.

The delegate of the USSR wanted the words 'shall ask' to be replaced by the optional formulation 'may ask'. Following his somewhat restrictive attitude at the time towards the competence of the Court, he suggested that this formulation should reflect a possibility and not an obligation so as to be in conformity with the equality of the rights of the Parties to the litigation. This proposal was not accepted. The Chairman wondered what would happen if the arbitrators did not ask the President of the International Court of Justice to appoint a chief arbitrator and he reminded the representatives of the fact 'that everyone knew that there were frequent instances of work being brought to a standstill because one Party refused to co-operate in the selection of an arbitrator'. The obligation of the arbitrators to address themselves to the President of the Court was accordingly maintained and the Soviet amendment was rejected by 23 votes to seven with seven abstentions.[8]

Paragraph 8

The arbitration procedure is both complex and costly and should only be followed in cases which are of some importance. Moreover, it is a fact that some countries are opposed to it because the use of arbitration does not fit in with their national policy.[9]

Stressing the fact that the Committee had adopted the simple arbitration formula only by a small majority, the UNESCO Commentary on the draft Convention already provided for a combination of a quorum and arbitration.

We have seen – in the commentary on paragraph 7 of this article – that the United States in particular was opposed to the arbitration procedure as its legislation did not permit arbitration on questions of fact. The issues concerning the value of a cultural property or its distance from a military objective are quite clearly questions of fact.

We have also seen that Mr Saba (UNESCO Secretariat) indicated a way forward to an acceptable compromise by proposing that, if arbitration were impossible, the decision should be taken by a qualified majority of the High Contracting Parties themselves. That proposal was accepted by the delegate of the United States and the delegate of the United Kingdom who submitted a proposal to preserve the text presented by UNESCO and adopted by the Main Commission but with the addition of the present paragraph 8 to overcome this problem. The proposal of the United Kingdom delegate was adopted by 29 votes to seven with one abstention and is therefore included in paragraph 8 of this article.

It is therefore hardly surprising that the Conference took all these considerations into account and came out in favour of a combination of the arbitration procedure on the one hand with the role of the High Contracting Parties on the other. In the latter procedure, each of the High Contracting Parties may declare, at the time when a dispute to which it is a Party arises, that it does not wish to apply the arbitration procedure for which provision is made in paragraph 7. In that case, the objection to a request for registration is submitted by the Director-General to the High Contracting Parties.

In this particular case, the objection is confirmed only if the High Contracting Parties so decide by a two-thirds majority of those voting.[10] The purpose of the proposal, supported by some and opposed by others, was to raise the level of the majority and reduce the possibility of objections.

Should the necessary majority not be obtained, the cultural property item, the registration of which had been opposed, would continue to obtain special protection. Since the objection procedure is applicable in time of war, in the event of disagreement between two countries the benefit of the doubt should be given in favour of special protection.[11] The delegate of Greece wanted the following words to be added to this paragraph: 'Should that majority not be obtained, the item will be considered as still being under special protection', so as to prevent the entry from being held up.

The vote will in principle be taken by correspondence unless the Director-General of UNESCO deems it essential to convene a meeting by virtue of the powers conferred upon him by Article 27 of the Convention. If the Director-General decides to call a vote by correspondence, he shall invite the High Contracting Parties to transmit their votes by sealed letter within six months from the day on which they were invited to do so. This time-limit was fixed by the Conference on a proposal from the delegate of Italy.

The adoption of this paragraph required an amendment to the text of Article 27 of the Convention in respect of meetings of the High Contracting Parties and the following words were added to paragraph 2: 'without prejudice to any other functions which have been conferred on it by the present Convention or the Regulations for its Execution'.

NOTES

1   *Records*, pp.324, 350, CBC/DR/122; *Records*, p.404.
2   *Records*, para. 1428, p.239.
3   *Records*, paras 1432–3, p.240.
4   *Records*, para. 1349, p.234.
5   *Records*, para. 1445, pp.240–41.
6   *Records*, para. 1453, p.241.
7   *Records*, para. 1702, p.261, CBC/DR/150, p.404.
8   *Records*, paras. 1361, 1365, p.235.
9   *Records*, para. 1340, p.233.
10 The discussion then turned to the size of the majority. The delegate of Poland maintained that 'an objection to the registration of an item should require a higher majority, for example, four-fifths, not of voters but of all the High Contracting Parties. For an article to be rejected the case should be exceptionally serious' (*Records*, para. 1783, p.269).
11 *Records*, para. 1789, pp.269–70. The delegate of Italy then stated that 'if a large majority did not decide to uphold it [the objection], the object should be registered'. *Records*, para. 1787, p.269.

Article 15 of the Regulations for the Execution of the Convention: Registration

1. *The Director-General of the United Nations Educational, Scientific and Cultural Organization shall cause to be entered in the Register, under a serial number, each item of property for which application for registration is made, provided that he has not received an objection within the time-limit prescribed in paragraph 1 of Article 14.*
2. *If an objection has been lodged, and without prejudice to the provision of paragraph 5 of Article 14, the Director-General shall enter property in the Register only if the objection has been withdrawn or has failed to be confirmed following the procedures laid down in either paragraph 7 or paragraph 8 of Article 14.*
3. *Whenever paragraph 3 of Article 11 applies, the Director-General shall enter property in the Register if so requested by the Commissioner-General for Cultural Property.*
4. *The Director-General shall send without delay to the Secretary-General of the United Nations, to the High Contracting Parties, and, at the request of the Party applying for registration, to all other States referred to in Articles 30 and 32 of the Convention, a certified copy of each entry in the Register. Entries shall become effective 30 days after the dispatch of such copies.*

Records: Text: pp.54, 56.
Minutes: paras 1313, 1336, 1367–70, 1427–8, 1443, 1709–10, 1715–18, 1767, 1773, 1814, 2077–83, 2088, 2092.
Working documents: pp.318, 324, 349, 404–5; CBC/DR/123/131/141/156/160/165.

The Conference adopted this article on the basis of the UNESCO Draft. Amendments were made to it, particularly in relation to the other articles, including Article 14 of the Regulations.

Paragraph 1

The Director-General of UNESCO shall cause to be entered in the Register under a serial number each item of property for which an application for registration is made, provided that this application has not been the subject of an objection within the time-limit laid down in the first paragraph of Article 14, that is, within four months of the day on which a copy of the application for registration was dispatched.

Paragraph 2

Where an objection has been lodged, the Director-General shall enter property in the Register only if the objection has been withdrawn or if it has not been confirmed following the procedures laid down in paragraphs 7 and 8 of Article 14.

The exception is also provided for on the basis of Article 14(5) which introduced a provisional registration in cases where a High Contracting Party, after applying for the entry of a cultural property in the Register in time of peace, becomes involved in an armed conflict before the registration has effectively been made. As we saw in paragraph 5 of Article 14 of the Regulations, in that case the cultural property concerned will at once be entered in the Register by the Director-General on a provisional basis pending the confirmation, withdrawal or cancellation of any objection that may be, or may have been, made. *In this way the benefit of the doubt has been given to the cultural property and not to the aggressor.*

Paragraph 3

To establish a link between the registration procedure and other provisions, paragraph 3 stipulates that, in the instance referred to by Article 11(3), the Director-General shall make the registration at the request of the Commissioner-General for Cultural Property.

This covers a situation in which a High Contracting Party, during an armed conflict, may be obliged by unforeseen circumstances to set up an improvised refuge and would like this refuge to be placed under special protection. As we have seen, in that case the Commissioner-General may authorize the High Contracting Party to use the distinctive emblem and he will notify his decision without delay to the delegates of the Protecting Powers who are concerned, each of whom may, within 30 days, order the immediate withdrawal of the emblem. But if these delegates have signified their agreement or if the time-limit of 30 days expires without an objection being lodged by any of the delegates concerned and if, in the view of the Commissioner-General, the improvised refuge fulfils the conditions laid down in Article 8 of the Convention, the Commissioner-General shall ask the Director-General of UNESCO to enter the refuge in the Register of Cultural Property under Special Protection.

Paragraph 4

As set out in the original UNESCO Draft, the Director-General shall forward without delay to the Secretary-General of the United Nations, to the High Contracting Parties and, at the request of the Party applying for registration, to all the other States referred to in Articles 30 and 32 of the Convention, a certified copy of each entry in the Register. Entries shall become effective 30 days after the dispatch of such copies.

The States referred to in Articles 30 and 32 are as follows: (1) all the States invited to the Conference which met at The Hague from 21 April to 14 May 1954; (2) any other State invited to accede to the Convention by the Executive Board of UNESCO.

Article 16 of the Regulations for the Execution of the Convention: Cancellation

1. *The Director-General of the United Nations Educational, Scientific and Cultural Organization shall cause the registration of any property to be cancelled:*
   - (a) *at the request of the High Contracting Party within whose territory the cultural property is situated;*
   - (b) *if the High Contracting Party which requested registration has denounced the Convention, and when that denunciation has taken effect;*
   - (c) *in the special case provided for in Article 14, paragraph 5, when an objection has been confirmed following the procedures mentioned either in paragraph 7 or in paragraph 8 of Article 14.*
2. *The Director-General shall send without delay, to the Secretary-General of the United nations and to all States which received a copy of the entry in the Register, a certified copy of its cancellation. Cancellation shall take effect 30 days after the dispatch of such copies.*

   Records: Text: p.56.
   Minutes: paras 1313, 1370–82, 1428, 1443, 1773–5, 1814, 2093–5.
   Working documents: pp.318, 406;
   CBC/DR/148/156/160.

During discussion of this article in the Main Commission, the delegate of Italy raised the question of whether provision should not be made for cancellation in cases where a cultural property entered in the Register was subsequently used for military purposes. The Chairman and the Swiss delegate pointed out that Article 8 already provided for that situation and stated that in that case the opposing Party was protected. Indeed, 'if the other Party to the conflict violated the Convention in respect of an object under special protection, the opposing Party was freed from its undertaking towards the object concerned for as long as that violation lasted'.[1] At the request of the Swiss delegate this interpretation was recorded in the minutes. However, doubts were expressed over the need to effect a cancellation as this would require a new registration or entry procedure at the time when the cultural property ceased to be used in violation of the Convention.

Paragraph 1

This article logically provides for the cancellation in the Register of a cultural property previously entered in it. The Director-General of UNESCO may cause the entry to be cancelled in three cases:

(a)   at the request of the High Contracting Party within whose territory the property is situated; the UNESCO Draft had referred to the High Contracting Party which had 'applied for it'; this amendment and clarification of the text were made at the request of the Secretariat;

(b)   if the High Contracting Party which requested registration has denounced the Convention and when that denunciation has taken effect. This paragraph is a logical addition to the Regulations since special protection (Article 8 of the Convention) and general protection (Article 4 of the Convention) can apply only on the territory of the High Contracting Parties;

(c)   in the special case provided for in Article 14(5), when an objection has been confirmed following the procedures referred to in Article 14(7) or (8). This paragraph was added on a proposal from the United Kingdom in order to make provision for the situations which were introduced into Article 14.[2]

Paragraph 2

As in the case of Article 15, paragraph 4, concerning applications for registration, in the event of cancellation, the Director-General shall forward without delay to the Secretary-General of the United Nations, and to all States which have received a copy of the registration, a certified copy of every cancellation in the Register. As in the case of registration, cancellation shall likewise take effect 30 days after this dispatch.

In order to bring this article into line with Article 15(4) , the reference to the Secretary-General of the United Nations, who was not mentioned in the article contained in the UNESCO Draft,[3] was added.

NOTES

1   *Records*, para. 1376, p.236.
2   See Commentary on Article 14 of the Regulations for the Execution of the Convention.
3   *Records*, para. 1773, p.268.

Article 9
Immunity of Cultural Property Under Special Protection

The High Contracting Parties undertake to ensure the immunity of cultural property under special protection of refraining, from the time of entry in the International Register, from any act of hostility directed against such property and, except for the cases provided for in paragraph 5 of Article 8, from any use of such property or its surroundings for military purposes.

Records: Text, p.14.

           Minutes: paras 463, 466, 491, 502, 506–37, 539, 551, 554, 556–7, 560, 579, 654°95, 772, 791, 973, 979, 1948–52, 1954, 1961, 1962.

           Working documents: pp.309, 344, 345, 347, 351–2, 380; CBC/DR/44/60/66/121.

Bibliography: Nahlik, Stanislaw Edward, 'La protection internationale des biens culturels en cas de conflit armé', *Recueil des cours de l'Académie de droit international*, Vol. 120, II, The Hague, 1967, pp.61–163; idem. 'On some deficiencies of the Hague Convention of 1954 on the Protection of Cultural Property in the Event of Armed Conflict', *Annuaire de l'Association des anciens de l'Académie*, Vol. 44, The Hague 1974, pp.100–108; idem. 'International law and the protection of cultural property in armed conflicts', *The Hastings Law Journal* (San Francisco), Vol. 27, No. 5, 1976, pp.1069–87; idem. 'Convention for the Protection of Cultural Property in the Event of Armed Conflict, The Hague 1954: General and Special Protection', in Istituto Internazionale di diritto umanitario (ed.), *La protezione internazionale dei beni culturali/The international protection of cultural property/ La protection internationale des biens culturels*, Rome, Fondazione Europea Dragan, 1986, pp.87–100.

Article 8 of the Convention defines cultural property placed under special protection. The purpose of Article 9 is to define the treatment accorded to this property, that is, to assure its immunity or absolute inviolability. For the purposes of the Convention immunity is defined as the prohibition from the time of entry in the International Register of any act of hostility directed against such property except for the cases provided for in paragraph 5 of Article 8 of the Convention and any use of such property or its surroundings for military purposes.

It was stressed that, having regard to the very high cultural value of the property recognized and entered in the Register following a procedure which provides for the possibility of objection to registration, any infringement of the Convention concerning such property will be of an extremely serious nature. The Party which commits such an infringement could not invoke the excuse of a lack of information given the publicity which surrounds the procedure envisaged and given the nature of the protected property.

The Main Commission adopted the United Kingdom proposal seeking the inclusion of the words 'from the time of entry in the International Register' which appeared in the UNESCO Draft and clearly show that the property benefiting from special protection cannot be used for military purposes even in peacetime. In this connection reference was also made to the suddenness of the outbreak of wars and to the resulting impossibility of removing military property or personnel from any particular location.

Acts of hostility constitute the whole range of actions and operations of war in the broad sense, regardless of whether they are committed by the opposing Party or by the Party to the conflict which has cultural property in its possession. The authors of Protocol I to the Geneva Conventions of 1977 preferred the term 'attack', which is defined in the military instructions of many countries as an offensive act whose purpose is to destroy enemy forces and gain ground. The definition adopted by the Protocol is wider since it also covers defensive acts (particularly, 'counter-attacks') and offensive acts since both of them may affect the protected objectives, in this case cultural property. The Commentary of the ICRC seems to identify both terms when it defines attacks as 'the use of armed force to carry out a military operation at the beginning or during the course of armed conflict.[1]

The fact that the Convention uses the term 'acts of hostility' signifies that the prohibition also extends to the cultural property in its own possession or on its own territory. The Convention therefore protects cultural property against destruction committed by all the Parties to the conflict, regardless of whether such destruction is the result of an attack or of the deterioration of objects under the control of a Party.

Article 9 of the Convention makes reference to paragraph 5 of Article 8. For the immunity to be ensured, it is essential for the cultural property to have been placed under special protection and, although situated near an important military objective, to be safeguarded against this natural disadvantage by an undertaking of the High Contracting Party to make no use of the objective in question in the event of an armed conflict and in particular, in the case of a port, railway station or aerodrome, to divert all traffic therefrom. As stipulated in that same paragraph, the diversion must be prepared in time of peace.

Paragraph 3 of Article 8 defines what is meant by use for military purposes.[2]

The exception in regard to 'immunity' in the case of paragraph 5 of Article 8 has been clearly expressed in Article 9 which, as we have seen, was not the case in Article 4. S.E. Nahlik has raised the question as to whether this exception is not contrary to the prohibition of reprisals. Indeed, the ban on reprisals also applies to cultural property under special protection even if no express mention is made of that prohibition. *A fortiori*, the ban on reprisals must also apply to special protection. S.E. Nahlik observes an inconsistency between the prohibition of reprisals on the one hand and the exception in regard to immunity on the other; this inconsistency may perhaps be explained by reference to the general principle of reciprocity (without forgetting the fact that the prohibition of reprisals must in itself be regarded as an exception to the principle of reciprocity).[3]

NOTES

1   Yves Sandoz, Christophe Swiniarski and Bruno Zimmermann (eds), *Commentary on the Additional Protocols of 8 June 1977 to the Geneva Conventions of 12 August 1949*, Geneva, ICRC/Martinus Nijhoff Publishers, 1987, para. 1882, p.603.
2   See Commentary on Article 8(3) of the Convention.
3   Stanislaw E. Nahlik, 'Convention for the Protection of Cultural Property in the Event of Armed Conflict, The Hague 1954: General and Special Protection', in Istituto internazionale di diritto umanitario, (ed.), *La protezione internazionale dei beni culturali/The international protection of cultural property/La protection internationale des biens culturels*, p.93.

Article 10
Identification and Control

During an armed conflict, cultural property under special protection shall be marked with the distinctive emblem described in Article 16, and shall be open to international control as provided for in the Regulations for the execution of the Convention.

Records: Text: p.14.
Minutes: paras 539–49, 696, 1465, 1469, 1472–6, 1963.
Working documents: pp.310, 392;
CBC/DR/49/143.

Article 6 of the Convention permits the distinctive marking of cultural property under general protection, while Article 10 covers that of cultural property under special protection. The details of the distinctive marking are set out in Article 16 and 17 of the Convention. Article 10 has two aspects: identification and control during an armed conflict.

IDENTIFICATION

The cultural property which is under special protection shall be marked with the distinctive emblem described in Article 16. Article 6 on the distinctive marking of cultural property under general protection introduces optional identification of this property. In the case of cultural property under special protection, distinctive marking is compulsory in periods of armed conflict.

The reference to armed conflict was maintained despite the French proposal which sought to extend protection to peacetime, which would have required cultural property to be already marked by distinctive emblems in peacetime. It was stated that cultural property under special protection *may* be marked by the distinctive emblem in peacetime but *must* be marked with that distinctive emblem in time of conflict.

INTERNATIONAL CONTROL

Cultural property under special protection shall be open to international control as provided for in the Regulations for the Execution of the Convention. The Commissioner-General for Cultural Property, the delegates of the Protecting Powers, the inspectors and experts may all monitor application of the Convention, make sure that there are no infringements (Articles 5, 6, 7 and 8 of the Regulations) or see that transport operations involve only the property stated in the request (Article 17(3) of the Regulations).

Article 11
Withdrawal of Immunity

1. *If one of the High Contracting Parties commits, in respect of any item of cultural property under special protection, a violation of the obligations under Article 9, the opposing Party shall, so long as this violation persists, be released from the obligation to ensure the immunity of the property concerned. Nevertheless, whenever possible, the latter Party shall first request the cessation of such violation within a reasonable time.*
2. *Apart from the case provided for in paragraph 1 of the present article, immunity shall be withdrawn from cultural property under special protection only in exceptional cases of unavoidably military necessity, and only for such time as that necessity continues. Such necessity can be established only by the officer commanding a force the equivalent of a division in size or larger. Whenever circumstances permit, the opposing Party shall be notified, a reasonable time in advance, of the decision to withdraw immunity.*
3. *The Party withdrawing immunity shall, as soon as possible, so inform the Commissioner-General for Cultural Property provided for in the Regulations for the Execution of the Convention, in writing, stating the reasons.*

Records: Text: p.16.
Minutes: paras 281, 469, 511, 513, 550–77, 696, 903, 906, 908–9, 968–1022, 1028, 1054, 1094, 1374, 1929, 1964–83.
Working documents: pp.310, 323–5, 329, 333, 340, 343, 347;
CBC/DR/9/48/50/59/65/96.

Bibliography: Eustathiades, T. 'La réserve des nécessités militaires et la Convention de La Haye pour la protection des biens culturels en cas de conflit armé', pp.183–209; Nahlik, Stanislaw E., 'La protection internationale des biens culturels en cas de conflit armé', *Recueil des cours de l'Académie de droit international*, Vol. 120, II, The Hague, 1967, pp.130–32.

The present article provides for certain forms of withdrawal of immunity as defined in Article 9 of the Convention. The first form, set out in paragraph 1, concerns the situation in which one of the High Contracting Parties is released from the obligation to ensure the immunity of a cultural property when the opposing Party commits a violation of the undertakings given under Article 9. The second form, set out in paragraph 2, relates to exceptional cases of unavoidable military necessity.

PARAGRAPH 1

Article 11, paragraph 1, introduces the notion of reciprocity in the area of special protection. By virtue of this provision, if one of the High Contracting Parties violates the obligations under Article 9 in respect of a cultural property placed under special protection (in other words if it commits any act of hostility directed against such property and, except for the cases provided for in Article 8(5), makes any use of such property or its surroundings for military purposes), the opposing Party shall, so long as this violation persists, be released from the obligation to ensue the immunity of the property concerned.

A request is optional in this instance. The article states that 'nevertheless, whenever possible, the latter Party (that is, the High Contracting Party) shall first request the cessation of such violation within a reasonable time'. What is meant by a reasonable time? This period, which is always short, can, in our view, only be determined in the light of the circumstances specific to each case.

PARAGRAPH 2

Article 11 is no doubt one of the most controversial provisions of the Convention. During the preparatory work, the desire to exclude the reservation of military necessity was clearly expressed by several delegations which were anxious to ensure that the Convention as a whole proved effective (see the Commentary on Article 4 of the Convention). The reservation of military necessity in the context of special protection seemed all the more serious as it gave the impression that 'one might legitimately take back with one hand something which had been parsimoniously granted with the other to an extremely limited number of cultural properties of "very great importance"'.[1]

Mr Morales Chacon, the delegate of Ecuador, considered such a reservation 'inadmissible if the spirit and fundamental postulates of the Convention were to be adhered to'. He thought that 'application of the provisions was difficult, if not impossible, as the military leadership of no country in the world could be entrusted with the supreme responsibility of deciding the preservation or destruction of the cultural heritage'.[2] The subjective nature of that approach was also underlined by the delegate of Spain. In his view, the future belligerents would believe themselves authorized to evade the obligations of the Convention by turning the exception into a permanent principle. Mr Brichet, the delegate of France, added that the French civilian and military authorities, when consulted on this question, would prefer this article to make no reference to imperative military necessities. The delegate of the USSR, Mr Kemenov, pointed out that the destruction of cultural property of exceptional value such as Westminster Abbey could not be justified by any military necessity whatsoever.[3]

On the other hand, the delegate of the United Kingdom hoped that it 'was clear...that, since the principle of military necessity had been included in the Convention with regard to general protection, it should necessarily appear with regard to special protection'. He saw this simply as a difference of degree.[4] He went so far as to say that to exclude such a reservation would make the Convention 'totally unacceptable to a number of countries'. It was precisely the desire of most of the delegates to secure the broadest possible ratification of the Convention which led to the rejection of the opposing motions (22 votes to nine with six abstentions in the Main Commission and 20 to seven with 14 abstentions in plenary session). This was the view expressed by the Rapporteur-General, Mr Brichet. It is therefore all the more regrettable that the countries which obtained satisfaction during the Conference did not sign and ratify this text or accede to it.

By comparison with the concept of general protection, the notion of military necessity in the case of special protection is more limited and accompanied in particular by a number of conditions which correspond to the other restrictions associated with special protection.

1. The expressions used are highly limitative. In the first place the text refers to *exceptional cases*. Secondly it refers to *unavoidable military necessity*, as compared with the term 'imperative military necessity' used in Article 4. Here some authors are of the opinion that 'it is not for a jurist to comment on the practical value of these adjectives' and they remain sceptical in this respect.[5] They also wonder whether the adjective 'unavoidable' will constitute a more effective barrier than the term 'imperative'. According to the dictionary definition, 'unavoidable' means 'inevitable, that cannot be avoided or escaped'.[6] While this adjective is impersonal, objective and independent of any decision, the term 'imperative' for its part has a

subjective character defined as follows: 'what characterizes the term "imperative" is the fact of combining the idea of the action with the idea of the determination of the speaker'.[7] This proposal takes the form of a command which demands obedience, execution, action.[8,9] The formulation used therefore gives fairly clear expression to the compromise which was reached at the Conference: a concession to those who insisted on the inclusion of military necessity on the one hand and the desire of the majority to ensure the protection of cultural property on the other.

2.   Particular attention was given to the determination of the *authority responsible* for the withdrawal of immunity. As we have seen, this matter was already discussed at the Conference in connection with Articles 4 and 11 of the Convention. The decision on the lifting of immunity was first to be entrusted to the 'staff of the large formation in charge of the operation involved' (UNESCO Draft). Then the United Kingdom proposal asked for the order to life immunity to be given only by 'the officer commanding a force the equivalent of a division in size or larger'. It was this latter wording which was included in the final text of the Convention.[10] The intention was to prevent a situation in which any officer was able to judge the existence of an unavoidable military necessity. There is no great difference between the two formulas,[11] except for the fact that the reference to 'staff' would have meant that an individual decision would have been replaced by a collective decision.

In addition, the delegate of France stressed the need to define the responsibility of the authority taking the decision. This 'official or body concerned should be responsible to national as well as international authorities'[12] and would have to submit reasons for any decision. The concern of the French delegate, which was expressed in more detail by the Japanese delegate, is reflected in Article 11(3) (notification of the withdrawal of immunity to the Commissioner-General for Cultural Property).

The United Kingdom proposal that the words 'or in exceptional circumstances confirmed' should be added after 'such necessity can be established' was not accepted. This new clause would have placed the decision on military necessity in the hands of an officer of a force the equivalent of a division in size or larger, *post factum* (that is, once it had been taken by a military commander of a rank lower than that of a divisional commander).[13] Approval of this proposal would have rendered the reservation completely ineffectual since it would have allowed the decision to lift immunity to be taken by any local commanding officer. For the same reason, the representatives at the Conference did not accept the United Kingdom proposal to the effect that unavoidable military necessity could be established by the commanding officer 'whenever military circumstances permit'.[14] Had this clause been adopted, the establishment of a case of unavoidable military necessity by the officer commanding a force at least equivalent to a division would no longer have been a condition for governing the legality of the waiver.

The lifting of immunity as it is defined in this paragraph leads us to take up the fundamental question which was raised by the delegate of Ecuador:[15] does the military commander, even at divisional level, have the necessary competence to assess the significance of what will be sacrificed by his decision? Despite this dilemma, the clause exists in the Convention and there is little likelihood of its being deleted even on the occasion of a reaffirmation and possible development of the rules relating to the protection of cultural property.

There are few ways of making this clause work. In fact there are only two: training and penalties. *Training* would consist in educating the senior military officers and making them understand the enormous responsibility which they bear to future generations. As to *penalties*, experience shows that in these situations the use of sanctions is both difficult and ineffectual (see the judgement handed down in the trial of the German High Command).[16] It is nevertheless important for military officers to be informed of the sanctions that they might incur if they omit to discharge their responsibilities and their duties.

This clause should help the authorities of the countries which have not yet acceded to the Convention by showing them just how few commitments are entailed in this accession. How can these authorities justify – given the minimum commitment involved – the fact that they still remain outside the system of relatively weak protection provided by the Convention? These remarks are directed in particular to the countries which, through their action at the Conference, substantially curtailed its scope and, after obtaining and minimizing the system of protection, have still not acceded to the Convention.

3. The lifting of immunity is *temporary*, 'for such time as that necessity continues'.

4. The *notification* 'a reasonable time in advance' of the withdrawal of immunity is required but unfortunately only 'whenever circumstances permit'.

PARAGRAPH 3

Paragraph 3 adds an obligation for the Party which withdraws immunity to so inform in writing, as soon as possible and stating the reasons, the Commissioner-General for Cultural Property in accordance with the conditions set out in the Regulations for the Execution of the Convention. The Conference accordingly filled two gaps in the text of the UNESCO Draft, thanks to the amendments tabled by the delegates of Japan and of Greece.[17]

The obligation to inform the Commissioner-General of the withdrawal of immunity relates to the two forms of withdrawal defined in paragraphs 1 and 2. In brief, the Party which decides to withdraw immunity must provide the following information. In the first formulation, set out in paragraph 1, which relates to the situation in which one of the High Contracting Parties is released from its obligation to ensure the immunity of a cultural property when the opposing Party violates the undertakings given under Article 9, the Party which withdraws immunity shall first request the opposing Party to cease the violation of the Convention and shall duly inform the Commissioner-General.

In the case of the second formulation, set out in paragraph 2, which relates to exceptional cases of unavoidable military necessity, the Party which withdraws immunity shall notify the opposing Party thereof sufficiently far in advance and shall duly inform the Commissioner-General.

It will be noted that the 'realists' obtained satisfaction in regard to the bulk of the amendments designed to limit the application of special protection. That is why T. Eustathiades wondered whether 'a way might not be found of counterbalancing the calculation of the realists who place such emphasis on military necessity in order to facilitate the adoption by the largest possible number of States of the undertakings set out in the Convention'.[18]

NOTES

1   T. Eustathiades, 'La réserve des nécessités militaires et la Convention de La Haye pour la protection des biens culturels en cas de conflit armé', in *Hommage d'une génération de juristes au Président Basdevant*, p.204.
2   *Records*, para. 569, p.178.
3   *Records*, para. 987, p.209.
4   *Records*, para. 986, p.208.
5   S.E. Nahlik, 'La protection internationale des biens culturels en cas de conflit armé', *Recueil des cours de l'Académie de droit international*, Vol. 120, II, The Hague, 1967, p.132. T. Eustathiades considers that the use of the term 'unavoidable' represents a higher degree of protection. He recalls the terminology used in other instruments of humanitarian law to conclude that 'in all cases where military necessity is qualified, the freedom of judgement of the person who applies the reservation is restricted to an extent which depends on the chosen qualification (important, imperative, absolute, unavoidable, urgent)': 'La réserve des néseccités militaires', p.205.
6   *The Oxford English Dictionary*, Vol. XI.
7   M. Bréal, *Essai de sémantique: science des significations*, Geneva, 1976, p.240.
8   *The Oxford English Dictionary*, Vol. V.

9 In his introduction to Article 11, Mr Saba, UNESCO's Legal Adviser, stressed that, 'in using the term "unavoidable" in connection with special protection, it was intended to give it a connotation even stronger than that implied by the expression "imperative military necessity" used in Article 4... This distinction should therefore be understood as reflecting the greater degree of protection provided for in Chapter II' (*Records*, p.310).

10 The United Kingdom delegate went still further in broadening the basis of decision making on the withdrawal of immunity: 'There would always be exceptional circumstances in which it would not be possible to refer back to divisional headquarters in time. A paratroop brigade thousands of miles away from any high command or a brigade in desperate straits in a battle, to quote only two instances, would have to take decisions on the spot, and the Convention should provide for that emergency in order that officers might not find themselves in the position of having violated the Convention.' That proposal was rejected by 22 votes to five with 11 abstentions (*Records*, para. 999, p.209). During the plenary session, Turkey supported the proposal of the United Kingdom delegate but this was rejected by 23 votes to ten with eight abstentions.

11 T. Eustathiades, 'La réserve des nécessités militaires', p.207.

12 *Records*, para. 572, p.179. In particular, he stated that the authority in question 'would have to submit the reasons for any decision according to a procedure similar to that used in naval law'.

13 *Records*, para. 1010, p.210.

14 *Records*, p.381 (CBC/DR/59).

15 *Records*, para. 569, p.178.

16 'the factual determination as to what constitutes military necessity is difficult... a commander must necessarily make quick decisions to meet the particular situation of his command. A great deal of latitude must be accorded to him under such circumstances' (*Law Reports*, Vol. XII, pp.93–4).

17 T. Eustathiades, 'La réserve des nécessités militaires', p.207.

18 Ibid., p.209.

Chapter III
Transport of Cultural Property

We may recall that the Instructions of 1863 'for the government of armies of the United States in the field' (Lieber Code) already made reference in Article 36 to the question of the transport of cultural property: 'if such works of art, libraries, collections or instruments belonging to a hostile nation or government, can be removed without injury, the ruler of the conquering State or nation may order them to be seized and removed for the benefit of the said nation. The ultimate ownership is to be settled by the ensuing treaty of peace. In no case shall they be sold or given away if captured by the armies of the United States, not shall they ever be privately appropriated or wantonly destroyed or injured.'[1]

At the end of the nineteenth century, Johann Caspar Bluntschli pointed out that international law could now rule that works of art must not be taken from the defeated nation because there is no direct or indirect way in which they can serve to make war, nor does seizing them force the enemy to sue for peace more quickly. Selling them and using the proceeds to make war is equally foreign to civilized ideas. Works of art are an integral part of the intellectual life of a people and a country, and war, which is only a passing storm, must respect, as far as possible, a nation's eternal rights.[2]

The Preliminary Draft Convention of 1938 laid down, in its Article 9, the basic principles that are now to be found in Article 12 of the 1954 Convention: immunity for the means of transport used, provided the transfer takes place under international supervision. The article also included a limitation that does not appear in the 1954 text, according to which the belligerent State shall be entitled to the immunity only once for the same works of art and solely in the direction of the host country.

The 1954 Hague Convention makes provision for two types of transport. The first, as specified in Article 12 of the Convention, is governed by conditions which provide that the opposing Party is informed of all relevant details some time in advance of the transfer and international supervision ensured. In this case transport enjoys the same immunity as that afforded to cultural property under special protection. The conditions governing this kind of transport are set out in the Regulations for the Execution of the Convention. The second type of transport, as specified in Article 13 of the Convention, covers situations in which it proves impossible to take the steps envisaged in Article 12 and where, for that reason, complete immunity cannot be provided.

Both types of transport may, under certain conditions, be entitled to the protection of the distinctive emblem. In both cases, the property is protected against seizure, placing in prize or capture (Article 14.1 of the Convention).

NOTES

1 'Instructions for the Government of Armies of the United States in the Field', prepared by Francis Lieber, promulgated as General Order No. 100 by President Lincoln, 24 April 1863. See Dietrich Schindler and Jiří Toman (eds), *The Laws of Armed Conflicts. A collection of conventions, resolutions and other documents*, third edition, Dordrecht, Martinus Nijhoff Publishers, 1988, p.8. See also J.G. Bluntschli, *Le droit international codifié*, fifth edition revised and amplified, Paris, Félix Alcan, 1895, p.493.
2 Johann Caspar Bluntschli, 'Code de droit international, article 650', in *Le droit international codifié*, p.366.

Article 12
Transport Under Special Protection

1. *Transport exclusively engaged in the transfer of cultural property, whether within a territory or to another territory, may, at the request of the High Contracting Party concerned, take place under special protection in accordance with the conditions specified in the Regulations for the Execution of the Convention.*
2. *Transport under special protection shall take place under the international supervision provided for in the aforesaid Regulations and shall display the distinctive emblem described in Article 16.*
3. *The High Contracting Parties shall refrain from any act of hostility directed against transport under special protection.*

Records: Text: p.16.
Minutes: paras 510, 581–92, 596–607, 696, 1034–6, 1043, 1047–8, 1668, 1985.

Working documents: pp.311–12, 318–19, 322, 344, 347, 382;
CBC/DR/67/68/118.

This first type of transport was regarded by the authors of this provision as the more appropriate. The conditions under which it takes place provide that the opposing Party is informed of all relevant details some time in advance of the transfer and international supervision ensured. In this case transport enjoys the same immunity as that afforded to cultural property under special protection. The conditions governing this kind of transport are set out in the Regulations for the Execution of the Convention; this provision is no more than an introduction and should be read and interpreted in the light of the text of those Regulations.

PARAGRAPH 1

Under this paragraph, transport exclusively engaged in the transfer of cultural property, whether within a territory or to another territory may, at the request of the High Contracting Party concerned, take place under special protection. The conditions for such transport are specified in more detail in the Regulations for the Execution of the Convention.

Although the Convention refers only to transport in this article it is logical that transport under special protection should concern the means of transport as well as the property that is transported. This is, moreover, clearly confirmed by the reference in Article 14, paragraph 1 of the Convention which, in prohibiting seizure, placing in prize or capture, refers to 'cultural property enjoying the protection provided for in Article 12 or that provided for in Article 13'. Here, respect for cultural property coincides with that for movable cultural property as laid down in Article 4 of the Convention.

A special provision – Article 15 – deals with the protection of personnel. The question of personnel was not included in the text concerning transport, even though this was expressly requested by the Swiss delegate.

During the Conference the Greek delegate also asked whether this protection concerned land, sea and air transport. The question was asked primarily because of the fact that private enemy property was not protected at sea or in the air. Ships transporting private property, for example, were not exempt from confiscation. Article 4 of the Eleventh Hague Convention referred only to ships on scientific missions and did not, therefore, cover the maritime transport of cultural property. For reasons of safety a government might wish to transport private collections by sea or air. He requested that a new paragraph should therefore be inserted to the effect that ships and planes, as well as the property transported, should in no case be subject to seizure.[1] This Greek proposal lay at the origin of the inclusion of Article 14, which did not appear in the UNESCO Draft.

The article makes it clear that the transport concerned here is exclusively that engaged in the transfer of cultural property. Any possibility of combining one transport with another is therefore ruled out.

Transport under special protection is carried out at the request of the High Contracting Party concerned. The expression 'High Contracting Party concerned' was defined at the Conference as an occupied country, an occupying one or one acting as a depositary.[2]

PARAGRAPH 2

This provision is simply a reference to the Regulations for the Execution of the Convention as regards the international nature of the supervision; the paragraph does also point out, however, that transport under special protection shall display the distinctive emblem described in Article 16.

Article 17, paragraph 3 of the Regulations contains provisions concerning international supervision. Transport under special protection must bear the distinctive emblem as defined in Article 16 of the Convention. As we shall see, the emblem is repeated three times in a triangular formation, as specified in Article 17, paragraph 1(b).

PARAGRAPH 3

The undertaking to refrain from any act of hostility towards transport under special protection is not subject to any reservation or derogation. Indeed, the representative of Japan at the Conference asked that the term 'refraining' be strengthened and proposed that it be replaced by 'prohibiting', the term 'refrain' being considered too weak.[3] The amendment was not accepted by the Drafting Committee.

The paragraph does not use the usual term 'respect', as it appears, for example, in Article 4 of the Convention, but refers to refraining from any act of hostility directed against transport. In the spirit of the Commentary on the Additional Protocols of 1977 the two expressions are equivalent. The Commentary defines 'respect' as meaning 'to spare, not to attack'.[4]

NOTES

1 *Records*, para. 583, p.180.
2 *Records*, para. 585, p.180.
3 *Records*, para. 510, p.173.
4 'The concepts of "respect" and "protection" are taken from the Conventions. The first concept was introduced as far back as the 1906 revision, the second at the time of the 1929 revision. *Respect* means "to spare, not to attack", while *protect* means "to come to someone's defence, to lend help and support". Thus it is prohibited to attack the wounded, sick or shipwrecked, to kill them, maltreat them or injure them in any way, and there is also an obligation to come to their rescue' (*Commentary on the Additional Protocols of 8 June 1977 to the Geneva Conventions of 12 August 1949*, Geneva, ICRC/Martinus Nijhoff Publishers, 1987, p.146. See also Jean S. Pictet (ed.), *The Geneva Conventions of 12 August 1949. Commentary*, Vol. I: *Geneva Convention for the Amelioration of the Condition of the Wounded and Sick in Armed Forces in the Field*, Geneva, ICRC, 1952, pp.134 *et seq.*

REGULATIONS FOR THE EXECUTION OF THE CONVENTION – CHAPTER III: TRANSPORT OF CULTURAL PROPERTY

We have seen that Article 12, paragraph 1, provides for the possibility of transport exclusively engaged in the transfer of cultural property, whether within a territory or to another territory, at the request of the High Contracting Party concerned. Paragraph 2 of Article 12 specified that such transport shall take place under special protection in accordance with the conditions specified in the Regulations for the Execution of the Convention. Articles 17 to 19 of these Regulations accordingly give details regarding transport of cultural property under special protection.

Article 17 of the Regulations for the Execution of the Convention: Procedure to Obtain Immunity

1. *The request mentioned in paragraph 1 of Article 12 of the Convention shall be addressed to the Commissioner-General for Cultural Property. It shall mention the reasons on which it is based and specify the approximate number and the importance of the objects to be transferred, their present location, the location now envisaged, the means of transport to be used, the route to be followed, the date proposed for the transfer, and any other relevant information.*
2. *If the Commissioner-General, after taking such opinions as he deems fit, considers that such transfer is justified, he shall consult those delegates of the Protecting Powers who are concerned, on the measures proposed for carrying it out. Following such consultation, he shall notify the Parties to the conflict concerned of the transfer, including in such notification all useful information.*
3. *The Commissioner-General shall appoint one or more inspectors, who shall satisfy themselves that only the property stated in the request is to be transferred and that the transport is to be by the approved methods and bears the distinctive emblem. The inspector or the inspectors shall accompany the property to its destination.*

> *Records*:   Text: p.58.
> Minutes: paras 1399, 2095.
> Working documents: pp.318–19, 406–7;
> CBC/DR/164.

Article 17 of the Regulations for the Execution of the Convention deals with the necessary procedure for ensuring special protection and obtaining immunity for cultural property and means of transport. Given its essentially technical and procedural nature, the article was adopted without discussion or amendment.

Paragraph 1

This article requires that the request of the High Contracting Party referred to in the first paragraph of Article 12 of the Convention be addressed to the Commissioner-General for Cultural Property. The first paragraph also specifies the content of the request, which must give the following particulars:

(a) the reasons that have given rise to the request;
(b) the approximate number and importance of the cultural objects to be transferred;
(c) the present location and intended new location of the property;
(d) the means of transport;
(e) the route to be followed;
(f) the intended date of the transfer; and
(g) any other relevant information.

Paragraph 2

The Commissioner-General for Cultural Property is accordingly responsible for taking the decision, in principle, on the transfer of cultural property. The reason for assigning this responsibility to the Commissioner-General is no doubt of a practical kind. Since he alone is called upon to make it, the decision may be reasonably expected to be taken swiftly and expeditiously under his authority and responsibility.

What does the Commissioner-General have to do when he receives such a request? First, he takes the opinions he feels to be appropriate before deciding. If he considers that the transfer is justified he consults the delegates of the Protecting Powers who are concerned, but only with regard to the measures envisaged for carrying out the transfer. Following these consultations he has to inform the Parties to the conflict concerned (that is, the occupied country, the occupying country and the depositary country) of the transfer and attach to such notification all the relevant information. This concerns more especially the particulars to be found in the request.

Paragraph 3

The Commissioner-General then proceeds to organize the transfer. For this purpose, he appoints one or more inspectors who must satisfy themselves that the transport contains only the property stated in the request, that it is being carried out by the approved methods and that the distinctive emblem is displayed.

The inspector or inspectors take part in the actual transfer procedure because, under this article, they are required to accompany the property to its final destination.

Article 18 of the Regulations for the Execution of the Convention: Transport Abroad

Where the transfer under special protection is to the territory of another country, it shall be governed not only by Article 12 of the Convention and by Article 17 of the present Regulations, but by the following further provisions:

(a)   *while the cultural property remains on the territory of another State, that State shall be its depositary and shall extend to it as great a measure of care as that which it bestows on its own cultural property of comparable importance;*

(b)   *the depositary State shall return the property only on the cessation of the conflict; such return shall be effected within six months from the date on which it was requested;*

(c)   *during the various transfer operations, and while it remains on the territory of another State, the cultural property shall be exempt from confiscation and may not be disposed of either by the depositor or by the depositary. Nevertheless, when the safety of the property requires it, the depositary may, with the assent of the depositor, have the property transported to the territory of a third country, under the conditions laid down in the present Article;*

(d)   *the request for special protection shall indicate that the State to whose territory the property is to be transferred accepts the provisions of the present Article.*

Records: Text: pp.58–60.
Minutes: paras 1400–11, 1662, 1667, 2095.
Working documents: pp.318, 324, 345, 349–50, 407;
CBC/DR/106/164.

We have seen that Article 12 of the Convention and Article 17 of the Regulations deal with transport either within the same territory or to another territory. The present article is exclusively concerned with transport abroad, that is, to the territory of another country.

Transfer under special protection to the territory of another country continues to be governed by Article 12 of the Convention and Article 17 of the Regulations. It is also governed by the special provisions that appear in this article, namely:

Paragraph (A)

While the cultural property remains on the territory of another State, that State shall be its depositary. As such, it shall extend to it as great a measure of care as that which it bestows upon its own cultural property of comparable importance. The article establishes equality of treatment for such property.

It may be that this other country to which the cultural property is to be transported is the Occupying Power. This reveals the importance of the role assigned to the Commissioner-General under Article 17, because such a transfer cannot be made without his collaboration. It is therefore all the more important to stress that Article 12 of the Convention and Article 17 of the Regulations are applicable to such transfers.

This paragraph is highly important inasmuch as it defines the status of cultural property on the territory of a foreign State as being on 'deposit'. The introduction of this qualification in the Regulations is based on general principles of law, the study of which in international law is very fragmentary, with much remaining to be done.[1] These principles incorporate others taken from domestic law whose logical nature seems to justify their transposition to international law. Many of these principles are borrowed from the law of obligations.

An in-depth study of the 'deposit' question lies outside the scope of this Commentary and so we shall confine ourselves to pointing out a number of features that characterize such a contract. In domestic law, deposit is an act by which a person receives the property of another in custody, binding himself to preserve it and return it in kind.[2] It is essentially an unpaid contract. No remuneration may be specified for the depositary (or 'depositee'), who is performing a friendly service for the depositor.[3] The depositor remains the owner and the depositary has only *alieno nomine* possession – the ministration of another's possession.

The depositary may not use the property without the permission of the depositor.[4] Since the time of Roman law it can be seen that the depositary has never had any right to make use of the property. What is involved is a real contract (the physical handing over of the property) and, from the viewpoint of rights, a contract in good faith, giving rise immediately – to the advantage of the *tradens* – to an obligation for the return of the property that has been deposited, this being sanctioned by the *actio depositi directa*, and opening up the subsequent possibility of a claim for indemnity – to the advantage of the *accipiens* – which he is entitled to pursue either in connection with the restitution action of the *tradens* or by a separate action of his own via the *actio depositi contraria*.[5]

The depositary may not return the deposit before the agreed time unless unforeseen circumstances make it impossible for him to keep the property any longer without endangering it or without prejudice to himself. Where no date has been agreed, he may return the property at any time.[6]

The depositary is responsible solely in the event of fraud or gross negligence on his part because he is providing an unpaid service. He is therefore relieved of responsibility in the case of loss of the property in all other circumstances. The depositary is entitled to claim all his expenses and compensation for any prejudice he has been caused. It is, then, a voluntary deposit created by the reciprocal consent of depositor and depositary. 'Necessary deposit' is the term used when the deposit is caused by *force majeure* in the event of an accident: fire, pillage, shipwreck and, hence, war as well.

From this summary of the deposit contract in domestic law we see that account was taken, at the 1954 Conference, of these main characteristics which were adapted to fit in with the circumstances of cultural property in a period of armed conflict.

In fact, the paragraph under discussion gives the safekeeping of cultural property on the territory of another (depositary) State the character of a deposit *sui generis* adapted to the needs of the protection of cultural property in the particular situation of such property in a period of armed conflict. In paragraph (a) the authors of this provision place a particular obligation on the depositary, namely to extend to such property at least as great a measure of care as that which it bestows upon its own cultural property of comparable importance. The principles of the deposit contract are also respected and utilized in paragraphs (b), (c) and (d).

Paragraph (B)

The depository State shall return the property only on the cessation of the conflict. The question that will no doubt arise is the definition of the 'end of conflict'. The government of Israel raised this question in its remarks and suggestions on the UNESCO Draft and asked for a more definite term. 'In many cases the cessation of the conflict does not solve the political problems with which the envisaged return of the property is necessarily linked.'[7]

The return of cultural property shall be effected within six months from the date on which it was requested. The UNESCO Draft proposed a shorter period (three months) and it was at the request of the United Kingdom that the period was lengthened[8] in view of the fact that, after a war, there was a great deal to be done in every field.

We have already seen who is authorized to request the return of cultural property. An important question raised at the Conference sought to establish to whom the cultural property concerned should be returned. The UNESCO Draft specified in paragraph (b) that the depositary State should return the property 'only to the State exercising sovereignty over the territory where the property was normally situated before the conflict'. Some delegations objected to this wording. The Italian delegate interpreted it this way: 'This meant that if State A possessed an item of cultural property situated in district X, which was then annexed by State B, the depositary State would have to return the property to State B. The undertaking to return such property to the annexing State was contrary to the very spirit of the Convention. If such property were privately owned, the problem became still more complicated, for the inhabitants of the annexed district would have the choice of being transferred to the country of their origin. The restitution of their property to the State annexing the district would be an injustice. The principle of international law involved was most intricate and it would be preferable not to regulate it in the Convention.[9] He proposed that, in the event of a dispute, it should be possible to appeal to the International Court of Justice. In the view of the Spanish delegate, 'not only was it dangerous to recognize the right of conquest, but also the new right of "cultural conquest" that the article allowed'.[10] The delegate of Israel considered, on the other hand, that after a war there were generally changes of territory. 'It would not be right to rule that if part of a country changed its territory by annexation, the cultural property should not be returned to it, but to the country to which it had previously belonged.'[11] The USSR delegate found the version proposed by UNESCO acceptable and considered that the question could not be left in the air. Even so, the proposal to delete from this article the expression used in the UNESCO Draft was accepted.[12] The question therefore remains open and unresolved.

Paragraph (C)

During the various transfer operations, and while it remains on the territory of another State, the cultural property shall be exempt from confiscation and may not be disposed of either by the depositor or the depositary.

We have already pointed out, in the commentary on Article 12, the importance of precautions in regard to the depositor – which may be the Occupying Power. This provision is included to prevent cultural property from becoming the object of transactions on the pretext of their protection. However, when the safety of the property requires it, the depositary may, with the assent of the depositor, have the property transferred to the territory of a third country, under the conditions laid down in this article. This concerns, more especially, a situation in which the territory of the depositary is, in turn, threatened with invasion or becomes the theatre of military operations. For a further transfer to take place the consent of the depositor must be obtained, and the same conditions as those governing the first transfer respected.

Paragraph (D)

The request for special protection shall indicate that the State to whose territory the property is to be transferred accepts the provisions of the present article.

NOTES

1   Charles Rousseau, *Droit international publique*, Vol. I, Paris, Sirey, 1970, p.375.
2   *Black's Law Dictionary*, fifth edition, St. Paul, Minn., West Publishing Co., 1979, p.394.
3   Ambroise Colin and Henri Capitant, *Cours élémentaire de droit civil français*, Vol. II, sixth edition, Paris, Dalloz, 1931, p.650. See also *Jenks; English Civil Law*, fourth edition by P.H. Winfield, Vol. I, London, Butterworth & Co., 1947, pp.163–5.
4   *Code suisse des obligations*, Article 474, para. 1.
5   Paul Frédéric Girard, *Manuel élémentaire de droit romain*, seventh edition, Paris, Rousseau, 1924, p.555. Cf. also W.W. Buckland, A.D. McNair and F.H. Lawson, *Roman Law & Common Law. A comparison in outline*, Cambridge University Press, 1952, pp.222, 277.
6   *Code suisse des obligations*, Article 476, paras 1 and 2.
7   *Records*, p.324.
8   CBC/DR/106, *Records*, p.407.
9   *Records*, para. 1401, p.237.
10 *Records*, para. 1402, p.238.
11 *Records*, para. 1403, p.238.
12 *Records*, para. 1409, p.238.

Article 19 of the Regulations for the Execution of the Convention: Occupied Territory

Whenever a High Contracting Party occupying territory of another High Contracting Party transfers cultural property to a refuge situated elsewhere in that territory, without being able to follow the procedure provided for in

Article 17 of the Regulations, the transfer in question shall not be regarded as misappropriation within the meaning of Article 4 of the Convention, provided that the Commissioner-General for Cultural Property certifies in writing, after having consulted the usual custodians, that such transfer was rendered necessary by circumstances.

Records: Text: p.60.
          Minutes: paras 1412–18, 2096.
          Working documents: pp.318, 345, 407;
          CBC/DR/107/164.

This article concerns an exceptional situation – the emergency transfer of cultural property by the Occupying Power on territory it is occupying although belonging to another High Contracting Party.

The wording of this article in the UNESCO Draft was as follows: 'Whenever in occupied territory the occupying authorities transfer cultural property to a refuge situated in the territory…'. On the proposal of the United Kingdom delegate, who considered that the term 'occupied territory' was ambiguous, the words 'occupying authorities' were replaced by the more specific expression 'a High Contracting Party occupying territory of another High Contracting Party'. The USSR delegate was in favour of keeping the UNESCO Draft wording mainly because the new text proposed by the United Kingdom was less clear in stating that it was a question of transferring property to a refuge situated in the same occupied territory. This point needs to be stressed because there was no doubt in the minds of the authors of the provision. It was therefore maintained that the article applied solely within the occupied territory and did not concern transport outside it.

In those circumstances – and only in those circumstances – the article releases the Occupying Power from the obligation to comply with the procedure laid down in Article 17 of the Regulations. The transfer is therefore not considered to be misappropriation within the meaning of Article 4 of the Convention. For this to be so, the Commissioner-General for Cultural Property has to certify, after consulting the usual custodians, that circumstances rendered the transfer necessary. Such certificates must be established in writing. The Commissioner-General is not entirely free to decide – he has to consult the 'usual custodians' in order to establish that 'the transfer is rendered necessary by circumstances' – but it is he who decides if these circumstances effectively exist. He is not bound to follow the advice of the 'usual custodians': he is simply required to consult them. The advice of the custodians could well have a determining effect on his decision.

The expression 'usual custodians' means the personnel normally entrusted with the protection of the property – in other words, the personnel responsible to the local authorities in the occupied territory.

In fact, the transfer of cultural property by the occupying authorities to a refuge situated on the territory of the occupied State cannot be regarded as a misappropriation prohibited by Article 4(2) of the Convention provided that the Commissioner-General for Cultural Property recognized by the Occupying Power certifies that circumstances justified the transfer.

Article 13
Transport in Urgent Cases

1. *If a High Contracting Party considers that the safety of certain cultural property requires its transfer and that the matter is of such urgency that the procedure laid down in Article 12 cannot be followed, especially at the beginning of an armed conflict, the transport may display the distinctive emblem described in Article 16, provided that an application for immunity referred to in Article 12 has not already been made and refused. As far as possible, notification of transfer should be made to the opposing Parties. Nevertheless, transport conveying cultural property to the territory of another country may not display the distinctive emblem unless immunity has been expressly granted to it.*
2. *The High Contracting Parties shall take, so far as possible, the necessary precautions to avoid acts of hostility directed against the transport described in paragraph 1 of the present Article and displaying the distinctive emblem.*

Records: Text: p.18.
Minutes: paras 581, 593–608, 696, 1034–5; 1037, 1043, 1947–8, 1985.
Working documents: pp.311, 318–19, 383–3;
CBC/DR/118.

There are many reasons for expressing doubts about the feasibility of the kind of transport operations described in Article 12. It seems to us that such protection will not be easy to carry out. We can see that, in practice, the organization of the system of supervision and the designation of the Protecting Powers and Commissioners-General are not easy to put into effect.

It was therefore helpful to provide a more flexible, practical and realistic formula included by the authors of the Convention in Article 13, though naturally without foreseeing the obstacles that arose subsequently when the Convention came to be applied.

Article 13 was designed at the outset to provide for evacuation to refuges at the opening of hostilities. It also applied in the case of transport not planned in peacetime but necessitated, in the course of a conflict, by unforeseen circumstances requiring immediate action.

In the former case – transfers of property at the commencement of the conflict – the point was made that, in theory, it would be desirable for evacuation transport to take place before a conflict broke out. However, there will often be many justifiable reasons, especially psychological reasons, militating against such transport being effected before general mobilization of the armed forces, which explain why measures of this type would not be taken. Moreover, in most cases hostilities break out suddenly or unforeseeably, so that such transfers cannot take place at the most suitable moment.

It is precisely for these reasons that this kind of situation needs to be anticipated in peacetime and the evacuation and movement of cultural property planned in detail. It is the duty of all persons with responsibility for this property in peacetime. The measures to be taken need to be thought out in advance in the same way as precautions against fire, flood, and so on. The civil authorities responsible for cultural property accordingly need to have close peacetime liaison with the military authorities so that if such a situation does arise the experts and technical staff, packing materials, trucks, trains and/or aircraft may be made available to the authorities responsible for civil protection and those responsible for cultural property. Evacuation plans and programmes need to be drawn up, those places where the property can be appropriately protected (in the country or abroad) identified and the most suitable routes selected away from the main roads, congested as they will be with military traffic or exposed to enemy attack. Provision will also need to be made for military escorts, and so on.

These measures and plans of action could also be relevant in the second case – transport and evacuation during a conflict when unforeseen circumstances make it necessary. This would be the case, for example, of transport to the improvised refuges referred to in the Regulations for the Execution of the Convention.

It has to be realized that the movement of cultural property always involves exposure to serious risk. One has only to think of the risks involved when there is no urgency at all in the transport arrangements, as with exhibits being conveyed for display at exhibitions. Such transfers should not, therefore, be contemplated unless they are imperative for the safety of the property to be protected and in cases of extreme urgency. The experts all consider that these risks are to be treated as greater than those arising because of enemy occupation. It will be a matter for the civil authorities, in cooperation with the military authorities, to weigh up these risks and assume their responsibilities, bearing in mind all the circumstances and not simply the importance of the physical protection of the property.

In all cases where, for various reasons, the transfer cannot be notified in advance or placed under international control – and cannot therefore be effected according to the requirement set out in Article 12 and the Regulations for the Execution of the Convention – Article 13 provides for a minimum of protection: the High Contracting Parties shall take 'so far as possible the necessary precautions to avoid acts of hostility directed against the transport described in paragraph 1 of the present article and displaying the distinctive emblem'. For these cases the Convention requires that transport display the emblem. 'In fact, even admitting that military necessities prevent the conferring of immunity on the transports as provided for in Article 12 of the Convention, it is desirable, because of the very great value of most property transferred to a refuge, that the transports should enjoy the right to carry the emblem, in order that the armed forces of the Parties to the conflict may realize that property is being transferred whose safeguarding is of concern to the international community as a whole.'[1]

The last sentence of the first paragraph stipulates the following: 'Nevertheless, transport conveying cultural property to the territory of another country may not display the distinctive emblem unless immunity has been expressly granted to it' – in other words, as provided for in Article 12 of the Convention. On this point, the UNESCO Draft stated: 'It might in fact be that such transport of cultural property to a foreign country was undertaken not in order to safeguard the property, but in order to sell or pledge it. In such a case, it could not be asked that the opposing Party should respect the transport, which might go to increase the financial resources of an enemy. Similarly, the emblem cannot be used if procedure for obtaining the immunity provided for in Article 12 has been begun but has not culminated in the result desired.'[2] It is therefore permissible to use the Convention's distinctive emblem only for transport within the country and provided the request for special protection has not been rejected. But the use of the emblem is not obligatory ('may'). Paragraph 2 specifies that the High Contracting Parties shall take, as far as possible, the necessary precautions to avoid acts of hostility directed against the transport described in paragraph 1 and displaying the distinctive emblem. The commitment of the High Contracting Parties is again limited by the words 'so far as possible'.

NOTES

1   *Records*, p.311.
2   Idem.

Article 14
Immunity from Seizure,
Capture and Prize

1. *Immunity from seizure, placing in prize, or capture shall be granted to:*
   (a) *cultural property enjoying the protection provided for in Article 12 or that provided for in Article 13;*
   (b) *the means of transport exclusively engaged in the transfer of such cultural property.*
2. *Nothing in the present Article shall limit the right of visit and search.*

Records: Text: p.18.
            Minutes: paras 605, 1035, 1038–9, 1167, 1173–91, 1985.
            Working documents: p.383;
            CBC/DR/118/132.

We noted, in our commentary on Article 12, that at the request of the Greek delegate, the Conference looked at the question of the form of transport (land, sea or air) mainly because of the fact that private enemy property is not protected at sea or in the air. Ships carrying private property are not exempt from seizure. Article 4 of the Eleventh Hague Convention of 1907 refers only to ships on scientific missions and does not, therefore, cover the maritime transport of cultural property. For reasons of safety a State may wish to transport private collections by sea or air. An additional paragraph was therefore requested to the effect that ships and aircraft and the property carried in them would in no case be subject to seizure. It is this Greek proposal that lies at the origin of the inclusion of Article 14 which did not appear in the UNESCO Draft; it was formulated by the Legal Committee on the basis of the Greek written proposal.[1]

PARAGRAPH 1

This article states that (a) cultural property enjoying the protection provided for in Article 12 or that provided for in Article 13 and (b) the means of transport exclusively engaged in the transfer of such cultural property shall be granted immunity from seizure, placing in prize or capture. It shows clearly that both cultural property and the means of transport enjoy the immunity granted them by this chapter.

Understanding of this provision is facilitated if one has a clear definition of the meaning of seizure, capture and prize, which according to this paragraph cannot be used against cultural property and means of transport. A first point worth noting is that there is no absolute distinction between these terms – particularly between seizure and capture – and often they are used as synonyms and for the same act.

Seizure

In law, seizure is defined as a procedure whereby movable or immovable property is placed in the hands of the judicial or the administrative authority in the private or public interest.[2] Seizure also occurs in Articles 23(g), 53 and 54 of the 1907 Hague Regulations respecting the Laws and Customs of War on Land. Articles 23(g) and 53 are of most interest to us, particularly in connection with the present article.[3]

Under Article 23(g), apart from the prohibitions instituted by special agreements, it is forbidden, among other things, 'to destroy or seize the enemy's property, unless such destruction or seizure be imperatively demanded by the necessities of war'.

Under Article 53 of the same Regulations: 'an army of occupation can only take possession of cash, funds and realizable securities which are strictly the property of the State, depots of arms, means of transport, stores and supplies and, generally, all movable property belonging to the State which may be used for military operations.

All appliances, whether on land, at sea or in the air, adapted for the transmission of news or for the transport of persons or things, exclusive of cases governed by naval law, depots of arms and, generally, all kinds of munitions of war, may be seized even if they belong to private individuals, but must be restored and compensation fixed when peace is made.'

Article 53 hence recognizes the Occupying Power's right to seize objects which could be used for purposes of war 'even though belonging to companies or to private persons'. The kind of seizure described in Article 53, paragraph 2, does not give the Occupying Power the right of ownership but neither does it constitute simple sequestration; it is an act of possession which is no obstacle to requisition as regulated by Article 52.

The Commentary on the 1949 Geneva Conventions draws a distinction between right of seizure and right of requisition. Whereas the right of seizure is exercised primarily in regard to State property (war booty), the right of requisition only concerns private property. 'There are, however, certain cases mentioned in Article 53, paragraph 2, of the Hague Convention in which private property can also be seized; but such seizure is only sequestration, to be followed by restitution and indemnity, whereas requisition implies a transfer of ownership.'[4]

Article 14 of the Convention therefore ensures immunity from seizure for cultural property enjoying the protection specified in Articles 12 and 13 of the Convention and for the means of transport assigned exclusively to the transfer of such property. Immunity from seizure, as defined here, embraces both public and private property; it is the nature of this property and the means of transport which precludes seizure.

Capture

Capture (*captura* in Latin) in the general sense of the word means the act of capturing, that is, taking a living being prisoner or taking possession of a thing. The term is mainly used for the capture of prisoners of war, an enemy, hospital ships, aircraft, wounded and shipwrecked persons and so on. In the law of naval warfare, capture is a purely military act whereby the commander of a warship or the maritime authority in a port substitutes his or its own authority for that of the captain of an enemy or neutral merchant vessel and whose effect is the confiscation of the ship in accordance with the law of prize jurisdiction.[5]

When enemy material is involved, the term 'capture' is often used as a synonym for the right to booty; this right can be exercised only in respect of movable property belonging to the enemy and results in the acquiring of ownership with no obligation in regard to restitution or compensation.

This article, therefore, provides immunity from capture for cultural property and its means of transport.

Prize

In feudal law, the right to take prize gave the lord the right to requisition anything he needed during his travels.

Unlike the rules of war on land, private property is not respected in naval warfare and the ancient custom of appropriating others' property is considered legitimate. In the law of armed conflict the term 'prize' has a double meaning. It means both (1) the naval operation whereby a belligerent State takes possession of an enemy or neutral merchant or cargo ship with a view to having its confiscation declared by the State's legal authorities, and (2) the ship or goods that are the object of the above operation. The term 'capture' is generally used when the right of 'prize' is invoked for vessels and 'seizure' when it is applied to goods or cargoes.[6]

A full study of the right of 'prize' lies outside the scope of this commentary and we would refer readers to the specialized literature on the subject.[7] We would, however, draw attention to the practice which has developed since the eighteenth century of making an exception for ships on scientific missions. Another exception is made for all types of hospital ship[8] and others, again, for the personal effects of crews and postal correspondence. Article 14 of the 1954 Hague Convention adds a further exception for cultural property and the means of transport involved. The right of prize relates both to enemy State property and to enemy private property.

PARAGRAPH 2

According to this paragraph, 'nothing in the present article shall limit the right of visit and search'.

The issue of capture was raised by the United States delegate because of the question of the transfer of cultural property by land transport and the crossing of front lines. Convoys could be a way used by the resistance or intelligence agents to transmit information of vital importance from the military standpoint. This question led to the adoption of an additional sentence regarding the right of the opposing Party to visit and search means of transport in order to ensure there were no military intelligence leaks.[9] However, in spite of the disagreement on the question of whether this clarification should appear in the article itself or simply in the minutes, the text of paragraph 2 was adopted by the Main Commission by 22 votes in favour with six abstentions.

NOTES

1   The provision that property was exempt from confiscation and might not be disposed of was, however, already included in Article 9, paragraph 3 of the 1938 Preliminary Draft Convention which probably served as a reference for the Greek delegate.

2   *Le Robert*, Vol. 6, p.119. According to *Black's Law Dictionary*, the seizure is 'the act performed by an officer of the law, under the authority and exigence of a writ, in taking into the custody of the law the property, real or personal, of a person against whom the judgment of a competent court has passed, condemning him

to pay a certain sum of money, in order that such property may be sold, by authority and due course of law, to satisfy the judgment. Or the act of taking possession of goods in consequence of a violation of public law. *Carey* v. *Insurance Co.*, 54 NW 18, 84 Wis. 80, 20 LRA 267, 36 Am.St. Rep. 907.

Seizure, even though hostile, is not necessarily capture, though such is its usual and probable result. The ultimate act or adjudication of the state, by which the seizure has been made, assigns the proper and conclusive quality and denomination to the original proceeding. A condemnation asserts a capture *ab initio*; an award of restitution pronounces upon the act as having been not a valid act of capture, but an act of temporary seizure only. *Appleton* v. *Crowninshield*, 3 Mass., 443. (*Black's Law Dictionary*, revised fourth edition, St. Paul Minn., West Publishing Co., 1968, p.1525).

3   Article 54 of the Hague Regulations deals only with the seizure and destruction of submarine cables.

4   Jean S. Pictet (ed.), *The Geneva Conventions of 12 August 1949. Commentary*, Vol. I, Geneva, ICRC, 1952, p.279.

5   Charles Rousseau, *Le droit des conflits armés*, Paris, Editions A. Pédone, 1983, p.313.

6   Ibid., pp.276–7.

7   Literature on the right of prize is vast. Among recent studies we recommend the following in particular: Charles Rousseau, *Le droit des conflits armés*, pp.274–353, Paris, Editions A. Pédone, 1983; G. Katevenis, 'Considerations on the law of prize jurisdiction over the enemy's ship in time of war', *Revue de droit pénal militaire et de droit de la guerre* (Brussels), IV-2, 1965, pp.359–68; N. Ronzitti (ed.), *The Law of Naval Warfare. A collection of agreements and documents with commentaries*, Dordrecht, Martinus Nijhoff Publishers, 1988, 888 pp. See also *Bibliography of international humanitarian law applicable in armed conflicts*, second edition, revised and amplified, Geneva, ICRC and Henry Dunant Institute, 1987, pp.241–7.

8   Geneva Convention of 12 August 1949 for the Amelioration of the Condition of the Wounded, Sick and Shipwrecked Members of Armed Forces at Sea, Articles 22–35.

9   This provision is also based on the practice of visit and search in prize law. In French terminology and practice, 'visite' denotes the action of a naval officer on board a merchant ship in both examining the ship's papers and carrying out a search (inspection of cargo, interrogation of passengers and crew). In United Kingdom practice a distinction is made between 'visit' (verifying the ship's right to its flag) and 'search' properly speaking. We see that Article 14, paragraph 2, also draws a distinction between 'visit' and 'search'. The same distinction is also made in the *Oxford Manual* adopted by the Institute of International Law on 9 August 1913 (Article 32).

Chapter IV
Personnel

Article 15
Personnel

As far as is consistent with the interests of security, personnel engaged in the protection of cultural property shall, in the interests of such property, be respected and, if they fall into the hands of the opposing Party, shall be allowed to continue to carry out their duties whenever the cultural property for which they are responsible has also fallen into the hands of the opposing Party.

Records: Text: pp.18, 20.
Minutes: paras 229, 540, 609–29, 696, 1034–5, 1050–53, 1985.
Working documents: pp.311–12, 318–19, 383;
CBC/DR/75/118.

Bibliography: Pictet, Jean S. (ed.), *The Geneva Conventions of 12 August 1949. Commentary published under the general editorship of Jean S. Pictet*, Vol. I, *Geneva Convention for the Amelioration of the Condition of the Wounded, Sick and Shipwrecked Members of Armed Forces in the Field*, Geneva, ICRC, 1952, pp.217–28.

The authors of this provision felt it necessary to include a rule in the Convention emphasizing respect for personnel responsible for cultural property and the principle of the continued functions of such personnel should they fall into the hands of the opposing Party, this being in the interests of the safeguarding of the cultural property concerned. The Preliminary Draft Convention of 1938 included, in Article 9 of the Regulations for its Execution, the following provision: 'During military occupation, the national staff appointed to preserve and guard refuges, museums or monuments must be retained in their employment, unless there is any legitimate military reason for their dismissal. They shall, however, be in the same position in elation to the military authorities of occupation as the civil population of the occupied territories.'

Taking as its basis the text of the 1949 Geneva Convention (and more particularly Articles 24 and 26 of the First Convention) the 1954 Hague Convention includes a provision concerning the protection of personnel, civilian or military, engaged in the protection of cultural property. The idea that such personnel should not only be respected but also protected in all circumstances had even been considered during the drafting of the article. The 1949 Geneva Conventions do not cover this kind of specialized personnel and therefore do not provide for their protection. However, some hesitation was felt about declaring that special protection would be imposed for such personnel. It was considered that absolute respect would not always be possible.

Article 15, therefore, refers only to respect for personnel – not its protection. On the other hand, Article 24 of the First Geneva Convention provides for respect and protection in all circumstances. The respect required for such personnel under the 1954 Hague Convention is markedly weaker.

Articles 24 to 26 of the First Geneva Convention refer, among other things, to six categories of personnel: army personnel, the staff of Red Cross Societies and other voluntary aid societies, the personnel of aid societies of neutral countries and, lastly, military personnel especially trained to act, should the need arise, as nurses or stretcher-bearers. Should they fall into the hands of the adverse Party, personnel designated in Articles 24 and 26 should not be deemed prisoners of war but allowed to continue to perform their duties (Article 28).

In this article the Hague Convention adopts a very general definition in regard to personnel, referring simply to 'personnel engaged in the protection of cultural property'. Respect is, hence, accorded on the basis of this personnel assignment and because the protection of cultural property is involved. Since this article is modelled on the First Geneva Convention, we may conclude that respect concerns both personnel attached to the army and civilian staff, even staff belonging to voluntary aid organizations for the protection of cultural property. It is for each Power to establish the composition of such personnel and to decide which persons it 'assigns' to that role.

In comparison with the Geneva Convention, Article 15 contains one important limitation, namely the reference to military necessity, when it states that such personnel shall be respected 'as far as is consistent with the interests of security'. This limitation had been strengthened by the proposal of the United States which asked that the words in the UNESCO Draft ('as far as possible') be replaced by the phrase which now appears in the Convention: 'as far as is consistent with the interests of security'. This is equivalent to the 'military necessity' mentioned in other articles of the Convention. The duty to ensure respect is thus diminished and the State can evade it as it wishes.

Emphasis was also laid, during the Hague Conference, on the need for personnel – few and far between in many countries – to be able to continue performing their duties. During the preparatory work the Greek delegate proposed that the words 'with the property for which they are responsible' be deleted. It seemed appropriate, in the interests of the safeguarding of cultural property, to give increased protection to specialized personnel who, if they fell into enemy hands, should be respected with or without the cultural property for which they were responsible. In that way, personnel with specialized knowledge could continue to use their skills to safeguard cultural property. The problem of the shortage of specialized personnel and the need to recover them was raised. The Greek proposal was indeed in favour of the protection of cultural property, its final wording being that found in the definitive text of the Convention according to which personnel 'shall be allowed to continue to carry out their duties whenever the cultural property for which they are responsible has also fallen into the hands of the opposing Party'. But it should also be noted, as stressed by the Italian delegate, that, 'apart from the cultural property for which they were responsible, such personnel should enjoy no special privileges'.[1] The final text of the Convention clearly confirms this twofold interpretation.

It should also be emphasized that, in order to enjoy respect, personnel must naturally abstain from any participation, even of an indirect kind, in acts of hostility.

The need to be able to call on specialized personnel stems from the fact that such staff must have specific knowledge in the preservation of and respect for cultural property. Special training is therefore required. This category of personnel must be chosen with particular care from among individuals who already have the necessary professional training or who, because of their occupation (having worked in establishments concerned with culture and the arts – teachers, for example) are best suited for it. In Switzerland, specialized teams and appropriately equipped mobile groups have been trained. The number of skilled persons is about 500–700, not counting auxiliary personnel.

In Italy, military personnel are chosen from among those who have acquired the necessary skills through the work they have done in civilian life. This mainly concerns education officials whose task, in the event of war, is to cooperate with the civil authorities responsible for the supervision of cultural property.

Under Article 17 of the Convention, personnel assigned to the protection of cultural property may use the distinctive emblem as a means of identification. Under Article 21 of the Regulations for the Execution of the Convention such persons may (optionally) wear an armlet bearing the distinctive emblem, issued and stamped by the competent authorities. They also carry a special identity card bearing the same emblem of which they may not be deprived without legitimate reasons, for example, if they are not entitled to carry it. Nor, subject to the same proviso, may they be deprived of their armlet.

It is as well to point out that, under Article 24 of the Convention, the High Contracting Parties may conclude special agreements for all matters they feel should be regulated separately, particularly as regards personnel assigned to the protection of cultural property. Such agreements may enter into greater detail regarding the role and status of personnel and extend their rights or protection but in no case may they diminish the protection afforded by the Convention for such personnel.

NOTE

1   *Records,* para. 621.

Chapter V
The Distinctive Emblem

The purpose of the distinctive emblem is to identify the cultural property for which general or special protection has been granted. It is not the first time that a distinctive emblem has been used to protect cultural property. As far back as 1874, at the Brussels Conference, the draft text for Article 16 concerning the protection of churches, hospitals and buildings dedicated to art, science or charitable purposes referred to the duty of the inhabitants to indicate such buildings by special visible signs. The Italian delegate, Colonel Lanza, stated that it was a drawback that these visible signs were not clearly specified.[1] The article finally adopted – Article 17 of the Project of an International Declaration concerning the Laws and Customs of War – did not go much further. It refers simply to the duty of the besieged to 'indicate the presence of such buildings by distinctive and visible signs to be communicated to the enemy beforehand'.[2] Article 27 of the Regulations respecting the Laws and Customs of War on Land of 1899 and 1907 contains the same provision (see also Article 36 of the 1954 Hague Convention). It should also be noted that historic monuments were added to the list of protected buildings in 1907.

Thus Article 27 of the Hague Regulations respecting the Laws and Customs of War, annexed to the Fourth Hague Convention of 1907 and Article 5 of the Ninth Hague Convention concerning Bombardment by Naval Forces in Time of War, had already envisaged the need for the distinctive marking of protected property. Article 5 of the Ninth Convention went further by instituting a special sign consisting of 'large, stiff rectangular panels divided diagonally into two coloured triangular portions, the upper portion black, the lower portion white' (see above). The reason for this is given in the Conference minutes: 'In view of the difficulty that may lie, in the case of bombardment by naval forces, in the way of a previous notification on the part of the inhabitants of the signs which they are going to use to mark the protected buildings, it seemed that the corresponding pro-

177

vision of the Regulations on land warfare ought to be supplemented in the project before us.'³

The Rules relating to aerial warfare and those concerning the use of radio in time of war, drawn up by the Commission of Jurists appointed to study and report on the revision of the laws of war, meeting in The Hague on 11 December 1922, were never adopted in legally binding form but they were recognized as an authoritative attempt to clarify and formulate rules of law governing the use of aircraft in war. To a great extent they correspond to the customary rules and general principles based on international treaties. Article 25 of these Rules states that 'buildings dedicated to public worship art, science or charitable purposes, historic monuments, hospital ships, hospitals and other places where the sick and wounded are collected, provided such buildings, objects or places are not at the time used for war purposes, must by day be indicated by marks visible to aircraft. The use of marks to indicate other buildings, objects or places than those specified above is to be deemed an act of perfidy. The marks used as aforesaid shall be, in the case of buildings protected under the Geneva Convention, the red cross on a white ground, and in the case of the other protected buildings, a large rectangular panel divided diagonally into two pointed triangular portions, one black and the other white. A belligerent who desires to secure by night protection for the hospitals and other privileged buildings above-mentioned must take the necessary measures to render the special signs referred to sufficiently visible.'

The Treaty on the Protection of Artistic and Scientific Institutions and Historic Monuments (Roerich Pact) signed in Washington on 15 April 1935 by the various States of North and South America introduced a distinguishing flag as illustrated: a red circle enclosing a triple sphere, all on a white ground (see p. 17 above).

The 1938 Preliminary Draft Convention was an important precedent and the source of the provisions in the 1954 Convention, particularly with regard to the use, placing and purpose of the distinctive emblem. Article 7 of the Preliminary Draft also states that monuments and museums shall be brought to the notice of the civil population, who shall be requested to protect them, and of the occupying troops who shall be informed that they are dealing with buildings the preservation of which is the concern of the entire international community. The distinctive emblem itself was simpler than that of the 1954 Convention: a light blue triangle inscribed in a white disc.

Since 1907 the question has become more complex. Developments in military technology, and more particularly aerial warfare, have led to a new approach to the distinctive sign problem. For some, such as the experts who prepared the UNESCO Draft Convention, use of too visible a sign could often be undesirable for tactical reasons. Whilst previously the aim was to ensure maximum visibility, in many cases today it has become necessary to secure better visibility on condition that this does not assist the enemy's direction finding. The UNESCO commentaries in 1954 suggest that the importance of identification has become less crucial than in 1907. For this reason the authors of the Convention attach paramount importance to the recording of property in the International Register of Cultural Property under Special Protection and the notification of States. These measures constitute the essential element in the identification of property and should facilitate its protection.

A similar interpretation was expressed during the preparatory work on the revision of the Geneva Convention.[4] The same view, however, was not altogether reflected in the approach adopted by the Geneva Conventions themselves, which state, in Article 42, paragraph 4 of the First Convention, for example, that 'Parties to the conflict shall take the necessary steps, in so far as military necessities permit, to make the distinctive emblems indicating medical units and establishments clearly visible to enemy land, air or naval forces, in order to obviate the possibility of any hostile action'. The same spirit also prevailed at the 1954 Conference, as is clear from the wording of Articles 16 and 17 of the Convention.

Another point to note is the Conference's reaffirmation of international humanitarian law (1974–77) and the need to strengthen it. Particular importance was attached to the visibility of the distinctive emblem and the development of modern identification techniques. Article 18 of Protocol I states that each Party to the conflict shall endeavour to ensure that medical and religious personnel, and medical units and transports, are identifiable. New methods of identification have been introduced, the reference here being to the Regulations concerning identification, Annex I to Additional Protocol I of 1977. The problem should also be studied and developed in connection with the identification of cultural property in the future.[5] As we shall see further below, in connection with Article 21 of the Regulations for the Execution of the Convention, possibilities for developing the identification of cultural property have been opened up and considerable initiative has been left here to the High Contracting Parties.

The provisions that follow should be read in conjunction with Article 6 of the Convention which concerns the general protection of cultural property and provides that 'in accordance with the provisions of Article 16, cultural property may bear a distinctive emblem so as to facilitate its recognition'. In this case the use of the emblem is optional.

These provisions should also be read in conjunction with Article 10 which provides that, during an armed conflict, cultural property under special protection shall be marked with the distinctive emblem described in Article 16, and shall be open to international control as provided for in the Regulations for the Execution of the Convention. In this case, marking with the emblem is optional in peacetime but compulsory in time of war.

Articles 16 and 17 that follow also need to be read in conjunction with Article 36 of the Convention which sets out the necessary provisions for States Parties to the Ninth Hague Convention of 1907 and the Washington Pact of 1935 in terms of the correlation between these agreements and the new Convention.

NOTES

1 *Actes de la Conférence de Bruxelles (1874)*, Brussels, F. Hayez, 1874, p.37.
2 This was included on the proposal of General Voigts-Rhetz who considered it was important that the special visible signs should be known to the besieging power so that it should not involuntarily fail to comply with the prescriptions set out in this article. He asked that the besieged party should be required to inform the besieging power about them in a way that left no room for uncertainty. (*Actes de la Conférence de Bruxelles (1874)*, p.201.)
3 *Proceedings of the Hague Peace Conference. Second International Peace Conference, The Hague, 15 June–18 October 1907, Acts and Documents*, Vol. III, The Hague, National Printing Office, 1907, pp.353–4.
4 Jean S. Pictet (ed.), *The Geneva Conventions of 12 August 1949. Commentary*, Vol. I, *Geneva Convention for the Amelioration of the Condition of the Wounded and Sick in Armed Forces in the Field*, p.319.
5 *Commentary on the Additional Protocols of 8 June 1977 to the Geneva Conventions of 12 August 1949*, pp.1125 *et seq.*

Article 16
Emblem of the Convention

1. *The distinctive emblem of the Convention shall take the form of a shield, pointed below, per saltire blue and white (a shield consisting of a royal-blue square, one of the angles of which forms the point of the shield, and of a royal-blue triangle above the square, the space on either side being taken up by a white triangle).*
2. *The emblem shall be used alone, or repeated three times in a triangular formation (one shield below) under the conditions provided for in Article 17.*

Records: Text: p.20.
Minutes: paras 389, 391, 400–401, 403, 408, 410, 540, 696, 1465, 1469, 1474, 1477–8, 1986.

Working documents: pp.309, 311–12, 333, 347, 383–4; CBC/DR/51/62/63/143.

Bibliography: Boylan, P.J., *Review of the Convention for the Protection of Cultural Property in the Event of Armed Conflict* (The Hague Convention of 1954), Paris, UNESCO, 1993, paras 7.1–7.4, pp.84–5; Bugnion, François, *L'emblème de la Croix-Rouge. Aperçu historique*, a study of M.D. Tensley's suggestions by the Henry Dunant Institute, Geneva, 1977, 132 pp.

The choice of the emblem described in this article was made in the light both of visibility experiments in other fields and the need to ensure that the emblem differed from those already used for other purposes. 'This sign, even though it is not as complicated as it sounds when you look at it, is nevertheless not easy to describe in words – but it seems that all the simpler emblems were already being used for other purposes such as traffic regulations!'[1]

An important question that has to be answered is when to display the emblem. Should it be peacetime (as is the case in Austria) or not until the outbreak of hostilities? For isolated and purpose-built refuges the answer would appear obvious: the emblem should be displayed as soon as the Convention enters into force or the moment the refuge is built or brought into use. The situation for other refuges (historic palaces, churches or important churches or monuments in major urban centres) is different. Displaying the distinctive emblem could raise aesthetic and even psychological difficulties, all the more so in the case of centres containing monuments.

Another problem could be caused by the suddenness of the outbreak of hostilities. Would the services involved have sufficient time and equipment to put up the emblems at the last moment, even supposing that the necessary preparations had been made in peacetime?

The Convention gives no answer to these questions and leaves it to the appropriate authorities of each High Contracting Party to decide in each individual case.

At the Conference the need for uniformity was stressed, whether the emblem was for general or for special protection, the purpose being to avoid confusion. Moreover, the Working Group[2] that proposed the emblem referred to in this article (and its repetition for special protection purposes) also stressed the need for visibility and simplicity. The shield shape was proposed by the Swedish representative. The expression that is used – 'per saltire blue and white' – is an heraldic term for the shape in which the colours should be set.

Emblem for the protection of cultural property (Article 16, para. 1)

The Hague Convention for the Protection of Cultural Property in the Event of Armed Conflict of 14 May 1954 prescribes a blue and white shield for the identification of such property. This blue and white shield displayed on any cultural property – museum, monument, building, archaeological site and so on – means that it is prohibited to use such property for military purposes.

To be visible from afar, the emblem must be extremely large. Its effectiveness is limited by conditions of visibility.

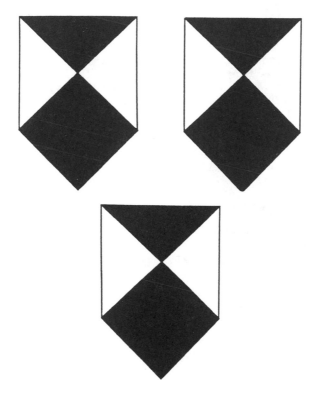

Emblem for the special protection of cultural property (Article 16, para. 2)

According to the Hague Convention of 14 May 1954, the transport of cultural property and cultural property of great significance shall receive special protection, marked by a group of three blue and white shields arranged in the shape of a shield. The triple emblem of protection for cultural property signifies that it is prohibited to use this property for military ends and that it must be specially protected.

Special protection is only granted if the property in question is registered in the International Register provided for this purpose. Transports under special protection are subject to international control.

NOTES

1   Stanislaw E. Nahlik, 'Protection of Cultural Property', in *International Dimensions of Humanitarian Law*, Geneva, Henry Dunant Institute, Paris, UNESCO, Dordrecht, Martinus Nijhoff Publishers 1988, p.207. In another article S.E. Nahlik also writes: 'As it so happened that the emblem had been drafted by a compatriot of mine who at the 1954 Conference served as a Rapporteur on the Working Group entrusted with the task of drafting the emblem, I asked him why he did not suggest something similar, more easily defined in words. His reply was that all geometrical figures had already been exploited for various other purposes. A proof, however, that his view was not entirely justified was furnished in the 1970s, at the Diplomatic Conference on Humanitarian Law, where one did succeed in establishing, for the purposes of civil defence, a much simpler and easily imaginable emblem: an equilateral blue triangle on an orange ground' (S.E. Nahlik, 'Convention for the Protection of Cultural Property in the Event of Armed Conflict, The Hague 1954, General and Special Protection', in Istituto internazionale di diretto umanitario, *La protezione internazionale dei beni culturali/ The international protection of cultural property/La protection internationel des biens culturels*, pp.87–9).

2   The Working Group consisted of representatives of the following States: Belgium, Byelorussia, France, Germany (Federal Republic), Greece, Iran, Italy, Japan, Poland, Sweden, United Kingdom, United States and Union of Soviet Socialist Republics. The Chairman was Mr Nyns (Belgium) and the Rapporteur Mr Zachwatowicz (Poland): *Records*, para. 1469, p.243.

Article 17
Use of the Emblem

1. *The distinctive emblem repeated three times may be used only as a means of identification of:*
   (a) *immovable cultural property under special protection;*
   (b) *the transport of cultural property under the conditions provided for in Articles 12 amd 13;*
   (c) *improvised refuges, under the conditions provided for in the Regulations for the Execution of the Convention.*
2. *The distinctive emblem may be used alone only as a means of identification of:*
   (a) *cultural property not under special protection;*
   (b) *the persons responsible for the duties of control in accordance with the Regulations for the Execution of the Convention;*
   (c) *the personnel engaged in the protection of cultural property;*
   (d) *the identity cards mentioned in the Regulations for the Execution of the Convention.*
3. *During an armed conflict, the use of the distinctive emblem in any other cases than those mentioned in the preceding paragraphs of the present Article, and the use for any purpose whatever of a sign resembling the distinctive emblem shall be forbidden.*
4. *The distinctive emblem may not be placed on any immovable cultural property unless at the same time there is displayed an authorization dated and signed by the competent authority of the High Contracting Party.*

Records: Text: pp.20, 22.
Minutes: paras 400–401, 403, 408, 696, 1465, 1569, 1479–86, 1923, 1987–91.
Working documents: pp.309–10, 312–13, 318, 384–5; CBC/DR/52/57/143.

The article describes the use of the two forms of the distinctive emblem of the Convention in precise terms: in one case it is repeated three times and in the other it is used alone.

PARAGRAPH 1

The distinctive emblem repeated three times may be used only in the following cases:

(a)   for immovable cultural property under special protection in accordance with Chapter 2 of the Convention;
(b)   for the transport of cultural property, under the conditions laid down in Articles 12 and 13;
(c)   for improvised refuges, under the conditions laid down in Article 11 of the Regulations for the Execution of the Convention.

During the experts' preparatory work prior to the Conference the idea had been envisaged of authorizing the use of the emblem on the material exclusively intended for the protection of cultural property in the event of armed conflict. However, it was feared that the volume of such material would diminish the importance of the emblem and it was also pointed out that in most cases such material would be located at the same place as the property under special protection and would therefore benefit from the protection afforded by the emblem identifying the property.

PARAGRAPH 2

The distinctive emblem may be employed alone only for:

(a)   cultural property that is not under special protection, in other words property under the general protection arrangements;
(b)   persons responsible for the duties of control in accordance with the Regulations for the Execution of the Convention, namely representatives for cultural property, the delegates of the Protecting Powers, the Commissioner-General for Cultural Property, inspectors and experts;
(c)   personnel engaged in the protection of cultural property in accordance with Article 15 of the Convention. (With regard to paragraph (c) it should be noted that, when the Parties use unpaid volunteers as personnel engaged in the protection of cultural property, they may use the emblem of the Convention for such personnel);[1]
(d)   the identity cards referred to in Article 21 of the Regulations for the Execution of the Convention.

PARAGRAPH 3

This paragraph imposes an absolute ban on the use of the distinctive emblem in cases other than those set out in the preceding paragraphs of the article or the use for any purpose whatsoever of a sign resembling the distinctive emblem in times of armed conflict.

Any misuse of the emblem would obviously expose those responsible to the sanctions applicable to breaches of the Convention (Article 28). Article 85 of Additional Protocol I considers that grave breaches of the Protocol are acts that are committed wilfully in violation of the relevant provisions of the Protocol and causing death or serious injury to body or health. Among such acts it mentions the perfidious use, 'in violation of Article 37, of the distinctive emblem of the red cross, red crescent or red lion and sun or of other protective signs recognized by the Conventions or this Protocol'. These emblems clearly include the protective emblem for cultural property.[2]

PARAGRAPH 4

The phrase 'an authorization duly dated and signed by the competent authority of the High Contracting Party'[3] was clarified during discussion in the Main Commission. Among other things it was made clear that the 'form of such authorization had not been otherwise defined and that it varied with the national customs of each country'. The form of the authorization would depend on the national regulations in force in the country concerned. It was also established that the copy of the authorization would be delivered by the relevant authorities and that only immovable cultural property was affected.[4]

PRACTICAL APPLICATION

UNESCO may provide technical help to the High Contracting Parties, particularly since few countries have as yet affixed the distinctive emblem on their cultural property. The countries that have done so could, in their turn, lend assistance to the other Parties to the Convention. The reports of the High Contracting Parties contain little information on the subject. Only the Federal Republic of Germany, Austria, the Netherlands and Switzerland give any details of measures taken – armlets, identity cards, information leaflets on immovable property, special stamps (Switzerland) – and on the use of the single or repeated form of the emblem.[5] Some countries, such as Switzerland, have produced explanatory notes regarding the shield for cultural property, the armlet and identity cards.

We feel we should also point out that a certain confusion seems to exist at times between the emblems of the Hague Convention and those concerning the cultural and natural heritage.

NOTES

1   Reply to Mr Malinoski of Poland dated 31 July 1961 (CA 12/20/2514).
2   *Commentary on the Additional Protocols of 8 June 1977*, para. 3498, p.999.
3   This wording replaced the phrase 'a certified copy of the authorization, duly dated and signed, issued by the competent authorities of the High Contracting Party' which appeared in the draft prepared by the Conference Working Group.
4   *Records*, paras 1485–6, p.244.
5   See the reports of the States or the summary in the Programme of Action, pp.108 *et seq.*

REGULATIONS FOR THE EXECUTION OF THE CONVENTION – CHAPTER V: THE DISTINCTIVE EMBLEM

Article 20 of the Regulations for the Execution of the Convention: Affixing of the Emblem

1. *The placing of the distinctive emblem and its degree of visibility shall be left to the discretion of the competent authorities of each High Contracting Party. It may be displayed on flags or armlets; it may be painted on an object or represented in any other appropriate form.*
2. *However, without prejudice to any possible fuller markings, the emblem shall, in the event of armed conflict and in the cases mentioned in Articles 12 and 13 of the Convention, be placed on the vehicles of transport so as to be clearly visible in daylight from the air as well as from the ground.*
   The emblem shall be visible from the ground:
   (a)   at regular intervals sufficient to indicate clearly the perimeter of a centre containing monuments under special protection;
   (b)   at the entrance to other immovable cultural property under special protection.

   Records: Text: pp.60, 62.
                Minutes: paras 1419, 1465, 1491, 2097–9.
                Working documents: pp.318, 408;
                CBC/DR/53/143/164.

Paragraph 1

According to the 1949 Geneva Convention, 'Parties to the conflict shall take the necessary steps, in so far as military considerations permit, to make the distinctive emblems indicating medical units and establishments clearly visible to the enemy land, air or naval forces in order to avoid the possibility of any hostile action' (Article 42, para. 4 of the First Convention).

The present provision – which concerns cultural property under both general and special protection – contains no reference to military considerations. What is more, it leaves considerable latitude to the Parties as regards positioning and the degree of visibility. This flexibility allows the competent authorities of the High Contracting Parties to develop the identification system in line with technical progress.

On the other hand, it should be noted that Additional Protocol I of 1977, whose Annex specifies quite precisely what means are to be used for identification, makes provision in Article 98 for the periodical review of the latter so that it may keep pace with technical developments.

Paragraph 2

For the period of armed conflict, the Regulations for the Execution of the Convention give general instructions concerning, among other things, visibility in the case of property placed under special protection. This provision lays down a minimum and leaves it to the Parties to ensure fuller coverage by the system, thus giving them a further opportunity to adjust the identification system to new technical facilities.

The question of visibility at sea was raised during the plenary session of the Conference. It was pointed out that the expression 'vehicles of transport' included, among other things, ships. Accordingly, where it is stated that the emblem shall be visible from the ground, the expression means that it must also be visible from the sea.[1]

Visibility

Even though the visibility requirement is compulsory only for property under special protection and, in the case of property under general protection, the question is left to the discretion of the competent authorities of each High Contracting Party, it seems important to draw the attention of the Parties to this matter.

Like any distinctive emblem, to be effective it has to be fully visible and identifiable within the visual range for which it is designed. Accordingly, it should make personnel, units and transport identifiable to the naked eye in daylight and in clear weather (absence of fog, snow, rain and so on) at the distance separating combatants when they shoot on sight. This distance varies significantly according to the nature of the armaments: infantry, armoured tanks, artillery, naval or air weapons, and so on.

The visibility of the distinctive emblem of the Geneva Conventions was tested by the Dutch and Swiss air forces in 1936 and, according to the experts, these tests are still valid today.[2] These visibility criteria need therefore to be borne in mind in interpreting paragraphs 1 and 2 of Article 20 of the Regulations for the Execution of the Convention.

In our view it would be desirable for the High Contracting Parties to be guided by the recent codification of international humanitarian law in the area of identification. Annex I to Additional Protocol I is based on recent technical developments and these conclusions should be used for the updating of the 1954 Convention. Before this revision can be undertaken it would be advisable for the General Conference of UNESCO to adopt a recommendation on the subject, basing itself on Annex I of Additional Protocol I of 1977 (see Annex).

NOTES

1   *Records*, paras 2097–9, p.288.
2   For more details, see *Commentary on the Additional Protocols of 8 June 1977*, pp.1167 *et seq*. The results of the Dutch tests, for a six-metre diameter red cross on a white six-metre side square, were as follows: from 1500m altitude, the red cross is visible to an observer knowing where it is; from 2500m, the red cross is scarcely visible even to an observer knowing where it is; from 3500m, the red cross is not visible.

Article 21 of the Regulations for the Execution of the Convention: Identification of Persons

1.   *The persons mentioned in Article 17, paragraph 2(b) and (c) of the Convention may wear an armlet bearing the distinctive emblem, issued and stamped by the competent authorities.*
2.   *Such persons shall carry a special identity card bearing the distinctive emblem. This card shall mention at least the surname and first names, the date of birth, the title or rank, and the function of the holder. The cad shall bear the photograph of the holder as well as his signature or his fingerprints, or both. It shall bear the embossed stamp of the competent authorities.*
3.   *Each High Contracting Party shall make out its own type of identity card, guided by the model annexed, by way of example, to the present Regulations. The High Contracting Parties shall transmit to each other a specimen of the model they are using. Identity cards shall be made out, if possible, at least in duplicate, one copy being kept by the issuing Power.*
4.   *The said persons may not, without legitimate reason, be deprived of their identity card or of the right to wear the armlet.*

Records: Text: p.62.
          Minutes: paras 1420–23, 2099.
          Working documents: pp.318, 408–9;
          CBC/DR/164.

This provision concerns the identification of persons engaged in the protection of cultural property, that is, those mentioned in Article 17 of the Convention, paragraphs 2(b) and (c). Identification is established by means of the armlet and the identity card.

Paragraph 1

The persons mentioned in Article 17, paragraphs 2(b) and (c) of the Convention (that is, persons responsible for the duties of control in accordance with the Regulations for the Execution of the Convention and personnel engaged in the protection of cultural property) *may* (it is not compulsory) wear an armlet bearing the distinctive emblem of the Convention issued and stamped by the competent authorities.

Paragraph 2

A card shall be issued to such personnel. It must bear the distinctive emblem. The paragraph also refers to the minimum of information that has to be shown on the card. The High Contracting Parties may, if they consider it useful, include other details as well.

With the possibility of abuse in the issue of these cards in mind, it was suggested that the card should mention the date on which its holder began to carry out his functions. This suggestion was not adopted because, on the one hand, the date of issue of the card would already constitute an indication and because, on the other, it was inevitable that the number of holders would grow as the dangers threatening cultural property due to events increased, and that many holders of these posts would be prevented from occupying them in time of armed conflict, particularly owing to their mobilization.[1]

The identity card issued by the competent authorities enables holders to prove that they belong to the personnel engaged in the protection of cultural property and are entitled to be respected (Article 15 of the Convention). It justifies, particularly in occupied territories and combat zones, the right to wear the distinctive emblem.

Paragraph 3

Identity cards should be prepared in peacetime. It would be dangerous to leave this task until a conflict began.

The Parties are free to make out their own type of identity card but should be guided by the model shown as an example in the Annex to the Regulations.

The competent authority designated in each country will have to perform a number of tasks in connection with the issue of the identity cards: management of indexes and duplicates, replacement of lost cards, prolongation of validity if required, and so on.

Transmitting the design of the card to other countries should take place in peacetime. In fact, the paragraph refers to transmission between the High Contracting Parties. This differs, then, from Additional Protocol I (Article 1 of Annex I) according to which the identity cards of permanent civilian medical and religious personnel must be transmitted to each other by the Parties to the conflict at the outbreak of hostilities. The procedure for such transmission is not laid down but it may be either directly or via the depositary. It would

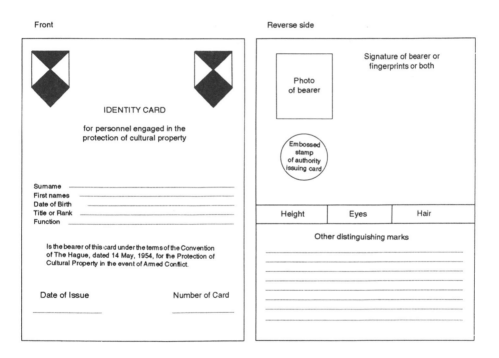

Identity card

Records: Regulations for the Execution of the Convention, Article 21.
Minutes: paras 1420–24.
Working documents: pp.319, 345, 385, 409.
Model: *Records*, p.64.
Working document: p.409.

seem desirable for the depositary to be responsible for this task. The High Contracting Parties should accordingly transmit specimens of the designs adopted for the cards to UNESCO. They should be accompanied by translations of the text into the other languages of the Convention. UNESCO should make itself responsible for transmitting these models to the other High Contracting Parties.

Paragraph 4

Holders may not be deprived of their card or of the right to wear the armlet. The object here is to provide protection against arbitrary decisions likely to interfere with the activity of personnel assigned to the protection of cultural property.

Such measures might be taken for legitimate reasons: because of the misuse of the card for purposes other than those for which it was issued, when the person has been found guilty of such acts.

NOTE

1   *Records* , p.319.

Chapter VI
Scope of Application of the Convention

Article 18
Application of the Convention

1. *Apart from the provisions which shall take effect in time of peace, the present Convention shall apply in the event of declared war or of any other armed conflict which may arise between two or more of the High Contracting Parties, even if the state of war is not recognized by one or more of them.*
2. *The Convention shall also apply to all cases of partial or total occupation of the territory of a High Contracting Party, even if the said occupation meets with no armed resistance.*
3. *If one of the Powers in conflict is not a Party to the present Convention, the Powers which are Parties thereto shall nevertheless remain bound by it in their mutual relations. They shall furthermore be bound by the Convention, in relation to the said Power, if the latter has declared that it accepts the provisions thereof and so long as it applies them.*

Records: Text: p.22.
Minutes: paras 544, 629–47, 696, 800–801, 803, 805, 1934, 1954, 1059, 1060–62, 1193, 1610, 1759, 1992, 2006.
Working documents: pp.313, 329, 347–8;
CBC/DR/69/77/88/118.

PREPARATORY WORK

Article 18 of the Convention is taken almost entirely from the text of Article 2 which is common to the Geneva Conventions of 12 August

195

1949. Many delegations at the Conference urged that this provision be maintained *in toto* without any change.

In our analysis of this article we have based ourselves on the Commentary on the Geneva Conventions, mentioning certain essential points, but we advise readers to read that Commentary,[1] which explains how the provision came into being.

Earlier conventions said nothing about the situations to which they applied. The reference to war or armed conflict seemed enough. This was the case with the Geneva Conventions of 1864, 1906 and 1929 and the Hague Conventions of 1899 and 1907. It was also the case with conventions relating to cultural property: the Fourth and Ninth Hague Conventions of 1907 and the Washington Pact of 1935.

As regards the Geneva Conventions, it was self-evident that they applied in time of war. The outbreak of hostilities should be preceded by a declaration, but when that was not the case or when, for one reason or another (such as non-recognition by one of the Parties of the government of the other), the state of war was not recognized by one of the two sides, the applicability of the Convention might be contested. It was for this reason that the ICRC, and also the Conference of Government Experts, recommended that the conventions should apply to 'any armed conflict, whether the latter is or is not recognized as a state of war by the Parties concerned' and in the case of occupation of territory in the absence of any state of war. The article was adopted by the XVIIth International Red Cross Conference in Stockholm in 1948 and submitted to the Geneva Diplomatic Conference in 1949.

PARAGRAPH 1

The first paragraph, disregarding the provisions which should take effect in time of peace, states that this Convention shall apply in the event of declared war or of any other armed conflict which may arise between two or more of the High Contracting Parties, even if the state of war is not recognized by one or more of them.

This provision, taken from the Geneva Conventions, deprives the belligerents of the pretexts they might invoke for evasion of their obligations. 'There is no longer any need for a formal declaration of war, or for recognition of the state of war, as preliminaries to the application of the Convention. The Convention becomes applicable as from the actual opening of hostilities. The existence of armed conflict between two or more Contracting Parties brings it automatically into operation.'[2]

The authors mention declared war in the context of a broader expression: that of armed conflict consisting of 'any difference arising between two States and leading to the intervention of armed forces' or similar forces. Thus the length of the conflict, the loss of life entailed, a simple police operation, acts of legitimate self-defence, undeclared hostilities and so on all constitute armed conflict.

In comparison with Article 2 common to the Geneva Conventions which states that the Conventions shall apply 'even if the state of war is not recognized by one of them' in 1954 Hague Convention refers to 'one or more of them'. This drafting change does not alter in any way the meaning of this provision as compared with Article 2 common to the 1949 Geneva Conventions.

The provision means that the Convention shall not be applied if all the parties to the conflict deny the existence of the state of war.[3] In Jean Pictet's view, 'even in that event it would not appear that they could, by tacit agreement, prevent the Conventions from applying. It must not be forgotten that the Conventions have been drawn up first and foremost to protect individuals, and not to serve State interests.'[4]

PARAGRAPH 2

According to paragraph 2, the Convention also applies to all cases of partial or total occupation of the territory of a High Contracting Party, even if such occupation meets with no armed resistance.

This provision was introduced in the Geneva Conventions as a result of the experience of the Second World War. It does not refer to occupation during hostilities because, in that case, the Conventions would be applicable immediately with the outbreak of hostilities or the declaration of war, as in paragraph 1. This paragraph refers solely to situations in which occupation takes place without war being declared and in the absence of hostilities or military operations.

Paragraph 3 of Article 5 should be brought to mind here, according to which any High Contracting Party whose government is considered their legitimate government by members of a resistance movement shall, if possible, draw their attention to the obligation to comply with those provisions of the Convention dealing with respect for cultural property.

PARAGRAPH 3

The draft common text for Article 2 was adopted by the XVII International Red Cross Conference in Stockholm in 1948 and was submitted to the Diplomatic Conference of Geneva in 1949. But it was not adequate. It was silent about relations between the belligerents Parties to the Convention and those which were not. The idea was then considered of making the provisions of the Conventions compulsory for a State deliberately remaining outside the convention system. It was asked whether a belligerent Party to the Convention should not, at least to a certain extent, be bound with regard to the opposing Party not a High Contracting Party. This idea, already present when the 1929 Conventions were being drafted, was taken up again. The ICRC suggested that the following be added to Article 2: 'In the event of an international conflict between one of the High Contracting Parties and a Power which is not bound by the present Convention, the Contracting Party shall apply the provisions thereof. This obligation shall stand unless, after a reasonable lapse of time, the Power not bound by the present Convention states its refusal to apply it, or in fact fails to apply it.'

Another approach was proposed by the Canadian and Belgian delegations to the Geneva Conference. The former suggested that the Convention should also apply to a Power not a Party to the Convention so long as that Power complied therewith. The Belgian delegation proposed that 'the Powers which are a Party to the Convention shall invite the Power which is not a Party to it to accept the terms of the said Convention; as from the latter Power's acceptance of the Convention, all Powers concerned shall be bound by it'. The ICRC proposal, like that of Canada, was resolutive: the signatory Powers were automatically bound and remained so as long as the non-signatory Party itself complied with the Convention. The Belgian proposal was suspensive: the Convention was binding on the signatories only from the moment that the non-signatory Party indicated its acceptance. All these proposals were rejected; the compromise formula that was agreed reads as follows.

First Sentence

The first sentence of article 2, paragraph 3 of the Geneva Conventions is identical with Article 18, paragraph 3, above. It is the response to the *clausula si omnes* already existing in the 1906 Geneva Convention and the Hague Conventions of 1899 and 1907. This clause signified that the Convention was applicable only if all Parties in the conflict were also bound. On that basis it only needed one belligerent not to be Party to the Convention for the application of the Convention to be ruled out for all the others. In the First World War, Monetenegro was not a Party to the Geneva Convention and, in the strict terms of the law, this meant there could be no application of the Convention in the world conflict. No one invoked this strict application of the law. Paul des Gouttes, author of the Commentary on the 1929 Convention, considered that, on this point, 'the facts, backed by the signatures of the signatories and by the humanitarian interests of all, outweighed the law'.[5]

Second Sentence

The second sentence of Article 2, paragraph 3, common to the Geneva Conventions, states: 'They shall, furthermore, be bound by the Convention in relation to the said Power, if the latter accepts and applies the provisions thereof.'

The Rapporteur of the Special Committee of the 1949 Diplomatic Conference of Geneva explained the reasons for this decision: 'As a general rule, a Convention could lay obligations only on Contracting States. But, according to the spirit of the four Conventions, the Contracting States shall apply them, in so far as possible, as being the codification of rules which are generally recognized. The text adopted by the Special Committee, therefore, laid upon the Contracting State, in the instance envisaged, the obligation to recognize that the Convention be applied to the non-contracting adverse State, in so far as the latter accepted and applied the provisions thereof.'[6]

The meaning of the phrase used in the 1949 Geneva Conventions is accordingly different. The Commentary on the 1949 Geneva Conventions states the following: 'The spirit and character of the Conventions conclusively indicate that the Contracting Party must apply their provisions from the moment hostilities break out until such time as the adverse Party has had the time and an opportunity to state his intentions. That is not perhaps a strictly legal solution based on a literal exegesis of the text; but it is to our thinking the only honourable and reasonable solution. It follows from the spirit of the Conventions, and is in accordance with their character, as we have already stated. It is also in accordance with the moral interest of the Contracting Party in so far as it invites the latter to honour the signature he has given before the world. It is in accordance even with his practical interest, because the fact of his making a beginning himself with the application of the Convention will encourage the non-Contracting Party to declare his acceptance, whereas any postponement of the application of the Convention by the Contracting Party is likely to give the non-Contracting Party a pretext for reserving his decision.

'There are two conditions to be fulfilled under this part of the paragraph – acceptance and *de facto* application of the Convention. What happens if the non-Contracting Party makes no declaration, but in actual fact applies the Convention? Before answering this question, let us see what is meant by "accepting" the provisions of the Convention.

'Is a formal and explicit declaration by a non-Contracting State indispensable? The Rapporteur of the Special Committee seems to say that it is. "A declaration", he wrote, "was necessary, contrary to the Canadian amendment, according to which an attitude on the part of the non-Contracting State in conformity with the Convention would have sufficed to make it applicable." He added, it is true, that it was not possible to lay down any uniform procedure in the matter, and that "the Convention would be applicable as soon as the declaration was made. It would cease to be applicable as soon as the declaration was clearly disavowed by the attitude of the non-contracting belligerent." Does it follow from this that, the second condition – namely the application of the Convention *de facto* – alone being fulfilled, the Contracting Party is released from its obligations?

'Closely as that may seem to follow from the letter of the text, it does not appear possible to maintain such an interpretation. It would make the application of the Convention dependent on a suspensive condition even more rigid than that of the Belgian proposal, which was itself regarded as being too strict. It would bring about a paradoxical – not to say monstrous – situation. It would entitle a Power to refuse to recognize rules solemnly proclaimed by itself, while its adversary, though not legally bound by these rules, was scrupulously applying them; and all this only because of the omission of the latter to make a declaration, or because of delay in the transmission of such a declaration!

'The two conditions laid down for the non-Contracting Power are that he should *accept* and *apply* the provisions of the Convention. In the absence of any further indication, there is no reason to assume that "acceptance" necessarily implies an explicit declaration. It can equally well be tacit. It may be implicit in *de facto* application. These considerations do not in any way minimize the importance of an explicit declaration by the non-Contracting Power. The latter should always make such a declaration, and with the least possible delay. The International Committee of the Red Cross for its part, when it offers its services at the beginning of a conflict, never fails to ask Parties to the conflict which are not legally bound by the Convention to declare their intention of applying it or of observing at least its essential principles, as the case may be.

'In practice any Contracting Power in conflict with a non-Contracting Power will begin by complying with the provisions of the Convention pending the adverse Party's declaration. It will be guided first and foremost by the latter's actions.'[7]

Now, having explained the meaning of the provision in the Geneva Conventions, let us return again to the 1954 Hague Convention. We can see that the wording of the second sentence of Article 18, paragraph 3 has been slightly modified as compared with the 1949

Geneva Conventions. Instead of 'accepts and applies the provisions thereof', Article 18, paragraph 3 of the 1954 Hague Convention states: *'if the latter has declared that it accepts the provisions thereof and so long as it applies them'*. As compared with Article 2 of the Geneva Convention, the acceptance has to be in the form of a declaration accompanied by effective application. The phrase 'accepts and applies' is far less formalistic and 'accepts' may be interpreted in conjunction with 'applies' as a single unit. By applying it, the Power concerned accepts it without any formal declaration.

The version adopted in the 1954 Convention can therefore be interpreted as a backward step, in the sense of the Belgian proposal submitted to the Geneva Conference, according to which the signatories were bound by the Convention only from the moment that the non-signatory Party gave its formal acceptance.

In 1962, and thus well before its ratification of the convention and the Protocol on 11 August 1967, the Federal Republic of Germany stated that in view of the fact that the ratification procedure would demand a considerable amount of time because of the federal nature of the Republic, in accordance with Article 18(3) of the Convention, it accepted as of now the provisions of the Convention and, for its part, now applied them. Hence all Parties to the Convention were, in accordance with Article 18(3), equally bound by the Convention *vis-à-vis* the Federal Republic of Germany.[8]

ADDITIONAL OBSERVATIONS

Application of the Convention to Armed Conflicts in which Peoples are Fighting for the Right of Self-determination

We have seen that the scope of application of the Convention was defined in Article 18 in almost the same terms as in Article 2 common to the Geneva Conventions. It gradually became clear that this provision was not appropriate for the increasing number of conflicts which were widespread from the 1960s onward: the wars of national liberation. The change in the definition of conflict proved to be one of the fundamental questions at the Diplomatic Conference on the Reaffirmation and Development of International Humanitarian Law Applicable in Armed Conflicts, Geneva (1974–77). The Conference adopted Article 1, paragraph 4, according to which: 'The situations referred to in the preceding paragraph [international armed conflicts] include armed conflicts in which peoples are fighting against colonial domination and alien occupation and against racist regimes in the exercise of their right of self-determination, as enshrined in the Charter of the United Nations and the Declaration on Principles of International

Law concerning Friendly Relations and Cooperation among States in accordance with the Charter of the United Nations.'

According to this provision, therefore, the rules of international humanitarian law, as they appear in the Geneva Conventions of 1949 and Protocol I of 1977, apply to wars of national liberation.

Two main schools of thought have developed with regard to this provision in the doctrine of international law. For some, the adoption of this article represents a consensus on the solution to be given to the problem of wars of national liberation, 'while indicating at the same time the interpretation that should prevail under the Geneva Conventions ... an interpretation which is subscribed to by a very large majority of the Parties to these Conventions'. 'Even if Protocol I is not accepted as a separate legal instrument by the handful of governments facing a war of national liberation, its provisions assert themselves as the proper interpretation of the Geneva Conventions.'[9] The fact that the *locus standi* of liberation movements was codified in Article 86, paragraph 3, of Protocol I vindicates earlier interpretations of the term 'Power' in the Geneva Conventions to include such movements, at least for the purpose of common Article 2, paragraph 3, of the Geneva Conventions, whose formula was more or less borrowed by Article 96 of the Protocol. This interpretation is interesting from the viewpoint of the 1954 Hague Convention which, as we have seen, took over almost the whole text of common Article 2.

The same authors conclude that, 'if a national liberation movement makes a declaration accepting the provisions of the Conventions, according to common Article 2, paragraph 3, these Conventions, as interpreted in the light of Protocol I, become applicable to the ongoing war of national liberation, regardless of the opposition of the adversary government, as long as it is itself bound by the Conventions'.[10]

The other view held by experts in international law is that, pending the entry into force of Protocol I, wars of national liberation are covered by common Article 3 of the 1949 Geneva Conventions (non-international armed conflicts). They consider that the scope of application of paragraph 4 of Article 1 is, at the moment, very restricted and limited, more especially, to the peoples of South Africa and Palestine.[11] For them, the resolutions and declarations of the General Assembly of the United Nations in no way create new law and paragraph 4 is not a codification of existing positive international law but a new rule of law.[12]

These two trends show there is no unanimity, either in interpretation by States or in doctrine. The question – of political interest, above all – should not be allowed to obscure the problem of the protection of cultural property which is the only issue that matters here. As regards the protection of cultural property, two points need to be made:

1   As far as the 1954 Hague Convention is concerned, the problem is much less acute than in the case of the Geneva Conventions. Indeed, the scope of the protection of victims of armed conflict in the four Conventions is incomparably wider for international armed conflict (where protection is covered by all 486 articles) than for non-international conflicts (where protection is confined to common Article 3 of the Geneva Conventions). In the case of the Hague Convention the protection of cultural property is limited in the case of Article 19 to at least the provisions of the Convention which relate to respect for cultural property. Even if application were limited to the strict minimum, that is, respect for cultural property within the meaning of Article 4 of the Hague Convention, it is still incomparably wider if compared with the situation of victims under the Geneva Conventions. We shall see below, in the Commentary on Article 19, that, in our opinion, the scope of physical application is far wider.

2   Many of the general provisions of the Hague Convention form part of customary international law which, also, constitutes an important basis for strengthening the application of the protection of cultural property in armed conflict, including wars of national liberation.

The question therefore remains somewhat academic for, as Frits Kalshoven says, the scope of application is very limited nowadays, the process of decolonization having more or less come to an end. But if a new conference or meeting of the High Contracting Parties were to be held, this question would probably be raised and it would be useful to solve the problem in a similar way to that chosen by the Diplomatic Conference of 1974–77, that is, by adopting one or more Protocols additional to the Hague Convention. This would give those States wishing to do so a chance to bring the scope of application of the Convention into line with the new conditions of conflicts and, for those which do not, to retain the traditional field of application set out in Article 18 of the Hague Convention.

Application of the Convention by the Armed Forces of the United Nations

It is interesting to return to the proposal made by the Greek delegate at the 1954 Hague Conference which was to add, after paragraph 2 of this article, a reference to collective action on behalf of the United Nations in the following terms: 'although it might be admitted that, in the case of collective action, the laws of war would be respected, it was important enough to state so, there or elsewhere, for the purposes of the Convention'.[13] This proposal was not taken up by the Conference but it should be remembered that the question is still of considerable interest in regard to both the Geneva Conventions and the present Convention. It is still desirable, as Mr Saba said at the Conference, for 'the Security Council and General Assembly to take a resolution deciding to apply the Convention'.

Even though the Hague Conference did not solve the problem of accession by the United Nations to the Convention, it adopted at least one resolution – Resolution I – in which it expressed the hope that the competent organs of the United Nations should decide, in the event of military action being taken in implementation of the Charter, to ensure application of the provisions of the Convention by the armed forces taking part in such action.[14]

Other organizations and academic centres[15] have expressed their agreement with accession, in an appropriate form, by the United Nations to the Geneva Conventions and the 1954 Hague Convention. We may mention here the Council of Delegates of the International Red Cross (1963), the International Conference of the Red Cross in Vienna, 1965 (Resolution XXV), the International Law Association (Helsinki Conference, 1966) and, lastly, the two resolutions of the Institute of International Law (1971 and 1975).[16]

Relevant examples in United Nations practice are the Regulations for the United Nations Force in Cyprus of 25 April 1964 which contain a general reference to respect for the Conventions in Article 40, according to which 'the Force shall observe and respect the principles and spirit of the general international Conventions applicable to the conduct of military personnel'.[17]

The exchange of letters constituting an agreement between the United Nations and Canada regarding the service with the United Nations Peace-Keeping Force in Cyprus of the national contingent provided by the Government of Canada (New York, 21 February 1966) contains information about the application of the Hague Convention in paragraphs 10 and 11. Interpreting Article 40 of the Regulations, the United Nations Secretary-General stated that 'The international Conventions referred to in this Regulation include, *inter alia*, the Geneva (Red Cross) Conventions of 12 August 1949 to which your Government is a party and the UNESCO Convention on the Protection of Cultural Property in the Event of Armed Conflict, signed at The Hague on 14 May 1954. In this connection and particularly with respect to the humanitarian provisions of these Conventions, it is requested that the Governments of the participating States ensure that the members of their contingents serving with the Force be fully acquainted with the obligations arising under these Conventions and that appropriate steps be taken to ensure their enforcement.'[18]

It is important to note, furthermore, that the troops serving with the United Nations forces are aware of their role as regards both respect for humanitarian agreements and the protection of cultural property. In practice, the lack of instructions on the subject has led the United Nations armed forces to undertake their action in the context of respect for the framework of these Conventions.[19] The *Peacekeeper's Handbook,* published by the International Peace Academy, refers to UNESCO's role in this area and notes that 'in the immediate aftermath of fighting it may be that only the United Nations Force can fulfil this responsibility. Inspections, removal to places of safety, supervision of restoration work wherever it may be required, are activities capable of being undertaken by Operations Economics.'[20]

NOTES

1   *Final Record of the Diplomatic Conference of Geneva of 1949,* Vol. II, Sec. B, Berne, Federal Political Department, p.108.
2   Jean S. Pictet (ed.), *The Geneva Conventions of 12 August 1949. Commentary,* Vol. I, p.32.
3   Sharon A. Williams, *The International and National Protection of Movable Cultural Property: a comparative study,* Dobbs Ferry, NY, Oceana Publications, 1978, p.43.
4   Jean S. Pictet (ed.), *The Geneva Conventions of 12 August 1949. Commentary,* Vol. IV, *The Geneva Convention Relative to the Protection of Civilian Persons in Time of War,* Geneva, ICRC, 1958, p.21.
5   Paul des Gouttes, *La convention de Genève pour l'amélioration du sort des blessées et des malades dans les armées en campagne du 27 juillet 1929, Commentaire,* Geneva, Comité international de la Croix-Rouge, 1930, p.188. Quoted in Pictet (ed.), *The Geneva Conventions of 12 August 1949,* Vol. I, p.34.
6   *Final Record of the Diplomatic Conference of Geneva of 1949,* Vol. II, Sec. B, Berne, Federal Political Department, p.108.
7   Jean S. Pictet (ed.), *The Geneva Conventions of 12 August 1949. Commentary,* Vol. I, pp.35–7.
8   Letter ref. ODG/SJ/2/467 of 2 March 1962.
9   Georges Abi-Saab, 'Respect of Humanitarian Norms in International Conflicts. Interstate wars and wars of national liberation', in *Modern Wars. The Humanitarian Challenge. A Report for the Independent Commission on International Humanitarian Issues,* London and New Jersey, Zed Books Ltd, 1986, p.83.
10 Ibid., p.83.
11 Frits Kalshoven, 'Reaffirmation and development of international humanitarian law applicable in armed conflicts: the Diplomatic Conference, Geneva, 1974–1977', Part I: 'Combatants and civilians', *Netherlands Yearbook of International Law* (Leiden), Vol. 8, 1977, p.122.
12 Michel Bothe, Karl Josef Partsch and Waldemar A. Solf, *New Rules for Victims of Armed Conflicts,* The Hague, Martinus Nijhoff Publishers, 1982, pp.48 *et seq.*
13 CBC/DR/88, *Records,* para. 633, p.187.
14 See Part IV, p.306.
15 See Finn Seyersted, *United Nations Forces in the Law of Peace and War,* Leiden, A.W. Sijthoff, 1966, pp.197, *et seq.* and especially pp.354–61. See also Yves

Sandoz, 'The application of humanitarian law by the armed forces of the United Nations Organization', *International Review of the Red Cross (Geneva): 60th Year*, September–October 1978, pp.274–84.

16   D. Schindler and J. Toman (eds), *The Laws of Armed Conflicts. A Collection of Conventions, Resolutions and other Documents*, Dordrecht, Martinus Nijhoff Publishers, 1988, pp.903–8.

17   ST/SGB/UNFICYP/1 of 25 April 1964, p.15; United Nations, *Treaty Series*, Vol. 555, p.126.

18   United Nations, *Treaty Series*, Vol. 555, p.126.

19   I.J. Rikhye, M. Harbottle and B. Egge, *The Thin Blue Line, International Peacekeeping and its Future*, New Haven, Yale University Press, 1974, p.88. See also Charles E. McConney, 'Draft Proposal for the Creation of a Permanent Monuments, Fine Arts and Archives Unit within the U.N. Peace-keeping forces (Summary)', in P.J. Boylan, *Review of the Convention for the Protection of Cultural Property in the Event of Armed Conflict* (The Hague Convention of 1954), Paris, UNESCO, 1993, Appendix XI, pp.221–3.

20   *Peacekeeper's Handbook*, New York, International Peace Academy, 1984, Chapter VIII, para. 39. See also ibid., para. 7: 'Section 2 – Operations Economics: The staff department in The United Nations Force in Cyprus (UNFICYP) responsible for economic assistance on the military side originally was known as Operation Economics and was a branch of the operations staff under the Chief Operations Officer. The designation "operations economics", or Ops E, would not necessarily be standard nomenclature in all circumstances; each peacekeeping operation would design its own specific organization and select an appropriate designation. In the event of the economic assistance programme assuming major significance or being extended to incorporate additional responsibilities, as was the case in Cyprus, the department very possibly would be detached from the operational staff structure and formed into its own separate organization. It should, however, be required to relate its operational work to that of the operations staff so that complete co-ordination can be achieved'.

Article 19
Conflicts not of an International Character

1. *In the event of an armed conflict not of an international charac-*
   ter occurring within the territory of one of the High Contracting
   Parties, each party to the conflict shall be bound to apply, as a
   minimum, the provisions of the present Convention which relate
   to respect for cultural property.
2. *The parties to the conflict shall endeavour to bring into force, by*
   means of special agreements, all or part of the other provisions
   of the present Convention.
3. *The United Nations Educational, Scientific and Cultural Or-*
   ganization may offer its services to the parties to the conflict.
4. *The application of the preceding provisions shall not affect the*
   legal status of the parties to the conflict.

Records: Text: pp.22, 24.
             Minutes: paras 133, 150, 631, 696, 1063–75, 1992, 2006.
             Working documents: pp.312–13, 343–4, 385;
             CBC/DR/81.
Bibliography: Boylan, P.J., *Review of the Convention for the Protec-*
                 tion of Cultural Property in the Event of Armed Con-
                 flict, (The Hague Convention of 1954), Paris,
                 UNESCO, 1993, paras 31.1–13.39, pp.115–26. Pictet,
                 Jean S. (ed.), *The Geneva Conventions of 12 August*
                 1949. Commentary, Vol. I, pp.37–61.

BACKGROUND AND PREPARATORY WORK

This article is also largely based on the Geneva Conventions, that is,
Article 3 common to all four Conventions (referred to hereinafter as
'Article 3'). It should, however, be remembered that the Preliminary
Draft International Convention of 1938 had, in Article 10, already
made provision for the situation of internal conflict defined in very
broad terms:

The High Contracting Parties, recognizing the necessity of extending the protection contemplated by this Convention to historic buildings and works of art threatened by disturbances or armed conflicts within a country, agree as follows:

1. They may lend their friendly assistance to the contending parties for the purpose of safeguarding the threatened historic and artistic treasures.
2. They may receive and shelter, in their respective territories, works of art coming from a country in which civil strife is prevalent and endangered by acts arising out of such strife.
3. Museums and collections of a public character may store works of art abroad during a period of civil strife. So long as such works remain abroad, the museums which deposited them shall be deemed their owners. Such deposits shall not be restored until the civil strife is at an end. During transport and for the period of their deposit, such works of art shall be exempt from confiscation, and may not be disposed of either by the depositor or by the depositary.
4. Works of art in private ownership may receive protection in foreign territory, provided that they are there deposited on the responsibility of and through the agency of a national museum or collection of a public character. The same rules concerning deposit and restoration shall apply and restoration may be affected only through the agency of the depositing institution.

Of relevance here is Article 11 of the Regulations for the Execution of the Convention annexed to the Preliminary Draft, according to which 'for the purposes of the application of Article 10 of the Convention, the Standing Committee of the Conference shall lend its good offices to the contending parties with a view to taking all necessary steps for the protection of monuments and works of art threatened by the operations'.

This provision, together with common Article 3 of the 1949 Geneva Conventions, lay at the origin of Article 19 of the 1954 Hague Convention. It helps us to gain a better understanding of the scope of its application, in particular *ratione materiae*.

The UNESCO Draft CBC/3, submitted to the 1954 Conference, borrowed the basic structure of common Article 3 of the 1949 Geneva Conventions. According to the UNESCO Commentary, the article concerned provided 'that at least the principles of the Convention relating to respect for cultural property should be applied in the event of a conflict not of an international character, i.e. generally, in fact, in the event of civil war. These provisions are based on those found in the Geneva Conventions of 1949. They may be thought to be imperfect; but the Red Cross, faced with the same textual difficulties, decided that they should not, for that reason, be omitted. The basis of the obligation prescribed by Article 19 for each adversary is that each of the latter is bound by contractual engagements undertaken by a community of which he is a part.'[1]

The United Kingdom was alone in proposing the deletion of Article 19 (judging it to be unworkable) or at least its weakening, inviting Parties to the conflict to 'endeavour' rather than 'be bound' to apply the provisions of the Convention and removing UNESCO's right take the initiative. The Legal Committee of the Conference did not agree with the United Kingdom's reasoning.[2] The USSR delegate, whose delegation had played an important part in the adoption of Article 3 at the Diplomatic Conference of 1949 in Geneva, replied to the United Kingdom to the effect that 'the article was perfectly clear. Paragraph 1 referred to the necessity of respecting and safeguarding cultural property and paragraph 4 implied that the application of its provisions would not affect the legal status of the Conflicting Parties. The subject had already been examined in sufficient detail at the 1949 Geneva Conference where a Special Committee and two Working Parties had worked on it for 20 days. A very detailed report had been submitted. Delegates from all countries had spoken and an Article 3 had finally been adopted, which appeared in all the Geneva Conventions and listed the provisions to be respected. While the question under discussion then had been the sick and wounded, and was now that of cultural property, the principle was the same and it should be remembered that the decisions then taken were adopted by 61 countries. It was a sufficiently weighty precedent and should be taken into consideration.'[3]

The article was adopted in its original form, with two changes for stylistic reasons.

PARAGRAPH 1

Under the terms of this paragraph, in the event of an armed conflict not of an international character occurring within the territory of one of the High Contracting Parties, each party to the conflict shall be bound to apply, as a minimum, the provisions of the present Convention which relate to respect for cultural property.

As in Article 3, the scope of application of Article 19 is not defined in any precise manner and we may conclude that it is the same as that of Article 3.

Definition of Armed Conflict not of an International Character

As the Commentary on the Geneva Conventions notes,[4] the scope of application was the burning question which arose again and again at the Diplomatic Conference of 1949 in Geneva. Many delegations feared that, because of its general and vague nature, it might be taken to cover any act committed by forced of arms, any form of anarchy, rebellion or even plain banditry. It was therefore proposed that the term 'conflict' should be defined or – and this would come to the same thing – that a list should be given of a number of conditions[5] on which the application of the Convention would depend. Finally, the idea of listing the conditions was abandoned: their formulation, apart from the fact that it would have to be approved, presented the danger of restricting the application of the Convention to certain more or less well-defined types of conflict, whereas the end in view was the maximum extension of protection to armed conflicts not of an international character. It would therefore seem, in this case as in other examples of the codification of law, that the normative power of common Article 3 lay in the absence of a precise definition of armed conflict not of an international character, as its application for some 40 years now appears to prove.

The criteria we have listed clearly show the distinction to be drawn between a genuine armed conflict and a mere act of banditry or an unorganized and short-lived uprising.

The Commentary goes on in these words: 'Does this mean Article 3 is not applicable in cases where armed strife breaks out in a country, but does not fulfil any of the above conditions which are not obligatory and are only mentioned as an indication? We do not subscribe to this view. We think, on the contrary, that the scope of application of the article must be as wide as possible. There can be no drawbacks since the article in its reduced form, contrary to what might be thought, does not in any way limit the right of a State to put down rebellion, nor does it increase in the slightest the authority of the rebel party. It merely demands respect for certain rules, which were already recognized as essential in all civilized countries, and embodied in the municipal law of the States in question, long before the Convention was signed. What government would dare to claim before the world, in a case of civil disturbances which could justly be described as mere acts of banditry, that, Article 3 not being applicable, it was entitled to leave the wounded uncared for, to torture and mutilate prisoners and take hostages? However useful, therefore, the various conditions stated above may be, they are not indispensable, since no government can object to observing, in its dealings with internal enemies, whatever the nature of the conflict between it and them, a few essential rules which it in fact observes daily, under its own laws, even when dealing with common criminals.'

Is it not in similar terms that the question of the protection of cultural property should be framed? After all, it is hardly possible that a government or an authority representing an insurrectional movement would justify the destruction of cultural property – which, for any government or authority, represents values that are in most cases part of the ideas for which the fighting was begun – on the grounds of uncertainty about the criteria for the definition of the conflict or some similar excuse.

The Commentary on the Geneva Conventions concludes: 'Speaking generally, it must be recognized that the conflicts referred to in Article 3 are armed conflicts, with armed forces on either side engaged in hostilities – conflicts, in short, which are in many respects similar to an international war, but take place within the confines of a single country. In many cases, each of the Parties is in possession of a portion of the national territory, and there is often some sort of front.'

It should be noted that both Article 3 and Additional Protocol II, when accepted by the government, become part of national law and as such are binding on both the government and national citizens, and therefore insurrectional movements as well.

By affording protection to cultural property, the government – like the rebel forces – is simply protecting the national heritage, the expression of the historical and artistic traditions of the nation in support of which they are fighting. To allow this property to be destroyed would therefore be the negation of the very aims of their struggle.

The ICRC has not limited its action to conflicts not of an international character. Many interventions have also taken place during internal disturbances and periods of tension, the ICRC basing its action on its Statutes and, above all, on the courageous initiative of the Committee which 'must, any place where there is a civil war, resolution, coup d'état, dictatorship and everywhere where there are political prisoners, remember that the latter are often more unhappy than prisoners of war and deserve its attention and concern'.[6]

In the same way as the ICRC, UNESCO might find itself having to interpret and define situations of conflict in order to determine whether an international or internal conflict or some other type of low-key conflict, was involved. It would risk, however, running counter to the provision in paragraph 3 of Article I of its Constitution, according to which 'the Organization is prohibited from intervening in matters which are essentially within their [States Members of the Organization] domestic jurisdiction'. In order to avoid possible and even probable friction with Member States, UNESCO has to refer to its general mandate for the protection of cultural property, which also derives from its Constitution.

The position of the ICRC is unquestionably easier because it is a private organization, whose activity is recognized by the international community as a whole.

In spite of all the difficulties it may encounter, UNESCO must fulfil the responsibilities entrusted to it by its Constitution but it must also comply with Article 19 of the Convention. It must expect criticism and opposition and accusations of interference in the internal affairs of States. But, in acting as it does, UNESCO is simply carrying out its mandate and ensuring respect for what represents the higher interest: the protection of cultural property. Surely it is preferable to be criticized and to face up to these criticisms, criticisms reflecting a passing interest, and to go ahead, in spite of everything, with the tasks and functions which are of such a fundamental nature?

In carrying out the duties assigned to it, UNESCO should be able to count on the understanding of all States, for it is on their behalf that it is acting.

Scope of Application *Rationale Personae*

In mentioning 'each party to the conflict', Article 19 (like Article 3 common to the Geneva Conventions) also refers to a non-signatory party, that is, one not existing at the moment of signature or ratification accession. According to the UNESCO Commentary, the basis of the obligation lies in the fact that each of the adversaries 'is bound by contractual engagements undertaken by a community of which he is a part'. The Commentary on the Geneva Conventions also expresses an opinion on the question of the justification for the obligation of the opposing party, rebelling against the established government:

> At the Diplomatic Conference doubt was expressed as to whether insurgents could be legally bound by a Convention which they had not themselves signed. But if the responsible authority at their head exercises effective sovereignty, it is bound by the very fact that it claims to represent the country, or part of the country. The 'authority' in question can only free itself from its obligations under the Convention by following the procedure for denunciation laid down in Article 158. But the denunciation would not be valid, and could not in point of fact be effected, unless the denouncing authority was recognized internationally as a competent government. It should, moreover, be noted that under Article 158 denunciation does not take effect immediately.
>
> If an insurgent party applies Article 3, so much the better for the victims of the conflict. No one will complain. If it does not apply it, it

will prove that those who regard its actions as mere acts of anarchy or brigandage are right. As for the *de jure* government, the effect on it of applying Article 3 cannot be in any way prejudicial; for no government can possibly claim that it is *entitled* to make use of torture and other inhuman acts prohibited by the Convention, as a means of combating its enemies.

Care has been taken to state, in Article 3, that the applicable provisions represent a compulsory minimum. The words 'as a minimum' must be understood in that sense. At the same time they are an invitation to exceed that minimum.[17]

As far as the situation of the non-signatory party is concerned, the following curious observation is also interesting. Whenever the 1954 Hague Convention refers to *Parties to the conflict*, the legislators have always and systematically used a capital 'P', as is customary, incidentally, in the international conventions entered into by the High Contracting Parties. One exception, however, is made in Article 19 where the expression used is 'parties to the conflict' with a small 'p'. On the basis of the text of the Convention one may see here an indication that this Article 19 (and those to which it refers) is binding not only on States but also on all other entities, parties to the conflict, whose statehood is not recognized or is in dispute.

Scope of Application *Ratione Materiae*

As far as the content of protection is concerned, the wording in Article 19 is 'apply, as a minimum, the provisions of the present Convention which relate to respect for cultural property'. What are these provisions? Clearly this definition of the content of Article 19 cannot be interpreted in a limitative and restricted fashion by reference to Article 4 of the Convention. If the authors of this provision had wanted to impose such a restriction they could have referred directly to this article instead of expressing themselves in such a general manner as they have done in the text of Article 19 itself. Indeed, the whole Convention deals with the protection of cultural property and this protection is defined in Article 2 as the safeguarding of and respect for such property.

Another argument speaks for a more qualified interpretation of this provision. We saw that the UNESCO Draft submitted at the Hague Conference was the result of a long process beginning well before the Second World War, and was itself the outcome of the Preliminary Draft International Convention for the Protection of Historic Buildings and Works of Art in Time of War proposed by the International Museums Office in 1938. Article 10 of this Preliminary Draft was formulated in a similar way to Article 3 common to the

Geneva Conventions adopted in 1949. As we have seen, it contained a number of provisions concerning safeguarding, placing in shelter, depositing abroad, restoration and transport. The authors of the draft text of Article 19 preferred a general reference rather than a list of all the practical provisions applicable in the case of non-international armed conflict. Limitation to a restrictive interpretation referring to Article 4 alone therefore seems inappropriate to us. All the general provisions relating to respect for cultural property accordingly need to be mentioned here.

In the matter of respect, the authors of this provision believed it probable that it would always be the High Contracting Party, namely the government of the country, that would be responsible for safeguarding measures. But that does not dispense an authority at the head of an insurrection from taking action against the foreseeable effects of an armed conflict, applying such measures as it deems appropriate. After all, would not that be part of its intention and its claim to constitute a possible future government?

But the main obligation lies in the area of respect which embraces both the provisions in Chapter I and those in Chapter II of the Convention, for special protection is no more than general protection reinforced. Clearly the rebel side cannot register property in the International Register. That is part of the government's exclusive competence. Once such property is registered it enjoys immunity. Property which is not, or not yet, under special protection still enjoys general protection.

The other chapters simply develop Chapters I and II, dealing, as they do, with technical measures or the personnel involved in ensuring respect for cultural property. Thus the chapters that follow must also – in our opinion be applied in the case of armed conflict not of an international character, provided that they relate to respect for cultural property.

By way of example, we may say that Article 12 concerning transport under special protection refers to the transfer of cultural property within a territory or to another territory. Such transport certainly relates to respect and must be protected by the High Contracting Parties but also by any other authority. In our view there is no doubt whatever that the provisions set out in Chapters III to I concern respect for cultural property and must be applied both in international and non-international armed conflicts.

The purpose of the Convention is to protect cultural property against the threat of destruction and it matters little whether the conflict that gives rise to that threat is international or domestic. The Convention is concerned with the threat of destruction. It is the protection (safeguarding and respect) of this property that constitutes the spirit and object of the Convention, and it is in the light of that spirit and that object that the Convention must be interpreted. This interpretation is also consistent with Article 31 of the 1969 Vienna Convention on the Law of Treaties according to which 'a treaty shall be interpreted in good faith in accordance with the ordinary meaning to be given to the terms of the treaty in their context and in the light of its object and purpose'.

The situation will be different when we come to discuss Chapter VII of the Convention, given that most of the provisions of that chapter concern international armed conflict. This applies in particular to Articles 21, 22, 26 and 27. It does not concern Article 20. Indeed, some provisions of the Regulations for the Execution of the Convention may be applied *mutatis mutandis* to domestic conflicts. It is also important to note that the authors of the Convention themselves excluded certain provisions of possible application to domestic conflicts. A case in point is the organization of control in Article 2 of the Regulations for the Execution of the Convention ('As soon as any High Contracting Party is engaged in an armed conflict to which Article 18 of the Convention applies...').

As regards assistance from UNESCO, paragraph 3 of Article 19 specifically provides for the possibility of the Organization offering its services to the parties to the conflict.

There is nothing to prevent the parties to the conflict from entering into special agreements (Article 24) for 'all matters concerning which they deem it suitable to make separate provision'. Indeed, on the contrary, it would be desirable to encourage the conclusion of such agreements and paragraph 2 of Article 19 urges parties to the conflict to endeavour to bring into force, by means of special agreements, all or part of the other provisions of the present Convention and in particular those concerning control and sanctions.

Dissemination is certainly not a prerogative of States. It would also be desirable for dissemination (Article 25) to be encouraged even at the level of the other parties to the conflict, as is the case with other humanitarian conventions.

It would also be desirable for parties to the conflict to impose penal or disciplinary sanctions (Article 28) upon those committing or ordering to be committed a breach of the present Convention.

Although the literature on the subject is sparse, it is interesting to quote the statement by S.E. Nahlik to the effect that the Convention remains in force, to a certain extent, even during conflicts that are not, properly speaking, of an international character.[8]

PARAGRAPH 2

As regards the content of protection, the Convention opens up the possibility for the parties to the conflict (and in fact invites them) to enlarge the protection of cultural property. This pressing invitation is expressed in the words, 'The parties to the conflict shall endeavour'. Although, in legal terms, a party to the conflict is not under any obligation to comply with Article 19, it is obliged to seek, by bilateral agreement, *a wider application*.

Paragraph 2 shows that the parties to the conflict are completely free to state their intention to apply the other provisions particularly as the conflict, as it lengthens, may assume the character of a full-scale ware and it would be in the interests of the parties to do so.

It appears to us that the 1954 Conference already had these trends in mind and that this was why it included in this article a scope for application *ratione materiae* whose content is very wide and where the conclusion of agreements could go even further than the Convention itself.

There are no grounds for the fear that entering into such agreements might be interpreted as implicit recognition. For one thing the parties to the conflict – and governments in particular – are free to specify in such agreements that their signature implies no recognition of the legitimacy of their adversary and, for another, paragraph 4 clearly states that 'The application of the preceding provisions shall not affect the legal status of the parties to the conflict'.

The meeting of experts in Vienna (1983) noted that it was unrealistic to hope that parties would enter into such agreements during the conflict dividing them. On the other hand, unilateral but concordant statements are possible and should be treated as 'special agreements' within the meaning of paragraph 2 of Article 19.

PARAGRAPH 3

The right of initiative conferred on UNESCO by this paragraph is based on Article 3 of the Geneva Conventions which grants the same right to an impartial humanitarian body, such as the International Committee of the Red Cross. In the French texts of the Geneva Conventions of 1949, this offer is formulated in a less affirmative way ('peut') than in Article 18 of the Hague Convention ('pourra'). There is no such distinction in the Spanish or Russian texts. The offer of services may be made to all entities – whether States or not – when they are parties to an armed conflict not of an international character.

The identical nature of this provision with that of Article 3 tells us that UNESCO should play a role in the protection of cultural property which should, *mutatis mutandis*, be similar to that of the ICRC for the protection of victims of armed conflicts.

Since paragraph 3 has also been copied from the text of the Geneva Conventions we may again refer to the conclusions of the Commentary on these Conventions. It is obvious that any organization can 'offer its services' to the parties to a conflict at any time, just as any individual can. 'To offer one's services costs nothing and, which is more important, in no way binds the recipient of the offer, since the offer need not be accepted.' The International Committee of the Red Cross has offered and will continue to offer its services whenever it considers that this is in the interests of the victims. UNESCO should do the same when cultural property is at risk.

The existence of provisions in a convention is useful for putting an offer of services into effect. 'Although the International Committee of the Red Cross has been able to do a considerable amount of humanitarian work in certain civil wars, in others the doors have been churlishly closed against it, the mere offer of charitable services being regarded as an unfriendly act – an inadmissible attempt to interfere in the internal affairs of the State. The adoption of Article 3 has placed matters on a different footing, an impartial humanitarian organization now being legally entitled to offer its services. The parties to the conflict may, of course, decline the offer if they can do without it. But they can no longer look upon it as an unfriendly act, nor resent the fact that the organization making the offer has tried to come to the aid of the victims of the conflict.'[9]

It should also be pointed out that the offer of services is supplementary and that responsibility for the application of Article 19 (as in the case of Article 3) lies first and foremost with the parties to the conflict and with the authorities of the countries which have been designated to supervise the protection of cultural property.[10]

As we have noted previously, the protection of cultural property is a complex subject and it may happen that a country is not able to ensure that protection by itself. Outside help offered by an international organization authorized by the community of States to provide such protection can only be received with satisfaction. The parties to the conflict can hardly refuse this aid without incurring full responsibility for any deterioration of the cultural property.

The nature of the body offering its services is obviously very important. In the case of the ICRC its character as a humanitarian and impartial body has been stressed. The legal basis offered to it by Article 2 is no more than confirmation of its practical and pragmatic role developed during the course of its history.[11]

The right of initiative introduced by Article 19 was not based on earlier experience, as was the case with the ICRC. This right in the case of armed conflicts not of an international character has been transposed to the 1954 Convention: to turn towards the ICRC as a reference for the purpose of developing this right in the area of cultural property is not, therefore, surprising. The transposition of this right was no doubt designed to ensure the effectiveness of protection but without any deep thought about consequences and practical possibilities.

In interpreting this provision we must be careful to avoid any automatic transfer based on ICRC experience. The profound difference between a private Swiss body (ICRC) and an intergovernmental organization (UNESCO) has to be borne in mind.[12] UNESCO is well aware of this difference and it is for that reason that it is seeking new modes of action in carrying out its mandate. The Director-General himself raised the problem in connection with the monuments of Angkor Vat: the Organization must be able to act independently of any but cultural considerations.[13]

Practical Application

In the practical application of its mandate, UNESCO will be called upon to make contact with the authorities of the parties to the conflict. It will encourage them to take preventive measures and, if relevant, such measures as are necessary in the event of the partial destruction of cultural property. Drawing on ICRC experience, UNESCO will do well to keep its approaches confidential. It is only in the event of flagrant and exceptional violations that it will be entitled to make them public and seek the support of the international community. UNESCO could proceed by making a general appeal to the parties to the conflict. An illustration of the difficulty of the UNESCO mandate is the case of Nigeria. Whereas the humanitarian action of the ICRC and other humanitarian organizations has been on a considerable scale in this country, UNESCO's offer of services was refused, although with the assurance that the provisions of the Convention would be observed.

PARAGRAPH 4

This is an essential provision without which the very existence if Article 19 (and Article 3 as well) would be unlikely. It is a kind of guarantee that, in the event of a civil war, the application of the Convention, however limited in scope, will not interfere with the legal government and its efforts – deemed to be legitimate – to quell the rebellion, or confer a status of belligerency, which would add to the adversary's authority and power. As regards Article 3, this provision was already suggested at the Conference of Government Experts convened by the ICRC in 1947. It states that the object of the article is the protection of cultural property alone and that this in no way interferes in a State's domestic affairs. In addition the fact that the legal government applies this article in no way represents recognition of any status whatsoever for the opposing party. The purpose of the article is confined to the protection of cultural property and in no way restricts what the government may do in order to put down rebellion.

Similarly, the application of the article does not entitle the opposing party —whoever it may be and whatever qualification it may give itself or claim – to special protection or any immunity. It is the carrying out of the mandate that matters. All political considerations which are not relevant to the accomplishment of this task should be set aside.

NOTES

1   *Records*, p.313.
2   *Records*, para. 1065, p.214.
3   *Records*, para. 1069, p.214.
4   *The Geneva Conventions of 12 August 1949. Commentary*, Vol. IV, pp.35–6.
5   The criteria defining armed conflicts listed at the 1949 Conference, though not in any way binding, are helpful in gaining an understanding of the concept of armed conflict not of an international character. The Commentary on the Conventions has drawn up the following list of criteria from the amendments discussed:

1.   That the Party in revolt against the *de jure* government possesses an organized military force, an authority responsible for its acts, acting within a determinate territory and having the means of respecting and ensuring respect for the Convention.
2.   That the legal government is obliged to have recourse to the regular military forces against insurgents organized as military and in possession of a part of the national territory.
3.   (a)   That the *de jure* government has recognized the insurgents as belligerents; or
     (b)   that it has claimed for itself the rights of a belligerent; or
     (c)   that it has accorded the insurgents recognition as belligerents for the purposes only of the present Convention; or
     (d)   that the dispute has been admitted to the agenda for the Security Council or the General Assembly of the United Nations as being a threat to international peace, a breach of the peace, or an act of aggression.
4.   (a)   That the insurgents have an organization purporting to have the characteristics of a State;
     (b)   that the insurgent civil authority exercises *de facto* authority over persons within a determinate portion of the national territory;

(c) that the armed forces act under the direction of an organized authority and are prepared to observe the ordinary laws of war;
(d) that the insurgent civil authority agrees to be bound by the provisions
of the Convention.

6   ICRC report of 1927, quoted by Jacques Moreillon, *Le Comité international de la
Croix-Rouge et la protection des détenus politiques*, Geneva, Institut Henry-Dunant,
1973, p.95. See also J. Toman, *UNESCO's Mandate for Implementation of the Hague
Convention for the Protection of Cultural Property in the Event of Armed Conflict*,
Paris, UNESCO, October 1983, p.68 *et seq.*

7   *The Geneva Conventions of 12 August 1949. Commentary.* Vol. IV, p.37.

8   Stanislaw E. Nahlik, 'Des crimes contres les biens culturels', *Annuaire de
l'Association des audieurs et anciens auditeurs de l'Académie de droit international de
La Haye*, The Hague, Vol. 29, 1959, p.20.

9   *The Geneva Conventions of 12 August 1949. Commentary*, Vol. IV, p.41.

10 Ibid., p.41.

11 On the proposal of Gustave Moynier, the ICRC offered its good offices for the
first time during the second Carlist war in Spain in 1872. For other examples,
see, in particular, Jacques Moreillon *Le Comité international*, p.24 *et seq.*

12 See commentary on Article 23.

13 *Le patrimoine culturel de l'humanité: une responsabilité commune*, Paris, UNESCO,
May 1982, pp.212. This study put forward several ideas: institution of a 'group
of wise men', joint action by UNESCO and ICRC, and so on.

Chapter VII
Execution of the Convention

Article 20
Regulations for the Execution of the Convention

The procedure by which the present Convention is to be applied is defined in the Regulations for its Execution, which constitute an integral part thereof.

Records: Text: p.24.
            Minutes: paras 698–704, 1098, 1588, 1992.
            Working documents: p.386;
            CBC/DR/142.

The idea of dividing the substance of the protection into two parts – a Convention and Regulations for its Execution – was already reflected in the Preliminary Draft prepared before the war by the International Museums Office. The division was maintained in the UNESCO Draft and approved by the Hague Conference. It was the Conference's Legal Committee which decided to propose to the Main Commission that it be clearly stated that the Regulations for the Execution of the Convention constitute an integral part thereof. The Conference examined this question and decided to maintain the division, mainly for practical reasons and because there was no time to revise the text as a whole.

Proposals were made to facilitate the revision of the Regulations, and it was finally decided to keep the same system of revision for both the Convention and the Regulations.

Article 21
Protecting Powers

The present Convention and the Regulations for its Execution shall be applied with the co-operation of the Protecting Powers responsible for safeguarding the interests of the Parties to the conflict.

Records: Text: p.24.
Minutes: paras 705–7, 709, 1079–80, 1084, 1098–1106, 1251, 1992.
Working documents: pp.313, 315, 330, 386.

Bibliography: *Commentary on the Additional Protocols of 8 June 1977*, pp.75–89, Abi Saab, G., 'Les mécanismes de mise en oeuvre du droit humanitaire', *Revue Générale de Droit International Public*, Vol. 82, No. 1, 1978, pp.103–29; idem. ;'The implementation of humanitarian law', in A. Cassese (ed.), *The New Humanitarian Law of Armed Conflict*, Naples, Giuffré, 1979, pp.310–46; Boylan, P.J., *Review of the Convention for the Protection of Cultural Property in the Event of Armed Conflict*, (The Hague Convention of 1954), Paris, UNESCO, 1993, paras 7.5–7.10, pp.85–8; Pictet, Jean S. (ed.), *The Geneva Conventions of 12 August 1949. Commentary*, Vol. I, pp.95–8; Sandoz, Y., 'Implementing international humanitarian law', in *International Dimensions of Humanitarian Law*, Geneva/Paris/Dordrecht, Henry Dunant Institute, UNESCO, Martinus Nijhoff Publishers, 1988, pp.259–82.

PREPARATORY WORK

The experts who prepared the UNESCO Draft studied various alternatives and concluded that there were three possible systems for controlling the application of the Convention and the Regulations for its Execution: 'The first system consists in establishing a special international organization to administer the Convention. Such a system, which would have to be built up from nothing by the Contracting Parties, has the drawback of being relatively complex and costly. The second system, which would be less costly, would involve using the services of UNESCO, an existing international organization which is already responsible for ensuring the protection of the world's cultural heritage. However, as it is of the utmost importance that non-Member States of UNESCO should accede to the Convention, it has been decided not to recommend that UNESCO should act as the supreme controlling authority. The third system, which is that adopted in the present draft, consists of having recourse to the aid of the Protecting Powers, which are traditionally called upon to watch over the interests of the Parties to the conflict, and have carried out valuable humanitarian work, especially during the last two world wars.'[1]

The Belgian delegate to the Conference noted that the control system was likely to be a little slow and recommended that complementary methods be sought, such as the temporary appointment of Commissioners-General and, in particular, the establishment of a Permanent Bureau.[2]

ANALYSIS OF THE TEXT

This provision incorporates almost the entire text of the first sentence of Article 8/8/8/9 common to the Geneva Conventions of 12 August 1949. The article states, in the French version, that the Convention and the Regulations for its Execution 'sont appliqués' with the cooperation, whereas the Geneva Conventions use the future, 'seront appliqués'.[3] This difference does not exist in the English version, which states 'shall be applied' in the two instances (for the 1954 Hague Convention and the 1949 Geneva Conventions). We may thus conclude that it was an editorial change introduced by the Committee of Experts responsible for preparing the UNESCO Draft, in which the modification is already present. The chronology should also be borne in mind, inasmuch as the authors of the provision may have wished to stress the fact that the Protecting Power had – very probably – already been appointed in the context of the Protecting Power control system under the Geneva Conventions.

We do not think that any change in the meaning of the provision is involved. We cannot therefore interpret it in the same way as the Commentary on the Geneva Conventions by describing the 'cooperation' to which the article refers as follows: an order given to the Parties to the conflict and to the Protecting Powers, in so far as they are Parties to the Convention.

In the case of the Parties to the conflict, it is an order addressed to them, since the Parties to the conflict are responsible for the application of the Convention. In the case of the Protecting Power, it is an order not to wait until the Party to the conflict, whose interests it is safeguarding, requests its cooperation. It must take the initiative by giving it.

Another difference between the text of the 1954 Convention and the Geneva Conventions of 1949 is the dropping of the words 'and under control', as a result of the fact that the control system provided for in the Hague Convention is organized differently from that set out in the Geneva Conventions of 1949. However, the Commentary on the UNESCO Draft submitted to the Conference envisaged the existence of such control, to be exercised by the delegates of the Protecting Powers, even though the reference to it had been deleted from the proposed text. At the same time, it provides that the higher mission and responsibility for control shall reside in the Commissioners-General.

Neither the present, very concise, provision nor the other articles of the Convention give details concerning the appointment of the Protecting Powers. This matter is accordingly left to general international law. In international law, the Protecting Powers may be appointed either in accordance with the Vienna Convention on Diplomatic Relations of 18 April 1961 (Article 46)[4] or in conformity with the provisions of the Geneva Conventions and Additional Protocol I. The Protecting Power thus appointed must act in accordance with the requirements laid down in the articles of these international conventions.

The Geneva Diplomatic Conference of 1974–77 gave each Party to the conflict the option of having one or two Protecting Powers: one under the 'Vienna mandate', the other under the 'Geneva mandate'. Theoretically, it is even possible to talk of a third mandate, that of 'The Hague'. We say 'theoretically' because, if a Protecting Power is appointed under one mandate or the other, it is reasonable to assume that it will be that Power which will be entrusted with a role in the protection of cultural property. But it is to be hoped that only one Protecting Power will be appointed, since a multiplicity of Powers would hardly be likely to simplify the situation. For the moment, this is all anticipation, since present policy clearly shows that States have little enthusiasm for the application of a control system.

Whereas the Geneva Conventions of 12 August 1949 entrusted control to the Protecting Powers or their substitute, the 1954 Convention and Regulations provide for a special and more complex control system. The organization of this control is based on three elements: the representatives of the High Contracting Parties engaged in a conflict, the Protecting Power and a Commissioner-General for Cultural Property appointed to the Party to the conflict. As we shall see, UNESCO also has an important part to play. This control system is described in the Regulations and exceeds the scope of this article. It will therefore be commented on in the pages that follow, in connection with the corresponding articles of the Regulations.

The reference to substitutes for the Protecting Powers, first mentioned in the UNESCO Draft, was deleted at the Conference.[5] Nevertheless, attention should be drawn to Article 6, paragraph 6, of the Regulations, according to which, if there is no Protecting Power, the Commissioner-General shall exercise its functions, as laid down in Articles 21 and 22 of the Convention.

The slender hope of seeing a control system established has led to a search for other means of protecting cultural property. The impasse in Cambodia, which persisted until 1989, and the grave threat of destruction which hung over the temples of Angkor prompted the Swiss authorities in 1973 to offer their assistance: 'Would Switzerland, a neutral country held in high esteem in certain Asian States, be in a position to lend its good offices to enable a solution to be found to this particularly disquieting and urgent problem, possibly in the form of an expert mission?'[6] Even though no action was taken on this proposal, the initiative shows how important it is to seek alternative solutions which might help to overcome temporary difficulties, or even solutions outside the context of conventions in order to ensure the effective protection of cultural property. The experience of the Red Cross in the protection of war victims constitutes an invaluable and imaginative guide to what needs to be done to achieve results.

According to the present article, the Convention and the Regulations for its Execution shall be applied with the cooperation of the Protecting Powers responsible for safeguarding the interests of the Parties to the conflict. The use of the word 'cooperation' implies that the role of the Protecting Powers is secondary to that of the Parties to the conflict themselves, which is fundamental.

The article does not go into details concerning the extent of such cooperation or the competence of the Protecting Powers. Earlier, the Commentary on the Geneva Conventions stated that 'All the occasions upon which a Protecting Power would have to intervene cannot be envisaged here, nor indeed the conditions under which such interventions take place. They will be determined by the circumstances of the conflict and the means at the disposal of the Protecting Power.' At the same time, other provisions of the Convention and the Regulations throw further light on this point, in particular: Article 22 (Conciliation procedure) of the Convention and Articles 4 (Appointment of Commissioner-General), 6 (Functions of the Commissioner-General), 8 (Discharge of the mission of control), 11 (Improvised refuges) and 17 (Transport – procedure to obtain immunity) of the Regulations, together with Article 5 of the Regulations which defines the functions of the delegates of the Protecting Powers.

In fact, the present article should be read in close conjunction with Articles 3 and 5 of the Regulations: Article 3 specifies the manner of appointment of delegates of Protecting Powers, while Article 5 briefly reviews their functions, thereby giving a clearer idea of the nature of the responsibilities to be entrusted to the Protecting Powers.

NOTES

1   *Records*, p.313.
2   *Records*, para. 705, p.189.
3   This difference is also reflected in the Spanish text ('se llevarán a la práctica' in the 1954 Convention and 'será aplicado' in the Geneva Conventions of 1949) and the Russian version ('primenyayutsya' in the 1954 Convention, and 'budet primenyat'sya'). These two texts are authentic in the case of the 1954 Hague Convention, but not in the Geneva Conventions of 1949. They are mentioned here for the purpose of illustration.
4   United Nations, *Treaty Series*, Vol. 500, pp.95 *et seq.*
5   *Records*, p.386.
6   Letters of 18 February 1973 from Mr G. Hammel to Mr René Maheu.

REGULATIONS FOR THE EXECUTION OF THE CONVENTION – CHAPTER I: CONTROL

We have placed the Commentary on the control system under Article 21, which is the only general provision of the Convention concerning control of the application of the protection of cultural property. In fact, there is no mention of control in the provisions of the Convention on general protection and only a single mention in Chapter II on special protection: Article 10 on identification and control, according to which 'during an armed conflict, cultural property under special protection shall be marked with the distinctive emblem described in Article 16, and shall be open to international control as provided for in the Regulations for the Execution of the Convention'. On the other hand, in the ten articles of the Regulations concerning control, there is no reference to special protection.

As we shall see, interpretation has followed from practice, particularly when the control system was applied in the case of the Middle East conflict.

Although control is a corner-stone of the application of international law, so far it has not had much success. Nor, in the area of humanitarian international law in general, has the system of control been as effective as had been hoped, particularly in view of the reluctance on the part of States to allow third parties to intervene in matters affecting their sovereignty. Armed conflict is undeniably both a matter of vital concern and a question of extreme delicacy, since it involves the very existence of each State.

The provisions on control do not envisage a particular role for UNESCO. However, it should not be forgotten that, in this case, Article 23 of the Convention also applies. Doctrine supports this view. Jean de Breucker states that control has been entrusted to the Protecting Powers and the Commissioner-General for Cultural Property, but without prejudice to UNESCO's right of initiative. This is also an innovation partly inspired by the proceedings of Geneva.[1]

In reading the following provisions concerning control, it is necessary to bear in mind this right of initiative set out under the terms of Article 23. This is another way in which UNESCO can exercise control over the application of the Convention. It is an important form of control, in particular as regards complaints or requests for investigations which may be addressed to UNESCO. It would be useful if UNESCO were to establish a procedure for handling such complaints and requests.

It should be recalled that the Preliminary Draft Convention of 1938 provided for an independent control system consisting of an International Verification Commission (Articles 3 to 5 of the Regulations of the Preliminary Draft) and an International Commission of Inspection (Article 7 of those Regulations).

Practical Application

Following the Middle East conflict in 1967, the States concerned appointed representatives for cultural property, together with Commissioners-General, in accordance with the procedure laid down in the Regulations for the Execution of the Convention.

NOTE

1   Jean de Breucker, 'Pour les vingt ans de la Convention de La Haye du 14 mai 1954 pour la protection des biens culturels', *Revue belge de droit international* (Brussels), Vol. XI, No. 2, 1975, pp.540 and 544.

Article 1 of the Regulations for the Execution of the Convention: International List of Persons

On the entry into force of the Convention, the Director-General of the United Nations Educational, Scientific and Cultural Organization shall compile an international list consisting of all persons nominated by the High Contracting Parties as qualified to carry out the functions of Commissioner-General for Cultural Property. On the initiative of the Director-General of the United Nations Educational, Scientific and Cultural Organization, this list shall be periodically revised on the basis of requests formulated by the High Contracting Parties.

Records: Text: p.42.
Minutes: paras 133, 792–6, 821, 1136–64, 1192, 1249, 1425–7, 2049.
Working documents: pp.315, 397;
CBC/DR/5/109/131/164.

The idea of establishing a list for the appointment of the commissioners is to be found in the Regulations appended to the Preliminary Draft Convention of 1938 (Article 1). This list was to consist of persons of acknowledged impartiality selected by the Standing Committee of the General Conference on the nomination of qualified institutions in the contracting countries: courts of justice, government departments, academies, universities and museums.

The 1954 Convention entrusts the Director-General of UNESCO with the task of compiling the international list of persons upon the entry into force of the Convention. However, his initiative is restricted. The list is to consist only of persons nominated by the High Contracting Parties as qualified to carry out the functions of Commissioner-General for Cultural Property. According to the Regulations, the list is to be periodically revised, but no time-limit has been fixed for its revision. The initiative, as far as revision is concerned, is left to the Director-General. But it is the only initiative he can take. He can call upon the High Contracting Parties, but must compile the list on the basis of requests previously formulated by the latter.

The persons on the list need not necessarily be nationals of the country proposing them. States may also nominate foreigners. The list is compiled by UNESCO in accordance with the proposals made by the High Contracting Parties. The Organization itself takes no initiative in this respect; it is simply a registry office for the names brought to its attention. UNESCO has become accustomed to compiling this list on a regular basis and communicating it to the High Contracting Parties through their UNESCO representatives. The list is updated by the UNESCO Secretariat. The latest version of the list is dated 31 March 1983. It has been revised on several occasions, most recently in 1986.

It is worth recalling that the UNESCO Draft allowed the Director-General greater initiative. According to the Draft, he was to compile the list alone, 'after taking whatever advice he thinks necessary, particularly that of the National Commissions for the Organization. The Director-General's choice was limited only by the requirement that the persons should be "of acknowledged impartiality" and "qualified to serve as Commissioner-General for Cultural Property or as chief arbitrator".'

It was on the initiative, more especially, of Spain[1] (following the precedent of the Arbitration Tribunal) and of the USSR that the original proposal was modified in favour of the High Contracting Parties which are now alone in nominating the persons on the list. The USSR wanted to add to this article the wording: 'As far as possible, this list should include representatives of all the States that are Parties to the Convention.' Spain wanted to stipulate the number of representatives by country.

The final text was prepared jointly by the delegates of the USSR, Spain and France.

NOTE

1   The delegate of Spain explained his amendment by stressing UNESCO's auxiliary function and the desire to avoid giving the Organization an executive role which would be 'initiatory and decisive in scope' and 'bind the Contracting Parties, instead of being merely a co-ordinating link' (*Records*, para. 1138, p.219).

Article 2 of the Regulations for the Execution of the Convention: Organization of Control

As soon as any High Contracting Party is engaged in an armed conflict to which Article 18 of the Convention applies:
(a)   It shall appoint a representative for cultural property situated in its territory; if it is in occupation of another territory, it shall appoint a special representative for cultural property situated in that territory.
(b)   The Protecting Power acting for each of the Parties in conflict with such High Contracting Party shall appoint delegates accredited to the latter in conformity with Article 3 below.
(c)   A Commissioner-General for Cultural Property shall be appointed to such High Contracting Party in accordance with Article 4.

> *Records*:   Text: p.42.
> Minutes: paras 796–825, 1193–8, 1249, 2049.
> Working documents: pp.315, 345, 397;
> CBC/DR/103/164.

Article 2 of the Regulations serves to introduce the control system. Accordingly, it refers briefly to the three control bodies or rather the three groups which make up the control: (a) national representatives, (b) delegates of the Protecting Powers, (c) Commissioners-General. The article specifies that the organization of control shall apply only in the case of international armed conflicts to which Article 18 of the Convention applies. This clarification was added at the request of the United Kingdom and the United States.[1] It concerns, then, the appointment both of representatives of the High Contracting Parties and of delegates of the Protecting Powers and Commissioners-General.

Paragraph (A)

According to this paragraph, each of the High Contracting Parties engaged in an armed conflict under the terms of Article 18 of the Convention shall appoint a representative for cultural property situated in its territory. Each of the Parties engaged in an international armed conflict is obliged to do so.

Paragraph (a) is even more positive where the occupation of another territory is concerned. It specifies that, if it is in occupation of a territory other than its own, the High Contracting Party shall appoint a special representative who must devote himself exclusively to the cultural property in the territory occupied. This person, then, is someone other than the representative appointed for cultural property in the territory of the Party itself. The article does not give details concerning the persons to be appointed as special representatives. They could be citizens of the High Contracting Parties, someone from the occupied territory or a subject of some other State. The appointment is accordingly left to the discretion of the High Contracting Party engaged in an international armed conflict.

When UNESCO communicates with High Contracting Parties to remind them of their obligations under the Convention, it would be desirable if they were also reminded of the obligation to appoint representatives both for the cultural property situated in their territory and for that situated in the territory they occupy.

The appointment of a representative is the exclusive responsibility of the High Contracting Party. Nevertheless, practical means of implementing this provision remain to be found. It is not a question of international control, that is, control exercised by a third party, but of means that depend solely upon the High Contracting Party and affect neither sovereignty nor the susceptibilities of States with regard to non-interference in their internal affairs. Yet the application of the provision is being met with an inexcusable silence. This task laid down by the Convention is probably one of the least difficult and States can hardly find valid reasons for avoiding application.

At the purely practical level, it would seem desirable to consider appointing a representative well before a conflict breaks out. We have already noted the role that the national committees could play in this connection even in peacetime, in particular by ensuring that the representative is adequately prepared for a task of this importance, which requires extensive knowledge, both cultural and technical.

Practical application   In the Cambodian conflict, when UNESCO provided a great deal of technical assistance in regard to the application of the Convention, the Rector of the University was appointed representative for cultural property.[2]

Following the Six-Day War, Israel's Ministry of Foreign Affairs sent a telegram to the Director-General of UNESCO assuring him that the Convention was being respected in the territories 'under Israel's authority'. A report on this subject was submitted to the 77th session of the Executive Board. In August 1967, Mr Abraham Biran, Director of the Department of Antiquities and Museums, was appointed as government representative for cultural property, in accordance with Article 2(a) of the Regulations.

It was intended from the outset that the Commissioner-General for Cultural Property would deal with this representative and with the delegates of the Protecting Powers.

Paragraph (B)

The general provision introducing Article 3 of the Regulations gives details concerning the appointment of delegates of the Protecting Power accredited to the opposing Party. This is a duty of the Protecting Power but, of course, such a Power must first be appointed. Article 21 of the Convention states only that the Convention and the Regulations shall be applied with the cooperation of the Protecting Powers responsible for safeguarding the interests of the Parties to the conflict. Neither the Convention nor the Regulations have anything more specific to say about the appointment of the Protecting Power. The latter may therefore be appointed in accordance with either the 'Vienna mandate' or the 'Geneva mandate', but it seems to us that there is nothing to prevent its being appointed – if necessary – in some other way more specifically adapted to the requirements of the protection of cultural property.

Paragraph (C)

The general provision introducing Article 4 of the Regulations gives details concerning the appointment of a Commissioner-General for Cultural Property. This paragraph specifies only that a Commissioner-General shall be appointed. Again, it is a question of an obligation upon each of the Parties to the international armed conflict.

In the course of the discussion between the representatives of the United States and the UNESCO Secretariat it was pointed out that 'as soon as a High Contracting Party was engaged in an armed conflict, a Commissioner-General for Cultural Property would be nominated for it so that if, for example, country A was at war with countries B, C, and D, only one Commissioner-General would be appointed to country A'.[3] This was also clearly specified in Article 4 of the Regulations.

A multiplicity of Commissioners-General, regarded as a disadvantage by the delegate of the United States, was not viewed as such by others, in particular the observer for the International Committee for Monuments, Artistic and Historic Sites and Archaeological Excavations, who considered that what the experts who met in 1952 had in mind was a Commissioner-General who would preside over the Commission composed of the delegates of the Protecting Powers.

NOTES

1 *Records*, para. 800, p.196, and pp.345, 397; CBC/DR/103.
2 André F. Noblecourt, *Protection des biens culturels*, Mission Report, 7–21 October 1970, Paris, UNESCO, 1970; Vladimir Elisseeff, *Rapport sur sa mission à Phnom Penh concernant l'application au Cambodge de la Convention pour la protection des biens culturels en cas de conflit armé*, 23 June–12 July 1970, Paris, UNESCO, 1970.
3 *Records*, para. 804, p.196.

Article 3 of the Regulations for the Execution of the Convention: Appointment of Delegates of Protecting Powers

The Protecting Power shall appoint its delegates from among the members of its diplomatic or consular staff or, with the approval of the Party to which they will be accredited, from among other persons.

Records: Text: p.44.
Minutes: paras 807, 826–38, 1249, 2050–52.
Working documents: pp.315, 324, 348, 398;
CBC/DR/110/164.
Bibliography: Pictet, Jean S. (ed.), *The Geneva Conventions of 12 August 1949. Commentary*, Vol. I, pp.98–9.

The procedure for appointing delegates of the Protecting Power, as described in the Regulations, is based on Article 8/8/9 common to the Geneva Conventions of 1949, even though it was not conceived in quite the same way as the procedure laid down in those Conventions.

In both cases – the 1954 Hague Convention and the Geneva Conventions of 1949 – the Protecting Powers choose their delegates from among their own diplomatic or consular staff: 'All members of the diplomatic and consular staff of the Protecting Power are *ipso facto* entitled, in virtue of their capacity as official representatives of their government, to engage in the activities arising out of the Convention. This rule covers, not only members of the staff who are *in service* when hostilities break out, but also those who are sent to relieve or *assist* them. It makes no difference whether they are assigned solely to the work of the Protecting Power as such, or whether they carry out other diplomatic or consular duties as well. No further formalities other than those entailed by their diplomatic or consular position in normal times (*agrément, exequatur*) are required.'[1]

However, when the Protecting Powers wish to choose delegates from among other persons, the matter is dealt with differently under the Hague Convention and the Geneva Conventions.

Under the Regulations for the Execution of the Convention, the choice is broader, since the delegates may be chosen 'with the approval of the Party to which they will be accredited' from among 'other persons', without further details. Under the Geneva Conventions of 1949, these other delegates may be appointed only from among their own nationals or from among the representatives of other neutral powers, but always with the approval of the Power to which they will be accredited. It is considered normal 'that the State of Residence should be entitled to refuse its consent, in particular when it has reason to fear that these auxiliary officials, knowing the country and perhaps having connections there, may take advantage of the facilities of movement and contact which their duties afford to engage in activities that have but little connection with the application of the Convention and may be harmful to the security of the State'.[2]

At the 1954 Hague Conference, Italy and the Soviet Union wished to extend the approval requirement to diplomatic and consular staff. The USSR requested 'that the Protecting Power appoint its delegates with the approval of the Party to which they would be accredited and, secondly, that such delegates would be chosen from among the members of the diplomatic or consular staff, or from among other persons'.[3] The USSR accordingly wanted a second approval, in addition to that already granted to the same staff when accredited to the country in which they must now carry out this new mandate of delegate of the Protecting Power. The USSR was supported by the delegate of Italy. However, the Conference did not consider this second approval to be necessary.[4]

NOTES

1 Jean S. Pictet (ed.), *The Geneva Conventions of 12 August 1949. Commentary*, Vol. I, p.98; *The Geneva Convention for the Amelioration of the Condition of the Wounded and Sick in Armed Forces in the Field*.
2 Ibid., p.98.
3 *Records*, para. 826, p.198. See also pp.342 and 348.
4 CBC/DR/110, *Records*, p.398.

Article 4 of the Regulations for the Execution of the Convention: Appointment of Commissioner-General

1. *The Commissioner-General for Cultural Property shall be chosen from the international list of persons by joint agreement between the Party to which he will be accredited and the Protecting Powers acting on behalf of the opposing Parties.*
2. *Should the Parties fail to reach agreement within three weeks from the beginning of their discussions on this point, they shall request the*

President of the International Court of Justice to appoint the Commissioner-General, who shall not take up his duties until the Party to which he is accredited has approved his appointment.

Records:　Text: p.44.
Minutes: paras 820, 839, 1199–1216, 1249, 1383–97, 2053.
Working documents: pp.326, 331, 345, 360, 408;
CBC/DR/136/164.

Paragraph 1

The Commissioner-General is appointed to the High Contracting Party engaged in an armed conflict. The Commissioner is chosen from the international list of persons, compiled in accordance with Article 1 of the Regulations, by joint agreement between the Party to which he will be accredited and the Protecting Powers acting on behalf of the opposing Parties.

In its comments on the UNESCO Draft, Belgium stressed the importance of the control system and of its application from the very outset of hostilities, the period when major damage to cultural property was chiefly to be feared. It was doubtful whether joint agreement between Parties in conflict could be achieved quickly, since the latter would be giving priority to many other measures just as urgent. It might be in the interests of the Aggressor Power to keep its hands free and to delay any agreement. At a later stage, the task of the Commissioner-General, inspectors and experts might also be hampered by delay on the part of the Power to which they were accredited in paying their remuneration and expenses.

These were the reasons behind the proposal made by the delegate of Belgium, who continued: 'This being so, it seems wise to consider whether the appointment of the Commissioner-General and the immediate institution of supervision should not be entrusted to a permanent independent body set up in peacetime and with a sufficient minima of financial resources for use if needed, the authority of which would be accepted by all Contracting Parties. Appointments by this body could, if preferred, be provisional only and subject to any later agreement within a specified period between the interested parties. The body in question would not, however, be UNESCO itself, since the Organization has rightly taken the view that it cannot assume such a role and must confine itself to purely administrative work.'[1]

Today, after many years of failure of the control system to function, it is legitimate to inquire whether the Director-General of UNESCO should not play some role in the appointment of a provisional Commissioner-General, who would serve until the procedure laid down in paragraphs 1 and 2 of the article had ended in the appointment of a Commissioner-General approved by the Parties. In particular, this would be desirable to ensure a rapid appointment at the very outset of the conflict (see, below, the recommendations of the 1983 meeting of experts).

Other proposals were put forward in the comments on the UNESCO Draft made prior to the Conference. France proposed the peacetime appointment of a Commissioner-General by means of periodic meetings of the High Contracting Parties. The Netherlands suggested that this appointment be made by the ICRC or by a special international body set up by the High Contracting Parties;[2] the United States proposed that it should be made by the Secretary-General of the United Nations,[3] while Switzerland proposed the Director-General of UNESCO, who could produce the guarantee of neutrality.[4] Finally, the delegate of Italy proposed that this role be entrusted to the President of the International Court of Justice, a solution which was finally accepted and incorporated in paragraph 2.

Following the 1967 conflict in the Middle East, the States concerned appointed representatives for cultural property, together with Commissioners-General, in accordance with the procedure laid down in the Regulations. Mr Karl Brunner (Switzerland) was appointed to Jordan, Lebanon, Egypt and Syria, and Mr J. Reinink (Netherlands) to Israel. When Mr Brunner died, he was replaced by Mr de Angelis d'Ossat (Italy). The two Commissioners resigned in 1977: Mr Reinink on 1 February and Professor de Angelis d'Ossat on 30 June. The replacement procedure has not yet led to the appointment of new Commissioners.

On the basis of the powers conferred upon UNESCO, under Article 23 of the Convention (Assistance of UNESCO), the meeting of experts (Vienna, 1983) expressed the wish that UNESCO should assess the results of the work of the Commissioners-General and that, on the basis of this study, their role should be examined, reconsidered and developed. The meeting also studied the possibility of UNESCO intervening in the procedure for the appointment of Commissioners-General, even though it is not authorized to do so under the present terms of the Convention and Regulations, the aim being to speed up the procedure for the appointment of Commissioners-General, but to avoid, for all that, taking the place of the Protecting Powers. The main objective was to ensure that the Commissioners were appointed as quickly as possible at the very outset of the conflict.

In particular, the meeting of experts raised the question of whether the Director-General should not play some part in the appointment of a provisional Commissioner-General who would intervene should the procedure laid down in paragraphs 1 and 2 of Article 4 of the

Regulations not lead to the desired result. This provisional Commissioner would perform the functions of the Commissioner-General until the latter was appointed under the prescribed procedure. The provisional Commissioners could be appointed by agreement between the Party to the conflict and the Director-General (or his representative), who would also obtain the approval of the opposing Party. The provisional Commissioners could be appointed from among the persons on the international list or, exceptionally, from among other persons whom the Director-General might suggest and who would possess both the required competence and the necessary impartiality. The appointment of a senior UNESCO official, who would act as the Director-General's representative, might even be envisaged.

At the 1983 meeting in Vienna, the experts recognized that 'UNESCO could not intervene in the negotiations for the appointment of Commissioners-General' but could 'provide its assistance in order to accelerate the procedure'.[5]

Paragraph 2

Following the discussion on the implementation of the control system and the appointment of Commissioners-General, the Working Party composed of Italy, the Netherlands and the USSR proposed that a special task be entrusted to the President of the International Court of Justice.

According to paragraph 2 of this article, should the Parties fail to reach agreement within three weeks from the beginning of their discussion on this point, they shall request the President of the International Court of Justice to appoint the Commissioner-General, who shall not take up his duties until the Party to which he is accredited has approved his appointment. The request must come from the Parties, that is both from the Party to which he is accredited and from the Protecting Powers of the opposing Parties. During the Conference the text submitted by the Working Party was amended, the words 'they may request' being replaced by 'they shall request' with the aim of making it mandatory upon the Parties to do so. The comment by the delegate of Switzerland was particularly pertinent here: 'a solution could not be obtained by saying they "might" do something, but only by asserting that they "must" ... It was essential to say at a certain time that there *must* be a Commissioner-General and if the Parties could not agree, he must be appointed by a third party.' Indeed if the system of control is rendered unworkable, will not the Convention become worthless?[6]

The appointment is, then, relatively simple to obtain if a request has been made beforehand. What should be done if this is not the case? Should not the initiative lie with the Director-General of UNESCO or even with the Director-General and the President of the International Court of Justice acting jointly? In our opinion, the question deserves examination.

As we shall see later, in the Commentary on Article 9 of the Regulations, there is a third possibility with regard to the appointment of a Commissioner-General. According to this third hypothesis, if the Parties are unable to proceed as laid down in paragraph 1 of the present article, or do not wish to follow the second procedure – that of Article 4, paragraph 2 – they may employ the formula according to which a neutral State may be requested to perform the functions of a Protecting Power with a view to such appointment. This involves, as it were, the designation of an ad hoc Protecting Power for the purpose of appointing a Commissioner-General. It is also possible to visualize a situation in which there are several Parties to the conflict and one or even several neutral States are asked to assist in the appointment of a Commissioner-General.

NOTES

1   *Records*, p.321, para. 1199, p.224.
2   *Records*, pp.348–9.
3   *Records*, para. 1216, p.225.
4   *Records*, para. 1216, p.225.
5   *Meeting of Legal Experts on the Convention for the Protection of Cultural Property in the Event of Armed Conflict (The Hague, 1954), Vienna, 17–19 October 1983*, Paris, UNESCO, 1984, p.11, para. 34 (CLT–83/CONF.641/1).
6   *Records*, para. 1389, p.237.

Article 5 of the Regulations for the Execution of the Convention: Functions of Delegates

The delegates of the Protectin Powers shall take note of violations of the Convention, investigate, with the approval of the Party to which they are accredited, the circumstances in which they have occurred, make representations locally to secure their cessation and, if necessary, notify the Commissioner-General of such violations. They shall keep him informed of their activities.

Records: Text: p.44.
          Minutes: paras 540, 840–44, 1249, 2050–53.
          Working documents: pp.316, 331, 398;
          CBC/DR/111/164.

We have seen that, as compared with the Geneva Conventions, the Hague Convention contains relatively few references to the specific activities of the Protecting Powers. This is probably why the Regulations include a general provision concerning the functions of delegates of the Protecting Powers.

The present article describes these functions, that is to say the functions of the delegates of the Protecting Powers, namely:

1   they take note of violations of the Convention, on their own authority;
2   they investigate, with the approval of the Party to which they are accredited, the circumstances in which these violations of the Convention have occurred; the UNESCO Draft made no reference to the approval of this Party. The words were included on the proposal of the Soviet delegation,[1] supported by the delegate of the United Kingdom;[2]
3   they make representation locally to secure their cessation; and
4   if necessary, they notify the Commissioner-General
5   the delegates keep the Commissioner-General informed of their activity.

There is also the general provision of Article 8 of the Regulations, according to which the delegates of the Protecting Powers shall in no case exceed their mandates. In particular, they shall take account of the security needs of the High Contracting Party to which they are accredited and shall in all circumstances act in accordance with the requirements of the military situation as communicated to them by that High Contracting Party.

The very restricted nature of the functions of the delegates of the Protecting Powers is rather surprising, especially when compared with the extensive functions laid down in the Geneva Conventions. The reason may lie in the different conception of the control system to be found in the Hague Convention. The authors of the system probably wanted to stress the specific and professional nature of these tasks, where cultural property is concerned, by entrusting them, in the first instance, to the Commissioners-General, experts and inspectors. Nor should it be forgotten that the Hague Convention also entrusts to the delegates of the Protecting Powers other functions which are mentioned more especially in Articles 6, paragraph 1; 11, paragraphs 2 and 3; and 17, paragraph 2 of the Regulations. Other functions are entrusted to the Protecting Power itself, under Articles 21 and 22 of the Convention and Article 4, paragraph 1 of the Regulations.

NOTES

1   *Records*, p.298; CBC/DR/111.
2   *Records*, para. 842, p.199.

Article 6 of the Regulations for the Execution of the Convention: Functions of the Commissioner-General

1. *The Commissioner-General for Cultural Property shall deal with all matters referred to him in connection with the application of the Convention, in conjunction with the representative of the Party to which he is accredited and with the delegates concerned.*
2. *He shall have powers of decision and appointment in the cases specified in the present Regulations.*
3. *With the agreement of the Party to which he is accredited, he shall have the right to order an investigation or to conduct it himself.*
4. *He shall make any representations to the Parties to the conflict or to their Protecting Powers which he deems useful for the application of the Convention.*
5. *He shall draw up such reports as may be necessary on the application of the Convention and communicate them to the Parties concerned and to their Protecting Powers. He shall send copies to the Director-General of the United Nations Educational, Scientific and Cultural Organization, who may make use only of their technical contents.*
6. *If there is no Protecting Power, the Commissioner-General shall exercise the functions of the Protecting Power as laid down in Articles 21 and 22 of the Convention.*

Records: Text: pp.44, 46.
        Minutes: paras 540, 816, 842, 845, 1103–5, 1249–56, 2054.
        Working documents: pp.315, 331, 334, 348–9, 398;
        CBC/DR/134/164.

The appointment of the Commissioner-General is a central feature of the control system under the Convention. In carrying out the functions entrusted to them by the present article, and indeed in all their doings, the actions of the Commissioners-General are governed by the general provision of Article 8. According to these terms, the Commissioners-General for Cultural Property (like the delegates of the Protecting Powers, inspectors and experts) shall in no case exceed their mandates and, in particular, *shall take account of the security needs of the High Contracting Party to which they are accredited. Moreover, they shall in all circumstances conform to the requirements of the military situation as communicated to them by that High Contracting Party.*

Paragraph 1

The Commissioner-General's first function is to deal with all matters referred to him in connection with the application of the Convention. This is a passive function since the Commissioner-General does not himself take any initiative. The initiative comes from elsewhere, being taken either by the Party to which he is accredited or by the delegates concerned, that is to say the delegates of the Protecting Powers of the opposing Parties.

The Commissioner-General 'deals with' these questions in conjunction with the Party to which he is accredited and with the delegates concerned. The words 'deal with', as used in the present article, have a very broad meaning,[1] signifying to take action concerning something so as to establish or modify it, by studying or examining it, by negotiating, and by endeavouring to solve a problem.

Paragraph 2

Paragraph 2 refers to the other powers of decision and appointment in the cases specified in the Regulations, involving more especially the following: Articles 7 (Inspectors and experts), 11 (Improvised refuges), 17 (Transport – procedure to obtain immunity), and 19 (Transport – occupied territory) of the Regulations.

Paragraph 3

Reference to the agreement of the Party to which the Commissioner is accredited did not feature in the UNESCO Draft for the delegates of the Protecting Power. This discrepancy was noted by the delegates of the Netherlands and the United Kingdom – and, as we have seen, the reference was also introduced in Article 5 of the Regulations.[2]

The Commissioner-General must obtain the special agreement of the Party to which he is accredited to be able to order an investigation, that is, to have it carried out by someone else (the inspectors or experts, for example), or to conduct it himself.

Paragraph 4

This paragraph authorizes the Commissioner-General to make any representations which he deems useful for the application of the Convention. The Commissioner-General may make these representations either to the Parties to the conflict or to their Protecting Powers. He is accordingly free to choose the most effective approach according to the circumstances.

Despite the objections of Switzerland, which considered this reference to the Parties to the conflict too general, the paragraph was retained in its original form and the proposed limitation to the Party to which the Commissioner-General is accredited and to the Protecting Powers was not adopted.[3]

Paragraph 5

The Commissioner draws up reports on the application of the Convention. He communicates them to the Parties concerned, that is, to the Parties to the conflict concerned, and to their Protecting Powers. Here, again, Switzerland wanted to limit the general reference and restrict it to the Party to which the Commissioner is accredited and to the Protecting Powers acting on behalf of the opposing Parties. This proposed restriction was not adopted either.[4]

The Commissioner-General sends copies of these reports to the Director-General of the United Nations Educational, Scientific and Cultural Organization. Since the reports have been sent to him for information, he may make use only of their technical contents with a view to taking action in the context of the assistance which UNESCO can provide under Article 23 of the Convention.

Paragraph 6

This paragraph was introduced into the Regulations by the delegate of Israel who considered it regrettable that the powers of conciliation and initiative could not be exercised in countries that did not benefit from the assistance of a Protecting Power.[5] Accordingly, the Convention conferred on the Commissioner-General an important power, namely the power to take the place of the Protecting Powers where there were none. In these circumstances, the Commissioner-General exercises the functions ascribed to the Protecting Power by Articles 21 and 22 of the Convention and, *with respect to this specific responsibility, he accordingly becomes a substitute for the Protecting Power*.

What are these functions laid down in Articles 21 and 22 of the Convention. They consist, first, in safeguarding the interests of the Parties to the conflict (in accordance with Article 21) and, second, lending their good offices (under paragraph 1 of Article 22) and taking other measures (under paragraph 2 of Article 22 of the Convention).

NOTES

1   From the Latin *tractare*; in old French the expression 'traiter' (deal with) meant 'lead, govern, decide'.
2   *Records*, para. 842, p.199.
3   *Records*, p.349.
4   Idem.
5   *Records*, para. 1251, p.288; CBC/DR/134, p.399.

Article 7 of the Regulations for the Execution of the Convention: Inspectors and Experts

1.   *Whenever the Commissioner-General for Cultural Property considers it necessary, either at the request of the delegates concerned or after consultation with them, he shall propose, for the approval of the Party to which he is accredited, an inspector of cultural property to be charged with a specific mission. An inspector shall be responsible only to the Commissioner-General.*
2.   *The Commissioner-General, delegates and inspectors may have recourse to the services of experts, who will also be proposed for the approval of the Party mentioned in the preceding paragraph.*

Records: Text: p.46.
          Minutes: paras 540, 845, 1257, 2055.
          Working documents: pp.315, 399;
          CBC/DR/164.

This article was adopted in the form proposed in the UNESCO Draft and there was no discussion concerning it at the Hague Conference.

In proposing this article, the experts who prepared the text doubtless had in mind the diversity of the functions reserved for the Commissioner-General and the delegates of the Protecting Powers. This diversity requires expertise, a profound knowledge of the various cultural domains that may be encountered, or specialization in the law of war or, again, in safeguarding or military techniques. A single individual, however able, could scarcely be expected to be competent in all these different areas and would therefore have to call upon specialists. The heavy burden on the Commissioner-General is another reason for appointing inspectors who could take over some of his functions. In their turn, the inspectors could, if necessary, have recourse to experts.

Finally, the sovereignty of the Party to which they are accredited is fully assured and respected, for nothing can be done without that Party giving its approval. The government representatives at the Conference felt completely satisfied with this respect for the authority of the State and did not make any other comments or amendments.

To remove any shadow of doubt, the authors of the Convention and the Regulations for its Execution included in the text Article 8 of the Regulations, consisting of a general clause ensuring respect for sovereignty and restricting the actions of the control bodies – in this case the inspectors and experts – exclusively to the fulfilment of their mandate.

Paragraph 1

Paragraph 1, which corresponds to the UNESCO Draft, allows the Commissioner-General to appoint inspectors charged with a specific mission, subject to the approval of the Party to which he is accredited.

The delegates concerned may request recourse to inspectors, or the initiative may come from the Commissioner-General himself. If the Commissioner-General takes the initiative, he must consult the delegates concerned, that is, the delegates of the Protecting Powers. However, the appointment of inspectors rests mainly with the Commissioner-General, since it is for him to judge whether it is necessary or not.

This requires that the Party to which the Commissioner-General is accredited approve the inspector he proposes. The use of the word 'propose' means that this Party plays a fundamental role, but from the moment it gives its consent, the inspector is no longer responsible to it, but only to the Commissioner-General. It should also be noted that the inspectors do not have a general control function; they are only responsible for a specific mission. Once they have carried out their mandate, their mission ends.

Paragraph 2

Paragraph 2, which corresponds to the UNESCO Draft, authorizes all those who are in any way responsible for control that is to say the Commissioner-General, the delegates and the inspectors, to have recourse to the services of experts. These experts are also proposed for the approval of the Party to which these control bodies are accredited.

Article 8 of the Regulations for the Execution of the Convention: Discharge of the Mission of Control

The Commissioners-General for Cultural Property, delegates for the Protecting Powers, inspectors and experts shall in no case exceed their man-

dates. In particular, they shall take account of the security needs of the High Contracting Party to which they are accredited and shall in all circumstances act in accordance with the requirements of the military situation as communicated to them by that High Contracting Party.

Records: Text: p.46.
Minutes: paras 1258–80, 2055.
Working documents: pp.315, 323, 345, 349, 399;
CBC/DR/104/128/133/164.

Article 8 is a general clause which specifies the duties of the control bodies. According to this article, the Commissioners-General for Cultural Property, delegates of the Protecting Powers, inspectors and experts *shall in no case exceed their mandates.* This excludes, then, any extensive interpretation of the mission entrusted to the control bodies. In particular, they must take account of the security needs of the High Contracting Party to which they are accredited and must in all circumstances act in accordance with the requirements of the military situation as communicated to them by that High Contracting Party.

This provision was envisaged in the UNESCO Draft which alluded to the duty 'to exercise in all circumstances absolute discretion', adding that 'on the other hand, provided that they confine themselves to their mission and respect the security requirements of that Party, their activities may be restricted only on the grounds of imperative military necessity'.

In accordance with the amendment proposed by the United States, the reference to the security of the State was strengthened, in particular by stipulating that the control bodies shall 'in all circumstances be guided by the requirements of the military situation as communicated to them by that High Contracting Party'. They must accordingly take account of the military situation not simply objectively, as it presents itself to them, but *as communicated to them by that High Contracting Party.* The delegate of the United States stressed that 'the limitations ... were not based on military necessity but rather on the needs of military security'. He proposed that reference should be made not to military necessity but to military security requirements.[1]

Some delegations to the Conference, such as the delegation of Greece, considered that the UNESCO Draft and its reference to imperative military necessity so reduced the scope of the powers of the Commissioners-General in this article as to render them, for practical purposes, nugatory.[2] What is the opinion, then, concerning the present version? The delegate of France preferred the UNESCO text but, curiously, the other delegations remained silent and the amendment proposed by the delegate of the United States was carried by 22 votes in favour, none against and 15 abstentions.[3]

NOTES

1   *Records*, para. 1264, p.229.
2   *Records*, p.323.
3   *Records*, para. 1279, p.229.

Article 9 of the Regulations for the Execution of the Convention: Substitutes for Protecting Powers.

If a Party to the conflict does not benefit or ceases to benefit from the activities of a Protecting Power, a neutral State may be asked to undertake those functions of a Protecting Power which concern the appointment of a Commissioner-General for Cultural Property in accordance with the procedure laid down in Article 4 above. The Commissioner-General thus appointed shall, if need be, entrust to inspectors the functions of delegates of Protecting Powers as specified in the present Regulations.

Records: Text: p.48.
            Minutes: paras 710, 1079, 1100, 1102, 1171, 1209, 1251, 1281, 1383–97, 2055.
            Working documents: pp.315–15, 345, 400;
            CBC/DR/112/164.

In the earlier drafts, based on the Geneva Conventions of 1949, it was provided that, where a country had no Protecting Power, a 'substitute could be appointed to fulfil all the duties of such a Power'. However, the Committee of Experts and the General Conference of UNESCO had already decided that this clause was valueless and a large part of the text had been deleted. The task of the substitute was reduced to the taking of a few steps concerning the appointment of the Commissioner-General. For the same reason, substitutes were not mentioned in the text of the Convention, either in Article 20 or 21, more especially.

It is interesting to note that the representative of the Secretariat summarized the Legal Committee's conclusions concerning Article 22 of the Convention as follows: 'Substitutes could offer their services in case of need but no obligation to do so was laid upon them.'[1]

We have seen that, where there is no Protecting Power, Article 6 of the Regulations entrusts the Commissioner-General with a number of functions assigned to the Protecting Power under Articles 21 and 22 of the Convention, that is, on the one hand, the safeguarding of the interests of the Parties to the conflict and, on the other hand, the lending of good offices in all cases where the Protecting Powers deem it useful in the interests of cultural property, particularly if there is disagreement between the Parties to the conflict as to the application or interpretation of the provisions of the Convention or the Regulations for its Execution. In these cases, the Commissioner-General becomes a kind of substitute for the Protecting Power. However, it is not to this substitute that reference is made in the present article.

Article 9 of the Regulations deals solely with the appointment of a Commissioner-General for Cultural Property in accordance with the procedure laid down in Article 4 of the Regulations. The article applies when a Party to the conflict does not benefit or ceases to benefit from the activities of a Protecting Power. In this case a neutral State may be asked to undertake the functions of a Protecting Power, but only with a view to the appointment of a Commissioner-General for Cultural Property.

The present article supplements the provisions of Article 4 which, as we have seen, provide for two ways of appointing the Commissioner-General:

1   Either the Commissioner-General for Cultural Property is chosen from the international list of persons by joint agreement between the Party to which he will be accredited and the Protecting Powers acting on behalf of the opposing Parties.
2   Or, should the Parties fail to reach agreement within three weeks from the beginning of their discussions on this point, they shall request the President of the International Court of Justice to appoint the Commissioner-General, who shall not take up his duties until the Party to which he is accredited has approved his appointment.

There is, then, a third possibility: if the Parties do not wish to proceed as laid down in paragraph 2 of Article 4, they can use the present formula, according to which a neutral State[2] may be asked to undertake those functions of a Protecting Power which concern the appointment of a Commissioner-General. It amounts to a kind of designation of an ad hoc Protecting Power, solely for the purpose of appointing a Commissioner-General. It is possible to visualize, then, a situation in which there would be several Parties to the conflict and one or several neutral States might be asked to appoint the Commissioner-General.

The main aim of the present article is to prevent the control system from being jammed because of the non-existence of Protecting Powers or the impossibility of using the second means of appointing Commissioners-General provided for in Article 4, paragraph 2 of the Regulations.

Second Sentence of Article 9

The article also provides for the possibility of appointing substitutes for the delegates of Protecting Powers. The Commissioner-General appointed in accordance with the procedure laid down in the article, that is, through the agency of a neutral State, may entrust ('shall, if need be, entrust') to inspectors the functions of delegates of Protecting Powers as specified in the Regulations. These are the functions mentioned in the Regulations and, in particular, in their Article 5.

NOTES

1 *Records*, para. 1171, p.222.
2 In the UNESCO Draft, it was provided that, in addition to a neutral State, the President of the International Court of Justice could be a substitute for a Protecting Power and be asked to undertake those functions which concern the appointment of a Commissioner-General (*Records*, CBC/3, p.399). The reference to the President of the Court was deleted on the proposal of the USSR (CBC/DR/112) supported by Italy and the Netherlands (CBC/DR/136). The delegate of Israel to the Conference drew attention to the incompatibility of the references to the President of the International Court of Justice in Articles 4 and 9 of the Regulations, since he might be called upon to exercise the two functions (*Records*, para. 1209, p.225).

Article 10 of the Regulations for the Execution of the Convention: Expenses

The remuneration and expenses of the Commissioner-General for Cultural Property, inspectors and experts shall be met by the Party to which they are accredited. Remuneration and expenses of delegates of the Protecting Powers shall be subject to agreement between those Powers and the States whose interests they are safeguarding.

Records: Text: p.48.
       Records: paras 1199, 1282, 2055.
       Working documents: pp.316, 320–21, 349, 400;
       CBC/DR/164.

In its comments on the UNESCO Draft, Belgium pointed out that the mission of the Commissioner-General, inspectors and experts might be impeded by delays on the part of the Power to which they were accredited in paying their remuneration and expenses.[1] The Conference did not, however, examine this proposal.

According to the present article, the remuneration and expenses of the Commissioner-General, inspectors and experts are, then, to be met by the Party to which they are accredited, which might considerably restrict their freedom of action. It might therefore perhaps be desirable, *de lege ferenda*, to give the Commissioner-General, inspectors and experts the status of international civil servants so as to ensure or, at least, foster their independence.

It will be noted that the 1938 draft of the International Museums Office envisaged granting international status to the officials responsible for cultural property. Furthermore, the persons entrusted with these tasks were not to be given other functions in their country, when the latter was involved in an armed conflict. Indeed, the scale of the responsibilities laid upon them required that they be fully available for the safeguarding of cultural property.

NOTE

1   *Records*, p.349, para. 1199, pp.223–4.

Article 22
Conciliation Procedure

1. *The Protecting Powers shall lend their good offices in all cases where they may deem it useful in the interests of cultural property, particularly if there is disagreement between the Parties to the conflict as to the application or interpretation of the provisions of the present Convention or the Regulations for its Execution.*
2. *For this purpose, each of the Protecting powers may, either at the invitation of one Party, of the Director-General of the United Nations Educational, Scientific and Cultural Organization, or on its own initiative, propose to the Parties to the conflict a meeting of their representatives, and in particular of the authorities responsible for the protection of cultural property, if considered appropriate on suitably chosen neutral territory. The Parties to the conflict shall be bound to give effect to the proposals for meeting made to them. The Protecting Powers shall propose for approval by the Parties to the conflict a person belonging to a neutral Power or a person presented by the Director-General of the United Nations Educational, Scientific and Cultural Organization, which person shall be invited to take part in such a meeting in the capacity of Chairman.*

Records: Text: pp.24, 26.
          Minutes: paras 708–34, 798, 1100, 1102, 1104, 1107, 1167, 1171–2, 1251, 1992.
          Working documents: pp.313, 344, 386; CBC/DR/82.
Bibliography: Pictet, Jean S. (ed.), *The General Conventions of 12 August 1949. Commentary*, Vol. I, pp.126–31.

As indicated in the Commentary on the UNESCO Draft, the experts convened to prepare for the Conference examined the question of possible disagreement between the Parties to the conflict as to the application or interpretation of the Convention or the Regulations. The first suggestion was that disputes of this kind might be submitted to the International Court of Justice, but this idea was rejected for two reasons: first, because it is hard to imagine two belligerents taking their dispute to the Court; second, because the Court is open only to States Parties to its Statute; and where a non-Party State is concerned, only on the conditions laid down by the Security Council.[1] This is why – by analogy with Article 11/11/11/12 common to the Geneva Conventions of 1949 – recourse was had to the Protecting Powers, by asking them to lend their good offices to settle disagreements.

Article 22 describes the good offices functions of the Protecting Power in almost identical terms to those of Article 11/11/11/12 common to the Geneva Conventions.

As far as the Geneva Conventions are concerned, this article was not entirely new. It was based on a similar text which appeared in Articles 83, paragraph 3, and 87 of the 1929 Geneva Convention relative to the treatment of prisoners of war. The article was adopted by the Diplomatic Conference of 1949 without much discussion. Nor should it be forgotten that the 1938 Preliminary Draft Convention also raised the question of possible disagreement between belligerents; its Article 13 accordingly provided that, in this case, 'the Contracting States entrusted with the interests of the belligerents and the Standing Committee of the General Conference shall lend their good offices for the settlement of the dispute'.

It is immediately clear that the application of this provision depends on the appointment of Protecting Powers. Indeed, if in a conflict Protecting Powers are not appointed, this provision ceases to have any practical effect.

PARAGRAPH 1

According to this paragraph, the Protecting Powers shall lend their good offices in all cases where they may deem it useful in the interests of cultural property. The application of the provision is not, then, restricted to cases of disagreement between the Parties to the conflict, but it is in situations of disagreement or dispute that recourse to the good offices of the Protecting Powers seems most likely.

Disagreement between the Parties to the conflict as to the application or interpretation of the provisions of the Convention or the Regulations for its Execution is mentioned in this article as only one example of a situation in which the 'usefulness' of lending good offices might be appropriate. The Protecting Powers could, then, lend their good offices in other situations, when they wish, for example, to propose a measure without knowing what might be the reaction of the Parties to the conflict. They can also withhold their good offices when there is disagreement between Parties to the conflict or they do not deem that their intervention would be useful in the interests of cultural property.

Thus the present article does not call upon the Protecting Powers to interpret the Convention or the Regulations, *but only to settle disagreements between the Parties to the conflict as to the application or interpretation of the Convention or the Regulations*, when they deem it useful.[2] The initiative is left to the Protecting Powers, who are the sole judges of the desirability of such intervention. The paragraph also leaves it to the Protecting Powers to choose the cases or situations in which they 'lend' their good offices; however, it does not specify the form, conditions or elements of their intervention nor the parties to which the good offices may be lent. The only restriction which the paragraph places on the Protecting Powers is the requirement that they lend their good offices 'in the interests of cultural property'.

The present article is silent on the form that these good offices might take. It merely provides, in paragraph 2, for the possibility of bringing representatives of the Parties to the conflict together. However, the Protecting Powers could resort to other forms of good offices which they may deem useful for seeking a compromise or avoiding the emergence of a dispute between the Parties to the conflict.

The authors of the Commentary on the Geneva Conventions point out that the interests of each of two belligerents could be protected either by the same State or by two different Protecting Powers. 'In the latter case, they can take action either severally or jointly. It is generally preferable to have an agreement concluded between the two Protecting Powers.'[3]

The authors of the Commentary on the Geneva Conventions also stress that, here, the task of the Protecting Powers is much heavier than that assigned to them by Convention II relative to the Treatment of Prisoners of War of 1929. In the case of the present Convention, the Protecting Powers would also act as representatives of all the High Contracting Parties, so that their action is the logical consequence of Article 21 of the Convention according to which 'the present Convention and the Regulations for its Execution shall be applied with the co-operation of the Protecting Powers responsible for safeguarding the interests of the Parties to the conflict'.

PARAGRAPH 2

Paragraph 2 gives an example of good offices. For this purpose, each of the Protecting Powers may, either at the invitation of one Party, of the Director-General of the United Nations Educational, Scientific and Cultural Organization, or on its own initiative, propose to the Parties to the conflict a meeting of their representatives, and in particular of the authorities responsible for the protection of cultural property, if considered appropriate on suitably chosen neutral territory.

As compared with Article 11/11/11/12 common to the Geneva Conventions, the present article contains an important innovation: whereas the Geneva Conventions leave the initiative for such a meeting to the representatives of the Protecting Powers and the Parties to the conflict, the 1954 Convention extends the same right to the Director-General of UNESCO.

According to the present paragraph, the Parties to the conflict are bound to give effect to the proposals for meeting made to them. The Protecting Powers shall propose for approval by the Parties to the conflict a person belonging to a neutral Power or a person presented by the Director-General of the United Nations Educational, Scientific and Cultural Organization, which person shall be invited to take part in such a meeting in the capacity of Chairman.

Article 22 is, then, more positive than common Article 11/11/11/12, which says that the Protecting Powers 'may' if necessary, propose'.

The person proposed for the chairmanship of such a meeting may be either a person belonging to a neutral Power or someone presented by the Director-General of UNESCO. The powers conferred upon UNESCO in this area are thus greater than those conferred by the Geneva Conventions upon the International Committee of the Red Cross. Article 11/11/11/12 does not, in fact, mention the chairmanship of a meeting of representatives of the Parties to the conflict, but only a person who will take part in it and who maybe either someone belonging to a neutral Power or someone delegated by the ICRC.

This example of a meeting of representatives of the Parties to the conflict was included both in the Geneva Conventions and in the present Convention on the basis of the experience gained in the First World War when such meetings led to the conclusion of agreements on humanitarian matters.[4] This was not the case during the Second World War.

There can be no doubt that direct contact between belligerents can be very useful for the purpose of ensuring the application of the various provisions of the Convention, in particular those relating to improvised refuges or the transport of cultural property.

NOTES

1   This question was also raised at the 1949 Diplomatic Conference of Geneva. The draft article recognizing the competence of the International Court of Justice in all matters relating to the interpretation or application of the Convention was not adopted and was converted into a resolution which was itself adopted without opposition. See Resolution 1, *International Red Cross Handbook*, twelfth

edition, Geneva, ICRC, Ligue, 1983, p.213. See also Jean S. Pictet (ed.), *The Geneva Conventions of 12 August 1949. Commentary*, Vol. I, p.131.

2   This question was also posed at the 1949 Diplomatic Conference of Geneva when a delegation objected to the reference to interpretation, alleging that interpretation was a matter not for the Protecting Powers but only for the Contracting Parties. 'Several delegations pointed out in this connection that there was no question of entrusting the interpretation of the Convention to the Protecting Powers, but only of allowing them to adjust differences arising in regard to its interpretation.' See Jean S. Pictet (ed.), *The Geneva Conventions of 12 August 1949. Commentary*, Vol. I, p.130.

3   Ibid., p.127.

4   Ibid., p.128.

Article 23
Assistance of UNESCO

1. *The High Contracting Parties may call upon the United Nations Educational, Scientific and Cultural Organization for technical assistance in organizing the protection of their cultural property, or in connection with any other problem arising out of the application of the present Convention or the Regulations for its Execution. The Organization shall accord such assistance within the limits fixed by its programme and by its resources.*
2. *The Organization is authorized to make, on its own initiative, proposals on this matter to the High Contracting Parties.*

Records: Text: p.26.
               Minutes: paras 735–7, 764–71, 1992.
               Working documents: pp.313, 344, 386;
               CBC/DR/83.

Bibliography: Boylan, P.J., *Review of the Convention for the Protection of Cultural Property in the Event of Armed Conflict* (The Hague Convention of 1954), Paris, UNESCO, 1993, pp.127–42; Nafziger, James A.R., 'UNESCO Centred Management of International Conflict over Cultural Property', *The Hastings Law Journal* (San Francisco), Vol. 27, No. 5, May 1976; Sandoz, Yves, 'Le droit d'initiative du Comité International de la Croix-Rouge', *German Yearbook of International Law*, Berlin, Vol. 22, 1979, pp.352–73; Toman, Jiří, *UNESCO's Mandate for implementation of the Hague Convention for the Protection of Cultural Property in the Event of Armed Conflict*, Paris, UNESCO, 1983.

This article, though modest, is one of the fundamental provisions on which the entire edifice for the protection of cultural property is built. The very existence of the most advanced protection provisions would be seriously threatened if there were not a structure and an institutional framework capable of ensuring the daily operation of the protection, the control of its application, the introduction of the new codification or simply the dissemination and fostering of awareness of the relevant rules. The example of the Red Cross in the domain of humanitarian international law is significant. The authors of the 1954 Convention based their work on the example of the Red Cross and the Geneva Conventions, to such an extent that reference has been made to the 'Red Cross of cultural property'.

HISTORICAL BACKGROUND

From the very beginnings of the protection of cultural property, it was clear that an institutional framework was needed to ensure the implementation of the rules concerning protection. During the First World War, and particularly after the destruction of the cities of Rheims, Louvain and Arras, efforts were made to reinforce the protection of cultural property. At a public meeting in Geneva, in April 1915, Mr de Berne, Mr Mauriaud and Mr Vetter suggested the establishment of an international body called 'the Golden Cross'. The idea, inspired by the Red Cross, gained ground. A conference, which met in Brussels in August 1915, prepared the broad outlines of a convention providing for the establishment of an international office for the protection of monuments in wartime. The failure of this conference led the Netherlands Archaeological Society (Nederlandsche Oudleidhundige Bond) to propose to the Queen of the Netherlands, in April 1918, the convening of another, international conference for the protection of monuments and historical and art objects against the perils of war. The report drawn up by Mr Van Eysinga envisaged control of the application of the rules by neutral States and the setting-up of an office to implement such control.[1]

The Hague Rules relating to aerial warfare and the use of radio in time of war, as established by the Commission of Jurists charged with studying and reporting on the revision of the laws of war, which met in The Hague on 11 December 1922, never entered into force. Nevertheless, they had considerable influence on future projects. In particular, paragraph 8 of Article 26 stated: 'An inspection committee consisting of three neutral representatives accredited to the State adopting the provisions of this article, or their delegates, shall be appointed for the purpose of ensuring that no violation is committed of the provisions of paragraph 7 [using the monument for military purposes or committing within such monument or zone any act with a military purpose in view]. One of the members of the committee of inspection shall be the representative (or his delegate) of the State to which has been entrusted the interests of the opposing belligerent.'

The idea of a neutral institution gained ground. In his report to the Director's Committee of the International Museums Office in 1936,

Mr de Visscher suggested that the neutral supervisory commission should be responsible to a central institution.

As for the Treaty of Washington, it did not provide for any control system and rested solely on the undertaking of the parties 'to adopt the measures of internal legislation necessary to ensure said protection and respect'.

As we have seen, the first article of the Preliminary Draft Convention of 1938 provided for the defence of monuments and works of art against the foreseeable effects of armed conflicts even in time of peace. As for paragraph 2 of Article 2 of the Preliminary Draft, it envisaged the possibility of the administrations of the Contracting States securing the technical collaboration of the International Museums Office in organizing that defence which, in this draft text, was a synonym for safeguarding. This provision formed a nucleus which was substantially developed in the 1954 Convention.[2]

In 1943, during the Second World War, the *Association internationale pour la protection des populations civiles et des monuments historiques en temps de guerre ou de conflits armés*, known as 'Lieux de Genève' (Geneva Zones), envisaged the establishment of a commission composed of neutrals which was to be responsible, in wartime, for the supervision of duly notified non-transportable historic monuments and the zones around those monuments, so as to ensure that no violation was committed.[3] When a convention was first mooted, the initial idea was to set up a permanent international body whose functions would have been similar to those of the International Committee of the Red Cross (ICRC). This project was abandoned so as to avoid adding to the number of international organizations, and it was decided to entrust the responsibility to an organization then in the process of being formed – UNESCO.

As we have seen, after the Second World War, it was quite natural that UNESCO should play a fundamental part in the protection of cultural property, as laid down in its Constitution. It therefore fell upon the Conference to determine the role it should play. In order to do this, the authors of the Convention took the Geneva Conventions as their model without, however, going as far as they had done.

On the basis of its very Constitution, UNESCO was accordingly given a special task in the application of standards concerning the protection of cultural property. The 1954 Hague Convention developed this task and introduced a number of clarifications with regard to its implementation. However, while granting UNESCO certain powers, the authors failed to take into account the fundamental difference between the various institutions responsible for controlling the application of humanitarian law.

In conferring certain rights and powers upon the ICRC, the authors of the Geneva Conventions took account of the particular and specific nature of that institution. The ICRC is, of course, a private Swiss body, an association governed by Article 60 *et seq.* of the Swiss Civil Code, and possessing legal personality. The special nature of the ICRC was recognized by the International Conferences of the Red Cross and by the Geneva Conventions.

When the States assigned the ICRC certain rights and duties, they did so in full awareness of the special structure of the Committee but also of the principles that have governed its activities throughout its history, in particular the principles of humanity, impartiality, neutrality and independence. It was its character as an impartial humanitarian body that won the trust of the States when they asked the ICRC to assume certain functions in periods of armed conflict, stressing that it was its total structural independence that imposed on the ICRC, at least in its activities under the Convention, a correspondingly greater obligation to remain faithful to itself.[4]

UNESCO on the other hand, is an intergovernmental organization composed of States that form part of the international community. Its powers and competence are established, by decision of the Member States, in its Constitution (the instrument creating a United Nations Educational, Scientific and Cultural Organization, signed at London on 16 November 1945).[5] The Organization's policy is laid down by its General Conferences, which reflect the points of view of all the States. For the Organization to play a role similar to that entrusted to the ICRC, the UNESCO Secretariat must be able to perform its functions in a way that conforms as closely as possible to the principles of humanitarian international law. For that, *States must first bear in mind and understand the functions that UNESCO has to perform in this area and give the Secretariat the fullest opportunity of carrying out those functions.*

GENERAL RIGHT OF CULTURAL INITIATIVE

It must be remembered that UNESCO's role in the protection of cultural property in the event of armed conflict is not based exclusively on the 1954 Hague Convention but has its origin in the Organization's Constitution[6] itself, which gives UNESCO a general mandate 'to maintain, increase and diffuse knowledge: by assuring the conservation and protection of the world's inheritance of books, works of art and monuments of history and science, and recommending to the nations concerned the necessary international conventions'.

In order to carry out this mandate in peacetime, UNESCO has adopted numerous recommendations and conventions, in particular the Convention on the Means of Prohibiting and Preventing the Illicit Import, Export and Transfer of Ownership of Cultural Property, adopted by the General Conference at its session in Paris on 14 November 1970,[7] and the Convention concerning the Protection of the World Cultural and Natural Heritage, approved by the General Conference at its seventeenth session in Paris on 16 November 1972.

In giving UNESCO this mandate, the States thereby recognized that the protection of cultural property was no longer an internal affair but a question of concern to the whole of humanity and the international community in general. As we noted in connection with Article 19, States can no longer cite paragraph 3 of Article I of UNESCO's Constitution and refuse any initiative on the pretext that it is an internal matter in which UNESCO has no right to intervene.

It should also be noted that the World Conference on Cultural Policies, held in Mexico City from 26 July to 6 August 1982, concluded that 'in a world torn by dissensions which imperil the cultural values of the different civilizations, the Member States and Secretariat of the United Nations Educational, Scientific and Cultural Organization must increase their efforts to preserve such values and take more intensive action to further the development of mankind. The establishment of a lasting peace is essential to the very existence of human culture.'

Moreover, under this same mandate, the international community also gave UNESCO the right to take cultural initiatives, such as formulating recommendations, adopting international conventions, offering its services, making proposals and giving advice, not only in situations of armed conflict but also in other exceptional situations, such as internal strife, natural disasters, and so on. Without that right, UNESCO would certainly not be able to carry out this mandate.

To perform the mission entrusted to it, UNESCO must remain faithful to its objective and work exclusively for its realization. In order to serve cultural property and hence the whole of the international community, it must remain aloof from politics so as to avoid confrontations. *It must also act impartially and help to settle disputes between its members.* Experience has shown that UNESCO is capable of fulfilling its mission, and that the action it has taken to protect cultural property is credible.

ANALYSIS OF THE TEXT

It is only in the actual text of the article entitled 'Assistance of UNESCO' that we find a precise definition of the assistance accorded by the Organization. This article was also included in the UNESCO Draft, so as to ensure, more especially, the existence of a permanent secretariat. The Conference adopted the text as it stood. As we shall see, only the United Kingdom asked for the article to be deleted, on account, more especially, of paragraph 2 which gave UNESCO a right of initiative. According to the United Kingdom delegate, UNESCO should not offer assistance but wait for requests for it. Despite the Secretariat's explanations, the United Kingdom delegate considered that an initiative coming from UNESCO might cause a State embarrassment. The United Kingdom proposal was rejected. In rejecting it, the Conference showed that it wished to confer upon UNESCO powers more extensive than a simple offer of services.[8]

The UNESCO Draft (CBC/3) also referred to the Director-General's role in the maintenance of the Register, in connection with conciliation procedures and in non-international conflicts. The role played by UNESCO was, hence, considered as a whole.

Paragraph 1

This paragraph refers to technical assistance in two areas: in organizing the protection of the cultural property of the High Contracting Parties and in connection with any other problem arising out of the application of the present Convention or the Regulations for its Execution.

This provision already appeared in the Draft submitted by UNESCO to the 1954 Hague Conference, and it was adopted unchanged. According to the Director-General's commentary on this article, the expression 'technical assistance' meant that UNESCO's role was a subsidiary one involving purely technical collaboration with the Contracting States, that is, having no financial implications. In formulating this provision, the authors of the text probably had in mind the rights and duties assigned by the Geneva Conventions to the ICRC. Thus Article 9/9/9/10 common to these Conventions gives the ICRC the right to propose humanitarian activity on behalf of the victims of conflicts, that is to say an activity devoid of 'any political or military consideration'.[9] In this area the ICRC acts totally independently, since it is this independence that 'characterizes its action' and 'would not permit of its acting as the agent of a particular Power'.[10]

As for the word 'technical' used in this article, we believe that it originates in and is based upon the text of Article 9/9/9/10 common to the Geneva Conventions of 1949. The authors wished thereby to prevent the request from the High Contracting Parties or UNESCO's offer of services from assuming a military or political character. Moreover, this interpretation adds to the clarity, efficacy and credibility of the provision.

This was also the spirit of the suggestion that within the context of the technical mandate more attention should be paid to settling the disputes that might arise between the States and that the adoption of positions that might aggravate them should be avoided. Accordingly, within the framework of this technical, indeed apolitical mandate, UNESCO *should employ techniques of dispute settlement such as conciliation and mediation.*[11]

It should also be noted that, according to Article 22 of the Convention, 'the Protecting Powers shall lend their good offices in all cases where they may deem it useful in the interests of cultural property, particularly if there is disagreement between the Parties to the conflict as to the application or interpretation of the provisions of the present Convention or the Regulations for its Execution'. However, as we have already pointed out, this provision would be inapplicable if the control system – in particular the appointment of Protecting Powers – had not been set up. In those circumstances, UNESCO would be alone in assisting the Parties to the conflict to settle any disputes.

UNESCO's technical assistance may be *initiated* either by a call upon the Organization from the High Contracting Parties or by UNESCO itself since, according to paragraph 2 of Article 23, the Organization is authorized to make, on its own initiative, proposals on this matter to the High Contracting Parties.

UNESCO's technical assistance may take various forms: for example, there is the assistance provided to States Parties to the Convention at national level for the establishment of national committees, as suggested in Resolution II of the 1954 Hague Intergovernmental Conference,[12] the affixing of distinctive emblems on the principal monuments, the compilation of records of protected property, the construction of refuges and other technical forms of protection, the preparation of protective packaging, protection against fire or the effects of bombardment.[13] For this purpose, UNESCO could send out experts or technical teams or collaborate with other international organizations or bodies, for example the United Nations Development Programme (UNDP).

UNESCO could advise the Contracting Parties, and an advisory service could be set up for that purpose. Such advice was given, for example, in connection with the inclusion of the Vatican City[14] and Libya[15] in the Register.

On the other hand, UNESCO rejected Japan's request, made within the context of technical assistance, to give an interpretation of the Convention, considering that the States alone were entitled to rule on that question.[16] Switzerland submitted a request for clarification concerning Article 34, to which the UNESCO Secretariat replied by referring Switzerland to certain passages of the records of the Hague Conference, but without going any further.

The last sentence of the first paragraph of Article 23 protects UNESCO against any excessive demands that might be made by the High

Contracting Parties. Thus UNESCO shall accord such assistance 'within the limits fixed by its programme and by its resources'.

The ICRC has been confronted by a similar problem. In 1949, upon undertaking the functions of substitute for the Protecting Power, the ICRC realized that 'The guarantees of efficacy are to be sought mainly in the financial and material resources which the organization has at its command and, even more perhaps, in its resources in qualified staff'.[17] The same idea was expressed by President of the ICRC at the 1972 Conference of Government Experts.[18]

Paragraph 2

As we saw in the introduction to the commentary on this article, at the Conference paragraph 2 failed to meet with the approval of the United Kingdom delegate. In the communication of 17 April 1953 (CBC/4, Add.2) it is stated that the United Kingdom 'objected very strongly to the proposal contained in paragraph 2 that UNESCO should, on its own initiative, make offers of assistance'. Difficulties would certainly arise if international organizations were to approach sovereign governments with suggestions as to what they should do. The United Kingdom considered that, as a matter of principle, UNESCO should not offer assistance, but should wait for requests for assistance.[19]

According to Mr Saba, the representative of the Director-General of UNESCO, the General Conference of UNESCO should accept the responsibilities inherent in this provision. At its seventh session, the General Conference had examined the assistance that UNESCO could provide in connection with certain technical matters, within the framework of its programme and budget. 'Paragraph 2 therefore only applied within the limits of the programme and budget. It would not imply special expenditure.' Mr Saba described this provision as a legitimate clause and gave examples of others that were applied without inconvenience. He did not consider that acceptance of the text would present the Organization with any difficulties.[20]

However, this reply, which affirmed UNESCO's availability, did not deal with the question of principle raised by the United Kingdom delegate, namely the question of State sovereignty, since the initiative accorded to UNESCO was clearly a right that limited the sovereignty of the State. It was this limitation that was questioned by the United Kingdom delegate, for 'if a country were approached by UNESCO with offers of assistance which it had not invited, it would be placed in an invidious and embarrassing position. The High Contracting Party should not be so approached.'[21]

Although States often take a restrictive position with respect to the intervention of international bodies in matters as sensitive as armed conflict, the United Kingdom proposal was rejected by the Main Commission, by 20 votes to four with six abstentions. We may conclude that the representatives of the States felt reassured by the notion of 'technical assistance' and by the statement of the UNESCO representative to the effect that this assistance would not involve expenditure over and above that provided for in the UNESCO programme and budget approved by its Member States.

At this point it is appropriate to recall a number of functions entrusted to UNESCO under the Convention:

1 Translation and communication of translations of the text of the Convention: UNESCO has the task of arranging for translations into the other official languages of its General Conference (Article 29, para. 2). Furthermore, the Director-General acts as intermediary for the communication of texts in other languages between the High Contracting Parties; this applies both to the Convention and to the Regulations for its Execution. The corresponding provision appears in Article 26, paragraph 1 (in the chapter concerning the Execution of the Convention), although it might have been more appropriate in Article 29.

2 In accordance with Article 31, paragraph 2, of the Convention, UNESCO is the depositary of the Convention. Among the functions performed by the Director-General are the following:

   (a) deposit of the instruments of accession of non-signatory States invited to the 1954 Conference (Article 32);

   (b) deposit of the instruments of accession of any other State invited to accede by the Executive Board of UNESCO (Article 32);

   (c) communication of the immediate effect given to ratifications or accessions deposited before or after the beginning of hostilities or occupation, in accordance with the situations referred to in Articles 18 and 19 of the Convention (Articles 33, para. 3, and 38);

   (d) receipt of notifications concerning the territorial extension of the Convention (Article 35);

   (e) receipt of instruments of denunciation (Article 37, para. 2);

   (f) informing the States referred to in Articles 30 and 32, and the United Nations, of the deposit of instruments of ratification, accession or acceptance (in accordance with Articles 31, 32 and 39) and of the notifications and denunciations provided for in Articles 37 and 38;

   (g) acceptance and transmission to each High Contracting Party of proposals for amendments, transmission of the replies received and notification of the decision of each of the High

Contracting Parties to adopt those amendments (Article 39, paras 1, 2 and 3);

(h) convening of the Conference of the High Contracting Parties to consider the proposed amendment, if requested to do so by more than one-third of the High Contracting Parties, and receipt of a formal instrument in this connection (Article 39, paras 4 and 6);

(i) request by the Director-General to the United Nations Secretariat for the registration of the Convention in accordance with Article 102 of the Charter;

(j) deposit of a copy of the Convention in the UNESCO archives (Article 40);

(k) delivery of a certified true copy of the Convention to all the States referred to in Articles 30 and 32, as well as to the United Nations.

The Director-General performs similar functions under the provisions of the Protocol for the Protection of Cultural Property in the Event of Armed Conflict (Articles 6 to 15 of the Protocol).

PRACTICAL APPLICATION: SOME EXAMPLES

In 1956 and 1957, at the request of the Member States of UNESCO concerned, Mr Gérard Garitte, Professor at the University of Louvain, undertook a mission to Egypt and Israel. On that occasion he prepared a detailed report on the state of the monastery of Saint Catherine (Sinai) and made several suggestions for its protection.[22] The ICRC was also interested in the monastery and its delegate, Mr Louis Guilland, visited it on 25 December 1956 'to ascertain whether it had suffered in any way at the hands of the Israelis'.[23] This is not the only example of its kind.

In 1969, when hostilities broke out between Honduras and El Salvador, the Director-General of UNESCO appealed to the two governments, suggesting that they become Parties to the Convention and take all the measures necessary to ensure the protection of cultural property in the territory of the two States. This appeal was made despite the fact that the two States were not (and still are not) Parties to the Convention.

Similar messages were sent in 1971 to India and Pakistan (Parties to the Convention), in 1974 to Cyprus and Turkey, in connection with the conflict in Cyprus (Cyprus and Turkey being Parties to the Convention), and in 1980 to Iraq and the Islamic Republic of Iran, both also Parties to the Convention.

In 1982, a mission was sent to Lebanon, at its request, to visit the archaeological site of the city of Tyre. In making his appeal for the preservation of the site and in taking his decision to send a mission, the Director-General of UNESCO acted in conformity with the provisions of the 1954 Hague Convention (particularly Article 23) but also on the basis of a special mandate conferred by Resolution 4/13 of the General Conference, adopted at its twenty-first session. Since the site was occupied by the Israeli army, the Director-General asked the Israeli authorities to cooperate and passed on to them the Lebanese request. This mission is an example of cooperation between governments, authorities of various kinds, the United Nations and also the general population, for the participants were struck 'by the indissoluble bond, at Tyre, between the archaeological sites, relics of an often very distant past, and the inhabitants of a modern city seeking to survive and prosper despite the numerous difficulties witnessed by the mission'. The mission was impeded only by the absence of Lebanese archaeologists, despite the approaches made to the Lebanese and Israeli authorities. The mission report, which is objective and impartial, made a number of recommendations, several of which could not be implemented without the assistance of UNESCO.[24]

In the conflict between the Islamic Republic of Iran and Iraq, the Executive Board of UNESCO and the Director-General intervened frequently to express their concern but also the desire that UNESCO should contribute to the search for a solution that would ensure the protection of human lives, educational, scientific and cultural institutions and the cultural and natural heritage threatened by the conflict. Jointly with the President of the General Conference, the Director-General sent a telegram to this effect to the Ministers of Foreign Affairs of both Member States. Following the resumption of the 'war of the cities', he had frequent contacts with the delegates of both countries and stressed, in particular, the importance of the provisions of the Hague Convention, proposing in this connection that UNESCO should study *in situ* the state of the heritage referred to in the Convention.[25] The resolutions of the twenty-third and twenty-fourth sessions of the General Conference and the decisions of the Executive Board appealed to the two States to end the war, seek a peaceful solution and observe all the international humanitarian principles and regulations, particularly those concerning the protection of the cultural and natural heritage, the environment and educational, scientific and cultural institutions.

The Director-General sent two personal representatives – Dr Abdulgani and Professor Lemaire – to the Islamic Republic of Iran (31 October to 7 November 1985) and to Iraq (11 to 15 January 1986). These representatives visited sites and monuments affected by the war which the authorities of the two countries wished to show them.

They were able to hold talks with the authorities of both States and learned that their governments considered themselves bound by the provision of the Convention. Accordingly, the two governments undertook rapidly to examine the possibility of implementing the procedure for the appointment of Commissioners-General for Cultural Property. The war between the Islamic Republic of Iran and Iraq ended before Commissioners-General could be appointed.

During the conflict in the Gulf, when in August 1990 Iraq invaded Kuwait, the Director-General of UNESCO appealed to both parties, asking the belligerents to comply with their obligations. He issued a number of statements in December 1990 and January 1991. In his Declaration of 7 February 1991 he appealed for the scrupulous observance of the duties imposed by international law, and in particular by the Hague Convention. In 1990, UNESCO took steps for the application of the 1954 Hague Protocol.

During the war in Yugoslavia, starting in 1991, the Director-General insisted in his communications on the need to comply particularly with Article 4 of the Hague Convention. In his appeal to the opposing Parties of 27 September and 7 October 1991, he asked the peoples and leaders of Yugoslavia to make peace prevail over violence and to respect common cultural heritage.[26] On 24 October a joint declaration by the Secretary-General of the United Nations and the Director-General of UNESCO solemnly appealed 'to all parties concerned to end the tragic conflict and to negotiate a peaceful settlement of their differences'. They requested all parties to respect the Hague Convention and the World Heritage Convention.[27] The UNESCO Executive Board and the General Conference expressed their full support for the Director-General and appealed 'to the conflicting parties in Yugoslavia to take all necessary measures, under the terms of the Hague Convention, to protect the cultural and natural heritage'.

In view of the destruction of cultural property in many towns and villages, the Director-General sent his principal private secretary on two occasions in 1991 to Belgrade and Zagreb to draw the attention of the civil and military authorities to their obligations.[28]

Several missions were sent to Yugoslavia (Belgrade, Dubrovnik, Ljubljana, Split and Zagreb). The Director-General's special envoys had talks with the authorities, both civilian and military, often at the highest level, on measures to be taken for the purpose of implementing the Convention. They have also been assessing damage in Croatia and Serbia. The Director-General's initiatives led to a programme of technical cooperation with the local authorities.

In November 1991, the Director-General of UNESCO decided to send two permanent observers to Dubrovnik when the city was surrounded by armed forces.[30] The inclusion of the Old City of Dubrovnik in the World Heritage List, and the subsequent international protection under the World Heritage Convention, placed special responsibility on the international community to help protect the city against possible destruction. The two permanent observers were sent first to Belgrade and Zagreb, where they received guarantees from the civil and military authorities that the city would be preserved. The United Nations flag was hung on the walls of the Old City to mark the concern of the international community and the effective presence of UNESCO. However, early in the morning of 6 December 1991, the city was bombed. The observers in Dubrovnik were able to call the Director-General from their shelter and UNESCO immediately sent a message to the Yugoslav authorities and to press agencies.[30] These authorities replied that the city had been bombed by error and that they had given instructions to cease bombing. A restoration programme in the Old City was devised with the assistance of UNESCO. According to the experts who saw the city following the bombing of 6 December, a number of buildings were burned, some of them almost completely, and many houses and historic monuments were attacked. However, the state of the Old City following the bombing was not as serious as that of other cities such as Vukovar which was also visited by a high-ranking UNESCO expert. UNESCO also offered its services for the restoration of the cultural heritage in these areas. A plan of action has been launched by UNESCO in Dubrovnik. It will concentrate on the repair of what was damaged during the bombing but may be extended later on to more important works on shoring up fragile structures endangered by the 1979 earthquake.[31]

The form of the Director-General's approach may differ from one case to another. First of all, a letter is sent to the Ambassador to UNESCO of the States concerned, followed by a telex to the Ministry of Foreign Affairs or to the Head of State. This might soon be followed by a meeting between the Director-General and the Ambassador to UNESCO. During the conflict in Yugoslavia, the Director-General, jointly with the Secretary-General of the United Nations, appealed to the parties to cease fighting and to respect the Hague Convention. As a rule, the authorities respond to the Director-General's request by assuring him that they will honour their obligations. The Director-General has sometimes had occasion to send a special envoy to draw the attention of the authorities to their obligations. Such was the case in recent major conflicts, including the one in former Yugoslavia.[32]

CONCLUSION

Study of Article 23 shows how great is the responsibility placed upon UNESCO in connection with the application of the present

Convention. This responsibility, together with its right of initiative, provides UNESCO with numerous possibilities for action. The initiative can be carried very far, without being scrupulously confined to the letter of the legal provisions. This no doubt leaves UNESCO exposed to criticism from those whose intentions are not always in keeping with the spirit of the Convention. But what does criticism matter when the action is consistent with the Organization's role and is, indeed, its duty? The fate of cultural property is at stake and it is that which counts.

NOTES

1   Bureau international pour la protection des oeuvres et monuments d'art en temps de guerre, proposed in *Journal de droit international*, 1918, pp.784 *et seq.*
2   'Preliminary Draft International Convention for the Protection of Historic Buildings and Works of Art in Time of War', League of Nations, *Official Journal* (Geneva), 19th year, No. 11, November 1938, p.930.
3   Secretary-General of the 'Lieux de Genève' (ed.), *La Guerre moderne et la protection des civils*, Geneva, Association internationale pour la protection de la population civile et des monuments historiques en temps de guerre ou de conflit armé, Geneva, 1943, pp.61 *et seq.*
4   Yves Sandoz, 'Le droit d'initiative du Comité international de la Croix-Rouge', *German Yearbook of International Law*, Berlin, Vol. 22, 1979, p.362.
5   United Nations, *Treaty Series*, Vol. 4, pp.276, *et seq.*
6   Idem.
7   *UNESCO's Standard-Setting Instruments*, Paris, UNESCO, 1980, No. IV.A.4.
8   *Records*, paras 735–7, 764–71, pp.191 and 193–4.
9   *The Geneva Conventions of 12 August 1949. Commentary*, Vol. I, 1952, p.109.
10 Idem, Vol. I, p.102.
11 James A.R. Nafziger, 'UNESCO Centred Management of International Conflict over Cultural Property', *The Hastings Law Journal* (San Francisco), Vol. 27, No. 5, May 1976, p.1070.
12 Thus, for example, in 1970, the Director-General sent an expert mission in response to a request from the Cambodian government for technical assistance with a view to the application of the 1954 Hague Convention. The expert entrusted with the mission participated more especially in the organization of the services provided for under the Convention (establishment of a national committee) and the affixing of distinctive emblems (PI/P No. 53 of 26 June 1970).
13 For a description of the various technical methods of protection, see A. Noblecourt, *Protection of Cultural Property in the Event of Armed Conflict*, Paris, UNESCO, 1958, 346 pp.
14 The UNESCO Secretariat made informal approaches with a view to inducing the Holy See to modify the wording of its request and obtaining a guarantee from the Italian government concerning the use of the Via Aurelia.
15 The UNESCO Secretariat informed Libya that its request might easily provoke opposition and deferred the sending of copies of that request to the Parties to the Convention despite the fact that Article 13, para. 3, of the Regulations requires such copies to be sent 'without delay'.
16 The request primarily concerned the Hague Protocol on the Prohibition of the

Exportation of Cultural Property from an Occupied Territory. One of the questions raised was whether the provision came into play only if the occupied territory was that of a Party to the Convention. Other questions related to settlement of the indemnity to the holders in good faith, the determination of the ownership of the property returned, and so on.

17   *The Geneva Conventions of 12 August 1949. Commentary*, Vol. IV, p.105.
18   Conference of Government Experts, 1972, *Report*, Vol. I, para. 5.46, subpara. 8.
19   *Records*, para. 736, p.191.
20   Ibid., p.194.
21   Ibid., p.194.
22   UNESCO Chronicle, Vol. III, No. 3, March 1957, pp.51 *et seq.*
23   Ibid., p.56.
24   UNESCO, *Rapport de la mission à Tyr*, 23 pp. A number of the recommendations have been implemented, for example the affixing of distinctive emblems.
25   129 EX/INF.3, Part I, p.17.
26   UNESCOPRESSE, No. 91-191, 91-206.
27   UNESCOPRESSE, No. 91-228.
28   E. Clément, 'Some Recent Practical Experience in the Implementation of the 1954 Hague Convention', *International Journal of Cultural Property* (Berlin, New York), No. 1, Vol. 3, 1994, pp.16–17; UNESCOPRESSE, No. 91-245.
29   UNESCOPRESSE, No. 91-251 and 263.
30   UNESCOPRESSE, No. 91-273.
31   E. Clément 'Some Recent Practical Experience', p.18.
32   Ibid., pp.16–17.

Article 24
Special Agreements

1. *The High Contracting Parties may conclude special agreements for all matters concerning which they deem it suitable to make separate provision.*
2. *No special agreement may be concluded which would diminish the protection afforded by the present Convention to cultural property and to the personnel engaged in its protection.*

    Records: Text: p.26.
                Minutes: paras 697, 738–9, 1077–92, 1108–9, 1992.
                Working documents: pp.313, 386;
                CBC/DR/70.
   Bibliography: Pictet, Jean S. (ed.), *The Geneva Conventions of 12 August 1949. Commentary*, Vol. I. pp.65–77.

Adopted by the Hague Conference in accordance with a proposal that appeared in the UNESCO Draft, this article reflects the text of Article 6/6/6/7 common to the Geneva Conventions of 12 August 1949. It is based on the same principle as that article, namely: 'The notion of special agreements ought, in the same way, to be interpreted in a very broad sense, and to be without any limitation as to form and time of conclusion. It is only the ground covered, extensive though it may be, which is subject to limitations, formulated in the interest of the protected persons.'[1]

If the outbreak of war is accompanied by the breaking off of diplomatic relations, this does not mean an end to legal relations. Quite the contrary: 'The legal phenomenon persists throughout war and despite war, attesting thereby to the perennial nature of the international law.'[2] In wartime, the law of armed conflicts applies. This law has been built up (by custom and convention) precisely for application in time of war, and it continues to develop in the course of armed conflicts. In this connection, it is worth recalling the cartels and capitulations which constituted the first bilateral treaties to contribute to customary law.

The Geneva Conventions of 1864, 1906 and 1929 already provided for arrangements between belligerents, and many such agreements were concluded in the course of both the First and the Second World

Wars. Moreover, Article 6/6/6/7 of the 1949 Geneva Conventions refers to the various provisions of the Conventions which already expressly mention the possibility of agreements between the Parties concerned.

At the 1954 Hague Conference, the present article was examined quickly and without much discussion. The only proposal was that made by the delegate of the United States who wanted to add a supplementary article for unforeseeable situations called 'Extension of the Convention'. According to this draft text, Parties to the conflict who considered the provisions of the Convention inadequate would be able to extend the Convention in order to deal with the situation confronting them at the outbreak of the conflict.

The new article was to apply 'upon the outbreak and during the course of hostilities' and such special agreements or amendments were to be arranged through the good offices of the Protecting Powers.[3] This provision was to be additional to Article 24, which concerns only the execution of the Convention. The new proposal was based on Article 23 of the first 1949 Geneva Convention concerning the conclusion of agreements for the recognition of hospital zones and localities. According to this article, the Protecting Powers and ICRC were invited to lend their good offices to facilitate the establishment and recognition of such zones and localities.

The USSR delegate saw in this provision a possibility of amending the Convention – which the Geneva Conventions did not envisage – and he therefore objected to the United States proposal which was rejected by the Main Commission of the Conference.

PARAGRAPH 1

The subject of the special agreements is very broadly defined and the High Contracting Parties may conclude such agreements for all matters concerning which they deem it suitable to make separate provision. This does not mean that the special agreement must relate exclusively to the subject-matter of the Convention. It may deal with much more wide-ranging problems, only one or two provisions being concerned with cultural property.

Nor need these agreements meet all the requirements of the law of treaties, since they fall rather into the category of conventions in simplified form. In the event of armed conflict, measures would have to be taken as quickly as possible, which would make it difficult to carry out all the formalities inherent in treaties and would give these agreements the character of temporary local arrangements. By their very nature, special agreements would generally have to be concluded by the executive bodies. It is even possible to envisage agreements arranged orally, which is acceptable in international law. They could also be concluded through third parties: the Protecting Powers or their substitute, UNESCO, or the Commissioners-General.

Special agreements may be concluded between the High Contracting Parties. This means that they may be concluded by the Parties to the conflict, by neutral States and the belligerents or the neutral States themselves. Finally, such agreements may be concluded in time of peace and during or after the end of hostilities.

PARAGRAPH 2

Whereas the first paragraph leaves a great deal of freedom as far as the conclusion of special agreements is concerned, the second imposes a significant restriction with respect to the protection of cultural property. According to this paragraph, a special agreement may not be concluded if its aim is to diminish the protection afforded by the present Convention to cultural property and to the personnel engaged in its protection.

The High Contracting Parties are not, then, free to conclude no matter what agreement and to modify the provisions of the Convention in an adverse or restrictive fashion. The protection afforded may not be diminished; neither may the obligations imposed by the Convention be restricted or waived. This 'saving clause' is similar to that contained in the Geneva Conventions. The restriction applies to all the provisions of the Convention and, no doubt under the influence of Article 6/6/6/7, there is a specific reference to the protection afforded to the personnel engaged in the protection of cultural property.

On the other hand, the 'saving clause' in no way prevents an extension of the duties of the High Contracting Parties in the interests of cultural property or the personnel engaged in its protection. As in the case of the Geneva Conventions, 'obligations under the Geneva Conventions must often be considered as representing a minimum, which the Powers are invited to exceed'.[4]

So far, no agreement of this kind has been concluded, except for that between the Holy See and Italy concerning the use of the Via Aurelia.

NOTES

1   Jean S. Pictet, *The Geneva Conventions of 12 August 1949. Commentary*, Vol. I, p.68.
2   Ibid., p.66.
3   *Records*, CBC/DR/70, p.387.
4   Jean S. Pictet, *The Geneva Conventions*, p.74.

Article 25
Dissemination of the Convention

The High Contracting Parties undertake, in time of peace as in time of armed conflict, to disseminate the text of the present Convention and the Regulations for its Execution as widely as possible in their respective countries. They undertake, in particular, to include the study thereof in their programmes of military and, if possible, civilian training, so that its principles are made known to the whole population, especially the armed forces and personnel engaged in the protection of cultural property.

Records: Text: pp.26, 28.
             Minutes: paras 131, 370, 373, 430–31, 444, 740–44, 1110–31, 1992.
             Working documents: pp.313–14, 338, 344, 387; CBC/DR/78/84.

Bibliography: Bredels, Jan, 'The dissemination of the Hague Conventions: in armed forces, the civilian population and academic circles', in Istituto internazionale di diritto umanitario, *La protezione internazionale dei beni culturalia/ The international protection of cultural property/La protection internationale des biens culturels*, pp.101–5; Pictet, Jean S. (ed.), *The Geneva Conventions of 12 August 1949. Commentary*, Vol. I, pp.347–392.

Knowledge of the rules concerning armed conflicts is of capital importance for all those called upon to apply them. The application of these rules requires, in fact, a rapid, spontaneous, almost immediate response, which means that the official, officer or ordinary soldier has little time available for interpreting them or taking a decision. He must therefore be familiar with the rules well before becoming involved in military action.

The authors of the first attempts to codify the law of war were aware of this problem. Gustave Moynier, one of the five founders of the Red Cross, wrote in the preface to the Oxford Manual: 'it is not sufficient for sovereigns to promulgate new laws. It is essential, too, that they make these laws known among all people, so that when war is declared, the men called upon to take up arms to defend the causes of the belligerent States may be thoroughly impregnated with the special rights and duties attaching to the execution of such a command.'[1]

The Fourth Hague Convention of 1907 does not contain any provision relating to dissemination. The first article of the Convention merely mentions military instructions. On the other hand, the text of the 1949 Geneva Conventions includes an important common article – Article 47/48/127/144 – drawn from the provisions of the Geneva Conventions of 1906 (Article 26) and 1929, which now forms the basis of the present provision.

The Preliminary Draft Convention of 1938 requested governments and military high commands to take steps to impress the idea of respect for cultural property on their troops, with a view to involving them in the protection of monuments and works of art (Article 3, para. 2). Both the UNESCO Draft and the debate at the Conference show that the legislators recognized the importance and the necessity of disseminating the provisions of the Convention, and the discussion was concerned only with the details.

The present provision applies both in time of peace and in time of war. It concerns civilian as well as military training. The inclusion of the study of the Convention in civilian training programmes is, however, qualified by the words 'if possible'. The same formula was used in Article 47/48/127/144 common to the Geneva Conventions. According to the Commentary on the Geneva Conventions, these words by no means imply that civilian training is less important than military training. The only reason for adding them is that 'education comes under the provincial authorities in certain countries with federal constitutions, and not under the central government. Constitutional scruples, the propriety of which is open to question, led some delegations to safeguard the freedom of provincial decisions.'[2]

In acceding to the Convention, the States Parties thus gave a firm undertaking to ensure the dissemination of its provisions. Most of the States which reported to the Director-General of UNESCO in 1962, 1967, 1970, 1979 and 1984 had responded to this undertaking and indicated that the study of the Convention had been included in the training programmes of military academies or those of the armed forces and that handbooks, brochures and guides had been distributed, together with articles in the press, for the information of the public and, in particular, schoolchildren. Similarly, conferences, exhibitions and special courses had been organized for museum personnel.[3]

The Report of the First Meeting of the High Contracting Parties (UNESCO/CUA/120 of 3 September 1962) stressed the importance of the measures to be taken at national level with a view to applying the Convention, such as the drawing up of inventories, the exchange of information (the various methods of disseminating the Convention employed in some countries might be useful to others), and so on.

In recent years, the Red Cross and, in particular, the ICRC have done much to develop the dissemnination of humanitarian international law. The activities of the Red Cross in this area are guided by its Programme of Action concerning the dissemination of humanitarian international law and the principles and ideals of the Red Cross. The protection of cultural property is part of humanitarian international law and it would therefore be desirable for UNESCO and the ICRC to cooperate more closely where the dissemination of the provisions of the Convention is concerned.[4]

Familiarity with the Convention is, first and foremost, a duty for the members of the armed forces. 'Within the armed forces, the main effort of instruction should be directed to privates, who are in the majority and who go into action on the battlefield; they should be the first to receive instruction. When teaching privates, consideration should be given to the most favourable circumstances, when the fighting man, almost or entirely alone, suddenly has to face the unexpected: an enemy who surrenders, a wounded soldier lying across his path, a civilian who moves into his line of fire just as he is about to squeeze the trigger, an objective which is found during an attack to be marked with a red cross, and so on. Such situations demand a response which should not only be immediate, but should be above all correct and in conformity with the law of war. These responses should be as automatic to every soldier as is his use of weapons.'[5]

Training begins at rank-and-file level, with the ordinary soldier being taught a few basic principles. Knowledge of the Conventions must be adapted to the various categories and ranks of the armed forces. Whereas the training for privates and NCOs should be restricted to the essentials, that intended for the ranks of lieutenant to captain and especially for commanding officers should be more thorough. Commanders-in-chief are supposed to have an in-depth knowledge of the humanitarian conventions, including the 1954 Hague Convention. It is they, above all, who bear the responsibility mentioned in the Commentary on Articles 4 and 11 of the Convention (military necessity).

It is also important to bear in mind the authorities, the police and the paramilitary bodies which might assume certain responsibilities in the event of armed conflict, especially in connection with the administration of an occupied territory. They too should be familiar with the principles of the Convention. It is interesting to note that at the Conference itself the delegate of France drew attention to the need to disseminate the provisions of the Convention among police forces.[6]

Article 82 of Additional Protocol I of 1977 provides for legal advisers to be available to the armed forces. These advisers have both peacetime tasks (consultation on dissemination for the armed forces) and wartime duties (specific advice for the military commanders who have to prepare or take decisions during the hostilities). Obviously, they need to be thoroughly trained in the protection of cultural property.

UNESCO is also aware of the need to train those who bear considerable responsibility for the protection of cultural property, in particular those concerned with the safeguarding and administration of cultural property in time of peace: curators of museums and art galleries, keepers of historic monuments and buildings, attendants, and so forth. A programme for middle-level personnel and senior specialists, organized at national, regional and international level, was to include courses on the protection of cultural property.[7] Provision has also been made to offer training for government officials, at university level, and for the general public as well.[8]

A final important consideration is the dissemination of the Convention and the Regulations for its Execution in the context of cultural education. In this way it is possible to arouse the interest of the entire population in the values that form part of the human cultural heritage and to bring home the need to safeguard that heritage.

NOTES

1 *The Laws of War on Land* (Oxford Manual), Institute of International Law, in D. Schindler and J. Toman (eds), *The Laws of Armed Conflicts*, Geneva, Henry Dunant Institute, 1981.
2 Jean S. Pictet (ed.), *The Geneva Conventions of 12 August 1949, Commentary*, Vol. I, p.349.
3 See J. Toman, *La protection des biens culturels en cas de conflit armé: projet d'un programme d'action. Etude et commentaire*, Paris, UNESCO, 1984, pp.150 *et seq.*
4 For further details, see J. Toman, *UNESCO's Mandate for Implementation of the Hague Convention for the Protection of Cultural Property in the Event of Armed Conflict*, Paris, UNESCO, 1983, pp. 40 *et seq.* See also resolution 5.12 adopted by the General Conference of UNESCO at its eighteenth session.
5 F. de Mulinen, 'The law of war and the armed forces', *International Review of the Red Cross*, eighteenth year, January–February 1978, pp.18–43.
6 *Records*, para. 1123, p.218.
7 *The Cultural Heritage of Humanity: a Shared Responsibility*, Paris, UNESCO, 1982 (CLT-82/WS/27).
8 See J. Toman, *La protection des biens culturels en cas de conflit armé: projet d'un progamme d'action. Etude et commentaire*, pp.158 *et seq.*

Article 26
Translations, Reports

1. *The High Contracting Parties shall communicate to one another, through the Director-General of the United Nations Educational, Scientific and Cultural Organization, the official translations of the present Convention and of the Regulations for its Execution.*
2. *Furthermore, at least once every four years, they shall forward to the Director-General a report giving whatever information they think suitable concerning any measures being taken, prepared or contemplated by their respective administrations in fulfilment of the present Convention and of the Regulations for its Execution.*

Records: Text: p.28.
            Minutes: paras 439–41, 745–57, 1132, 1992.
            Working documents: pp.314, 344, 387;
            CBC/DR/76/85.

Bibliography: Boylan, P.J., *Review of the Convention for the Protection of Cultural Property in the Event of Armed Conflict* (The Hague Convention of 1954), Paris, UNESCO, 1993, paras 8.1–8.8, pp.89–90, appendix VII, pp.199–200; Pictet, Jean S. (ed.), *The Geneva Conventions of 12 August 1949. Commentary*, Vol. I, p.350; idem. 'The Protection of Cultural Property in the Event of Armed Conflict', *Information on the Implementation of the Convention for the Protection of Cultural Property in the Event of Armed Conflict* (The Hague, 1954), SHC/MD/1, Paris, 19 May 1967, 42 pp.; idem. 'The Protection of Cultural Property in the Event of Armed Conflict (The Hague, 1954), SHC/MD/6, Paris, 30 April 1970, 31 pp.; idem. 'The Protection of Cultural Property in the Event of Armed Conflict', *Information on the Implementation of the Convention for the Protection of Cultural Property in the Event of Armed Conflict* (The Hague, 1954),CC/MD/41, Paris, July 1979, 29 pp.; idem., 'The Protection of Cultural Property in the Event of Armed Conflict', *Information on the Imple-*

> mentation of the Convention for the Protection of Cul-
> tural Property in the Event of Armed Conflict (The
> Hague, 1954), CLT/MD/3, Paris, December 1984,
> 41 pp.; idem. 'The Protection of Cultural Property
> in the Event of Armed Conflict', *Information on the
> Implementation of the Convention for the Protection of
> Cultural Property in the Event of Armed Conflict* (The
> Hague, 1954), CC/MD/11, Paris, December 1989,
> 39 pp.

The present article contains two different provisions: communication of official translations and forwarding of reports on measures in fulfilment of the Convention.

PARAGRAPH 1

The High Contracting Parties must communicate official translations of the present Convention and the Regulations for its Execution to one another through the Director-General of UNESCO.[1] So far, the following States have transmitted their translations to UNESCO: Austria, Bulgaria, former Czechoslovakia, Israel, Netherlands, Norway, Romania, Switzerland, Thailand and former Yugoslavia. However, other countries with a special interest in the application of the Convention have taken or could take useful initiatives in this respect. According to the report by V. Elisseeff, the Cambodian National Committee has had abridged texts of the Convention prepared in Cambodian, Chinese, French and Vietnamese.[2]

The reports of the States Parties to the Convention do not give a very precise idea of the number of translations in existence. A reminder could be issued to States when the next report is requested. Furthermore, when preparing the first meeting of the Contracting Parties, UNESCO drew up a list of discrepancies in the translation of the authentic texts of the Convention. No measures have, however, been taken to correct the texts. It would be desirable for such measures to be taken at a future meeting of the High Contracting Parties.[3]

Like many other provisions of the Convention, the present paragraph is based on Article 48/49/128/145 common to the Geneva Conventions. However, unlike the present paragraph, the common article of the Geneva Conventions also provides for the communication of laws and the regulations for their implementation, which is not the case here. The authors of the provision probably thought that these implementing texts would be communicated under the following paragraph concerning reports on measures taken in fulfilment of the Convention. But why not say so? In our opinion, that would have been preferable. This omission could be remedied in a future revision.

Where a country uses more than one official language, several official translations maybe communicated.

PARAGRAPH 2

The submission of reports to international organizations on the application of conventions is a common practice developed, more especially, within the context of the International Labour Organization and in the area of human rights.

The paragraph states that the Contracting Parties must give whatever information they think suitable. It is then left to the High Contracting Parties to decide what kind of information they wish to communicate in these reports.[4]

As we have seen, under paragraph 1, the High Contracting Parties must communicate to one another the official translations of the Convention and the Regulations for its Execution, but nothing is said about communicating the laws and regulations for their implementation as in the texts of the Geneva Conventions of 1949 (Common Article 48/49/128/145) and Protocol I of 1977 (Article 84). The 1938 Preliminary Draft Convention also provided for the communication of the texts of laws and regulations (Article 3, para. 4).

The delegations to the Conference were, in principle, in favour of the communication of reports. The United Kingdom delegation was alone in asking for the deletion of the article concerning reports, arguing that they were of no real use and that it was enough to fix a time-limit in Article 34, according to which the signatories to the Convention must take all necessary measures to ensure its application.[5] The delegate of the USSSR stressed the importance of reports as a vehicle for exchange, in so far as they strengthened the cultural links between states.[6] The delegate of Greece asked that reports be submitted every year,[7] but it was agreed that the four-year cycle should be retained. The text clearly indicates that these reports must be forwarded 'at least once every four years' and cannot be interpreted as a mere proposal or example, as some delegations appeared to think.[8]

The Commentary on the UNESCO Draft made it clear that States unwilling to disclose certain information were under no obligation to do so: the text 'accordingly authorizes States to communicate only such information as they think suitable. Further, this exchange of information is to take place through the Director-General of UNESCO, who will judge as to the desirability and the time of giving effect to it.'[9]

During the discussions in the Main Commission, the representative of the UNESCO Secretariat pointed out that at the Florence Conference in 1950 an agreement had been reached on 'the procedure for the submission and examination of Member States' reports on action taken in pursuance of conventions and recommendations adopted by the General Conference'. According to this agreement, 'In addition to the normal annual reports, Member States shall submit to the General Conference special reports on the action taken to give effect to conventions or recommendations adopted by the General Conference. Initial reports relating to any convention or recommendations adopted shall be transmitted not less than two months prior to the opening of the second ordinary session of the General Conference following that at which such recommendations or conventions were adopted. The General Conference may further request Member States to submit by prescribed dates, additional reports giving such further information as may be necessary.'

Considering the case of Article 26, para. 2, to be identical from the legal standpoint, the Secretariat representative noted that neither the United Kingdom delegate nor any other delegate had objected to that agreement. The Main Commission rejected the United Kingdom proposal to delete Article 26, which was finally adopted in its original version unopposed.[10]

PRACTICAL APPLICATION

UNESCO first applied Article 26, paragraph 2, in 1962, that is, six years after the Convention entered into force. The Director-General, with the meeting of Contracting Parties in view, requested the States Parties to the Convention to send him special reports, in accordance with a schedule appended to letter MUS/BC/7R1.[11]

By 28 February 1962, nine States had submitted reports and information to the UNESCO Secretariat. These were analysed in document CA/RBC.1/3 of 15 June 1962 to which the texts of the reports are annexed. In addition to these nine States, six other States Parties to the Convention submitted a late reply, and their reports were also appended to the analysis.[12]

Another series of reports was requested from the Contracting Parties in 1965 (letter MUS/BC 15/1 to 53 of 16 April 1965). At the same time, the Director-General approached the Member States not yet Parties to the Convention (DG/3.2/221/300 of 16 April 1965) and asked them to inform him whether their governments had taken or were contemplating taking certain measures for the protection of their cultural property in the event of armed conflict. Sixteen States Parties and four non-Parties to the Convention replied.[13]

A further series was requested on 30 March 1969: 16 States Parties sent reports and four States non-Parties information on the measures they were contemplating.[14] A somewhat longer interval preceded the next request for reports, which States received in March 1977. This time 19 replied.[15] A fresh series was requested in 1983. Twenty-four States replied to this invitation, which was issued within the context of the thirtieth anniversary of the Convention. After receiving this series of reports, the UNESCO Secretariat analysed them and prepared a file containing details of all the information it had been able to obtain.[16]

This analysis of the new 1989 Reports enabled us to draw a number of conclusions concerning the way the reporting system had worked up to December 1989. Of the 84 States Parties to the Convention, 45 sent in one or more reports. In addition, reports have been received from six States which were not Parties, giving a total of 51 States: 26 in Europe, nine in Asia/Oceania, five in Africa, eight in the Middle East, and three in Latin America. The number of replies received on each occasion were as follows: 15 in 1962, 20 in 1967 and 1970, 17 in 1979, 24 in 1983, and 25 in 1989. Thirty-three States have never submitted any information on the application of the Convention. On the other hand, only one State had replied regularly and submitted reports from the time of its ratification of the Convention: Germany; five States sent five reports, four States sent four reports, eight States sent three reports, 14 States sent two reports and 19 States sent one report. According to the analysis of the six periodic report compilation done by Mr Boyland, not one of the High Contracting Parties has submitted reports on each occasion. He estimates that only about 20 per cent of those that should have been prepared by States Parties under the terms of the Convention have actually been submitted.[17]

As for the quality of the information received, there was a great deal of unevenness in the presentation of the reports. Some countries listed the measures taken and contemplated in application of the various articles of the Convention, while others took a selective approach. Some were content just to mention a measure, whereas others gave a systematic and detailed description of the measures taken in application of an article (safeguarding measures, dissemination, military measures, legislation). The most detailed information to be supplied related to Articles 3 (safeguarding) and 25 (dissemination). The information relating to Articles 7 (military measures), 28 (sanctions), 34 (effective application) and, particularly, 4 (respect for cultural property) was sparser and less precise. Information on identification was given whenever the country had taken measures in this area.

With the exception of the Islamic Republic of Iran in its last report in 1983, the countries directly affected by an armed conflict provided very little information on the measures taken in time of war. They merely stated that the Convention had been scrupulously respected and that they had collaborated in the application of control, without giving details. This reticence calls for thought.

It should be noted that the latest series of reports was requested in 1987. Twenty-five States replied and the reports were published in December 1989.

The meeting of experts held in Vienna in 1983 suggested to the Director-General that he remind States Parties that the submission of reports was a legal obligation which could not be evaded without infringing Article 26, paragraph 2, of the Convention.[18] A number of measures were suggested in the Secretariat's study of this question.[19]

NOTES

1   The Federal Republic of Germany even asked that a reference to laws and regulations for their implementation be added (CBC/DR/76).
2   UNESCO document, 85 EX/9 of 10 September 1970, para. 7.
3   List of 30 March 1961 appended to Memorandum CA/12/Memo 7645 of 2 April 1961.
4   See statement by the Soviet delegate at the 1954 Hague Conference (*Records*, para. 752, p.192).
5   *Records*, p.344, CBC/4, Add. 2.
6   *Records*, para. 752, p.192.
7   CBC/DR/13, which was finally withdrawn (*Records*, paras 441–2, pp.167, 377).
8   *Records*, para. 752, p.192.
9   *Records*, para. 324, CBC/3.
10   *Records*, para. 757, p.193.
11   UNESCO document CA/RBC.1/3, Annex I. See also J. Toman, *UNESCO's Mandate for Implementation of the Hague Convention for the Protection of Cultural Property in the Event of Armed Conflict*, p.115.
12   CA/RBC.1/3, Add. 1, 2, 3, 4, 5, 6.
13   These reports were published in UNESCO document SHC/MD/1.
14   These reports were published in UNESCO document SHC/MD/6.
15   See CC/MD/41, July 1979.
16   See J. Toman, *La protection des biens culturels en cas de conflit armé: projet d'un programme d'action. Etude et commentaire*, pp.66–8.
17   P.J. Boylan, *Review of the Convention*, paras 8.1–8.8, pp.89–90, appendix II, pp.199–200.
18   *Meeting of Legal Experts on the Convention for the Protection of Cultural Property in the Event of Armed Conflict (The Hague, 1954), Vienna, 17–19 October 1983. Final Report*, Paris, UNESCO, 1983, p.9, para. 28. (CLT-83/CONF.641/1).
19   See J. Toman, *La protection des biens culturels en cas de conflit armé: projet d'un programme d'action. Etude et commentaire*, pp.71–7.

Article 27
Meetings

1. *The Director-General of the United Nations Educational, Scientific and Cultural Organization may, with the approval of the Executive Board, convene meetings of representatives of the High Contracting Parties. He must convene such a meeting if at least one-fifth of the High Contracting Parties so request.*
2. *Without prejudice to any other functions which have been conferred on it by the present Convention or the Regulations for its Execution, the purpose of the meeting will be to study problems concerning the application of the Convention and the Regulations for its Execution, and to formulate recommendations in respect thereof.*
3. *The meeting may further undertake a revision of the Convention or the Regulations for its Execution if the majority of the High Contracting Parties are represented, and in accordance with the provisions of Article 39.*

Records: Text: p.28.
Minutes: paras 438, 440–41, 758, 1132–5, 1200–1202, 1218–45, 1704, 1778–9, 1993–4, 2041–4.
Working documents: pp.314, 322–3, 344, 388–9; BC/DR/86/89/119/129/130/158.

Bibliography: UNESCO, *First Meeting of the High Contracting Parties to the Convention for the Protection of Cultural Property in the Event of Armed Conflict, UNESCO House, Paris, 16–25 July 1962*, Paris, UNESCO, 1962 (UNESCO/CUA/120); idem. *Report on the results of the consultation of States Parties to the Convention concerning the advisability of convening a meeting of the High Contracting Parties to the Convention for the Protection of Cultural Property in the Event of Armed Conflict*, UNESCO, Paris, May 1971 (87 EX/32).

PRELIMINARY WORK PRIOR TO THE CONVENING OF THE HAGUE CONFERENCE IN 1954

The origin of this provision is already to be found in the Preliminary Draft Convention of 1938. According to Article 12 of this text, 'the High Contracting Parties agree to meet from time to time in general conference to decide conjointly upon measures for ensuring the application of this Convention and to review, if necessary, the Regulations for its Execution'.

In the course of the work carried out in preparation for the Conference, UNESCO expressed the following view:

> If the Convention is to remain effective and if its application is to be gradually extended and improved, it is highly desirable that the States Parties to it should maintain direct contact with each other, otherwise than through the inter-communication of reports by means of UNESCO. This can only be achieved by exchanges of views between the States in question. As a result of such exchanges, it may be found that the Convention or the Regulations for its Execution stand in need of revision in certain respects.
>
> How should this periodical conference discharge its function? It was considered desirable to avoid swelling the number of standing committees equipped with secretariats and involving fresh expense, and also to avoid overlapping. It was noted, in this respect, that there were already bodies like UNESCO, the International Council of Museums and the International Committee on Monuments, which had made and published studies constituting a substantial source of information. A second source of useful information, for the purpose of adapting and improving the Convention, derives from the obligation, undertaken by the signatory States, to furnish reports on the measures taken by them with a view to applying the Convention.
>
> No permanent body, therefore, was deemed necessary; and a reasonable and economical solution for this problem appeared to be that the periodical meeting proposed should be held, in principle, every four years, preferably at the same time as a session of the General Conference of UNESCO, from which it would remain independent.[1]

DISCUSSIONS AT THE 1954 HAGUE CONFERENCE

The role of the periodic meetings gave rise to long discussions at the Conference, and a number of amendments were proposed.

France proposed that the procedure for the appointment of Commissioners-General be linked to the institution of 'Periodic Meetings' by entrusting them, for example, with the establishment of a nominal list of Commissioners-General.[2] The United Kingdom asked for the article to be deleted, but Italy, on the other hand, wanted to make the meetings more useful by proposing that they also be entrusted with the problems that might arise in connection with registration in the International Register.[3]

Italy also wanted coordination in the execution of the Convention: 'Most multilateral conventions, e.g. the Red Cross Convention, the Universal Convention for the Protection of Copyright, referred to the establishment of a permanent committee to ensure the application of the convention. No qualified body for such a task existed within UNESCO and it was from that fact that the idea arose of establishing, within the UNESCO framework, a body ensuring the application of the Convention which would make it possible for recourse to a complicated arbitration procedure to be avoided. The choice of property to be placed under general protection had been left to each country. How could their number be reduced if the list submitted by every country was too long? While in cases of disagreement, recourse might be had to the objection procedure, the latter was unpleasant and to avoid it required preliminary control by a body comprising the main Contracting Parties to the Convention. That body would have other duties, such as the choice of the Commissioners-General and other permanent tasks. The meetings referred to in Article 26 of the Draft would thus be more frequent. The name, whether council, coordinating committee or permanent bureau was of little importance. What was important was that such a body should be representative of the governments and should enjoy some discretion in the compilation of the lists of property falling under general protection. While an exchange of such lists was essential – it was also provided for in the Washington Pact – a general examination with the object of making recommendations to those governments that had submitted lists which were too long was also necessary.'[4]

Some delegations were opposed to the introduction of regular intervals between meetings, to any power of revision and to the discussion of reports. In the decision taken at the Conference it was their opinion that prevailed.[5]

Even though the idea of a committee was abandoned by the Conference, it was not completely forgotten. The Secretary-General of the Belgian National Commission for UNESCO suggested later the establishment of a Consultative Committee responsible for monitoring the execution of the Convention and for interpreting it. Such a committee might be composed of two delegates from the International Committee for Monuments and the International Council of Museums, together with two jurists (in line with the example of the Universal Copyright Convention).

FIRST MEETING OF THE HIGH CONTRACTING PARTIES IN 1962[6]

At the first meeting of the High Contracting Parties in 1962 – the only one to be held so far – the Netherlands government asked for the question of the interpretation of the Convention to be placed on the agenda. The problem involved, in particular, the interpretation of the expressions 'adequate distance', 'centres containing monuments' and 'other immovable cultural property of very great importance'. The meeting was unable to arrive at a more precise definition of those terms, because of its limited competence and because of the different circumstances which prevailed in the various particular cases and made it impossible to adopt uniform and universally valid rules. The meeting deemed it preferable 'to consider setting up an ad hoc body in the form of an advisory committee consisting of experts on the different matters covered by the Convention'.[7]

PARAGRAPH 1

Thus, according to the text adopted, which appears in the Convention, the Director-General may decide to convene, on his own initiative, meetings of representatives of the High Contracting Parties. To do so, however, he must obtain the approval of the Executive Board of UNESCO. At the same time, he must convene such a meeting if at least one-fifth of the High Contracting Parties so request. In this case, the approval of the Executive Board is not required.

PARAGRAPH 2

With regard to the competence of these meetings, the paragraph states that 'without prejudice to any other functions which have been conferred on it by the present Convention or the Regulations for its Execution, the purpose of the meeting will be to study problems concerning the application of the Convention and of the Regulations for its Execution, and to formulate recommendations in respect thereof'.

The meeting will accordingly be competent to take action in two areas: first, it must settle questions specifically entrusted to it by the Convention or the Regulations for its Execution: secondly, it will be competent to undertake, as it thinks fit, study of problems concerning the application of the Convention and the Regulations for its Execution, in respect of which it may formulate recommendations.

With regard to the first area of action introduced by the phrase 'without prejudice to any other functions which have been conferred on it by the present Convention or the Regulations for its Execution', the representative of the UNESCO Secretariat at the Hague Conference, Mr Saba, took as an example Article 14, paragraph 8, of the Regulations, concerning objection to an application for registration. In that case, the Director-General had the choice between a vote by correspondence and the convening of a meeting under Article 27 of the Convention.[8] The Convention also contains another reference to the meeting of the High Contracting Parties in Article 39 of the Convention, mentioned in paragraph 3 of the present article.

In the context of the whole range of questions concerning the application of the Convention and the Regulations for its Execution, the second area of action follows from the very general reference authorizing the meeting to study any problem of application, whatever the two instruments may provide. We shall see later, in connection with the practical application of this article, that the only meeting to be held, in 1962, adopted this very extensive interpretation and had no hesitation about discussing numerous problems relating to the very substance of the application of the Convention, the system of control and the interpretation of the text.

PARAGRAPH 3

What we have just said concerning the extensive interpretation of paragraph 2 is simply confirmed by paragraph 3, which gives the meeting very broad competence even with respect to the revision of the Convention. According to the present paragraph, the meeting may undertake a revision of the Convention or the Regulations for its Execution. This high degree of competence, fairly unusual in the law of treaties, especially in our times, is, however, accompanied by a number of requirements. First of all, the majority of the High Contracting Parties must be represented at the meeting, which means that the majority of all the States bound by the Convention must be present. Moreover, the other conditions mentioned in Article 39 must be satisfied.[9]

PRACTICAL APPLICATION

The first and only meeting of the High Contracting Parties was held at UNESCO from 16 to 25 July 1962.[10] Thirty-nine States participated and 18 States non-Parties to the Convention sent observers. If for no other reason than the broad participation of both Parties and non-Parties to the Convention, the meeting must be deemed a success, which should encourage UNESCO to hold another meeting of this kind.

This first – and so far only – meeting had no proposed amendments before it; it confined its proceedings to examination of problems concerning the application of the Convention. It considered that 'to encourage other States to become Parties to the Convention and to facilitate its application, it ought also to make some suggestions for future action'.

The government of the Netherlands asked the meeting of High Contracting Parties to interpret Article 8 of the Convention, but the meeting was unable to define the terms more precisely and proposed instead the establishment of an advisory committee responsible for certain tasks such as the study of a specific problem.

The participants also agreed that the Convention and the measures taken in conformity with its provisions were 'an effective means of protecting cultural property against the dangers to which it is exposed even in time of peace'.[11]

In the course of the discussion at this first meeting of the Contracting Parties' reports, the Polish delegation found an opportunity to draw attention to certain flaws in the text of the Convention:

(1) Should there be difficulties in interpreting the Convention and should the procedure which it lays down for its application prove inadequate, the Committee which it was recommended to set up might prove to have a useful part to play.
(2) On the other hand, in the case of clauses likely to weaken the effectiveness of the Convention, such as the possibility of waiving special protection in the event of unavoidable military necessity, there would be no other means of remedying the matter than to contemplate a revision of the Convention, in the manner provided for the Convention itself.[12]

The meeting set up a group of experts to examine certain problems concerning the application of the Convention, and their report was appended to the report of the meeting.

At the conclusion of the general discussion, the importance of the following points was stressed:

(a) the desirability of ensuring that as many States as possible become Parties to the Convention;
(b) the importance of action to be taken at the national level for the implementation of the Convention, such as the preparation of inventories, exchanges of information, etc.;
(c) the part that should be played, in compliance with resolution II adopted by the Hague Conference, by the National Committees set up to advise on the implementation of the Convention.

The meeting also adopted a resolution stressing the anxiety aroused by the arms race.

In 1970, at the request of the Executive Board, the Director-General of UNESCO consulted the States Parties to the Convention on the advisability of convening a new meeting of the High Contracting Parties. Twenty-three States replied, of which 19 were in favour, with various qualifications, and four against. The results of this consultation could not be interpreted as an express request on the part of at least one-fifth of the High Contracting Parties. After examining the replies received and taking budget resources into account, the Executive Board endorsed the point of view of the Director-General and decided that it would not be advisable to convene a meeting 'in the present circumstances'.[13]

The legal experts, who met in Vienna in October 1983, considered that it would be useful for a meeting of the High Contracting Parties – if one were convened – to examine the important developments in the practical application of the Convention, the new developments in the nature of conflicts, the results of the reaffirmation and development of humanitarian international law in the years 1974 to 1977 and, above all, the adoption of two articles concerning the protection of cultural property in the context of the Additional Protocols to the Geneva Conventions.

The advisability of convening a meeting of the High Contracting Parties in the near future was ruled out, for several reasons: 'On the one hand, if such a meeting were convened, this would risk giving the impression that amendments were necessary to make the Convention more effective. In the present context and, in particular given the arms reduction talks, any amendment process risked leading to inconclusive results. In these circumstances, the experts considered that it was preferable to direct efforts towards a better application of the Convention in its present form. On the other hand, the interest of States which were not parties to the Convention could more appropriately be encouraged by convening a conference of all the Member States of UNESCO.'[14]

It was also considered useful to start by endeavouring to raise the level of awareness of States with respect to the application of the Convention and to promote ratification of and accession to this important instrument. It was also necessary to make an assessment of the current situation and to encourage States to prepare for such a meeting before one was actually convened,[15] so as to ensure its total success.

In 1988, the permanent delegate of the Islamic Republic of Iran, Mr Feiz, informed the Executive Board of UNESCO that he had requested the Director-General to convene a meeting of the High Contracting Parties to the Hague Convention. This information did not elicit any response from the members of the Board.

NOTES

1 UNESCO Commentary, CBC/3, *Records*, p.314.
2 *Records*, p.322.
3 *Records*, paras 1133–6, pp.219, 344.
4 *Records*, para. 1201, p.244; see also CBC/DR/129, 139, pp.388–9.
5 The Italian amendment was rejected by 20 votes to five with ten abstentions (*Records*, paras 1218–46, pp.225–7.
6 See below under, 'Practical application', p.294.
7 For further details concerning the committee, see CUA/120, pp.3 *et seq*. See also J. Toman, *UNESCO's Mandate for Implementation of the Hague Convention for the Protection of Cultural Property in the Event of Armed Conflict*, pp.78 *et seq.*, Paris, UNESCO, 1983.
8 *Records*, paras 1777–8, pp.268–9.
9 See the Commentary on Article 39 of the Convention, p.000
10 Report of the meeting, document UNESCO/CUA/120 of 3 September 1962.
11 Ibid., p.4, para. 19.
12 Ibid., p.5, para. 19.
13 Document 87 EX/32 Draft, item 4.4.1.
14 *Meeting of Legal Experts on the Convention for the Protection of Cultural Property in the Event of Armed Conflict (The Hague, 1954), Vienna, 17–19 October 1983. Final Report*, Paris, UNESCO, 1983, p.10, para. 31 (CLT-83/CONF.641/1).
15 See J. Toman, *La protection des biens culturels en cas de conflit armé: projet d'un programme d'action. Etude et commentaire*, pp.60–62.

Article 28
Sanctions

The High Contracting Parties undertake to take, within the frame-work of their ordinary criminal jurisdiction, all necessary steps to prosecute and impose penal or disciplinary sanctions upon those persons, of whatever nationality, who commit or order to be committed a breach of the present Convention.

Records: Text: p.30.
            Minutes: paras 281, 760–62, 903, 1494, 1608–26, 1995.
            Working documents: pp.314, 324, 341–2, 347–8, 389–90;
            CBC/DR/28/71/87/124/146.

Bibliography: Bassiouni, Cherif, 'Reflections on criminal jurisdiction in international protection of cultural property', *Syracuse Journal of International Law and Commerce,* (Syracuse, New York), 1983, Vol. 10, No. 2, pp.218–322; idem., *International Crimes: Digest/Index of International Instruments 1815–1985,* Vol. 2, New York, Oceana Publications, 1986, pp.195–227; Boylan, P.J., *Review of the Convention for the Protection of Cultural Property in the Event of Armed Conflict* (The Hague Convention of 1954), Paris, UNESCO, 1993, paras 9.1–9.25, pp.91–8; Breucker, Jean de, 'Pour les vingt ans de la Convention de La Haye du 14 mai 1954 pour la protection des biens culturels', *Revue belge de droit international* (Brussels), Vol. XI, No. 2, 1975, pp.525–47; Nahlik, Stanislaw E., 'Des crimes contre les biens culturels', *Annuaire de l'Association des auditeurs et anciens auditeurs de l'Académie de droit international de La Haye,* Vol. 29, The Hague, 1959, pp.14–27.

HISTORICAL BACKGROUND

The rules concerning the protection of cultural property form part of the laws and customs of war, and violations of those rules are commonly called 'war crimes'. The Fourth Hague Convention of 1907 deals only with the responsibility of the belligerent Party (Article 3), but leaves States entirely free to punish or not to punish the actions of their own troops and to include individual responsibility in their national legislation. In keeping with the spirit of the Fourth Hague Convention, the Peace Treaty with Germany, signed at Versailles on 28 June 1919, ordered the return of property, rights and interests to the rightful owners. The Joint Arbitration Tribunal was to determine the amount of reparations.

The Roerich Pact of 1935 also left it to governments to adopt the internal legislative measures necessary to ensure that cultural property was respected and protected.

The Preliminary Draft Convention of 1938 requested the High Contracting Parties 'to take steps to punish in time of war any person looting or damaging monuments and works of art' (Article 3, para. 3). But the Preliminary Draft also contains another interesting provision: Article 11 stipulates that the International Commissions of Inspection shall satisfy themselves while military operations are proceeding that no breach of the provisions of this Convention is committed. Offences committed in breach of the provisions would be established by the commission operating in the territory in which they were committed.

PREPARATORY WORK

The UNESCO Draft,. which stressed the necessity of an effective system of sanctions, assigned modest objectives to the sanctions to be included in the Convention. The UNESCO Secretariat itself described this as an extremely simple approach, accounted for largely by the fact that criminal international law is still in its infancy. Thus, according to the UNESCO Draft, the aim of the Conference should be to induce the Contracting Parties to take 'all necessary measures to prosecute and impose penal or disciplinary sanctions upon those persons ... who commit or order to be committed a breach of the present Convention'. It was not considered indispensable to give a detailed list of the many breaches that might be committed. In order to meet the objections of certain States whose penal system depends on the principles of public law, which it was not intended to change, it was decided that States would undertake repressive measures only within the framework of their criminal jursidiction.[1]

In his comments, the delegate of the United Kingdom pointed out that 'because of the vague and all-embracing definition of cultural property in Article 1, there is a danger that people might break the Convention quite unwittingly. It is wrong that sanctions should apply to breaches committed through ignorance'. He proposed that the word 'knowingly' should, therefore, be inserted between 'who' and 'commit'.[2] For his part, the delegate of Italy considered that the word 'prosecute' was superfluous.[3] The Conference did not take up these two requests.

On the other hand, the delegate of the USSR proposed a more detailed article[4] based on Article 146 of the Fourth Geneva Convention. In his opinion, the article should comprise, in particular, effective sanctions and the possibility of the accused persons being handed over for trial to another Party concerned, if that Party were to possess evidence constituting counts of indictment against such persons. His draft included a definition of acts contrary to Article 11 of the Convention and sanctions to be imposed in the event of misuse of the distinctive emblem. Finally, the delegate of the USSR asked that the necessary measures be taken to put an end to any other acts contrary to the provisions of the Convention. The Conference decided to base the text on the UNESCO Draft and did not take these proposals into account.

The discussion which took place at the Conference bear witness to the restrictive attitude on the part of governments: for example, when reference was made to cases of *force majeure* or when it was proposed that there should be no provision concerning sanctions.

The experts who prepared the UNESCO text added a list of possible breaches. They understood that they had no chance of having this text accepted by all the States, particularly those with a federal constitution.

ANALYSIS OF THE TEXT

The 1954 Convention did not go much beyond the previous provisions concerning the protection of cultural property (Fourth Hague Convention of 1907, Roerich Pact of 1935). According to the present article, the High Contracting Parties undertake to take, within the framework of their ordinary criminal jurisdiction, all necessary steps to prosecute and impose penal or disciplinary sanctions upon those persons, of whatever nationality, who commit or order to be committed a breach of the present Convention. The question is, then, left to national law.

The wording of the text is modelled on paragraph 1 of Article 49/50/129/146 common to the Geneva Conventions. The States undertake to enact the necessary legislation. This legislation must already be implemented in time of peace. In our opinion, the legislation should lay down a sanction for each breach.

PRACTICAL APPLICATION

The reports of the High Contracting Parties throw little light on this subject. Some States merely note in their reports that the provisions of the penal code or the military penal code are consistent with the spirit of the Convention (Austria, Hungary, Switzerland). Others cite the law or the articles of the pertinent laws (Byelorussian SSR, Iran, Italy, the Netherlands, Yugoslavia).

The Federal Republic of Germany indicated that the criminal law provides for sanctions against the commanding officers and members of the armed forces. Special penal provisions are envisaged to supplement the general body of laws in force (penal code, military penal law, regulations governing members of the armed forces). The following acts are considered to be offences: damaging or looting property, misusing or damaging the distinctive emblem, interfering with, assaulting, insulting or threatening persons charged with the protection of property and control tasks.

In Article 261 (offences against international law) Chile defines offences against places of worship, libraries, museums, archives and works of art.

The representative of one government raised the question of whether a Party to the Convention was obliged to prosecute and impose penal sanctions upon persons having committed breaches outside the territory subject to the criminal jurisdiction of the State in question. The answer is yes, because that is the aim of this provision. It may reasonably be assumed that the country has at its disposal general legislation concerning the protection of its own cultural property and that the criminal act directed against that property would, in any event, be covered by those provisions. What remains to be done – according to Article 28 of the Convention – is *to prosecute those who have committed criminal acts outside the territorial jurisdiction of the State.*

Because the provision is so succinct and leaves all the regulating to national legislation, it is impossible to give it a uniform interpretation. There is one positive side to the article: it is made quite clear that the Convention may not be infringed with impunity.

The limited nature of the sanctions provided for by the Convention has been criticized as a step backwards relative to the previous provisions. However, it was pointed out that, even though the Convention fails to deal with the civil consequences, Article 3 of the Fourth 1907 Hague Convention is applicable. According to this provision, 'A belligerent party which violates the provisions of the said Regulations shall, if the case demands, be liable to pay compensation. It shall be responsible for all acts committed by persons forming part of its armed forces.' S.E. Nahlik has rightly remarked that 'the restitution of the object removed or, if it can no longer be returned, the restitution of another object of the same kind and the same cultural (and not economic) value is likely to satisfy the owner. In fact, this is the solution which, for centuries, has generally been recognized under customary law.'[5] The reluctance on the part of the Conference to venture further along the path of sanctions has been attributed to the fact that the International Law Commission was in the process of drawing up an international penal code which, however, contained only a very general clause since, in its Article 2, paragraph 12, it mentions 'acts committed in violation of the laws and customs of war'. Nahlik has compiled a list of crimes against cultural property which it would be useful to bear in mind should this question be reconsidered in the future.[6]

Finally, we should mention the most recent experience in the field of sanctions for the destruction of cultural property in time of armed conflict. Following the serious violations of international humanitarian law committed on the territory of former Yugoslavia as from 1991, the United Nations Security Council adopted on 25 May 1993 Resolution 827 (1993) establishing 'an international tribunal for the sole purpose of prosecuting persons responsible for serious violations of international humanitarian law', and adopted the Statute of the International Tribunal.

The Statute defines the competence of the Tribunal by referring to the violations of international humanitarian law, both conventional and customary. It refers *expressis verbis* to the 1949 Geneva Conventions. No reference is made to the 1954 Hague Convention. The violation of cultural property is included in Article 3 of the Statute: *Violations of the laws and customs of war.* The article says, *inter alia*:

> The International Tribunal shall have the power to prosecute persons violating the laws and customs of war. Such violations shall include, but not be limited to:
>
> ...
> (b)   wanton destruction of cities, towns or villages, or devastation not justified by military necessity;
> (c)   attack, or bombardment, by whatever means, of undefended towns, villages, dwellings, or buildings;
> (d)   seizure of, destruction or wilful damage done to institutions dedicated to religion, charity and education, the arts and sciences, historic monuments and works of art and science;
> (e)   plunder of public or private property.

The authors of the Statute expressed in this article the customary rules of international law, as interpreted and applied by the Nuremberg Tribunal in the wording used by the 1907 Hague Regulations. No reference was made to the 1954 Hague Convention.

CONCLUSION

Some authors consider that the history of jurisprudence and international relations reveals a trend that should logically lead to the singling out, among international crimes, of those which more particularly threaten humanity's cultural heritage. These criminal acts are called 'crimes against cultural property'.[7]

In so far as it defined more precisely the nature of these crimes, the Additional Protocol I of 1977 represented a step forward in this respect. However, it did not establish a special category of crimes against cultural property, but included them in the category of war crimes, to which they already belonged according to the 1907 Hague Regulations. In fact, Article 85, paragraph 4 of Protocol I states: '(d) making the clearly recognized historic monuments, works of art or places of worship which constitute the cultural or spiritual heritage of peoples and to which special protection has been given by special arrangement, for example, within the framework of a competent international organization, the object of attack, causing as a result extensive destruction thereof, where there is no evidence of the violation by the adverse Party of Article 53, subparagraph (b), and when such historic monuments, works of art and places of worship are not located in the immediate proximity of military objectives'. These acts are regarded as a serious breach of the Protocol when committed deliberately and in violation of the Geneva Conventions and Protocol I.

According to paragraph 5 of the same article: 'Without prejudice to the application of the Conventions and of this Protocol, grave breaches of these instruments shall be regarded as war crimes.'

LIST OF OFFENCES AND WAR CRIMES AGAINST CULTURAL PROPERTY COMPILED BY S.E. NAHLIK

In the doctrine, S.E. Nahlik, former professor of international law at Cracow University, included a list of crimes against cultural property.[8]

I General Injunctions

1. General principle of respect for private property; institutions dedicated to religion, charity and education, the arts and sciences, even when State property, shall be treated as private property (Articles 46, para. 1 and 56, para. 1 of the 1907 Regulations).

2 Prohibition of any act of hostility directed against cultural property (Articles 4, para. 1, and 9 of the 1954 Convention).
3 Prohibition of any act directed by way of reprisals against cultural property (Article 4, para. 4 of the 1954 Convention).
4 Prohibition of any act of hostility directed against transport under special protection (Article 12, para. 3 of the 1954 Convention).
5 Principle of respect for and facilities to be accorded to personnel engaged in the protection of cultural property (Article 15 of the 1954 Convention).

II Prohibition of Destruction

6 General prohibition of the destruction of enemy property, unless such destruction is imperatively demanded by the necessities of war (Article 23, letter (g) of the 1907 Regulations).
7 Prohibition of any wilful destruction of institutions dedicated to religion, charity and education, the arts and sciences, and of historic monuments and works of art and science (Article 56 of the 1907 Regulations).
8 Prohibition of attack or bombardment, by whatever means, of towns, villages, dwellings or buildings which are undefended (Article 25 of the Regulations and Article 1, para. 1 of the Ninth Convention of 1907).
9 Injunction, before commencing a bombardment, except in the case of assault, to do everything within the power of the officer in command of an attacking force to warn the authorities (of the place to be bombarded) (Article 26 of the Regulations and Article 6 of the Ninth Convention of 1907).
10 Injunction, during sieges and bombardments, to take all necessary steps to spare, as far as possible, buildings dedicated to religion, art, science, or charitable purposes, historic monuments … provided that they are not being used at the time for military purposes (Article 27, para. 1 of the Regulations and Article 5, para. 1 of the Ninth Convention of 1907).
11 Injunction, in the event of occupation of the territory of the other belligerent, to ensure that its cultural property is safeguarded and preserved (Article 5, paras 1 and 2 of the 1954 Convention).

III Prohibition of Pillage

12 Prohibition of the pillage of a town or place, even if taken by assault (Article 28 of the Regulations and Article 7 of the Ninth Convention of 1907).

13   Prohibition of pillage during the exercise of military authority over the territory of a hostile State (Article 47 of the Regulations of 1907).

14   General prohibition of the seizure of the property of institutions dedicated to religion, charity and education, the arts and sciences (Article 46, para. 2, Article 56, para. 1, and Article 53, *a contrario*, of the Regulations of 1907).

15   Prohibition of the capture of vessels charged with religious, scientific or philanthropic missions (Article 4 of the Eleventh Convention of 1907).

16   Prohibition of the requisitioning of movable cultural property situated in the territory of a Contracting Party (Article 4, para. 3, second sentence of the 1954 Convention; cf. Article 52 of the Regulations of 1907).

17   General prohibition of the seizure of enemy property, unless such seizure is imperatively demanded by the necessities of war, and a special prohibition of any seizure of institutions dedicated to religion, charity and education, the arts and the sciences and of historic monuments and works of art and science (Article 23, letter (g) and Article 56, paras 1 and 2 of the Regulations of 1907).

18   Prohibition of the seizure, capture or placing in prize of cultural property being transported and means of transport exclusively engaged in the transfer of such cultural property (Article 14 of the 1954 Convention).

19   Injunction addressed to States in occupation of enemy territory to regard themselves only as the administrator or usufructuary of public buildings and immovable property belonging to the hostile State (Article 55 of the Regulations of 1907).

20   Injunction addressed to States in occupation of enemy territory to prohibit, prevent and, if necessary, put a stop to any form of theft, pillage or misappropriation of, and any acts of vandalism directed against, cultural property (Article 4, para. 3, first sentence of the 1954 Convention).

21   Injunction addressed to all the Parties to prevent the exportation of cultural property from an occupied territory, to take into custody cultural property imported either directly or indirectly from any occupied territory and, at the close of hostilities, to return such property to the competent authorities of the territory previously occupied (paras 1, 2 3 and 5 of the 1954 Protocol).

IV   Prohibition of Wilful Damage

22   Prohibition of any wilful damage done to institutions dedicated to religion, charity and education, the arts and sciences, and to

historic monuments and works of art and science (Article 56, paras 1 and 2 of the Regulations of 1907).

V Injunctions Concerning Property Belonging to the Enjoined State Itself

23 Injunction addressed to all the Contracting Parties to prepare in time of peace for the safeguarding of cultural property situated within their own territory against the foreseeable effects of an armed conflict (Article 3 of the 1954 Convention).

24 Prohibition (by hypothesis) of the use for military purposes of buildings dedicated to religion, art, science or charitable purposes and historic monuments, and of the use of cultural property and its surroundings either for military purposes or for purposes likely to expose it to destruction or damage in the event of armed conflict (Article 27, para. 1 of the Regulations and Article 5, para. 1 of the Ninth Convention of 1907, Articles 4, paras 1 and 9 of the 1954 Convention).

25 Injunction to mark with distinctive emblems at least the cultural property under special protection (Article 10 of the 1954 Convention; cf. Articles 27, para. 2 of the Regulations and 5, para. 2 of the Ninth Convention of 1907).

26 Injunction addressed to any Contracting Party whose government is considered their legitimate government by members of a resistance movement to draw, if possible, their attention to the obligation to respect cultural property (Article 5, para. 3 of the 1954 Convention).

VI Abuse of Privileges Granted by the Conventions

27 Prohibition of the use of the distinctive emblem in cases other than those specified by the Convention (Article 17, para. 3 of the 1954 Convention).

28 Prohibition (by hypothesis) of the lifting of the immunity to which the cultural property of the opposing Party is entitled in circumstances other than those specified by the Convention and of taking advantage of the military necessity clause in circumstances other than those specified by the Convention (Article 4, para. 2 of the 1954 Convention).

VII   Injunction to Take the Necessary Measures to Ensure the Application of the Convention

29   Injunction to take all necessary measures to ensure the effective application of the Convention within a period of six months after its entry into force, and in particular to disseminate the text, to include the study of the text in training programmes, to introduce the principles into military regulations, and so on (Articles 34, para. 1, 25 and 7 of the Convention and para. 11 of the Protocol of 1954).

VIII   Injunction Addressed to the International Control Personnel

30   Injunction addressed to the Commissioners-General for Cultural Property, delegates of the Protecting Powers, inspectors and experts in no case to exceed their mandates, to take account of the security needs of the Contracting Party to which they are accredited and so on (Article 8 of the 1954 Regulations).

NOTES

1   *Records*, p.314.
2   Ibid., p.344.
3   Ibid., p.347.
4   *Records*, CBC/DR/71, p.390.
5   Stanislaw E. Nahlik, 'Des crimes contre les biens culturels', *Annuaire de l'Association des auditeurs et anciens auditeurs de l'Académie de droit international de La Haye*, Vol. 29, The Hague, 1959, p.21.
6   See list of offences and war crimes against cultural property at the end of the present article.
7   Ibid., p.27.
8   Stanislaw E. Nahlik, 'Des crimes contre les biens culturels', pp.24–7.

Final Provisions

Article 29
Languages

1. *The present Convention is drawn up in English, French, Russian and Spanish, the four texts being equally authoritative.*
2. *The United Nations Educational, Scientific and Cultural Organizations shall arrange for translations of the Convention into the other official languages of its General Conference.*

Records: Text: p.30.
             Minutes: paras 1493–8, 1996–7.
             Working documents: pp.313–14, 344, 389–80;
             CBC/DR/72/97/142.

The Convention has four authentic languages, English, French, Russian and Spanish, which are thus equivalent. By signature, ratification and accession, the High Contracting Parties accept the four texts as being equally authoritative. Interpretation of the text must, therefore, be based on all four versions.

The multiplicity of authentic texts may create difficulties if there are discrepancies and contradictions. A possible difference between the texts may, where necessary, give rise to a correction procedure. In the course of preparing the first meeting of the Contracting Parties, UNESCO drew up a list of discrepancies in the translation of the authentic texts of the Convention. However, so far, nothing has been done to correct these texts. Appropriate action would be desirable, for example, at a future meeting of the High Contracting Parties.[1]

According to paragraph 2, UNESCO should arrange for translations into other official languages of the General Conference, which are, apart from the four authentic languages of the Convention, Arabic, Chinese, Hindi and Italian. At present, the UNESCO Secretariat possesses texts of the Convention in all these languages, except Hindi.

This provision was included for technical reasons, in particular to avoid having to print the texts in these four additional languages. The delegate of China asked that the minutes of the Conference should record that, in his view, there should also be official texts of the Convention in Arabic, Chinese, Hindi and Italian.[2]

NOTES

1 List of 30 March 1961 appended to Memorandum CA/12/Memo 7645 of 2 April 1961.
2 *Records*, para. 1496, p.244.

Article 30
Signature

The present Convention shall bear the date of 14 May 1954 and, until the date of 31 December 1954, shall remain open for signature by all States invited to the Conference which met at The Hague from 21 April 1954 to 14 May 1954.

Records: Text: p.30.
Minutes: paras 1499–1517, 1580, 1586, 1998–2000.
Working documents: pp.314, 390–91;
CBC/DR/90/142.

The Conference chose the commonest procedure for introducing the Convention into positive law. It thus conformed to the system prevailing at the time. The same system has been followed in numerous multilateral treaties, including the Geneva Conventions of 1949.

According to this classical system, a distinction is made between the conclusion of a treaty and its entry into force: the conclusion of the treaty ends with the adoption of the text and signature; its entry into force is covered by Articles 31 to 33.

The first version, to be found in the UNESCO Draft, was broader. It proposed the opening of the Convention for signature by all the Member States of UNESCO, the United Nations and the Specialized Agencies and by other States invited by the Executive Board of UNESCO. The delegation of the Ukrainian SSR proposed that only the States represented at the Conference be permitted to sign. This proposal was accepted, but with the word 'represented' replaced by 'invited', which broadened its scope.

For practical reasons,[1] the time-limit for signature was made to coincide with the end of 1954. It is as well, in this connection, to recall Article 18(a) of the Vienna Convention on the Law of Treaties of 23 May 1969 (obligation not to defeat the object and purpose of a treaty prior to its entry into force), according to which a signatory State must refrain from acts which would defeat the object and purpose of a treaty until it shall have made its intention clear not to become a party to the treaty. To some extent, this idea had already been accepted by the Permanent Court of International Justice (PCIJ) in the matter of certain German interests in Polish Upper Silesia.[2]

NOTES

1 The Conference took into account the fact that the General Conference of UNESCO would be held only in November of the same year and that the report made at that time might encourage certain States to add their signature.
2 Permanent Court of International Justice, The Hague, 1926, Series A, No. 7, p.30.

Article 31
Ratification

1. *The present Convention shall be subject to ratification by signatory States in accordance with their respective constitutional procedures.*
2. *The instruments of ratification shall be deposited with the Director-General of the United Nations Educational, Scientific and Cultural Organization.*

Records: Text: p.30.
              Minutes: paras 1518, 2001.
              Working documents: p.314, 391;
              CBC/DR/142.
Bibliography: Boyan, P.J., Review *of the Convention for the Protection of Cultural Property in the Event of Armed Conflict*, (The Hague Convention of 1954), Paris, UNESCO, 1993, paras 11.1–11.21, pp.103–8.

PARAGRAPH 1

Paragraph 1 of this article is the natural and indispensable complement to Article 30 of the Convention concerning signature. According to this paragraph, the Convention shall be subject to ratification by signatory States in accordance with their respective constitutional procedures. Ratification is a formal act by which a Power definitively accepts the text of the Convention (and in accordance with Article 20 of the Convention, the Regulations for its Execution as well), previously signed by its plenipotentiaries. This act, performed by the competent body under the domestic law of each State, is alone capable of giving the Convention its mandatory force and causing the State to be bound by it.[1] It is interesting to see the trend in ratifications and accessions to the Convention since signature:

Years	Number of States becoming Parties to the 1954 Convention	Important events concerning the Convention
1954		Signature of the Convention
1955	1	
1956–57	18	Entry into force of the Convention: 7 August 1956
1958–59	11	
1960–61	17	
1962		Meeting of High Contracting Parties
1962–63	5	
1964–65	4	
1966–67	3	
1968–69	3	
1970–71	4	
1972–73	1	
1974–75	1	
1976–77	2	
1977		Additional Protocols of 8 June 1977 to the Geneva Conventions of 12 August 1949 and adoption by the Diplomatic Conference of Geneva of Resolution 20 inviting States to become parties to the 1954 Hague Convention.
1978–79	0	
1980–81	5	
1982–83	0	
1984		Thirtieth anniversary of the adoption of the Hague Convention in 1954
1984–85	3	
1986–87	1	
1988–89	2	
1990–91	0	
1992	5	
1993	3	

The ratification of and accession to the Convention are entirely in the hands of the States. A number of measures have been proposed for drawing their attention to this important Convention: information campaign, appeal, dissemination, action taken by the National Commissions for UNESCO, and so on.[2]

There is also the possibility of 'notification of succession', whereby a newly independent State maintains its participation in a treaty concluded in its name, before independence, by the former governing Power.

PARAGRAPH 2

Ratification is effected by the deposit of the instrument of ratification, which demonstrates the intention of the State concerned to be bound by the Convention *vis-à-vis* the other States which have ratified or acceded to it. According to the present paragraph, the instruments of ratification shall be deposited with the Director-General of the United Nations Educational, Scientific and Cultural Organization. That is, the Director-General has been designated as the depositary of the Convention.

NOTES

1 For the present status of ratifications and accessions, see Annex VI.
2 See J. Toman, *La protection des biens culturels en cas de conflit armé: projet d'un programme d'action. Etude et commentaire*, pp.42–53.

Article 32
Accession

From the date of its entry into force, the present Convention shall be open for accession by all States mentioned in Article 30 which have not signed it, as well as any other State invited to accede by the Executive Board of the United Nations Educational, Scientific and Cultural Organization. Accession shall be effected by the deposit of an instrument of accession with the Director-General of the United Nations Educational, Scientific and Cultural Organization.

Records: Text: pp.30, 32.
                 Minutes: paras 1509, 1521–36, 1580, 1586, 2002.
                 Working documents: pp. 314, 321, 344, 391;
                 CBC/DR/91/98/139/142.
Bibliography: Boylan, P.J., *Review of the Convention for the Protection of Cultural Property in the Event of Armed Conflict*, (The Hague Convention of 1954), Paris, UNESCO, 1993, paras 11.1–11.21, pp.103–8.

The Convention is open for accession by all States mentioned in Article 30 which have not signed it, as well as any other State invited to accede by the Executive Board of the United Nations Educational, Scientific and Cultural Organization.[1] The Hague Conference chose, then, to be more restrictive than the Geneva Conventions of 1949 which are open for accession by all States which have not signed them.

Accession, as its definition shows, is possible only after the Convention has entered into force (Article 33 of the Convention). It is effected by depositing an instrument of accession with the Director-General of the United Nations Educational, Scientific and Cultural Organization, the depositary. It produces exactly the same effects as ratification, to which it is equivalent in every respect. The procedure for accession is the same as for ratification.

At the Hague Conference, many States were motivated by a desire to broaden participation in the Convention to the greatest possible extent. The Legal Committee submitted two proposals to the Main Commission: the first, simple, proposal, based on the Geneva Conventions of 1949, was to leave the Convention open for accession by all the States which had not signed it; the second, more restrictive, suggestion was to leave the Convention open for accession by the States mentioned in Article 30 (that is, those which had been invited to the 1954 Hague Conference) and States invited to accede by the Executive Board of the United Nations Educational, Scientific and Cultural Organization.

The first text, modelled on the Geneva Conventions of 1949, was calculated to encourage the widest accession to the Convention. It was not adopted by the Main Commission, which was more inclined to side with the delegates who had asked for a definition of the State with a view to preventing abuse by groups of individuals claiming to be governments. To ensure a certain degree of control, they preferred that this task be assigned to the Executive Board of UNESCO.[2]

At its 53rd session, the Executive Board of UNESCO invited the States which had not been invited to the Hague Conference but had become members of UNESCO a little later. Accordingly, the Convention is open for ratification or accession by all Member States of UNESCO. Moreover, although not members of UNESCO, Liechtenstein and the Holy See are among the High Contracting Parties to the Convention and the Protocol of 1954.

It is interesting to note that, of the present total number of High Contracting Parties, namely 82 States on 31 March 1993, 37 signed and ratified the Convention, 38 acceded to it and seven deposited a notification of succession.

NOTES

1   For the present status of ratifications and accessions, see Annex VI.
2   *Records*, paras. 1521–36, pp.246–7.

Article 33
Entry into Force

1. *The present Convention shall enter into force three months after five instruments of ratification have been deposited.*
2. *Thereafter, it shall enter into force, for each High Contracting Party, three months after the deposit of its instrument of ratification or accession.*
3. *The situations referred to in Articles 18 and 19 shall give immediate effect to ratifications or accessions deposited by the Parties to the conflict either before or after the beginning of hostilities or occupation. In such cases the Director-General of the United Nations Educational, Scientific and Cultural Organization shall transmit the communications referred to in Article 38 by the speediest method.*

> *Records*:   Text: p.32
> Minutes: paras 1537–41, 2003–12, 2045–7.
> Working documents: pp.315, 329–30, 344, 348, 391–2;
> CBC/DR/99/142.

Considering the uncertainty in which the world lives, particularly as regards the possibility of armed conflict breaking out, the authors of the Convention were anxious for it to enter into force as quickly as possible. This is why the time-limit for entry into force was made so short and the number of prior ratifications required is so low.

PARAGRAPH 1

Under the terms of this paragraph, the Convention is to enter into force three months after five instruments of ratification have been deposited. Accordingly, this date applies only to the five States which have ratified the Convention; moreover, it falls three months after the fifth State has deposited its instruments of ratification.

This date is also important from another standpoint: it is the date on which the Convention becomes an integral part of international law. Henceforward, the Convention exists as such. Failing the five necessary ratifications, it would never be more than a mere historical document. After these five ratifications, a signatory State may become a Party to the Convention by accession.[1]

The Convention entered into force on 7 August 1956. The entry of the Convention into force in a country has national consequences. All the provisions accordingly become applicable. However, many are intended to be implemented only in the event of armed conflict. Others, as we have seen, must be applied immediately, even in time of peace.

The number of States which must become Parties to the Convention was fixed at five. As with the Geneva Conventions, this number was reduced to the strict minimum (two for the Geneva Conventions of 1949 and the Additional Protocols of 1977). This is because these conventions form part of humanitarian international law and are intended to be universal.

The time-limit for the Convention to enter into force was fixed at three months. This is even shorter than that which applies to the Geneva Conventions, namely six months. In the case of the Geneva Conventions, the reason was that States had to be given time to take the national measures (legislative and administrative) necessary to enable them to assume new obligations.[2] The UNESCO Draft proposed, and the Conference accepted, another approach. The two requirements were separated into two phases. The time-limit for the Convention to enter into force was fixed at three months, but another provision was also adopted: Article 34 (Effective application), which gives the High Contracting Parties an additional period of six months from the date of entry into force to take all necessary measures to ensure the effective application of the Convention.

PARAGRAPH 2

For each State ratifying it thereafter, the Convention is to enter into force three months after the deposit of its instrument of ratification or accession. At the end of that period, such State will be bound by the Convention *vis-à-vis* all the Powers that have ratified it or acceded to it at least three months previously. Subsequently, it will find itself bound *vis-à-vis* other Powers as they, in their turn, effect ratification and, for each of them, the three-month period elapses.

PARAGRAPH 3

In their common Article 62/61/141/153, the Geneva Conventions made provision for the Conventions to take immediate effect. Prompted by this provision, the Hague Conference included in the text wording according to which the situations referred to in Articles 18 and 19 shall give immediate effect to ratifications or accessions deposited by the Parties to the conflict either before or after the beginning of hostilities or occupation.

In fact, in such situations it is not possible to let things take their course. The Convention will enter into force from the beginning of hostilities or occupation, if the ratification has been deposited beforehand, and from deposit, if the ratification is deposited after hostilities begin.

The article mentions the situations referred to in Articles 18 and 19 whose aim, as we have seen, is to define the situations in which the Convention will be applicable. These are as follows: declared war or any other armed conflict, even if the state of war is not recognized by one of the Parties (Article 18, para. 1), partial or total occupation of the territory, even if it meets with no armed resistance (Article 18, para. 2) and, finally, armed conflicts not of an international character (Article 19).

In all such cases, the Director-General of the United Nations Educational, Scientific and Cultural Organization shall transmit the communications referred to in Article 38 by the speediest method. The usual form of notification is no longer necessary and the means most appropriate to the circumstances (telegram, telex, fax, and so on) may be used.

NOTES

1   Jean S. Pictet (ed.), *The Geneva Conventions of 12 August 1949. Commentary*, Vol. I, pp.405–6.
2   Ibid., p.406.

Article 34
Effective Application

1. *Each State Party to the Convention on the date of its entry into force shall take all necessary measures to ensure its effective application within a period of six months after such entry into force.*
2. *This period shall be six months from the date of deposit of the instruments of ratification or accession for any State which deposits its instrument of ratification or accession after the date of the entry into force of the Convention.*

Records: Text: p.32.
Minutes: paras 749, 1542–53, 2013.
Working documents: pp.315, 333, 344, 348, 392;
CBC/DR/142.

This article lays down a period of six months for the effective application of the Convention. This means taking the measures required by the Convention in peacetime and the measures intended to prepare for the application of the Convention should war break out.

PARAGRAPH 1

As we saw in Article 33, the Conference decided on a relatively short period (three months) for the entry into force of the Convention. To enable the High Contracting Parties to take all the necessary measures to ensure the effective application of the Convention, the Conference adopted the present article, which gives them an additional period of six months from the date of its entry into force to discharge that obligation.

PARAGRAPH 2

During the preparatory work, the delegates of Switzerland and Japan stressed that the period proposed was too short for States to carry out the tasks which the Convention required of them. A slight change in this period – from three to six months – in paragraph 2 was accepted. However, the Chairman pointed out that this period related only to the taking of preparatory measures for the safeguarding of cultural property; this did not necessarily mean that 'the preparations were to be completed'. It is in this sense that the present provisions should be understood.

For the States which ratified the Convention before its entry into force, the period of six months began on the date on which the Convention entered into force at international level, 7 August 1956. For the other States – those which ratify or accede to the Convention after the date of its entry into force – the period begins to run from the moment at which the Convention enters into force for each State. As we have seen, a period of three months must elapse before the Convention enters into force for States depositing their instruments of ratification or accession after its entry into force.

PRACTICAL APPLICATION

The reports of the High Contracting Parties do not provide much information about the implementation measures. Some States merely note that the Convention acquires the force of law in the country as a result of its ratification and publication in the *Official Journal*. Other reports give the chronology of the ordinances and decrees adopted which in some cases may even pre-date the Convention. Although the information may be far from systematic, it nevertheless shows that the definition of a consistent policy of cultural property protection goes hand in hand with the drafting of increasingly detailed legislation,[1] covering aspects as varied as:

1 the definition of competence, administrative and budgetary, at national (federal), regional and local level;
2 the organization of protection services and personnel (recruitment, functions);
3 the definition of cultural property, its classification, registration and documentation (criteria);
4 the notion of respect for and utilization of the cultural heritage;
5 the notion of State protection;
6 practical measures for restoring and safeguarding cultural property in peace and war: standards and directives;
7 construction, town-planning and land use and their relationship with the protection of cultural property;
8 military ordinances, the penal code, offences and sanctions;
9 regulations concerning the importation and exportation of cultural property, and so forth.

NOTE

1 See, in particular, the reports of the following countries: Byelorussian SSR and Ukrainian SSR, Czechoslovakia, the Netherlands, Norway, Poland, Romania, San Marino, Switzerland and USSR.

Article 35
Territorial Extension of the Convention

Any High Contracting Party may, at the time of ratification or accession, or at any time thereafter, declare by notification addressed to the Director-General of the United Nations Educational, Scientific and Cultural Organization that the present Convention shall extend to all or any of the territories for whose international relations it is responsible. The said notification shall take effect three months after the date of its receipt.

Records: Text: pp.32, 34.
         Minutes: paras 1554–69, 1574–5, 1885, 1890, 2014–21.
         Working documents: pp.344, 348, 392;
         CBC/DR/73/142/158.

In the past, and even at the time of the conclusion of the Hague Convention in 1954, the colonial Powers had adopted the practice of including in many treaties a final clause known as the 'colonial clause', which served to exclude the colonial territories from the application of the treaties they concluded. Today, following the almost total disappearance of the colonial phenomenon in its classical form, this question has lost much of its practical importance. Such a clause is now likely to be of interest only to highly decentralized States, particularly where economic treaties are concerned.

The Vienna Convention on the Law of Treaties of 1969 confined itself to a general rule concerning the territorial scope of treaties. According to Article 29, 'Unless a different intention appears from the treaty or is otherwise established, a treaty is binding upon each party in respect of its entire territory.' Thus the decision with regard to territorial space was left to the High Contracting Parties to each treaty.

This colonial clause is to be found in a good number of international conventions of the period.[1] It is, then, hardly surprising that the question of the colonial clause should have been raised by certain Powers. On the other hand, there is no colonial clause in the Geneva Conventions of 1949.

At the 1954 Hague Conference, the Soviet Union, for ideological, political and legal reasons, recommended another clause which would render the Convention equally relevant or applicable 'to the metropolitan territories of signatory States and to all non-self-governing and trust territories or colonies administered or governed by such States'.[2] The Legal Committee of the Hague Conference adopted, by a majority, the text of the UNESCO Draft, according to which 'Any High Contracting Party may, at the time of ratification or accession, or at any time thereafter, declare by notification addressed to the Director-General of the United Nations Educational, Scientific and Cultural Organization that the present Convention shall extend to all or any of the territories for whose international relations it is responsible' (CBC/3). However, the Committee decided also to submit to the Main Commission a text proposed by a minority of the Committee and based on the Soviet proposal (CBC/DR/73), leaving it to the higher bodies of the Conference to choose between these two proposals.

The United Kingdom delegate explained that it was not his intention to restrict the number of territories to which the Convention would apply. If he had pressed for the adoption of the majority draft, it was rather out of respect for democratic constitutional procedure which would leave it to the territories in question to decide for themselves whether or not to ratify the Convention.

Finally, the plenary session of the Conference chose the majority draft, amended by the Secretariat, which now constitutes the present article.

NOTES

1   See, for example, General Agreement on Tariffs and Trade (1947), Article 26, para. 4(a); Convention on the Intergovernmental Maritime Consultative Organization (1948), Articles 9 and 58; Convention on the Nationality of Married Women (1957), Article 7; Treaty Establishing the European Economic Community (1957), Article 227.
2   *Records*, p.392, CBC/DR/73.

Article 36
Relation to Previous Conventions

1. *In the relations between Powers which are bound by the Conventions of the Hague concerning the Laws and Customs of War on Land (IV) and concerning Naval Bombardment in time of War (IX), whether those of 29 July 1899 or those of 18 October, 1907, and which are Parties to the present Convention, this last Convention shall be supplementary to the aforementioned Convention (IX) and to the Regulations annexed to the aforementioned Convention (IV) and shall substitute for the emblem described in Article 5 of the aforementioned Convention (IX) the emblem described in Article 16 of the present Convention, in cases in which the present Convention and the Regulations for its Execution provide for the use of this distinctive emblem.*

2. *In the relations between Powers which are bound by the Washington Pact of 15 April, 1935 for the Protection of Artistic and Scientific Institutions and of Historic Monuments (Roerich Pact) and which are Parties to the present Convention, the latter Convention shall be supplementary to the Roerich Pact and shall substitute for the distinguishing flag described in Article III of the Pact the emblem defined in Article 16 of the present Convention, in cases in which the present Convention and the Regulations for its Execution provide for the use of this distinctive emblem.*

Records: Text: p.34.
Minutes: paras 1570, 2024–8.
Working documents: pp.312, 315, 393;
CBC/DR/142.

The purpose of this article is to establish how the new provisions will take over from the former rules. The new Convention will be binding only on the States which are Parties to it. The former Conventions will continue to govern the relations between the Parties to those Conventions.

Thus the present article constitutes a rule affirming the coexistence of the treaties concerning the protection of cultural property. It does not have the aim of abrogating the earlier treaties. This article, which has its origins in the UNESCO Draft and is modelled on the Geneva Conventions of 1949, was adopted by the Conference without significant change.

PARAGRAPH 1

The first paragraph begins by dealing with the relations between the High Contracting Parties to the 1954 Hague Convention which are also bound by the Hague Conventions concerning the Laws and Customs of War on Land (IV) and concerning Naval Bombardment in Time of War (IX), whether those of 29 July 1899 or those of 18 October 1907.

Among these High Contracting Parties, the present 1954 Hague Convention is to be supplementary to the aforementioned Convention (IX) and to the Regulations annexed to the aforementioned Convention (IV). Thus the 1899 and 1907 Hague Conventions and their action are in no way affected by the present provision, not even as between High Contracting Parties to the present Convention. This is understandable, since in the Preamble itself to the 1954 Convention it is stated that, in preparing the Convention, the High Contracting Parties were 'guided by the principles concerning the protection of cultural property during armed conflict, as established in the Conventions of The Hague of 1899 and of 1907 and in the Washington Pact of 15 April 1935'. It should also be borne in mind that the Regulations annexed to Convention I of The Hague constitute not only a codification of the law of armed conflicts but also an expression of customary law.

With regard to the use of the distinctive emblem the situation is, however, different. The provisions of the 1954 Convention are to substitute for the emblem described in Article 5 of the aforementioned Convention (IX) the emblem described in Article 16 of the present Convention, in cases in which the present Convention and the Regulations for its Execution provide for the use of this distinctive emblem. Accordingly, among the High Contracting Parties to the present Convention, the old distinctive emblem is replaced by the new one. On the other hand, the distinctive emblem – as described in Article 5 of the Convention (IX) of The Hague of 1907 – is to continue in use among States which are not bound by the 1954 Convention or in the relations between those States and the States which are bound by the 1954 Convention.

PARAGRAPH 2

Paragraph 2 of the present article deals with the relations with the Roerich Pact of 1935.[1] In the relations between Powers which are bound by the Washington Pact of 15 April 1935 on the Protection of Artistic and Scientific Institutions and Historic Monuments (Roerich Pact) and which are also Parties to the present Convention, the latter Convention is to be supplementary to the Roerich Pact. As in the case of the 1899 and 1907 Hague Conventions, the present provision indicates that the 1954 Convention seeks only to supplement the Roerich Pact. It does not, then, replace the Pact, even in the relations between High Contracting Parties to the 1954 Convention, particularly as the Roerich Pact also covers other questions and other situations. It will be recalled that in the Preamble to the 1954 Convention it is stated that, in preparing the present Convention, the High Contracting Parties were 'guided by the principles concerning the protection of cultural property during armed conflict, as established in the Conventions of The Hague of 1899 and of 1907 and in the Washington Pact of 15 April 1935'. On the other hand, for States which are Parties to both instruments, in the relations between Parties to the 1954 Convention, the Convention provides for the substitution of the emblem defined in Article 16 for the distinguishing flag described in Article III of the Pact, in cases in which the present Convention and the Regulations for its Execution provide for the use of this distinctive emblem.

As for the Washington Pact of 1935, although signed by 21 States of the Western Hemisphere, it was ratified by only ten, namely: Brazil (5 August 1936), Chile (8 September 1936), Colombia (20 February 1937), Cuba (26 August 1935), Dominican Republic (2 November 1936), El Salvador (1 May 1936), Guatemala (16 September 1936), Mexico (2 October 1936), United States of America (13 July 1935) and Venezuela (11 November 1936).[2] Thus, the following States are currently bound by both instruments: Brazil (ratification, 12 September 1958), Cuba (ratification, 26 November 1957), Dominican Republic (accession, 5 January 1960), El Salvador (signatory only), Guatemala (accession, 2 October 1985) and Mexico (ratification, 7 May 1956). It is, then, only in the case of five States bound both by the Roerich Pact and by the 1954 Hague Convention that the Convention supplements the Roerich Pact and the distinctive emblem of the Pact is replaced by that of the 1954 Convention.

NOTES

1   See pp.19 *et seq.*
2   Status of ratification as at 28 January 1994.

Article 37
Denunciation

1. *Each High Contracting Party may denounce the present Conven-*
   tion, on its own behalf, or on behalf of any territory for whose
   international relations it is responsible.
2. *The denunciation shall be notified by an instrument in writing,*
   deposited with the Director-General of the United Nations Edu-
   cational, Scientific and Cultural Organization.
3. *The denunciation shall take effect one year after the receipt of*
   the instrument of denunciation. However, if, on the expiry of this
   period, the denouncing Party is involved in an armed conflict,
   the denunciation shall not take effect until the end of hostilities,
   or until the operations of repatriating cultural property are com-
   pleted, whichever is the later.

Records:	Text: pp.34, 36.
	Minutes: paras 1573–78, 1885, 1890, 2016, 2019, 2029–39.
	Working documents: pp.315, 329, 344, 348, 393; CBC/DR/74/101/142.

PARAGRAPH 1

The present article gives each High Contracting Party the possibility of withdrawing unilaterally from the community of States Parties to the Convention. The UNESCO Draft contained this provision which had also been taken from the text of the Geneva Conventions of 12 August 1949 (Article 63/62/142/158).

Even if a State withdraws from the Convention, it remains bound by the principles and customary rules of modern international law, although that is not mentioned either in the Preamble or in the text of the present article.[1]

The Soviet Union, faithful to its conception of the trusteeship system and firm in its opposition to colonialism in all its forms, requested that the phrase 'on its own behalf, or on behalf of any territory for the conduct of whose foreign affairs it is responsible' be deleted, since 'Legal situations varying according to the countries concerned should not be created, nor could it be alleged that the present wording ... had been adopted for democratic reasons'.[2] However, considering that, as we have seen, the Conference retained the 'colonial clause' (Article 35), it is not particularly surprising that it should also have retained the reference to the territories mentioned in the present article.

PARAGRAPH 2

The denunciation must be notified by an instrument in writing, to be deposited with the Director-General of UNESCO, the depositary of the Convention.

PARAGRAPH 3

The denunciation does not have immediate effect. In normal circumstances – in peacetime – it is to take effect one year after the receipt of the instrument of denunciation. However, if, on the expiry of this period, the denouncing Party is involved in an armed conflict, the denunciation shall not take effect until the end of hostilities, or until the operations of repatriating cultural property are completed, whichever is the later. This second sentence was introduced to cover the case in which a Power, on the point of engaging in hostilities or expecting to become involved, might want to free itself as speedily as possible from the obligations imposed upon it by the Convention. Therefore, for a denouncing Power involved in an armed conflict on the expiry of the year following its denunciation, the denunciation will not take effect until the end of hostilities or possibly even later, namely until the operations of repatriating cultural property are completed. Such restitution may be required under a peace treaty, but must actually be put into effect.

ADDITIONAL COMMENT

Taking the common article of the Geneva Conventions of 1949 as its model, the UNESCO Draft referred in paragraph 4 of the present article to the 'Martens clause': the denunciation shall in no way impair the obligations which the Parties to the conflict shall be bound to fulfil by virtue of the principles of the law of nations, as resulting from usages established among civilized peoples.

This provision was rejected by eight votes to seven with 29 abstentions, at the pressing invitation of Mr Eustathiades, the delegate of

Greece, who feared that the paragraph 'might be interpreted as meaning that the Convention, in cases where it might be applied, would be opposed to the general principles of international law .... Those principles would remain valid for all items not specifically regulated by the Convention.'[3]

In our opinion, the fears of the Greek delegate were not justified, as shown by experience with the Geneva Conventions of 1949. Moreover, the Commentary on the Geneva Conventions stressed the usefulness of this reference which 'reaffirms the value and permanence of the lofty principles underlying the Convention. These principles exist independently of the Convention and are not limited to the field covered by it. The clause shows clearly ... that a Power which denounced the Convention would nevertheless remain bound by the principles contained in it in so far as they are the expression of inalienable and universal rules of customary international law.'[4]

NOTES

1 See the 'Additional comment' on the present article.
2 *Records*, para. 2016, p.284, CBC/DR/74, p.393.
3 *Records*, paras 2029–39, p.285.
4 Jean S. Pictet (ed.), *The Geneva Conventions of 12 August 1949. Commentary*, Vol. I, p.413.

Article 38
Notifications

The Director-General of the United Nations Educational, Scientific and Cultural Organization shall inform the States referred to in Articles 30 and 32, as well as the United Nations, of the deposit of all the instruments of ratification, accession or acceptance provided for in Articles 31, 32 and 39 and of the notifications and denunciations provided for respectively in Articles 35, 37 and 39.

Records: Text: p.36
            Minutes: paras 1579–84, 2004–5, 2011–12, 2040, 2045–6.
            Working documents: pp.315, 329–330, 348, 393;
            CBC/DR/92/142.

The Hague Convention introduced a general provision concerning notifications. There is no such provision in the Geneva Conventions, which deal with this question separately in the articles concerning ratification, accession or denunciation.

   Article 38 does not call for lengthy comment. According to this article, the Director-General of UNESCO must inform the States referred to in Articles 30 and 32, that is, all the States invited to the 1954 Hague Conference and any other State invited to accede to the Convention by the Executive Board of UNESCO, as well as the United Nations, of the deposit of all the instruments of ratification, accession or acceptance provided for in Articles 21, 32 and 39 and of the notifications and denunciations provided for respectively in Articles 35, 37 and 39.

NB: it should be noted that the word 'accept' (acceptance) refers to the acceptance of amendments formulated in accordance with Article 39.

Article 39
Revision of the Convention and of the Regulations for its Execution

1. *Any High Contracting Party may propose amendments to the present Convention or the Regulations for its Execution. The text of any proposed amendment shall be communicated to the Director-General of the United Nations Educational, Scientific and Cultural Organization who shall transmit it to each High Contracting Party with the request that such Party reply within four months stating whether it:*
   (a) *desires that a conference be convened to consider the proposed amendment;*
   (b) *favours the acceptance of the proposed amendment without a conference; or*
   (c) *favours the rejection of the proposed amendment without a conference.*

2. *The Director-General shall transmit the replies, received under paragraph 1 of the present article, to all High Contracting Parties.*

3. *If all the High Contracting Parties which have, within the prescribed time-limit, stated their views to the Director-General of the United Nations Educational, Scientific and Cultural Organization, pursuant to paragraph 1(b) of this article, inform him that they favour acceptance of the amendment without a conference, notification of their decision shall be made by the Director-General in accordance with Article 38. The amendment shall become effective for all the High Contracting Parties on the expiry of 90 days from the date of such notification.*

4. *The Director-General shall convene a conference of the High Contracting Parties to consider the proposed amendment if requested to do so by more than one-third of the High Contracting Parties.*

5. *Amendments to the Convention or to the Regulations for its Execution, dealt with under the provisions of the preceding paragraph, shall enter into force only after they have been unanimously adopted by the High Contracting Parties represented at the conference and accepted by each of the High Contracting Parties.*

6. *Acceptance by the High Contracting Parties of amendments to the Convention or to the Regulations for its Execution, which have been adopted by the conference mentioned in paragraphs 4 and 5, shall be effected by the deposit of a formal instrument with the Director-General of the United Nations Educational, Scientific and Cultural Organization.*

7. *After the entry into force of amendments to the present Convention or to the Regulations for its Execution, only the text of the Convention or of the Regulations for its Execution thus amended shall remain open for ratification or accession.*

Records: Text, pp.36, 38.
Minutes: paras 1219, 1237, 1589–91, 1883, 2040.
Working documents: pp.314–15, 320, 326–7, 330, 334, 341, 344, 347, 395–6;
CBC/DR/95/145.

Bibliography: Boylan, P.J., *Review of the Convention for the Protection of Cultural Property in the Event of Armed Conflict* (The Hague Convention of 1954), Paris, UNESCO, 1993, paras 18.1–18.10, pp.143–5; Leca, J., *Les techniques de révision des conventions internationales*, Paris, Librairie générale de droit et de jurisprudence, 1961, IV, 330pp.; United Nations, *Multilateral treaties in respect of which the Secretary-General performs depositary functions. Annex: Final Clauses* (ST/LEG/SER.D/1.Annex).

Originally, in the UNESCO Draft, the revision procedure was divided into two phases. During the *first* phase, which was to last two years, any revision was to be left to the initiative of the General Conference of UNESCO. This was because it was expected that the Convention would be adopted by the Member States of UNESCO within the context of the Organization's General Conference. As soon as it was decided to give the Convention a broader scope and a certain independence *vis-à-vis* UNESCO, this idea was dropped.

In the *second* phase, responsibility for the revision procedure was to revert to the meeting of representatives of the High Contracting Parties, and in fact this was the formula that was adopted. The procedure also called for amendments to the Convention to be adopted unanimously, and amendments to the Regulations for its Execution by a two-thirds majority. This measure would scarcely have been practicable if the Regulations were to form part of the Convention. The procedure of separation between two assemblies was therefore abandoned, together with the difference with regard to voting.

The procedure adopted is original and characterized by a desire to achieve flexibility in the revision of the Convention and the Regulations for its Execution. In particular, it reflects the desire to avoid having to install elaborate diplomatic machinery within the framework of a conference for revising the texts. This was the reason for introducing a written procedure, consultation by correspondence similar to the procedure laid down in Article 31 of the Convention on Road Traffic of 19 September 1949.[1] There are two ways of revising the Convention and the Regulations.

WRITTEN PROCEDURE (PARAS 1, 2 AND 3)

Any Party may propose an amendment. The text is communicated to the Director-General who transmits it to the other Parties which have a choice between the formal system of a conference (subpara. (a)) and the written procedure without a conference (subparas (b) and (c)). In the second instance, the Director-General must ask the High Contracting Parties whether they accept (subpara. (b)) or, on the contrary, reject (subpara. (c)) the proposed amendment. The Director-General must transmit the replies to the Contracting Parties, which are thus always kept fully informed of developments.

According to paragraph 3, if all the Parties unanimously accept the proposed amendment, the Director-General must make notification of their decision, and the amendment becomes effective on the expiry of 90 days from the date of dispatch of the notification. Unanimity being required, one negative vote or one abstention on the part of a single State would be enough to derail the entire procedure.

Despite the interest in this mechanism, there is little chance of this type of procedure producing results, except where technical questions or editorial corrections are involved.

FORMAL PROCEDURE: REVISION BY SPECIAL CONFERENCE (PARAS 1, 4, 5 AND 6)

The Director-General will convene a special conference if requested to do so by more than one-third of the High Contracting Parties. Amendments submitted under this procedure can enter into force only on two conditions: first, they must be unanimously adopted by the Contracting Parties represented at the conference; second, they must be accepted by each of the High Contracting Parties. To exclude any shadow of doubt, the Convention provides for this acceptance to be effected by the deposit of a formal instrument with the Director-General.

Paragraph 7 specifies that, after the entry into force of amendments, only the amended text of the Convention or of the Regulations for its Execution shall remain open for ratification or accession by other Parties not yet bound by the Convention. This paragraph confirms the impossibility of two texts, one not amended and the other amended, existing simultaneously, since the procedure requires the unanimity of all the Contracting Parties. In fact, the text that is not amended ceases to exist the moment it is replaced by a new text accepted by all the High Contracting Parties. This also corresponds to the solution adopted later in Article 59, paragraph 1, of the Vienna Convention on the Law of Treaties of 1969.

At the Conference, the principle of unanimity on which the present article is based was already beginning to seem too severe. The delegate of Switzerland, for example, proposed that an amendment should enter into force as soon as it had been adopted by two-thirds of the States represented at the meeting concerned and accepted by four-fifths of the States Parties to the Convention[2]

PROSPECT OF A REVISION

The *Neue Züricher Zeitung* of 29 May 1954 (No. 1322) gave a very realistic appraisal of the achievements of the Convention. It wrote: 'Despite obvious omissions, the Hague Convention for the Protection of Cultural Property in Time of War may nevertheless be regarded as an important document. For all its shortcomings, this Convention raises hopes that in future wars much cultural property may be saved from destruction. The Convention has been realistically drafted and seems likely to be respected by the belligerents. As an imperfect convention, it is of more practical value than an "absolutely perfect" one with clearly no chance of being observed in the event of war.'

Like the Geneva Conventions of 1949, the 1954 Convention is a post-war achievement deriving, in particular, from the widespread destruction inflicted during the Second World War on the States that participated in the Hague Conference. This achievement must be preserved at all costs. If one day it had to be revised, the method of revision should, in our view, be similar to that chosen by the Conference on the Reaffirmation and Development of Humanitarian International Law in 1974–77, that is, a form of additional protocol. Accordingly, the text of the Convention and the Regulations for its Execution would not be affected, but its revision would still be possible for the States that so wished.

The meeting of legal experts held in Vienna in 1983 came up with the idea that a new conference centred on revision should deal with all the international instruments relating to the protection of cultural property. This conference would have to be prepared with special care, in particular by in-depth studies of the problems posed by the application of these instruments and by an extensive campaign to raise public awareness, supported by the National Commissions for UNESCO, national and international organizations and private associations.

However, the time for such a revision has not yet arrived. Much still remains to be done to ensure the effective application of the existing provisions which offer the international community a solid and adequate basis for affording minimum protection. It is more important to spread knowledge of the 1954 Convention and to give UNESCO the means of implementing it.

NOTES

1   United Nations, *Treaty Series*, Vol. 125, p.3.
2   *Records*, p.348.

Article 40
Registration

In accordance with Article 102 of the Charter of the United Nations, the present Convention shall be registered with the Secretariat of the United Nations at the request of the Director-General of the United Nations Educational, Scientific and Cultural Organization.

IN FAITH WHEREOF the undersigned, duly authorized, have signed the present Convention.

Done at The Hague, this fourteenth day of May, 1954, in a single copy which shall be deposited in the archives of the United Nations Educational, Scientific and Cultural Organization, and certified true copies of which shall be delivered to all the States referred to in Articles 30 and 32 as well as to the United Nations.

Records: Text: pp.38, 40.
          Minutes: paras 1586–87, 2040.
          Working documents: pp.344, 396;
          CBC/DR/93/102/142.

The Convention also includes a registration provision similar to that in Article 64/63/143/159 common to the Geneva Conventions. It should also be borne in mind that the Member States of the United Nations are under an obligation to register the international treaties they conclude, failing which they would be unable to invoke them with a United Nations body. The present article recalls this provision of the Charter of the United Nations: Article 102.

The Convention was registered with the Secretariat of the United Nations under No. 3511 on 4 September 1956. It was published in the *United Nations Treaty Series*, Vol. 249, pp.240–357.

Registration was entrusted – by the present article – to the Director-General of UNESCO. This is a task consistent with the duties of the depositary and it was the 1969 Vienna Convention on the Law of Treaties which added this function to those of the depositary (Articles 77(g) and 80, para. 2, of the Vienna Convention).

The original copy of the Convention was deposited with the UNESCO Secretariat in Paris and certified true copies were delivered to the signatory States as well as to the Member States of the United Nations which acceded to the Convention.

PART III
PROTOCOL FOR THE PROTECTION OF CULTURAL PROPERTY IN THE EVENT OF ARMED CONFLICT, SIGNED AT THE HAGUE ON 14 MAY 1954

The High Contracting Parties are agreed as follows:

I

1. Each High Contracting Party undertakes to prevent the exportation, from a territory occupied by it during an armed conflict, of cultural property as defined in Article 1 of the Convention for the Protection of Cultural Property in the Event of Armed Conflict, signed at The Hague on 14 May 1954.
2. Each High Contracting Party undertakes to take into its custody cultural property imported into its territory either directly or indirectly from any occupied territory. This shall either be effected automatically upon the importation of the property or, failing this, at the request of the authorities of that territory.
3. Each High Contracting Party undertakes to return, at the close of hostilities, to the competent authorities of the territory previously occupied, cultural property which is in its territory, if such property has been exported in contravention of the principle laid down in the first paragraph. Such property shall never be retained as war reparations.
4. The High Contracting Party whose obligation it was to prevent the exportation of cultural property from the territory occupied by it shall pay an indemnity to the holders in good faith of any cultural property which has to be returned in accordance with the preceding paragraph.

II

5. Cultural property coming from the territory of a High Contracting Party and deposited by it in the territory of another High Contracting Party for the purpose of protecting such property against the dangers of an armed conflict, shall be returned by the latter, at the end of hostilities, to the competent authorities of the territory from which it came.

III

6. The present Protocol shall bear the date of 14 May 1954 and, until the date of 31 December, 1954, shall remain open for signature by all States invited to the Conference which met at The Hague from 21 April 1954 to 14 May 1954.
7. (a) The present Protocol shall be subject to ratification by signatory States in accordance with their respective constitutional procedures.

(b)   *The instruments of ratification shall be deposited with the Director-General of the United Nations Educational, Scientific and Cultural Organization.*

8.   *From the date of its entry into force, the present Protocol shall be open for accession by all States mentioned in paragraph 6 which have not signed it as well as any other State invited to accede by the Executive Board of the United Nations Educational, Scientific and Cultural Organization. Accession shall be effected by the deposit of an instrument of accession with the Director-General of the United Nations Educational, Scientific and Cultural Organization.*

9.   *The States referred to in paragraphs 6 and 8 may declare, at the time of signature, ratification or accession, that they will not be bound by the provisions of Section I or by those of Section II of the present Protocol.*

10.   (a)   *The present Protocol shall enter into force three months after five instruments of ratification have been deposited.*

(b)   *Thereafter, it shall enter into force, for each High Contracting Party, three months after the deposit of its instrument of ratification or accession.*

(c)   *The situations referred to in Articles 18 and 19 of the Convention for the Protection of Cultural Property in the Event of Armed Conflict, signed at The Hague on 14 May 1954, shall give immediate effect to ratifications and accessions deposited by the Parties to the conflict either before or after the beginning of hostilities or occupation. In such cases, the Director-General of the United Nations Educational, Scientific and Cultural Organization shall transmit the communications referred to in paragraph 14 by the speediest method.*

11.   (a)   *Each State Party to the Protocol on the date of its entry into force shall take all necessary measures to ensure its effective application within a period of six months after such entry into force.*

(b)   *This period shall be six months from the date of deposit of the instruments of ratification or accession for any State which deposits its instrument of ratification or accession after the date of the entry into force of the Protocol.*

12.   *Any High Contracting Party may, at the time of ratification or accession, or at any time thereafter, declare by notification addressed to the Director-General of the United Nations Educational, Scientific and Cultural Organization, that the present Protocol shall extend to all or any of the territories for whose international relations it is responsible. The said notification shall take effect three months after the date of its receipt.*

13. (a) Each High Contracting Party may denounce the present Protocol, on its own behalf, or on behalf of any territory for whose international relations it is responsible.
 (b) The denunciation shall be notified by an instrument in writing, deposited with the Director-General of the United Nations Educational, Scientific and Cultural Organization.
 (c) The denunciation shall take effect one year after receipt of the instrument of denunciation. However, if, on the expiry of this period, the denouncing Party is involved in an armed conflict, the denunciation shall not take effect until the end of hostilities, or until the operations of repatriating cultural property are completed, whichever is the later.

14. The Director-General of the United Nations Educational, Scientific and Cultural Organization shall inform the States referred to in paragraphs 6 and 8, as well as the United Nations, of the deposit of all the instruments of ratification, accession or acceptance provided for in paragraphs 7, 8 and 15 and the notifications and denunciations provided for respectively in paragraphs 12 and 13.

15. (a) The present Protocol may be revised if revision is requested by more than one-third of the High Contracting Parties.
 (b) The Director-General of the United Nations Educational, Scientific and Cultural Organization shall convene a Conference for this purpose.
 (c) Amendments to the present Protocol shall enter into force only after they have been unanimously adopted by the High Contracting Parties represented at the Conference and accepted by each of the High Contracting Parties.
 (d) Acceptance by the High Contracting Parties of amendments to the present Protocol, which have been adopted by the Conference mentioned in subparagraphs (b) and (c), shall be effected by the deposit of a formal instrument with the Director-General of the United Nations Educational, Scientific and Cultural Organization.
 (e) After the entry into force of amendments to the present Protocol, only the text of the said Protocol thus amended shall remain open for ratification or accession.

In accordance with Article 102 of the Charter of the United Nations, the present Protocol shall be registered with the Secretariat of the United Nations at the request of the Director-General of the United Nations Educational, Scientific and Cultural Organization.

In faith whereof the undersigned, duly authorized, have signed the present Protocol.

Done at The Hague, this fourteenth day of May, 1954, in English, French, Russian and Spanish, the four texts being equally authoritative, in a single copy which shall be deposited in the archives of the United Nations Educational, Scientific and Cultural Organization, and certified true copies of which shall be delivered to all the States referred to in paragraphs 6 and 8 as well as to the United Nations.

Records: Text: pp.68–75.
Minutes: paras 107, 114–15, 119, 127, 143, 148, 152, 341, 355, 379, 1465, 1624–6, 1628–1701, 1721, 1751–2, 1755–6, 1825–93, 2103–39, 2173, 2198, 2205–6, 2218.
Working documents: pp.310, 319–20, 324, 331, 342, 350–51, 410–14;
CBC/DR/7/64/79/117/138/153/155/157/159.

Bibliography: Eustathiades, Constantin T., 'La protection des biens culturels en cas de conflit armé et la Convention de La Haye du 14 mai 1954', *Etudes de droit international, 1929–1959*, Vol. III, Athens, Klissiounis, 1959, pp.504–8; Hall, Ardelia R., 'US program for return of historic objects to countries of origin, 1944–1954', *The Department of State Bulletin* (Washington, DC), Vol. XXXI, 4 October 1954, No. 797, pp.493–8; Nahlik, Stanislaw Edward, 'La protection internationale des biens culturels en cas de conflit armé', *Recueil des cours de l'Académie de droit international*, Vol. 120, II, The Hague, 1967, pp.61–163; Stavraki, Emmanuelle, 'La Convention pour la protection des biens culturels en cas de conflit armé: une Convention du droit international humanitaire', LLD thesis, Paris University I – Pantheon-Sorbonne, 1987–88, pp. 365–80 (mimeographed).

HISTORICAL BACKGROUND

The practice of seizing works of art has often been condemned in the past. In 1812, Sir Alexander Croke had a collection of prints and paintings returned to the Philadelphia Academy of Arts on the grounds that the arts and sciences are recognized by all civilized countries as forming an exception to the strict laws of war. They are considered not as being owned by a particular nation but as the property of the entire human race. To return them would therefore be in conformity with the law of nations, as practised by all civilized countries. The appropriation of a nation's art treasures has always been regarded as a trophy of war which adds to the glory of the victor and the humiliation of the vanquished. Doctrine and the international conventions both take the view that cultural property, even when belonging to the State, must be treated as privately owned, that is, as fully protected against seizure, destruction or defacement.

The Treaty of Peace between the Allied and Associated Powers and Germany, signed at Versailles on 28 June 1919, contains three provisions – Articles 245 to 147 – concerning the restitutions. According to Article 245, the German government had 'to restore to the French Government the trophies, archives, historical souvenirs or works of art carried away from France by the German authorities in the course of the war of 1870–1871 and during the last war...'. Germany had to restore to the British government the original Koran of the Caliph Othman and the skull of the Sultan Mkwawa (Article 246). It had to return to the University of Louvain the manuscripts, incunabula, printed books, maps and collection items corresponding in number and value to those destroyed in the burning by Germany of the Library of Louvain, and to deliver to Belgium in order to enable Belgium to reconstitute two great artistic works: the leaves of the Triptych of the Mystic Lamb, painted by the Van Eyck brothers, and the leaves of the Triptych of the Last Supper, pained by Dierick Bouts (Article 247).

PREPARATORY WORK

The adoption of the Protocol was a response to the events of the Second World War which saw not only the destruction of cultural property but also the systematic pillage of the occupied territories: 'The occupying powers practised a new technique to cloak the dispossession of the rightful owners of works of art with a semblance of legality. By demanding huge daily indemnities from the occupied countries, they made deliberately forced transactions appear free commercial dealings.'[1]

Pillage was prohibited by the 1907 Hague Regulations, but that prohibition was not enough. Accordingly, the 18 powers included in the Joint Declaration of 5 January 1943 a provision condemning acts of pillage committed in the occupied or subject territories:

> The Governments of...
> Hereby issue a formal warning to all concerned, and in particular to persons in neutral countries, that they intend to do their utmost to defeat the methods of dispossession practised by the governments with which they are at war against the countries and peoples who have been so wantonly assaulted and despoiled.

Accordingly the governments making this Declaration and the French National Committee reserve all their rights to declare invalid any transfers of, or dealings with, property, rights and interests of any description whatsoever, which are, or have been, situated in the territories which have come under the occupation or control, direct or indirect, of the governments with which they are at war, or which belong, or have belonged, to persons (including juridical persons) resident in such territories. This warning applies whether such transfers or dealings have taken the form of open looting or plunder, or of transactions apparently legal in form, even when they purport to be voluntarily effected.

The UNESCO draft was based on the Joint Declaration of 1943.

The proclamation of the Allied High Command to the German people, dated 20 September 1945 (Section VI, 19b), provided for the return of displaced cultural property. In addition, in decrees of the Federal Council dated 10 December 1945 and 22 February 1946, Switzerland, a country that had stayed neutral throughout the conflict, took some quite remarkable practical steps towards seeking out and reclaiming property removed from the occupied territories during the war. The first of these decrees extended the right to reclaim property to the case in which dispossession resulted from an act performed voluntarily by the owner but 'under the influence of fraud or of well-grounded fear for which the occupying power, or the military or civilian representatives of that power must be held responsible'.[2]

It is also worth noting the dispute between Poland and Canada concerning cultural property from the collection of the Royal Palace of Wawel in Cracow, which in 1940 was deposited as the property of the Polish State in the Bank of Montreal in Ottawa and in the Provincial Museum in Quebec City. This property was returned to Poland in 1959.[3]

Article 5 of the Convention originally included a provision on the return of movable property. Later, this question was incorporated in a special protocol. Thus the UNESCO draft submitted to the 1954 Hague Conference contained a special protocol with a single simple provision which stated.

1. If, during an occupation, a cultural property has changed hands and been exported, the restitution of that property may be required of its last holder within a period of ten years from the date on which it becomes possible to bring an action for restitution before a competent magistrate. If, however, the last holder can show proof that the property changed hands as a result of a legal transaction carried out without extortion of consent, the action for restitution shall be dismissed.

The other provisions of the Protocol are merely the final clauses. The commentary on the UNESCO Draft explained the significance of this provision. 'The Protocol establishes the principle of the restitution of cultural property that has changed hands and been exported during a period of occupation. Such restitution may be claimed within a time-limit of at least ten years beginning from the date on which the action for restitution can be brought before the competent judge. The provisions of this Protocol imply that, where cultural property has changed hands during a period of occupation, there has been no proper consent thereto and the transaction is therefore vitiated. The last holder may, of course, furnish proof to the contrary. Where the property has changed hands on the national territory and has not been exported, the case is one for the national legislation alone.'[4]

In his comments, the delegate of Israel expressed the view that the second part of the paragraph practically nullified the intent and purpose of the first clause of the paragraph, since 'it would always be possible to use some legal fiction, by which cultural property acquired by extortion or other illegal means can be made over to such acquirers in the guise of "a legal transaction" carried out without extortion of consent. The Government of Israel thinks that in such cases, where the final acquirer is a bona-fide party, he should still be compelled to restitute the property against payment of compensation in the amount paid by him. It should be left to the original owner of such property to decide whether he prefers to pay compensation and regain his property, or to leave the property in the hands of the bona-fide acquirer. It will, of course, be always open to the original owner to institute proceedings for reimbursement against such persons as may be responsible for the first extortion and for the further disposal of the property thus extorted.'[5]

The delegate of the Netherlands considered that incorporating the question of the return of property in a special protocol, the signing of which would be optional, would weaken the legal safeguards. He asked for this question to be embodied in the text of the Convention. The delegate of Belgium, on the other hand, said that incorporation in a separate protocol would enable countries whose legislation was not consistent with the provisions in question to refrain from signing the Protocol without thereby depriving other countries of those measures.[6]

The delegate of the Netherlands also proposed adding to the first sentence of the first paragraph a clause stipulating that the State, as well as a private owner, is entitled to lodge claims for the restitution of property. He also asked for the period of ten years to be reduced to five. He further pointed out that the point at which that period was supposed to begin was not clearly defined: 'As the text stands there are three possibilities: (1) at the end of hostilities, (2) at the moment when the rightful claimant can begin his investigations, or (3) at the moment when the rightful claimant can institute an action for restitution in the appropriate court. The last interpretation seems the best.'[7] Finally, he proposed that the words 'without extortion of consent' should be replaced by 'in a regular and normal way' or 'in a regular or normal way' or 'in good faith'.

These suggestions, though constructive, met with a negative response. For example, the delegate of the United States proposed that this question should not be dealt with at the Conference.[8]

Some important observations were made by the representative of the International Institute for the Unification of Private Law who sharply criticized the Protocol submitted by UNESCO, saying that the rule formulated in the Protocol 'in any case could not be adopted as it stood because it confounded matters entirely different in nature'[9] and pointing out, in particular, that aspects of private and public law were both covered in one and the same provision. After explaining these two aspects, the Institute's representative proposed new provisions as regards the protection of private interests:

A.   If, during an occupation, a cultural property has changed hands and been exported, the restitution of that property may be required of its last holder within a period of ten years from the date on which it becomes possible to bring an action for restitution before a competent magistrate. Nevertheless the claimant to the property shall be required to prove that the transfer of the property was vitiated by lack of consent on his part or that the acquirer took advantage of the occupation and the transfer was made on inequitable terms. The claimant shall in any case be required to prove that any third party to whom the property shall since have passed knew or should have known of these circumstances at the time he made the purchase.

B.   Each High Contracting Party undertakes to recognize, as enforceable in law, on its territory, judgements on the ownership of cultural property delivered by the judicial authorities of the other contracting parties, provided only:
(a)   that the judgement has been delivered in virtue of the substantive provisions set out above;
(b)   that, under the rules in force in the State where the judgement is to be given effect, the authority which delivered such judgement was competent to hear the case;
(c)   that the judgement delivered is considered as *res judicata* under the law of the country in which it was delivered;
(d)   that, likewise according to the law of the said country, the parties have been duly summoned and represented or declared in default;
(e)   that the judgement does not conflict with a judgement de-

livered on the same subject by the authorities of the State in which the judgement is invoked;
(f) that nothing in such judgement is prejudicial to public order.

As regards the protection of national interests (public law):

Each High Contracting Party undertakes to accept the restrictions on the export of cultural property existing under the law of the other High Contracting Parties and, for the period of any war, to prohibit the import of such property into their territory.
In particular each High Contracting Party undertakes:
– so far as possible to prevent, by means of Customs controls, the entry into their territory of cultural property, the export of which is prohibited or restricted under the law of the other Contracting Parties, unless the competent authorities of the country of origin shall have issued the permit prescribed under its law;
– to undertake the sequestration and return to the government of the country of origin – at its request and without prejudice to the question of ownership – of cultural property introduced into their contravention of the provisions in force in the country of origin.[10]

The criticisms made by the representative of the Institute were taken up by the delegate of Switzerland, who introduced an amendment which echoed the Institute's proposal with a few modifications, that is, he proposed to replace the text of the Protocol with the following text:[11]

The High Contracting Parties are agreed as follows:

1. (a) If, during an occupation, a cultural property has changed hands and been exported, its last holder is required to return such property on the following terms.
   (b) The claimant has the burden of proving that the cultural property in question left his hands either without his consent or through a transaction effected under the influence of well-grounded fear or otherwise vitiated by lack of consent or fraud, or else made on inequitable terms. Furthermore, if such property has once again changed hands, its restitution may be required of its last holder only against fair compensation, unless the claimant can prove that the last holder knew or should have known of the circumstances of the previous transfer when he acquired possession of the said property.
   (c) The claimant shall be considered to have made the transfer under the influence of well-grounded fear if the circumstances were such as to have induced the belief that, had he not

made such a transfer, he himself or some person closely connected with him would have been exposed to some serious imminent danger in respect of his life, his person, his honour or his property.

(d)   Action for restitution must be instituted within a maximum time-limit of five years from the end of the occupation, provided that such time-limit shall only begin to run from the date when action for restitution can be brought before the competent judge.

(e)   Each High Contracting Party undertakes to recognize as enforceable in law, on its territory, judgements delivered by the judicial authorities of the other High Contracting Parties, in implementation of the provisions of subparagraphs (a), (b) and (c) above, provided that:

(i)   under the law of the country where execution of the judgement is invoked, the authority which delivered such judgement was competent to hear the case;

(ii)   the judgement delivered is considered as *res judicata* under the law of the country in which it was delivered;

(iii)   likewise according to the law of the said country, the parties to the dispute have been duly summoned and appeared or been represented or duly declared in default;

(iv)   the judgement does not conflict with a judgement delivered on the same subject by the authorities of the country where execution of the judgement is invoked;

(v)   nothing in such judgement is prejudicial to the public order of the country in which execution of such judgement is invoked.

2.   (a)   If the territory of a High Contracting Party is occupied in whole or in part by foreign forces and if, before such occupation, the said Party had enacted legislation limiting the export of cultural property, the other High Contracting Parties shall, for the duration of the occupation, sequestrate property or prevent its direct or indirect importation into their territory from the territory of the aforementioned Party when such importation would be in violation of the legislation in question.

(b)   In the case envisaged under subparagraph (a) above, the other High Contracting Parties shall undertake to return to the Government of the said Party, at its request, such cultural property as they have sequestrated. Such restitution shall not prejudge any legitimate claim in respect of the property in question that might be made by any party under private law.

While expressing his regret that questions of public law were not included in the Convention, the delegate of Switzerland suggested the possibility of having two protocols, one on the aspects of private law and the other on those of public law.[12] The Swiss draft and that of the Institute included these two aspects.

During the Conference, a clearer text was demanded.[13] The delegate of the Netherlands renewed his request for restitution to be incorporated in the Convention but, in the light of the explanations offered by the representative of the International Institute for the Unification of Private Law, he proposed that the regulations concerning national interests should be included in the Convention and those concerning the protection of private interests in the special Protocol.[14] A solution was found on the basis of the amendment proposed by the delegates of Belgium and the Netherlands (CBC/DR/64) which formed the basis of the discussions in the Legal Committee (CBC/DR/153).

In the course of the debate, the delegate of the United Kingdom, supported by the delegate of the United States, proposed that examination of the question of the Protocol should be postponed since it required further study. Most delegates were unwilling to accede to this request. At the suggestion of the delegate of Belgium, it was agreed to propose the inclusion in the final clauses of a provision concerning the revision of the Protocol, which would enable the governments of the United Kingdom and the United States to sign the Protocol since they would then feel less irrevocably committed.[15]

Some delegates supported the incorporation of the provisions in the Convention. The delegate of Yugoslavia pointed out that the notion of sanctions was included in the Convention. However, the Main Commission decided to adopt a special Protocol on the return of property in order to enable certain large States to sign the Convention.[16]

Resolution III of the Hague Conference expresses the hope that the Director-General of UNESCO would convene a meeting of the High Contracting Parties as soon as possible. This was an Italian initiative (CBC/DR/151) aimed at enabling the Parties to proceed with a study of the return of property.[17]

After a further examination, when it had been decided to adopt a special Protocol, the Legal Committee submitted a new text (CBC/DR/157). As we shall see, the discussion in the Main Commission centred chiefly on paragraph 9 of the Protocol.

When the Main Commission began to debate Section III of the Protocol, the UNESCO Secretariat's representative proposed that the texts should be adopted as a whole, as in fact they were, with the exception of paragraphs 12 and 13 on colonies and trust territories. The representatives of the Socialist countries, supported by the delegate of Greece, requested that the colonial clause should be deleted, whereas the colonial powers insisted that it should be retained. The amendments proposed by the USSR (CBC/DR/73 and 74) were rejected by 14 votes to 13 with six abstentions. Thus the colonial clause remained in the Protocol.

At the Conference's plenary meeting, paragraphs 4 and 6 of the Legal Committee's draft (CBC/DR/157) were deleted. Section I (paras 1 to 4) was adopted by 33 votes to seven with five abstentions, Section II by 19 votes with 17 abstentions[18] and Section III by 20 votes to one with 14 absentions. The Protocol was then adopted by 23 votes with 12 abstentions.

TEXTUAL ANALYSIS

As we have seen, the text adopted retained only the aspects of public international law within the international competence of States, the private law aspects having been abandoned. The provisions adopted concerned only the safeguarding of each country's cultural heritage.

Paragraph 1

According to this paragraph, each High Contracting Party undertakes to prevent the exportation of cultural property (as defined in Article 1 of the Convention for the Protection of Cultural Property in the Event of Armed Conflict, signed at The Hague on 14 May 1954) from a territory occupied by it during an armed conflict. The paragraph thus covers all cultural property, movable and immovable, irrespective of its origin or ownership.

The delegate of Greece also raised the question of archaeological sites and of prohibiting the exportation of property that had been excavated. He asked that the occupying Power should be forbidden to carry out excavations unless assisted by the proper national authorities.[19]

The paragraph deals with the exportation of cultural property from the occupied territory by a High Contracting Party, irrespective of whether that territory belongs to a Contracting Party or not.

The paragraph does not say how the Contracting Party is to prevent exportation, the measures to be taken being left to its own judgement and discretion. On this point, the 1970 Convention is much more precise: see Articles 6 and 7 of the 1970 Convention.

Paragraph 2

To enable the aims of the Protocol to be achieved, each High Contracting Party undertakes to take into its custody cultural property imported into its territory either directly or indirectly from any occupied territory. The property is taken into custody either automatically upon importation or, failing this, at the request of the authorities of that territory.

In the course of the discussion in the Main Commission, it was made clear that the property is taken into custody by the State itself and not by a private individual.[20]

Paragraph 3

The decisions taken by the courts after the Second World War, citing the 1907 Hague Regulations, were based on the return of cultural property seized during the occupation of foreign territory.[21]

According to this paragraph, each High Contracting Party undertakes to return, at the close of hostilities, to the competent authorities of the territory previously occupied, cultural property which is in its territory, if such property has been exported in contravention of the principle laid down in the first paragraph of the Protocol. Cultural property which is in the territory of a High Contracting Party shall never be retained as war reparations. Its return is unconditional.

The delegate of Norway proposed that 'restitution cannot, however, be required later than 20 years after the object has got into the hands of the present holder, this holder having acted in good faith in acquiring it'. This proposal was not accepted by the Conference, and it may be concluded that there is no time-limit for lodging a claim for the return of property.[22]

On ratifying the Protocol, Norway entered a reservation, according to which 'restitution of cultural property in accordance with the provisions of Sections I and II of the Protocol could not be required more than 20 years from the date on which the property in question had come into the possession of a holder acting in good faith'.[23] The Byelorussian SSR, Bulgaria, Chad, Czechoslovakia, the German Democratic Republic, India, Italy, Madagascar, Mexico, the Netherlands, Poland, Romania, San Marino, Spain, the United Arab Republic and the USSR made comments on this reservation.[24] By *note verbale* dated 3 October 1979, Norway gave notice of its decision, taken on 24 August 1979, to withdraw the reservation.[25]

The cultural property is returned to the competent authorities of the occupied territory and not to private individuals, which may be regarded as recognition of the superiority of national over individual interests and rights.[26]

Paragraph 4

The High Contracting Party whose obligation it was to prevent the exportation of cultural property from the territory occupied by it shall pay an indemnity to the holders in good faith of any cultural property which has to be returned in accordance with the preceding paragraph. This obligation thus constitutes a sort of sanction, a consequence of failure to fulfil the requirements of the first paragraph of the Protocol.

The delegate of Italy criticized the text proposed by the Legal Committee for not dealing with the case of cultural property in the territory of a third country which is also under an obligation to take into custody and return the property. He asked if provision could not be made for the costs incurred by that third party to be reimbursed by the country to which the property is returned.[27] The delegate of the Netherlands helped to clarify this point. In his view, paragraph 4 would work against the occupying Power (B) as long as there was no exportation of cultural property coming from the territory of B. If, however, such property was exported to a third country (C), then, in the opinion of the delegate of Italy, C would also be obliged to pay an indemnity, whereas, according to the delegate of the Netherlands, only B would be answerable. It could be that the country C had merely done its duty by safeguarding the property in question and, consequently, should not be obliged to pay an indemnity.[28]

The delegate of Switzerland considered the reference to bona-fide holders to be too restricted: 'The injured person or body might well, in some cases, be in a third country. The property might fall into the hands of a bona-fide or mala-fide holder who might resell it. There was also the case of a buyer of an object of cultural property who concluded the sale, paid in advance but did not yet possess the object. On the object's arrival, the State applied paragraph 2, and took it into custody. The buyer could never benefit from the provisions of paragraph 4, as he was not holder and had never received the object.'[29] The delegate proposed that paragraph 4 should be supplemented.

The draft prepared by the Legal Committee (CBC/DR/157) contained the following additional provision: '4. If a State whose territory was previously occupied is not a Party to the present Protocol, the return of the property shall only take place, if that State undertakes to fulfil the obligation mentioned in paragraph 6.'[30] According to this paragraph 4, 'any occupied State could, even if not a Party to the Protocol, have its cultural property that had been exported, returned. But paragraph 6 obliged only the High Contracting Parties to reimburse an amount equivalent to the real value received in the territory previously occupied for the property returned. It could certainly be said that that undertaking was an implied condition for restitution for States that were not Party to the Protocol, but the Legal Committee had been of the opinion that a specific provision on that point would be useful.'[31]

At the Conference's plenary meeting, the delegate of Greece requested that paragraph 6 be deleted, on the grounds that an occupied country, sometimes perhaps ruined, could not be asked to bear the costs of indemnification. These ought to be borne by the occupying Power which had violated the provisions of paragraph 5 of the draft. In his view, it would be preferable for problems of this type to be settled by peace treaties or national law.[32] Paragraph 6 (originally proposed by Belgium and the Netherlands) was deleted by 12 votes to five with 22 abstentions. Accordingly, paragraph 4 of the draft was also removed.

Thus paragraph 4 of the final text of the Protocol imposed the obligation to pay an indemnity only on the occupying Contracting Party and not on the Parties into whose territory the property was imported or on the authorities of the territory previously occupied.

The paragraph does not stipulate the form which indemnification should take. This question, a matter of private law, is for the Parties or the national courts to decide.

Paragraph 5

Cultural property coming from the territory of a High Contracting Party and deposited by it in the territory of another High Contracting Party for the purpose of protecting such property against the dangers of an armed conflict shall be returned by the latter, at the end of hostilities, to the competent authorities of the territory from which it came.

This paragraph originated in the Polish proposal submitted to the Main Commission;[33] it features in the Legal Committee document CBC/DR/157.

The provision applies when cultural property has been transported abroad without benefiting from the provisions of Articles 12 and 13 of the Convention which, as we have seen, afford special protection to property transported abroad. It is a question of property deposited by a High Contracting Party in the territory of another Party as a precautionary measure, before an armed conflict breaks out.

Paragraphs 6 to 8

NB: See, *mutatis mutandis*, the commentary on the provisions of the Convention.[34]

Paragraph 9

According to this provision, the States referred to in paragraphs 6 and 8 of the Protocol may declare, at the time of signature, ratification or accession, that they will not be bound by the provisions of Section I or by those of Section II of the present Protocol. This paragraph derives from an oral proposal made by the delegate of the Netherlands during the meeting of the Main Commission of the Conference on 11 May 1954.[35] The discussion turned upon the question of reservations in international conventions. The proposal of the delegate of the Netherlands was adopted by 21 votes to ten with two abstentions.

At the Conference's plenary meeting, the Socialist countries vigorously opposed the separation of the two sections, but the paragraph was adopted by 19 votes to two with 12 abstentions.

The Protocol was signed as a separate document on 14 May 1954 by 22 States. Ten States attending the Conference, and which signed the Convention, refused to sign the Protocol: Andorra, Australia, Hungary, Ireland, Israel, New Zealand, Portugal, Romania, the United Kingdom and the United States of America.

Paragraphs 10 to 15

NB: See, *mutatis mutandis*, the commentary on the provisions of the Convention.[36]

Practical Application

At the meeting of the High Contracting Parties in 1962, the delegate of Poland suggested that the Protocol should be incorporated in the Convention in the form of a chapter on the restitution of property and, if necessary, on reparations.[37]

The request for a report on the implementation of the Convention, issued to States by the Director-General of UNESCO in 1982, included, for the first time, among the particulars requested, details of the measures adopted by States in connection with the importation and exportation of cultural property. Only a few reports provide information on this point, particularly concerning legislative measures.[38] In general, the information supplied is inadequate.

P.J. Boylan, in his report on the Hague Convention, comes to the same conclusion on the practical non-existence of examples 'of States Parties to the Protocol taking action of any kind in order to bring its provisions into practical effect to "freeze" trade in, or any kind of transfer or movement of, cultural property from areas affected by either international or internal armed conflicts. On the contrary, regularly over the past few decades the showrooms of dealers and auction salerooms in the major art "importing" nations appear to be full of materials that should raise grave suspicions that they originated in countries and regions of the world afflicted by international and civil wars. The almost universal disregard by actual or potential "importing" countries of the principles of the 1954 Hague Protocol is one of the most serious breaches of the fundamental principles and objectives of the 1954 Convention, and all High Contracting Parties should be asked to review their policy and practice in this respect. In particular, as a very minimum, all States Parties to the Protocol ought to impose an almost automatic embargo on all imports of cultural property from, or reasonably suspected to be from, countries and regions in which there is armed conflict.'[39]

During the 1990 Gulf conflict, UNESCO took steps for the application of the 1954 Hague Protocol. The Kuwaiti authorities had complained to UNESCO that Iraqi officials had transferred from Kuwaiti museums to Baghdad a number of items – such as terracotta figurines, pottery, bronzes, ceramics, seals, jewels, rare books, manuscripts and jewels – from pre-history and Islamic and Arabic periods.[40] UNESCO insisted again and again that Iraq should apply not only the Convention but also the Protocol. Both States were Parties to the Convention and to the Protocol. Kuwait acceded to the Convention on 6 June 1969 and to the Protocol on 11 February 1970. Iraq ratified the Convention and Protocol on 21 December 1967.

In their reply, the Iraqi authorities stated that they had placed all these objects, together with the contents of the other Iraqi museums, in safe keeping away from the dangers of the war. They mentioned that these measures were taken in order to protect the totality of the cultural heritage of Iraq, 'including that of its Province of Kuwait, and the contents of its museums. They added that in taking these measures they were in fact applying precisely the text and spirit of the Convention. The matter was the subject of a resolution of the United Nations Security Council (Resolution S/RES/686 – 1991) by which it requested Iraq to return to Kuwait items exported from that country, including cultural items. Thousands of objects were returned under the supervision of the United Nations between 14 September and 20 October 1991.[41]

This example illustrates the manner in which the United Nations Security Council can assist in the implementation of the principles of the Hague Protocol.

NOTES

1   CBC/3, *Records*, p.319.
2   Ibid.
3   Emmanuelle Stavraki, *La Convention pour la protection des biens culturels en cas de conflict armé: une Convention du droit international humanitaire*, pp.366–7. See also Karl von Becker, 'On the obligation of subjects of international return of cultural property to its permanent place', *Annuaire de l'Association des anciens de l'Académie* (The Hague), 1974; S.E. Nahlik, 'The case of the Polish collections in Canada. Legal considerations', *Polish Yearbook of International Affairs*, (Warsaw), 1959–60, pp.172–90; J.G. Castel, *Polish Art Treasures in Canada 1940–1960: a Case History*, paper delivered at the 68th annual meeting of the American Society of International Law, Washington DC, 25–27 April 1974.
4   *Records*, p.320.
5   Ibid., p.324.
6   Ibid., p.350.
7   Ibid., p.331.
8   Ibid., p.342.
9   Ibid., p.351.
10 Ibid., p.357.
11 CBC/DR/7, *Records*, pp.410–11.
12 *Records*, para. 152, p.123.
13 Ibid., para. 114, p.111.
14 Ibid., para. 127, p.113.
15 Ibid., paras 1645–90, pp.258–60.
16 Ibid., pp.260–61.
17 Ibid., paras 1750–56, pp.266–7.
18 When it came to a vote, it was a question of choosing between the wording 'to the competent authority of the territory from which it came' and 'to the High Contracting Party which deposited such property'. In fact, the choice fell on the first version (*Records*, paras 2124–6, p.290).
19 Ibid., para. 1641, p.257.
20 Ibid., para. 1637, p.256.
21 '*Rosenberg* v. *Fischer*, Switzerland (Chamber of the Restitution of Assets Seized in Occupied Territories), 3 June 1948', *International Law Reports*, Vol. 13, 1948, pp.467, *et seq*. The Court also mentioned the fact that the seizure had not been dictated by military necessity.
22 Imprescriptibility with respect to the return of cultural property can also be deduced from historical examples. See S.E. Nahlik, 'La protection internationale des biens culturels en cas de conflit armé', *Recueil des cours de l'Académie de droit international* (The Hague), Vol. 120, II, 1967, p.147.
23 Letter CL/1522 of 30 October 1961.
24 Letters CL/1606 of 27 November 1962 and CL/2351, Add. of 14 August 1974.
25 Letter LA/Depositary/1979/23 of 6 December 1979.
26 S.E. Nahlik, 'La protection internationale des biens culturels en cas de conflit armé', p.157.
27 *Records*, para. 1630, p.255.

28   Ibid., para. 1637, p.256.

29   Ibid., para. 1642, p.257.

30   '6. The government of the territory previously occupied shall reimburse, to the High Contracting Party mentioned in paragraph 5 [para. 5 of the draft is identical to the present para. 4 of the Protocol], which has indemnified the holder in good faith, an amount equivalent to the real value received in the territory previously occupied in exchange for an exported cultural property.'

31   *Records*, para. 1826, p.272.

32   Ibid., para. 204, p.289.

33   Ibid., paras 1644, 1663–70, pp.257, 259.

34   Articles 30 to 32 of the Convention, pp.329–35. For the present status of the ratifications of and accessions to The Hague Protocol, see Annex VI.

35   *Records*, para. 1828, p.272.

36   Articles 33, 34, 35, 37, 38, 39 and 40 of the Convention, pp.336–43 and 347–57.

37   S.E. Nahlik, 'La protection internationale des biens culturels en cas de conflit armé', *Recueil des cours de l'Académie de droit international*, p.142.

38   The following countries replied to the question concerning the Protocol: Czechoslovakia, Iran, Jordan, Kuwait, Liechtenstein, Nigeria, Pakistan, San Marino and USSR.

39   P.J. Boylan, *Review of the Convention for the Protection of Cultural Property in the Event of Armed Conflict* (The Hague Convention of 1954), Paris, UNESCO, 1993, para. 10.9, p.101.

40   UNESCOPRESSE, No. 91–106.

41   E. Clément 'Some Recent Practical Experience in the Implementation of the 1954 Hague Convention', *International Journal of Cultural Property* (Berlin, New York), Vol. 3, No. 1, 1994, pp.16–17.

PART IV
RESOLUTIONS
ADOPTED BY THE 1954
HAGUE CONFERENCE

Even though the resolutions adopted by the 1954 Hague Conference are not mandatory, they are a useful demonstration of the spirit in which the authors adopted the Convention and the Protocol. We have drawn attention to them in the course of our discussion of the various articles of the Convention and the Protocol.

RESOLUTION I

The Conference expresses the hope that the competent organs of the United Nations should decide, in the event of military action being taken in implementation of the Charter, to ensure application of the provisions of the Convention by the armed forces taking part in such action.

Records: Text: p.78.
               Minutes: paras 2149–59.
               Working documents: p.414;
               CBC/DR/152/162.

RESOLUTION II

The Conference expresses the hope that each of the High Contracting Parties, on acceding to the Convention, should set up, within the framework of its constitutional and administrative system, a national advisory committee consisting of a small number of distinguished persons: for example, senior officials of archaeological services, museums, etc., a representative of the military general staff, a representative of the Ministry of Foreign Affairs, a specialist in international law and two or three other members whose official duties or specialized knowledge are related to the fields covered by the Convention.

The Committee should be under the authority of the Minister of State or senior official responsible for the national service chiefly concerned with the care of cultural property. Its chief functions would be:

(a)   to advise the government concerning the measures required for the implementation of the Convention in its legislative, technical or military aspects, both in time of peace and during an armed conflict;

(b)   to approach its government in the event of an armed conflict or when such a conflict appears imminent, with a view to ensuring that cultural property situated within its own territory or within that of other

355

countries is known to, and respected and protected by the armed forces of the country, in accordance with the provisions of the Convention;

(c) *to arrange, in agreement with its government, for liaison and co-operation with other similar national committees and with any competent international authority.*

Records: Text: p.78.
Minutes: paras 2160–63, 2169–72.
Working documents: pp.4141–15;
CBC/DR/40/163.

RESOLUTION III

The Conference expresses the hope that the Director-General of the United Nations Educational, Scientific and Cultural Organization should convene, as soon as possible after the entry into force of the Convention for the Protection of Cultural Property in the Event of Armed Conflict, a meeting of the High Contracting Parties.

Records: Text: p.80.
Minutes: paras 2165, 2166.
Working documents: p.415;
CBC/DR/151.

PART V
THE PROTECTION OF CULTURAL PROPERTY IN TIME OF ARMED CONFLICT AND THE CONVENTION ON THE MEANS OF PROHIBITING AND PREVENTING THE ILLICIT IMPORT, EXPORT AND TRANSFER OF OWNERSHIP OF CULTURAL PROPERTY (PARIS, 14 NOVEMBER 1970)

The 1970 Convention on the means of prohibiting and preventing the illicit import, export and transfer of ownership of cultural property (referred to hereinafter as the 1970 Convention) was a decisive step in the international campaign against the illicit traffic in cultural property. Even though the idea of such a convention had long been entertained, it was not until the 1960s that a start was made on drafting the text.[1] The Convention aims to protect movable cultural property, without distinction between time of peace and time of war. It also contains a provision concerning the occupation of a country by a foreign power. A few remarks on this question will be found at the end of this part of the commentary.

The 1970 Convention[2] is a multilateral agreement which is indirectly applied. Its implementation depends on the High Contracting Parties, which must adopt legislation enabling it to be introduced at national level. The title of the Convention gives the impression of a broad measure, but its field of application is in fact quite limited, as illustrated by the provisions of Article 7(b)(i).

No reference was made in this Convention to the Hague Protocol of 1954.

DEFINITION OF CULTURAL PROPERTY

The definition of 'cultural property' is accordingly very different from that given by the 1954 Convention and Protocol. Regret has been expressed that the 1970 Convention should have chosen another (clumsier) definition of cultural property, different from that given in Article 1 of the 1954 Hague Convention[3] and also applicable to the 1954 Protocol.

The definition given in Article 1 of the 1970 Convention consists of a general description and a list of the property to be protected. According to this article, 'for the purposes of this Convention, the term "cultural property" means property which, on religious or secular grounds, is specifically designated by each State as being of importance for archaeology, prehistory, history, literature, art or science and which belongs to the following categories'. The categories listed include the following movable objects:

1   rare collections and specimens of fauna, flora, minerals and anatomy;
2   property relating to history;

3   products of archaeological excavations;
4   elements of historical monuments or archaeological sites which have been dismembered;
5   antiquities more than 100 years old;
6   objects of ethnological interest;
7   property of artistic interest;
8   rare manuscripts and incunabula, old books, documents and publications;
9   postage, revenue and similar stamps, singly or in collections;
10   archives;
11   articles of furniture more than 100 years old and old musical instruments.

The main difference when compared with the Convention and Protocol of 1954 is that the 1954 instruments give a single definition, whereas the 1970 Convention allows each State to adopt its own definition of what it considers to be of importance for archaeology, prehistory, history, literature, art or science, while at the same time restricting its choice to the listed categories of movable property.

PRACTICES REGARDED AS ILLICIT UNDER THE CONVENTION

As we have seen, the aim of the 1954 Hague Protocol was to 'prevent the exportation [of cultural property] from an occupied territory'. Under this Protocol, each of the High Contracting Parties is asked to prevent this type of exportation from territory occupied by it during an armed conflict. The Contracting Parties must take imported cultural property into their custody, return it, at the close of hostilities, to the competent authorities of the territory previously occupied and pay an indemnity to the holders in good faith.

The 1970 Convention defines illicit practices in Articles 3 and 11.

The Illegality of Import, Export and Transfer of Ownership (Article 3)

Without drawing any distinction between time of peace and time of war, Article 3 of the 1970 Convention introduces a prohibition by declaring that 'the import, export or transfer of ownership of cultural property, effected contrary to the provisions adopted under this Convention by the States Parties thereto, shall be illicit'. Thus the notion of illicitness is defined in relation to national law and only transfers effected contrary to the regulations adopted by each State Party can be termed illicit at the international level. Accordingly, the application of the Convention, the decision concerning the scope of the prohibitions and hence the success or failure of the Convention are determined by the national legislation of the States Parties.

The Illegality of Export and Transfer of Ownership Under Compulsion Arising from Occupation (Article 11)

A special provision concerning occupation was included in the Convention. Even though the Convention is not restricted to occupation in time of war, Article 11 is particularly relevant in periods of armed conflict. According to Article 11, 'the export and transfer of ownership of cultural property under compulsion arising directly or indirectly from the occupation of a country by a foreign power shall be regarded as illicit'.

Whereas Article 3 defines illicitness in relation to national legislation, by indicating that the acts in question are contrary to the provisions adopted under the Convention by the States Parties thereto, Article 11 defines the illicitness arising from occupation without linking it with or referring to national law.

Article 11 of the 1970 Convention supplements Articles 1 to 4 of the 1954 Hague Protocol. It reinforces the undertaking of the High Contracting Parties to 'prevent the exportation [of cultural property] from an occupied territory' as far as the movable property defined in Article 1 of the 1970 Convention is concerned. The prohibition on export does not concern just the territories occupied by the occupying power, but is addressed to all the States Parties to the 1970 Convention: Article 1 of the 1954 Protocol is intended to prevent 'the exportation [of cultural property] from a territory occupied by it'. Article 11 treats as illicit 'the export and transfer of ownership of cultural property under compulsion arising directly or indirectly from the occupation of a country by a foreign power'. Export and transfer are thus regarded as illicit not only with respect to the occupying power but also with respect to all powers Parties to the Convention.

Contrary to Article 1 of the 1954 Protocol, Article 11 of the present Convention concerns not just the export but any transfer of ownership of cultural property under compulsion.

In Article 1 of the 1954 Protocol, the prohibition is restricted to periods of armed conflict. The occupation referred to in Article 11 may take place even outside the context of an armed conflict. The term 'occupied country' must be understood to mean the permanent control of a given territory by armed forces.[4]

Export and transfer of ownership are deemed to be under compulsion when effected against the will of the lawful owner. In recognizing the illicitness of these operations, the 1970 Convention thereby declares any such transfers null and void and thus makes possible the recovery of the property when the occupation is over.[5]

OBJECTIVE AND *RAISON D'ETRE* OF THE CONVENTION

The 1954 Hague Protocol does not mention its aims or the underlying reasons for its adoption and existence. The 1970 Convention is clearer on this point, recognizing that the illicit import, export and transfer of ownership of cultural property 'is one of the main causes of the impoverishment of the cultural heritage of the countries of origin' (Article 2, para. 1).[6]

The Convention notes that international cooperation constitutes one of the most efficient means of protecting each country's cultural property against all the dangers resulting from such activities. States Parties undertake to oppose such practices with the means at their disposal and particularly by removing their causes, putting a stop to current practices, and helping to make the necessary reparations (Article 2, paras 1 and 2), that is, to combat the illicit traffic. The measures to be taken are merely cited as examples. The undertaking with respect to 'reparations' does not signify the restitution of the property, but States Parties are nevertheless bound to lend each other assistance in order to ensure the return of property illicitly exported.

PROTECTIVE MEASURES

The Convention contains numerous protective measures relating to the import, export and transfer of ownership of cultural property effected contrary to the provisions adopted under the Convention by the States Parties thereto. In particular, these measures must be implemented by the laws and regulations of the States Parties to the Convention. They particularly concern the illicit acts mentioned in Article 3.

Protection Against Illicit Import, Export and Transfer of Ownership (Article 3)

National Protection Service (Article 5)

The States Parties to the Convention undertake to set up one or more national services for the protection of the cultural heritage with a qualified and sufficiently numerous staff. This service is to carry out the following functions:

1   contributing to the formation of draft laws and regulations;
2   establishing and keeping up to date a list of important public and private cultural property whose export would constitute an appreciable impoverishment of the national cultural heritage;
3   promoting the development of institutions required to ensure the preservation and presentation of cultural property;
4   organizing the supervision of archaeological excavations;
5   establishing ethical principles for the acquisition of cultural property;
6   taking educational measures;
7   seeing that appropriate publicity is given to the disappearance of any items of cultural property.

Export Controls

All the States Parties must adopt a control system by introducing an export certificate, prohibiting the exportation of cultural property unless accompanied by such a certificate, and publicizing this prohibition (Article 6).

Import Controls

It is not enough to take measures to control exportation. These measures must be accompanied by effective import controls, as provided for in Article 7. According to this provision, the States Parties undertake to take the following measures:

1   to prevent museums and similar institutions within their territories from acquiring cultural property which has been illegally exported;
2   whenever possible, to inform the State of origin of an offer of such cultural property illegally removed;
3   to prohibit the import of cultural property stolen from a museum or a religious or secular public monument or similar institution; this prohibition is restricted to stolen property and thus is narrower in scope than the prohibition on exportation under Article 6;
4   at the request of the State of origin (Party to the Convention), to take appropriate steps to recover and return any cultural property thus stolen and imported. Thus only the State of origin can make this request, through diplomatic offices. The requesting State must bear the expenses. Each State Party is to establish the

procedure for returning property. The term 'restitution' is used where the cultural property has been removed from the territory of a State without its consent and in violation of its laws concerning the exportation of cultural property. The term relates only to cultural property that has been the subject of illicit trafficking.[7]

Penalties

The Contracting Parties undertake to impose penalties for infringement of the export and import prohibitions referred to under Articles 6(b) and 7(b).

Protection Under Article 11

The prohibition in Article 11 is a direct measure which the States Parties to the Convention must respect. However, the 1970 Convention does not contain any provision concerning the implementation of the prohibition in Article 11. It seems to us, therefore, that the measures of protection against illicit import, export and transfer of ownership (Articles 5 to 7) should be applied *mutatis mutandis* to this prohibition.

For States Parties to the 1954 Protocol and for the situations mentioned in Article 1, the Protocol provides for precise and specific measures, without waiting for national legislation to be adopted:

1   the taking of property into custody (Article 2);
2   the return of property at the close of hostilities and the forbidding of its retention as war reparations;
3   the obligation to pay an indemnity to the holders in good faith of cultural property which has to be returned in accordance with Article 3 of the Protocol (Article 4).

It should also be noted that Member States of UNESCO, whether or not Parties to the 1954 Convention and Protocol, may request the good offices of the Intergovernmental Committee for Promoting the Return of Cultural Property. This Committee for promoting the return of cultural property to its countries of origin or its restitution in case of illicit appropriation was set up in 1978 by the UNESCO General Conference.[8]

The 1970 Convention also proposed particular measures concerning the pillage of archaeological or ethnological materials (Article 9) and educational measures (Article 10).

It may be concluded that the main purpose of these measures is the application of the prohibitions in Article 3. According to that article, the Convention depends directly on the national legislative measures adopted, and this holds true not only for the definition of illegality but also for the implementation of the Convention.

NOTES

1 We have already drawn attention to UNESCO's interest in the protection of movable property in time of peace, in particular archaeological excavations. See the Recommendation on International Principles Applicable to Archaeological Excavations, adopted by the UNESCO General Conference (New Delhi) on 5 December 1956, and particularly paragraph 32 concerning excavations in occupied territory. See also p. 76.

2 For the text of the Convention (see Annex VII), *UNESCO's Standard-Setting Instruments*, Paris, UNESCO, 1980, I.A.4; *UNESCO Conventions and Recommendations Concerning the Protection of the Cultural Heritage*, Paris, UNESCO, 1983, pp.57–73. On 30 April 1994, 81 States were Parties to the Convention, which entered into force on 24 April 1972. For further details, see, in particular: P.J. Boylan, *Review of the Convention for the Protection of Cultural Property in the Event of Armed Conflict*, (The Hague Convention of 1954), Paris, UNESCO, 1993, paras 10.1–10.10, pp.99–101; Ridha Fraoua, *Convention conçernant les mesures à prendre pour interdire et empêcher l'importation, l'exportation et le transfert de propriété illicites des biens culturels* (Paris, 1970); idem., *Commentaire et aperçu de quelques mesures nationales d'exécution*, Paris, UNESCO, 1986 (CC-86/WS/40), 123 pp.; Lyndel V. Prott, 'The 1970 UNESCO Convention on illicit traffic – present practice and future development', Istituto internazionale di diritto umanitario, *La protezione internazionale dei beni culturali/The international protection of cultural property/La protection internationale des biens culturels*, pp.121–38; Sharon A. Williams, 'Recent developments in restitution and return of cultural property', ibid., pp.139–58, and *International Journal of Museum Management and Curatorship* (Guildford, Surrey), No. 3, 1984, pp.117–19; Lyndel V. Prott and P.J. O'Keefe, *National Legal Control of Illicit Traffic in Cultural Property*, Paris, UNESCO, 1983, 144pp.

3 Stanislaw E. Nahlik, 'Convention for the protection of cultural property in the event of armed conflict, The Hague 1954: general and special protection', in Istituto internazionale di diritto umanitario, *La protezione internazionale dei beni culturali/The international protection of cultural property/La protection internationale des biens culturels*, p.88.

4 Ridha Fraoua, *Commentaire et aperçu...*, p.85.

5 Ibid.

6 Article 4 lists the categories of property which form part of the cultural heritage of a State, but covers only the movable cultural property defined in Article 1 of the Convention. It is silent on the legal status of this property (public or private). It only mentions the relationship between certain property and the cultural heritage, a relationship which may take the form of a bond which is national (property created by nationals), territorial (property created within the territory of the State by foreign nationals resident within the territory, property found within the national territory) or contractual (property acquired, exchanged, received or purchased with the consent of the country of origin).

7 This term must be distinguished from the term 'return', which is applied in connection with cultural property removed from the territory of origin during colonization.

8 Emmanuelle Stavraki, 'L'UNESCO et le Comité intergouvernemental pour la

promotion du retour des biens culturels à leur pays d'origine ou de leur restitution en cas d'appropriation illégale, Thesis for a doctorate in law, mimeo, Paris, University of Paris I – Pantheon-Sorbonne, 1987–88, p.28.

PART VI
THE PROTECTION OF CULTURAL PROPERTY IN TIME OF ARMED CONFLICT AND THE CONVENTION FOR THE PROTECTION OF THE WORLD CULTURAL AND NATURAL HERITAGE (PARIS, 16 NOVEMBER 1972)

The Convention for the Protection of the World Cultural and Natural Heritage (or 1972 Convention) was adopted by the UNESCO General Conference at its seventeenth session in Paris on 16 November 1972.[1]

Even though the Convention is not specifically aimed at the protection of the cultural heritage in wartime, that question is included. In the preamble to the Convention, the UNESCO General Conference notes 'that the cultural heritage and the natural heritage are increasingly threatened with destruction not only by the traditional causes of decay [which, in our opinion, must also include international and non-international armed conflicts] but also by changing social and economic conditions which aggravate the situation with even more formidable phenomena of damage or destruction'.

According to the text of the preamble, it is incumbent on the international community as a whole to participate in the protection of the cultural and natural heritage of outstanding universal value. Thus the 1972 Convention strengthens the protection of certain cultural property 'of outstanding universal value'. The definition of the property protected by the Convention is narrower than that given in the 1954 Hague Convention, since only immovable property is protected.[2]

According to Article 3 of the 1972 Convention, it is for each State Party to identify and delineate the different properties situated on its territory covered by the definition of the cultural and natural heritage; that is, to determine eligibility for the special and particular protection described in Article 11, namely inclusion in the World Heritage List established by the Intergovernmental Committee on the basis of the inventories submitted by States. The Convention also emphasizes that 'the duty of ensuring the identification, protection, conservation, presentation and transmission to future generations of the cultural and natural heritage referred to in Articles 1 and 2 and situated on its territory' belongs primarily to each State Party to the Convention.

As far as armed conflict is concerned, there are two provisions of special interest. Firstly, according to Article 6, paragraph 3, 'Each State Party to this Convention undertakes not to take any deliberate measures which might damage directly or indirectly the cultural and natural heritage referred to in Articles 1 and 2 situated on the territory of other States Parties to this Convention'. Secondly, in accordance with Article 11, paragraph 4, the Intergovernmental Committee for the Protection of the World Cultural and Natural Heritage (called the World Heritage Committee) 'shall establish, keep up to date and publish, whenever circumstances shall so require, under the title of

"List of World Heritage in Danger", a list of the property appearing in the World Heritage List for the conservation of which major operations are necessary and for which assistance has been requested under this Convention. This list shall contain an estimate of the cost of such operations. The list may include only such property forming part of the cultural and natural heritage as is threatened by serious and specific dangers, such as the threat of disappearance caused by accelerated deterioration, large-scale public or private projects or rapid urban or tourist development projects; destruction caused by changes in the use or ownership of the land; major alterations due to unknown causes; abandonment for any reason whatsoever; the outbreak or the threat of an armed conflict; calamities and cataclysms; serious fires, earthquakes, landslides; volcanic eruptions; changes in water level, floods, and tidal waves. The Committee may at any time, in case of urgent need, make a new entry in the List of World Heritage in Danger and publicize such entry immediately.'

This provision was further developed in the *Operational Guidelines for the Implementation of the World Heritage Convention*, prepared by the International Council on Monuments and Sites (ICOMOS) and the International Union for the Conservation of Nature and Natural Resources (IUCN); drawn up in 1982 and last revised in February 1994 (WHC/2, Revised), it makes clear that the inclusion of a property in the List of World Heritage in Danger is an exceptional initiative and a temporary emergency measure. The Operational Guidelines include in Part II the following provisions relating to the establishment of the List of World Heritage in Danger.

A   GUIDELINES FOR THE INCLUSION OF PROPERTIES IN THE LIST OF WORLD HERITAGE IN DANGER

In accordance with Article 11, paragraph 4, of the Convention, the Committee may include a property in the List of World Heritage in Danger when the following requirements are met:

1   the property under consideration is on the World Heritage List;
2   the property is threatened by serious and specific danger;
3   major operations are necessary for the conservation of the property;
4   assistance under the Convention has been requested for the property; the Committee is of the view that its assistance in certain cases may most effectively be limited to messages of its concern, including the message sent by inclusion of a site on the List of World Heritage in Danger and that such assistance may be requested by any committee member or the Secretariat.

B   CRITERIA FOR THE INCLUSION OF PROPERTIES IN THE LIST OF WORLD HERITAGE IN DANGER

A World Heritage property – as defined in Articles 1 and 2 of the Convention – can be entered on the List of World Heritage in Danger by the Committee when it finds that the condition of the property corresponds to at least one of the criteria in either of the two cases described below.

Cultural Properties

1   *Ascertained danger*: the property is faced by specific and proven imminent danger, such as:
   (a)   serious deterioration of materials;
   (b)   serious deterioration of structure and/or ornamental features;
   (c)   serious deterioration of architectural or town-planning coherence;
   (d)   serious deterioration of urban or rural space, or the natural environment;
   (e)   significant loss of historical authenticity;
   (f)   important loss of cultural significance.
2   *Potential danger*: the property is faced by threats which could have deleterious effects on its inherent characteristics. Such threats are, for example:
   (a)   modification of juridical status of the property diminishing the degree of its protection;
   (b)   lack of conservation policy;
   (c)   threatening effects of regional planning projects;
   (d)   threatening effects of town planning;
   (e)   outbreak or threat of armed conflict;
   (f)   gradual changes due to geological, climatic or other environmental factors.

Natural properties

1   *Ascertained danger*: the property is faced with specific and proven imminent danger, such as:
   (a)   a serious decline in the population of the endangered species or the other species of outstanding universal value which the property was legally established to protect, either by natural factors such as disease or by man-made factors such as poaching;

(b) severe deterioration of the natural beauty or scientific value of the property, as by human settlement, construction of reservoirs which flood important parts of the property, industrial and agricultural development including use of pesticides and fertilizers, major public works, mining, pollution, logging, firewood collection, and so on;

(c) human encroachment on boundaries or in upstream areas which threaten the integrity of the property.

2 *Potential danger*: the property is faced with major threats which could have deleterious effects on its inherent characteristics. Such threats are, for example:

(a) a modification of the legal protective status of the area;

(b) planned resettlement or development projects within the property or so situated that the impacts threaten the property;

(c) outbreak or threat of armed conflict;

(d) the management plan is lacking or inadequate, or not fully implemented.

In addition, the factor or factors which are threatening the integrity of the property must be those which are amenable to correction by human action. In the case of cultural properties, both natural factors and man-made factors may be threatening, while in the case of natural properties, most threats will be man-made and only very rarely will a natural factor (such as an epidemic disease) be threatening to the integrity of the property. In some cases, the factors threatening the integrity of a property may be corrected by administrative or legislative action, such as the cancelling of a major public works project or the improvement of legal status.

The Committee may wish to bear in mind the following supplementary factors when considering the inclusion of a cultural or natural property in the List of World Heritage in Danger.

(a) Decisions which affect World Heritage properties are taken by governments after balancing all factors. The advice of the World Heritage Committee can often be decisive if it can be given *before* the property becomes threatened.

(b) Particularly in the case of *ascertained danger*, the physical or cultural deteriorations to which a property has been subjected should be judged according to the *intensity* of its effects and analysed case by case.

(c) Above all in the case of *potential danger* to a property, one should consider that:

   – the threat should be appraised according to the normal evolution of the social and economic framework in which the property is situated;

- it is often impossible to assess certain threats – such as the threat of armed conflict – as to their effect on cultural or natural properties;
- some threats, such as demographic growth, are not imminent in nature, but can only be anticipated.

(d) Finally, in its appraisal the Committee should take into account *any cause of unknown or unexpected origin* which endangers a cultural or natural property.

The report also examined procedural questions. In particular, we note that, when drawing up a programme for corrective measures, the Committee may ask the Secretariat to ascertain, in cooperation with the State Party concerned, the present condition of the property, the dangers to which it is exposed and the feasibility of undertaking corrective measures. The Committee may further decide to send a team of qualified observers from the International Union for Conservation of Nature and Natural Resources (now the World Conservation Union) (IUCN), the International Council on Monuments and Sites (ICOMOS), and the International Centre for the Study of the Preservation and Restoration of Cultural Property (ICCROM) in Rome or other organizations to visit the property, evaluate the nature and extent of the threats and propose the measures to be taken.

USE OF THE WORLD HERITAGE EMBLEM AND THE NAME, SYMBOL OR DEPICTION OF WORLD HERITAGE SITES

At its second session, the Committee adopted the World Heritage emblem which had been designed by Mr Michel Olyff. This emblem symbolizes the interdependence of cultural and natural properties: the central square is a form created by man and the circle represents nature, the two being intimately linked. The emblem is round, like the world, but at the same time it is a symbol of protection. The Committee decided that the two versions proposed by the artist could be used, in any colour, depending on the use, the technical possibilities and considerations of an artistic nature. In practice, however, the second version is usually preferred by States Parties and has been used by the Secretariat for promotional activities.

Properties included in the World Heritage List should be marked with the emblem which should, however, be placed in such a way that it does not visually impair the property in question.

States Parties to the Convention should take all possible measures to prevent the use of the emblem of the Convention and the use of the name of the Committee and the Convention in their respective countries by any group or for any purpose not explicitly recognized and approved by the Committee. The World Heritage emblem should, in particular, not be used for any commercial purposes unless specific authorization is obtained from the Committee.

The name, symbol or depiction of a World Heritage site, or of any element thereof, should not be used for commercial purposes unless written authorization has been obtained from the State concerned regarding the principles of using the said name, symbol or depiction, and unless the exact text or display has been approved by that State and, as far as possible, by the national authority specifically concerned with the protection of the site. Any such utilization should be in conformity with the reasons for which the property has been placed on the World Heritage List.

World Heritage emblem (adopted by the World Heritage Committee at its second session)

Finally, it should also be pointed out that the objective of the 1972 Convention is not just to provide protection but also and especially to organize international assistance, under Articles 13 and 15 to 26. In this respect, the Convention goes further than the 1954 Hague Convention.

The question of the desirability of a closer link between the 1954 and 1972 Conventions, with regard to special protection has been raised. S.E. Nahlik suggests that any revision of the 1954 Convention might include an amendment to Article 8 of the Convention so as to accord special protection to property appearing in the World Heritage List.[3]

This issue was also discussed by the Bureau at its seventeenth session (Paris, June 1992) and the new provision was included in the revised text of the Operational Guidelines, adopted at the seventeenth session of the World Heritage Committee in Cartagena, Colombia, 4–11 December 1993.[4] This new text reads as follows.

I Links with Other Conventions and Recommendations

The World Heritage Committee has recognized the collective interest that would be advanced by closer co-ordination of its work with other international conservation instruments. These include the 1949 Geneva Convention, the 1954 Hague Convention, the 1970 UNESCO Convention, the Ramsar Convention and CITES, as well as other regional conventions and future conventions that will pursue conservation objectives, as appropriate. The Committee will invite representatives of the intergovernmental bodies under related conventions to attend its meetings as observers. Similarly, the Secretariat will appoint a representative to observe meetings of the other intergovernmental bodies upon receipt of an invitation. The Secretariat will ensure through the World Heritage Centre appropriate co-ordination and information sharing between the Committee and other conventions, programmes and international organizations related to the conservation of cultural and natural heritage.

This provision is a further step on the way to achieving better protection of the cultural property. Other improvements must follow. In his report to the Cartagena session of the World Heritage Committee on the implementation of the World Heritage Convention, Mr B. von Droste, Director of the UNESCO World Heritage Centre, indicated the need for further revision of the Operational Guidelines in particular to create emergency assistance procedures to provide heritage assistance in cases of armed conflict or natural catastrophes.[5]

The World Heritage Committee continues to give attention to situations of armed conflict. At the Cartagena session in 1993 it vigorously condemned the destruction of the heritage in Bosnia Herzegovina which was in flagrant contradiction with international law, and called for emergency assistance.

NOTES

1 The Convention is registered with the United Nations Secretariat under No. 15.511 (9.03.1977). It entered into force on 17 December 1975. On 30 March 1994, 137 States were bound by the Convention, see Annex III; *UNESCO's Standard-Setting Instruments*, Paris, UNESCO, 1980, IV.A.5; *Conventions and Recommendations of UNESCO Concerning the Protection of the Cultural Heritage*, Paris, UNESCO, 1983, pp.79–98; P.J. Boylan, *Review of the Convention for the Protection of Cultural Property in the Event of Armed Conflict* (The Hague Convention of 1954), Paris, UNESCO, 1993, paras 12.1–12.18, pp.109–13.

2 Article 1 of the 1972 Convention defines 'cultural heritage' as follows:

  – Monuments: architectural works, works of monumental sculpture and painting, elements or structures of an archaeological nature, inscriptions, cave dwellings and combinations of features, which are of outstanding universal value from the point of view of history, art or science.
  – Groups of buildings: groups of separate or connected buildings which, because of their architecture, their homogeneity or their place in the landscape, are of outstanding universal value from the point of view of history, art or science.
  – Sites: works of man or the combined works of nature and man, and areas including archaeological sites which are of outstanding universal value from the historical, aesthetic, ethnological or anthropological points of view.

  See also Operational Guidelines, paras 23 to 42.

3 Stanislaw E. Nahlik, 'Convention for the protection of cultural property in the event of armed conflict, The Hague 1954: General and special protection', in Istituto internazionale di diritto umanitario, *La protezione internazionale dei beni culturali/The international protection of cultural property/La protection internationale des biens culturels*, pp.97–8.

4 UNESCO document: WHC-93/CONF.002/LD.2, p.53.

5 Ibid., Annex IV, p.9.

PART VII
PROTOCOLS ADDITIONAL TO THE GENEVA CONVENTIONS OF 12 AUGUST 1949 AND RELATING TO THE PROTECTION OF VICTIMS OF INTERNATIONAL AND NON-INTERNATIONAL ARMED CONFLICTS, OF 8 JUNE 1977[1]

INTRODUCTION

The Additional Protocols, drawn up by the Conference on the Reaffirmation and Development of International Humanitarian Law, contain two provisions concerning the protection of cultural property, these being Article 53 of Protocol I and Article 16 of Protocol II. The Conference also adopted Resolution 20 urging States not Parties to the Hague Convention of 1954 to become Parties to it. In this resolution, the Conference expressed its satisfaction at the adoption of Articles 53 and 16 of the Protocols and recognized 'that the Convention for the Protection of Cultural Property in the Event of Armed Conflict and its Additional Protocol, signed at The Hague on 14 May 1954, constitute an instrument of paramount importance for the international protection of the cultural heritage of all mankind against the effects of armed conflict and that the application of this Convention will in no way be prejudiced by the adoption of the article [Article 53 of Protocol I] referred to in the preceding paragraph'.

TEXT OF THE PROVISIONS OF ADDITIONAL PROTOCOLS I AND II OF 8 JUNE 1977

Additional Protocol I Relating to the Protection of Victims of International Armed Conflicts

Article 53   Protection of Cultural Objects and Places of Worship

Without prejudice to the provisions of the Hague Convention for the Protection of Cultural Property in the Event of Armed Conflict of 14 May 1954, and of other relevant international instruments, it is prohibited:

(a)   *to commit any acts of hostility directed against the historic monuments, works of art or places of worship which constitute the cultural or spiritual heritage of peoples;*
(b)   *to use such objects in support of the military effort;*
(c)   *to make such objects the object of reprisals.*

Official Records of the Diplomatic Conference on the Reaffirmation and Development of International Humanitarian Law Applicable in Armed Conflicts, Geneva, 1974–77:

OR I: Part 1, p.148; OR III: pp.213–15 (Article 47 bis); OR VI: pp.170–73, CDDH/SR.41, paras 157–81; pp.194–5, idem., Annex (Netherlands); pp.205–8, CDDH/SR.42, paras 2–18; p.225, Annex (Federal Republic of Germany); pp.219–20, idem., Annex (Australia); p.224 (Canada); p.240 (United States); pp.230–1 (Italy); p.234 (Poland); pp.238–9 (United Kingdom); p.227 (Holy See); OR XI: p.118, CDDH/III/SR.15, paras 6 and 8; p.121, para. 22; pp.123–5, paras 31 and 39–40; pp.127–8, CDDH/III/SR.16, para. 5; pp.129–30, paras 10, 15–16 and 19; p.134, para. 32; pp.220–22, CDDH/III/SR.24, paras 19–25 and 28–30; p.223, para. 39; p.400, CDDH/III/SR.37, paras 59–60;

OR XV: p.211, CDDH/III/SR.37, paras 59, paras 10–11; p.216, paras 42–4; p.219, para. 61; p.220, paras 65 and 68–9; pp.277–8, CDDH/215/Rev.1, paras 68–70; p.307, idem., Annex; pp.332–3, CDDH/II/224; pp.394–5, CCDH/236/Rev.1, para. 60; p.437, CDDH/III/353; p.456, CDDH/407/Rev. 1, paras 20–30; p.520, CDDH/III/391.

Bibliography: Bothe, M., K.J. Partsch and Waldemar A. Solf, *New Rules for Victims of Armed Conflicts. Commentary on the two 1977 protocols additional to the Geneva Conventions of 1949*, The Hague, Martinus Nijhoff Publishers, 1982, pp.328–34; Levie, Howard S. (ed.), *Protection of War Victims: Protocol I to the 1949 Geneva Conventions*, Vol. 3, Dobbs Ferry, Oceana Publications, 1980, pp.208–26; Preux, Jean de, 'La Convention de la Haye et le récent développement du droit des conflits armés', in Istituto internazionale di diritto umanitario, *La protezione internazionale dei beni culturali/The international protection of cultural property/La protection internationale des biens culturels*, Rome, Dragan European Foundation, 1986, pp.107–17; Sandoz, Yves, Christophe Swiniarski and Bruno Zimmermann (eds), *Commentary on the Additional Protocols of 8 June 1977 to the Geneva Conventions of 12 August 1949*, Geneva, ICRC, Martinus Nijhoff Publishers, 1987, pp.639–49.

Additional Protocol II Relating to the Protection of Victims of Non-international Armed Conflicts

Article 16: Protection of Cultural Objects and Places of Worship

Without prejudice to the provisions of the Hague Convention for the Protection of Cultural Property in the Event of Armed Conflict of 14 May 1954, it is prohibited to commit any acts of hostility directed against historic monuments, works of art or places of worship which constitute the cultural or spiritual heritage of peoples, and to use them in support of the military effort.

Official Records of the Diplomatic Conference on the Reaffirmation and Development of International Humanitarian Law Applicable in Armed Conflicts, Geneva, 1974–77:

OR I: Part 1, p.196; OR III: p.213, CDDH/III/17; OR IV: pp.65–6 (Article 20 bis); OR II: pp.114–18, CDDH/SR.51, paras 56–93; pp.125–8, CDDH/SR/52, paras 1–25; pp.141–3, CDDH/SR.53, paras 1–12; pp.156–63, idem., Annex (Finland, Holy See, India, Indonesia, Netherlands, United Kingdom). OR XV: p.107, CDDH/III/SR/49, para. 3; pp.110–11, paras 13–17, 19 and 21; p.211, CDDH/III/SR.59, para. 11; p.220, paras 65 and 68–9; pp.394–5, CDDH/236/Rev.1, paras 60–63; p.437, CDDH/III/353; p.456, CDDH/407/Rev.1, para. 30; p.466, para. 68; p.501, idem., Annex II; p.520, CDDH/III/391.

Bibliography: Bothe, M., K.J. Partsch and A. Waldemar Solf, *New Rules for Victims of Armed Conflicts. Commentary on the two 1977 protocols additional to the Geneva Conventions of 1949*, pp.685–9; Levie, Howard S. (ed.), *The Law of Non-international Armed Conflict. Protocol II to the 1949 Geneva Conventions*, Dordrecht, Martinus Nijhoff Publishers, 1987, pp.507–26; Preux, Jean de, 'La Convention de La Haye et le récent déeloppement du droit des conflits armés', pp.107–17; Sandoz, Yves, Christophe Swiniarski and Bruno Zimmermann (eds), *Commentary on the Additional Protocols of 8 June 1977 to the Geneva Conventions of 12 August 1949*, pp.1466–70; Smith, Daniel, 'New protections for victims of international armed conflicts: the proposed ratification of Protocol II by the United States', *Military Law Review* (Charlottesille), Vol. 120, Spring 1988, pp.72–5.

COMMENTARY ON AND PRINCIPAL CHARACTERISTICS OF ARTICLE 53 OF PROTOCOL I AND ARTICLE 16 OF PROTOCOL II ON THE PROTECTION OF CULTURAL PROPERTY AND PLACES OF WORSHIP

Preparatory Work

At the first Conference of governmental experts on the reaffirmation and development of international humanitarian law applicable in armed conflicts, held in 1971, the protection of cultural property was mentioned in the proposals (working papers) presented by the experts representing Mexico, the Netherlands, Sweden, Switzerland and the United Arab Republic.[2] The ICRC draft submitted to the second conference of experts in 1972 contained a single general provision concerning respect for civilian property, but no specific provisions relating to cultural property (Article 47). Only in the amendment submitted by the experts of Egypt, Mexico, the Netherlands, Sweden and Switzerland was there a reference to religious, educational or cultural institutions.[3]

Because of this limited interest, but mainly because of the existence of the precise provisions of the Hague Convention, the ICRC did not consider it necessary to include an article on cultural property in the draft Protocols submitted to the Diplomatic Conference of 1974–77.

At the Conference's second session, a proposal, in the form of an amendment, was submitted to Committee III, in the first instance by the delegate of Greece, later joined by the delegates of Spain and Jordan and, in 1975, by those of the Holy See, Uruguay and Venezuela. Article 53 was derived from this proposal, which read as follows: 'It is forbidden to attack historic monuments and to destroy or endanger works of art which constitute the cultural heritage of a country [of mankind or places of worship]. Such objects shall not be made the object of reprisals.'[4]

Although all the delegations quickly agreed to the protection of historic monuments and works of art, the question of places of worship led to lengthy discussions. Some considered that all places of worship should be protected without exception, while others considered that this should apply only to some important places 'which constitute the heritage of peoples'.

Following the discussion of draft Article 16 of Protocol II, Committee III returned to this matter and adopted a second version of the article in which any reference to places of worship has disappeared. The reasons for this were, firstly, that places of worship in general were mentioned in Article 52, paragraph 3, of Protocol I and mentioned as one of several examples of objects normally used for civilian purposes; thus places of worship were presumed to have a civilian character and enjoy the general protection afforded to objects of that sort. Secondly, it was considered that places of worship already benefited from the protection afforded to historic monuments and works of art under the terms of Article 53 of Protocol I.

In the plenary meetings, the Conference considered that it was useful to reintroduce the reference to places of worship in Article 53, specifying that the provision only applied to those which constituted the 'spiritual heritage of peoples'. The article was finally adopted by consensus.[5]

The question of introducing the protection of cultural property and places of worship into Protocol II gave rise to heated controversy, in particular concerning the question whether places of worship should be mentioned and whether there should be an express provision that it was without prejudice to the application of the Hague Convention. The draft was introduced as an amendment by 11 States in 1976.[6]

Two delegations to the Conference, while supporting the principle that cultural objects should be protected, considered that this rule should not be included in a simplified instrument, seeing that many other rules relating to the conduct of hostilities had been eliminated. The delegate of Finland took the view that the inclusion of the article, which contained no general rules on the methods and means of combat, upset the protective and humanitarian balance of the Protocol. Together with the delegate of the United Kingdom, he considered that the main idea behind Protocol II should be to protect people against unnecessary suffering and destruction; anything else would result in the true aims of the Protocol being distorted.[7] The delegate of the Netherlands would have preferred Article 16 to make express mention of the possibility of a waiver.[8] Article 16 of Protocol II was adopted by 35 votes to 15 with 32 abstentions.

In connection with Articles 53 and 16 of the Protocols, we should also mention Resolution 20 adopted by the Geneva Diplomatic Conference of 1974–77. As we have already noted, this resolution recognized that the 1954 Hague Convention and Protocol constituted an instrument of the utmost importance and that the adoption of Article 53 would have no adverse effect of the application of the Convention. It accordingly urged States to become Parties to the Convention.[9]

In its Conclusions, the Symposium organized by the International Institute of Humanitarian Law on the occasion of the thirtieth anniversary of the Hague Convention stressed the need to harmonize the text of other international instruments, and especially Additional Protocols I and II of 1977 to the four Geneva Conventions of 1949, with the 1954 Hague Convention.[10]

General Protection of Civilian Objects

As a preliminary to the analysis of Article 53 of Protocol I, it might be useful to recall the text of Articles 48 and 52 of the Protocol concerning the general protection of civilian objects:

Article 48: Basic Rule

In order to ensure respect for and protection of the civilian population and civilian objects, the Parties to the conflict shall at all times distinguish between the civilian population and combatants and between civilian objects and military objectives and accordingly shall direct their operations only against military objectives.

Article 52: General Protection of Civilian Objects

1. *Civilian objects shall not be the object of attack or of reprisals. Civilian objects are all objects which are not military objectives as defined in paragraph 2.*
2. *Attacks shall be limited strictly to military objectives. In so far as objects are concerned, military objectives are limited to those objects which by their nature, location, purpose or use make an effective contribution to military action and whose total or partial destruction, capture or neutralization, in the circumstances ruling at the time, offers a definite military advantage.*
3. *In case of doubt whether an object which is normally dedicated to civilian purposes, such as a place of worship, a house or other dwelling or a school, is being used to make an effective contribution to military action, it shall be presumed not to be so used.*

Paragraph 1 of Article 52 establishes the general principle of the immunity of civilian objects. These objects must not be the object of attack or of reprisals. Civilian objects are objects which are not military objectives, that is objects 'which by their nature, location, purpose or use make an effective contribution to military action' and 'whose total or partial destruction, capture or neutralization, in the circumstances ruling at the time, offers a definite military advantage'. As soon as these two elements are present, we are dealing with a military objective within the meaning of Protocol I. This definition is broadly based on the previous work mentioned in our commentary on Article 8 of the Convention.

According to paragraph 3, 'in case of doubt whether an object which is normally dedicated to civilian purposes, such as a place of worship, a house or other dwelling or a school, is being used to make an effective contribution to military action, it shall be presumed not to be so used'.

Textual Analysis of Articles 53 and 16 of Additional Protocols I and II

In relation to Article 52, Article 53 constitutes special protection. Thus cultural objects benefit from special protection similar to that afforded to hospitals and medical installations. If they lose this special protection, they remain protected in case of attack if they satisfy the conditions of Article 52. Thus Article 52 grants general protection to cultural objects and places of worship which cannot be described as constituting 'the cultural or spiritual heritage of peoples'.

The two provisions – Article 53 of Protocol I and Article 16 of Protocol II – are almost identical. We will therefore examine them side by side. The two provisions have the following features in common.

Reference to the Hague Convention of 1954 and Other International Instruments

Both texts refer to the 1954 Conventions, the French text of Protocol I using the term 'sans préjucide', that is, 'without prejudice to', that of Protocol II the even stronger expression 'sous réserve', that is, 'subject to' the application of the Hague Convention of 1954. This difference is not found in the English, Spanish and Russian texts, which in both Protocols use the expressions 'without prejudice', 'sin perjuicio' and 'bez ushcherba', respectively. It therefore does not seem that the authors of these provisions actually intended to give them different meanings. The reference to the Hague Convention of 1954 makes it clear that the Protocols have no effect on the application of the Convention.

However, since this distinction is made in the French text, let us attempt to explain it. The expression 'sans préjudice' means that the provision in no way impairs other provisions, in this case those of the Hague Convention, and lies outside their sphere of application. The expression 'sous réserve' goes further. It implies that the application of other provisions, hence those of the Hague Convention, is unaffected by the article in question and that, when these provisions apply and fully protect the cultural property, the article is not applicable. On the other hand, the latter article would be applicable if the protection afforded were not complete. In our opinion, this distinction is justified, particularly as regards the material aspects of protection. In fact, the provisions of the Convention go beyond Article 16 and thus the material sphere of application already embraces all the protection this article can offer, except for places of worship that are not of great historical value. It will also be noted that Article 16 is not the subject of any express waiver. In particular, there is no reservation with respect to military necessity, as is the case with the Hague Convention.

Article 53 refers to 'other relevant international instruments'. These words do not appear in Article 16. Thus the reference in Article 53 concerns, in particular, the Hague Conventions of 1899 and 1907 which, in fact, are not applicable in non-international armed conflicts. On the other hand, it should not be forgotten that the Roerich Pact also applies in time of peace, as do the Conventions of 1970 and 1972, whose importance for the protection of endangered cultural property we have already noted.[11] The delegate of the Federal Republic of Germany explained his vote by saying that he understood that Article 53 was not 'intended to replace the existing customary law prohibitions reflected in Article 27 of the 1907 Hague Regulations respecting the Laws and Customs of War on Land protecting a variety of cultural and religious objects'.[12] The delegates of Canada and the United States expressed similar views.[13]

As Article 16 of Protocol II does not contain a reference to other international instruments, it may be assumed that the authors of this provision had concluded that the Hague Conventions of 1899 and 1907 did not apply to non-international armed conflicts. On the other hand, the Roerich Pact applies in time of peace and in time of war, and we consider that also to be the case where the UNESCO Conventions of 1970 and 1972 are concerned.

Field of Application

As regards Protocol I, Article 53 is certainly to be welcomed since it makes it possible to act in a broader field of application, that is, that of Protocol I. This relates especially to the fact that other conflicts, in particular those mentioned in Article 1, paragraph 4 of Protocol I, are affected by this provision, which thus ensures the protection of cultural objects in most of the international conflicts that exist in the world today.

The situation is different with respect to non-international armed conflicts, where the field of application is reduced in relation to the scope of Article 19 of the Hague Convention. Indeed, the field of application of Article 16 is different from that of Article 19 of the Convention, which was based on Article 3, common to the Geneva Conventions. The field of application of Article 16 is narrower, since Article 1 of this Protocol, introduced into the definition of non-international armed conflict new elements which reduced its scope. According to Article 1, non-international armed conflicts are those 'which are not covered by Article 1 of the Protocol Additional to the Geneva Conventions of 12 August 1949, and relating to the Protection of Victims of International Armed Conflicts (Protocol I) and which take place in the territory of a High Contracting Party between its armed forces and dissident armed forces or other organized armed groups which, under responsible command, exercise such control over a part of its territory as to enable them to carry out sustained and concerted military operations and to implement this Protocol'.

Article 16 of Protocol II includes several elements which had previously been discussed at the 1949 Conference.

Article 1, paragraph 2 of Protocol II excludes from the field of application cases of internal unrest and tension, which thus are governed by the principles of international law applicable in time of peace. These rules concern human rights and also the international conventions for the protection of cultural property intended for time of peace, in particular the Convention for the Protection of the World Cultural and Natural Heritage, adopted by the UNESCO General Conference on 16 November 1972. However, as we have seen, some of these situations would also be covered by Article 19 of the Convention, whose scope is wider than that of Article 16 of Protocol II. These situations would also be covered by UNESCO's general mandate, which we dealt with under Article 23.

Objects of Protection

The property protected by the Hague Convention (Article 1 of the Convention) is broadly defined to include both the historic monuments and the works of art mentioned in Articles 53 and 16. The Protocols introduce only one innovation relative to the Hague Convention of 1954, since they also protect places of worship, not only as part of the cultural heritage but also as part of the spiritual heritage, that is, irrespective of their cultural value. In fact, customary law and the 1954 Convention adopt the criterion of the nature of the objects and their importance for the heritage of peoples. The Protocols opt for the criterion of purpose or use and thus ensure the protection of places of worship on that basis.

In explaining their vote, some delegates stressed that Article 53 provided special protection for a limited group of objects which, because of their acknowledged importance, formed part of humanity's special heritage. For these delegates, 'other monuments, works of art or places of worship which are not so recognized, none the less represent objects normally dedicated for civilian purposes and are therefore presumptively protected as civilian objects in accordance with the provisions of Article 47 [52]'.[14] In relation to Article 52, Article 53 constitutes special protection.

We have mentioned the discussion about introducing places of worship into this provision. In explaining his vote, the United Kingdom delegate said it was clear that this article was not intended to apply to all places of worship without exception.[15] The Holy See, on the other hand, considered that the introduction of notions such as 'spiritual' and 'places of worship' constituted an undeniable step forward in a humanitarian sense in that it showed 'a better understanding of what was most mysterious and most precious in man's heritage; and in that it extended better protection to the material embodiments of that heritage'.[16]

According to Jean de Preux, from the grammatical standpoint, the formula finally adopted in the Protocols is not really clear: 'For our part, particularly in view of the discussions that took place during the Diplomatic Conference, we conclude that the phrase "which constitute the spiritual heritage of peoples" is not so much an explanatory as a selective clause and, as already noted, a very severe one at that, and consequently only places of worship of exceptional importance are covered by this provision'.[17]

The two articles of the Protocols describe the heritage as 'the cultural or spiritual heritage of peoples'. Thus they give this heritage an international value that extends beyond the borders of a single nation. The words 'cultural or spiritual heritage of peoples' apply to all the items listed. The Hague Convention refers to property of 'great importance to the heritage'. The provisions therefore do not differ greatly, except for the introduction of the spiritual element.

Article 1 of the Hague Convention refers to property 'of great importance to the heritage', whereas the Protocols speak of objects 'which constitute the heritage'. This terminological difference would appear not to have any material consequences.

States which are not bound by the 1954 Convention but are Parties to Protocol I must respect the objects protected under the terms of Article 8 of the Hague Convention, without the procedural conditions of the Convention having to be fulfilled.[18]

The provisions of the two Additional Protocols relate to movable and immovable objects, and also to renovated and restored objects.[19]

Acts of Hostility

The Hague Convention says that the Parties must refrain from any act of hostility. The Protocol uses a stronger expression: it prohibits the committing of such acts, which is more affirmative than the language of the Convention. It prohibits acts directed against the objects protected. Accordingly, it is not necessary for damage to have been inflicted for the article to be infringed.[20]

According to another commentary on the Protocols, an act of hostility includes the destruction of any specially protected object, by any Party to the conflict, either by way of attack of by demolition of objects 'under its control'.[21]

Waivers

Article 4, paragraph 2, of the Hague Convention permits the obligations to be waived 'in cases where military necessity imperatively requires'. There is no express mention of such a waiver in the text of the Protocols, but this does not mean that if the objects were used in support of the military effort they would retain the protection conferred by the articles of the Protocols.[22] Article 53 is not subject to any waiver, which further adds to its importance. The military necessity clause applies in the case of Parties to the Convention. These States Parties are thus freed of their obligations under Articles 53 and 16 of the Additional Protocols in the event of imperative military necessity, given that the Protocols are applicable 'without prejudice' to the provisions of the Hague Convention. However, an attack may not be launched against an objective which is not a military objective within the meaning of the Protocol. 'The prohibition on attacking objects which are not military objectives as well as the definition of the latter given in Article 52, paragraph 2, also apply when the Hague Convention of 1954 is applicable: thus the effect of Article 52 of Protocol I is to limit the possibilities of derogations allowed by the Hague Convention. This is an important development for the protection of cultural objects.'[23]

States which are not Parties to the Convention do not have the right of recourse to military necessity and must apply Articles 53 and 16 in all circumstances.

The authors of the Protocols probably did not want to include any possibility of waiver in this provision because of its general and concise nature and because the provision applied only to the most important cultural and spiritual objects. The authors of the amendment which led to the adoption of the two articles certainly had no intention of restricting the protection afforded to cultural property in any way whatsoever; on the contrary, they were anxious to strengthen it.

Use of Cultural Objects in Support of the Military Effort

The Hague Convention of 1954 prohibits the use of cultural property for purposes (even non-military) likely to expose it to destruction or damage in the event of armed conflict and asks Contracting Parties to refrain from any act of hostility directed against such property. The prohibition in the Protocols is, in a way, more general, since it prohibits use 'in support of the military effort' without mentioning the possible consequences for the objects concerned. This is a blanket prohibition and does not necessarily have to be associated with a threat of destruction of the property or damage to it.

The reasons given by certain delegates for the way they voted at the Diplomatic Conference enable us to understand this provision more clearly. In particular, the delegate of the Netherlands said he understood 'that the illegitimate use of those historical objects for military purposes would deprive them of any effective protection in the event of attacks directed against their use for military purposes'. An identical interpretation was given by the delegates of the Federal Republic of Germany and the United States.[24] This prohibition constitutes the indispensable counterpart of subparagraph (a) requiring the adversary to respect the objects.

The 'military effort' implies any military activity for the purpose of waging war. 'In support of the military effort' means that it is forbidden to take advantage of these objects or to use them for military action. 'If the protected objects were used in support of the military effort, this would obviously constitute a violation of Article 53 of the Protocol, though it would not necessarily justify attacking them. To the extent that it is admitted that the right to do so does exist with regard to objects of exceptional value, such a right would depend on their being a military objective, or not, as defined in Article 52 (General protection of civilian objects), paragraph 2. A military objective is an object which makes "an effective contribution to military action" for the adversary and whose total or partial destruction, capture or neutralization "in the circumstances ruling at the time, offers a definite military advantage" for the attacker. Those conditions are therefore stricter than the simple condition that they must be "in support of the military effort". For example, it is not permitted to destroy a cultural object whose use does not make any contribution to military action nor a cultural object which has temporarily served as a refuge for combatants, but is no longer used as such. In addition, all preventive measures should be taken to terminate their use in support of the military effort (warnings, injunctions, etc.), in order to prevent the destruction or damage of cultural objects. However, if it is decided to attack anyway, the principle of proportionality should be respected, which means that the damage should not be excessive in relation to the concrete and direct material military advantage anticipated, and all the precautions required by Article 57 (Precautions in attack) should be taken.'[25]

Reprisals

Article 53 of Protocol I prohibits reprisals, but this prohibition is not to be found in Article 16. The Hague Convention also prohibits reprisals. Thus States Parties to the Hague Convention are bound by this prohibition in both international and non-international armed conflicts.

In explaining its vote, Australia said it was against the provision on reprisals in Article 53. It reaffirmed the position it had taken during the discussion of Article 52, when it had requested the prohibition of reprisals against the persons protected, and considered that the adoption of other prohibitions on reprisals would not assist in the development of international law for humanitarian purposes.[26]

In connection with Article 53, it is also necessary to draw attention to the other provisions of Protocol I which considerably strengthen the protection of cultural property.

Violation of the Provisions on the Protection of Cultural Property

In accordance with Article 85, paragraph 4, of Protocol I: '(d) making the clearly-recognized historic monuments, works of art or places of worship which constitute the cultural or spiritual heritage of peoples and to which special protection has been given by special arrangement, for example, within the framework of a competent international organization, the object of attack, causing as a result extensive destruction thereof, where there is no evidence of the violation by the adverse Party of Article 53, subparagraph (b), and when such historic monuments, works of art and places of worship are not located in the immediate proximity of military objectives' is considered to be a grave breach of the Protocol, when committed wilfully and in violation of the Geneva Conventions or Protocol I.

This provision has been rightly criticized because of its complexity and lack of precision and clarity. It also mingles elements derived from the Hague Convention and Article 53 of Protocol I.

For there to be a grave breach, the attack must be wilful and committed in violation of the Geneva Conventions or Protocol I. Thus, as far as cultural property is concerned, the paragraph is limited to Article 53.

This also follows from the beginning of subparagraph (d), which refers to attacks on clearly-recognized historic monuments, works of art or places of worship which constitute the cultural or spiritual heritage of peoples. However, a further requirement is added since these must – at the same time – be objects to which special protection has been given by special arrangement, for example, within the framework of a competent international organization. What arrangement is intended? Is this a reference to the Hague Convention or to regional or bilateral arrangements? Is the reference to a competent international organization meant to call to mind UNESCO and the Organization of American States? Since other organizations active in this field do not spring readily to mind, why not be more specific?

Thus we must interpret this reference as including UNESCO (Article 8, para. 6, of the Convention and Article 12 of the Regulations for its Execution) and the Organization of American States (Roerich Pact, Article 9), which are at present the only organizations working in this field.

According to the rest of the subparagraph:

1   the attack causes extensive destruction, although there is no evidence of the violation by the adverse Party of Article 53, subparagraph (b);
2   the objects must not be used in support of the military effort (Article 53, subparagraph (b));
3   the historic monuments, works of art and places of worship in question are not located in the immediate proximity of military objectives.

The definition of a grave breach thus goes beyond Protocol I and its Article 53 and also covers the protection afforded by the Hague Convention of 1954 or the Convention of 1972.[27] Accordingly, wilfully launching an indiscriminate attack, knowing that it will cause damage to civilian objects that is excessive in relation to the direct material military advantage anticipated, is a grave breach of the Protocol and a war crime. As regards the cultural objects specially protected by Article 53, the fact of wilfully making them the object of an attack and thereby causing extensive destruction thereof, where there is no evidence of their use, by the adverse Party, in support of the military effort and when these objects are not located in the immediate proximity of military objectives, also constitutes a grave breach of the Protocol and a war crime (Article 85, para. 4(d)).

Unusually for a penal clause, the article says nothing about the perpetrator of the act violating the provisions concerning the protection of property. Such an act could be committed by the commander of a small army unit as well as by an officer of the highest rank.[28]

According to paragraph 5 of the same article, 'Without prejudice to the application of the Conventions and of this Protocol, grave breaches of these instruments shall be regarded as war crimes.' According to the Commentary on the Additional Protocols, 'This paragraph, which was considered indispensable or self-evident by some delegations, seemed out of place or dangerous to others. The former emphasized the need to confirm that there is only one concept of war crimes, whether the specific crimes are defined under the law of Geneva or The Hague and Nuremberg law. Without denying that grave breaches of the Conventions and the Protocol are indeed war crimes, the latter preferred those instruments to stick to their own terminology in view of their purely humanitarian objectives. Finally, the paragraph was adopted by consensus, despite some reservations, once a formula had been added which guaranteed the application of the Conventions and the Protocol. The expression "without prejudice to" means that the affirmation contained in this paragraph will not affect the application of the Conventions and the Protocol. In the French text the expression used is "sous réserve".'[29]

Article 85, paragraph 3(f), of the Protocol also includes among grave breaches and war crimes the perfidious use of the distinctive emblem of the red cross, red crescent or red lion and sun or of other protective signs recognized by the Conventions or Protocol I. Thus the perfidious use of the protective emblem for cultural property, an internationally recognized protective sign, constitutes a grave breach and a war crime.

Non-defended Localities

According to Article 59, a locality may be declared to be non-defended if it is open to occupation by an adverse Party, under the conditions laid down in the Protocol (para. 2(a)–(d)). Parties to the conflict are prohibited from attacking non-defended localities, by whatever means. Paragraph 5 provides for the possibility of the Parties to the conflict agreeing on the establishment of non-defended localities, even if such localities do not fulfil the conditions laid down.

Even when the locality does not fulfil the conditions of paragraph 2, it continues to enjoy the protection provided by the other provisions of the Protocol and the other rules of international law applicable in armed conflict, that is, including the instruments for the protection of cultural property.

Demilitarized Zones

According to Article 60, a demilitarized zone is established by agreement, which may be concluded in peacetime as well as after the outbreak of hostilities. Special conditions are laid down in paragraph 3. The Parties to the conflict may not extend their military operations to zones on which, by agreement, they have conferred the status of demilitarized zone, if such extension is contrary to the terms of this agreement.

CONCLUSION

The relationship between Protocol I and the Hague Convention should be examined in the light of Article 30 (Application of successive treaties relating to the same subject-matter) of the Vienna Convention on the Law of Treaties of 1969:

1. Subject to Article 103 of the Charter of the United Nations, the rights and obligations of States parties to successive treaties relating to the same subject-matter shall be determined in accordance with the following paragraphs.
2. When a treaty specifies that it is subject to, or that it is not to be considered as incompatible with, an earlier or later treaty, the provisions of that other treaty prevail.
3. When all the parties to the earlier treaty are parties also to the later treaty but the earlier treaty is not terminated or suspended in operation under article 59, the earlier treaty applies only to the extent that its provisions are compatible with those of the later treaty.
4. When the parties to the later treaty do not include all the parties to the earlier one:
   (a)   as between States parties to both treaties, the same rule applies as in paragraph 3;
   (b)   as between a State party to both treaties and a State party to only one of the treaties, the treaty to which both States are parties governs their mutual rights and obligations.
5. Paragraph 4 is without prejudice to article 41, or to any question of the termination or suspension of the operation of a treaty under article 60 or to any question of responsibility which may arise for a State from the conclusion or application of a treaty the provisions of which are incompatible with its obligations towards another State or another treaty.

On the basis of the notion of special protection in accordance with Article 53 and another special protection in accordance with Article 8 of the Hague Convention, Jean de Preux draws the following conclusion: 'If it is accepted that Article 53 of Protocol I and Article 8 of the 1954 Hague Convention relate to the same subject-matter, which seems uncertain, since the definition of Protocol I appears to be more restricted, then, in the light of Article 30 of the Vienna Convention, the situation is as follows: between two States Parties to the Protocol, one of which is a Party to the 1954 Hague Convention while the other is not, the Protocol prevails; between two States Parties to the Protocol and to the 1954 Hague Convention, the Convention prevails, inasmuch as the Protocol states that it is not to be considered as incompatible with the Convention ("without prejudice" clause). Thus there has been no progress, unless it is considered that the two instruments do not relate to exactly the same subject-matter, since the definitions are not identical. This solution would enable us to conclude that, within the framework of the rules applicable to the protection of civilian objects against the effects of hostilities, the 1954 Hague Convention continues to govern exclusively cultural property not covered by the definition of Article 53 of Protocol I and of Article 16 of Protocol II. As for objects specially protected by the Protocols, waivers would be prohibited.'[30]

NOTES

1 As of 31 August 1995, 143 States were Parties to Protocol I and 135 States Parties to Protocol II. For the text of the Additional Protocols of 1977, see the *Official Records of the Diplomatic Conference on the Reaffirmation and Development of International Humanitarian Law Applicable in Armed Conflicts*, Geneva (1974–77), Berne Federal Political Department, 1978, Vol. 1, pp.115–219; United Nations, *Treaty Series*, Vol. 1125, pp.3–434, 609–99; *The Laws of Armed Conflicts. A Collection of Conventions, Resolutions and other Documents*, D. Schindler and J. Toman (eds), third revised and completed edition, Dordrecht/Martinus Nijhoff Publishers, Geneva/Henry Dunant Institute, 1988, pp.621–718; *International Review of the Red Cross* (Geneva), No. 197–8, August–September 1977, special double issue, pp.3–101; *International Legal Materials*, (Washington, DC), Vol. 16, No. 6, 1977, pp.1391–1449; *American Journal of International Law* (Washington, DC), Vol. 72, 1978, pp.457–509.

2 'Non-military objects ... such as medical, religious, educational or cultural institutions...': Article 14, CE/Com.III/44, Conference of Government Experts on the Reaffirmation and Development of International Humanitarian Law Applicable in Armed Conflicts (Geneva, 24 May–12 June 1971), *Report on the Work of the Conference*, ICRC, 1971, p.98.

3 CE/Com.III/PC 64. Conference of Government Experts on the Reaffirmation and Development of International Humanitarian Law Applicable in Armed Conflicts – Second Session (Geneva, 4 May–3 June 1972), *Report on the Work of the Conference*, ICRC, Geneva, 1972, Vol. II (Annexes), p.76.

4 CDDH/III/17, CDDH/III/17/Rev.1 and CDDH/III/17/Rev.2, *Official Records of the Diplomatic Conference on the Reaffirmation and Development of International Humanitarian Law Applicable in Armed Conflicts, Geneva (1974–1977)*, Berne, Federal Political Department, 1978, Vol. III, p.214. The words in square brackets appear in Doc. CDDH/III/17/Rev.2.

5 CDDH/SR.42/paras 1–11, *Official Records of the Diplomatic Conference on the Reaffirmation and Development of International Humanitarian Law Applicable in Armed Conflicts, Geneva (1974–1977)*, Berne, Federal Political Department, 1978, Vol. VI, pp.205–6.

6 CDDH/III/GT/95, 25 May 1976.

7 CDDH/SR/53, *Official Records of the Diplomatic Conference on the Reaffirmation and Development of International Humanitarian Law Applicable in Armed Conflicts, Geneva (1974–1977)*, Berne, Federal Political Department, 1978, Vol. VII, pp.156–7 and 163.

8 'It is our understanding, however, that a derogation for imperative reasons of military necessity is indeed implied in Article [16] by virtue of the clear reference to the aforementioned Hague Convention .... It goes without saying that cessation of immunity from attack during such time as the cultural object is

used by adversary armed forces is an example of such military necessity': CDDH/SR/53, *Official Records of the Diplomatic Conference on the Reaffirmation and Development of International Humanitarian Law Applicable in Armed Conflicts, Geneva (1974–1977)*, Berne, Federal Political Department, 1978, Vol. VII, p.162.

9   See Annex IX.

10 Istituto internazionale di diritto umanitario, *La protezione internazionale dei beni culturali/The international protection of cultural property/La protection internationale des biens culturels*, Rome, Dragan European Foundation, 1986, pp.10–11.

11 Thus, unlike the commentary on the Protocols, we do not think that this omission has no consequences for the material protection. See Yves Sandoz, Christophe Swiniarski and Bruno Zimmermann (eds), *Commentary on the Additional Protocols of 8 June 1977 to the Geneva Conventions of 12 August 1949*, Geneva, ICRC, Martinus Nijhoff Publishers, 1987, p.1468.

12 CDDH/SR.42, *Official Records of the Diplomatic Conference on the Reaffirmation and Development of International Humanitarian Law Applicable in Armed Conflicts, Geneva (1974–1977)*, Berne, Federal Political Department, 1978, Vol. VI, p.225.

13 Ibid., pp.224 and 240.

14 Ibid., pp.240–41 and, for the explanation of the Canadian vote, p.224.

15 Ibid., pp.238–9.

16 Ibid., p.227.

17 Jean de Preux, 'La Convention de La Haye et le récent développement du droit des conflits armés', in Istituto internazionale di diritto umanitario, *La protezione internazionale dei beni culturali/The international protection of cultural property/La protection internationale des biens culturels*, p.113.

18 Waldemar A. Solf, 'Cultural property, protection in armed conflict', in Rudolf Bernhardt (ed.), *Encyclopedia of Public International Law*, Amsterdam, North-Holland Publishing Company, 1985, Vol. 9, p.68.

19 CDDH/215/Re.1, paras 68–70, *Official Records of the Diplomatic Conference on the Reaffirmation and Development of International Humanitarian Law Applicable in Armed Conflicts, Geneva (1974–1977)*, Berne, Federal Political Department, 1978, Vol. XV, pp.277–8.

20 Sandoz, Swiniarski and Zimmermann (eds), *Commentary on the Additional Protocols of 8 June 1977 to the Geneva Conventions of 12 August 1949*, p.647, para. 2070.

21 M. Bothe, K.J. Partsch and W.A. Solf, *New Rules for Victims of Armed Conflicts*, The Hague, Martinus Nijhoff Publishers, 1982, p.334, para. 2.5.2.

22 See the statements made by certain States at the Geneva Diplomatic Conference of 1974–77, CDDH/SR.42, Annexes.

23 Sandoz, Swiniarski and Zimmermann (eds), *Commentary on the Additional Protocols of 8 June 1977 to the Geneva Conventions of 12 August 1949*, p.648, note 30.

24 In ratifying the Protocols, the Netherlands gave Article 53 the following interpretation: 'It is the understanding of the Government of the Kingdom of the Netherlands that if and for so long as the object and places protected by this article, in violation of paragraph (b), are used in support of the military effort they will thereby lose such protection.' A similar statement was made by Italy at the time of ratification. When it signed the Protocols, the United Kingdom followed suit: 'in relation to Article 53, that if the objects protected by the article are unlawfully used for military purposes they will thereby lose protection from attacks directed against such unlawful military uses' (United Nations, *Treaty Series*, Vol. 1125, 1979, pp.432–3, 699). In recommending the ratification of Protocol II, the Government of the United States suggested the adoption of Article 16, which it interpreted as follows: 'The United States understands that Article 16 establishes a special protection for a limited class of

objects that, because of their recognized importance, constitute a part of the cultural and spiritual heritage of people and that such objects will lose their protection if they are used in support of the military effort' (State Department Report submitted to President Reagan, S. Treaty Doc. No. 2, 100th Congress, 1st Session (1987), p.7). See CDDH/SR.41, SR.42, *Official Records of the Diplomatic Conference on the Reaffirmation and Development of International Humanitarian Law Applicable in Armed Conflicts, Geneva (1974–1977)*, Berne, Federal Political Department, 1978, Vol. VI, pp.195, 225, 241.

25 Sandoz, Swiniarski and Zimmermann (eds), *Commentary on the Additional Protocols of 8 June 1977 to the Geneva Conventions of 12 August 1949*, p.648, para. 2079.
26 CDDH/SR.41 *Official Records of the Diplomatic Conference on the Reaffirmation and Development of International Humanitarian Law Applicable in Armed Conflicts, Geneva (1974–1977)*, Berne, Federal Political Department, 1978, Vol. VI, pp.176–7.
27 Sandoz, Swiniarski and Zimmermann (eds), *Commentary on the Additional Protocols of 8 June 1977 to the Geneva Conventions of 12 August 1949*, p.1003, citing E.J. Roucounas, 'Les infractions graves au droit humanitaire', *Revue hellénique de droit international*, Athens), Vol. 31, Nos 3–4, 1978, pp.113–14.
28 Bothe, Partsch and Solf, *New Rules for Victims of Armed Conflicts*, pp.519–20, para. 2.24.
29 Sandoz, Swiniarski and Zimmermann (eds), *Commentary on the Additional Protocols of 8 June 1977 to the Geneva Conventions of 12 August 1949*, pp.1003–4, paras 3521–3.
30 Jean de Preux, 'La Convention de La Haye et le récent développement du droit des conflits armés', in Istituto internazionale di diritto umanitario, *La protezione internazionale dei beni culturali/The international protection of cultural property/La protection internationale des biens culturels*, p.116.

Annex I
Treaty on the Protection of Artistic and Scientific Institutions and Historic Monuments (Roerich Pact), Signed at Washington, 15 April 1935

The High Contracting Parties, animated by the purpose of giving conventional form to the postulates of the resolution approved on 16 December 1933, by all the States represented at the Seventh International Conference of American States, held at Montevideo, which recommended to 'the Governments of America which have not yet done so that they sign the "Roerich Pact", initiated by the "Roerich Museum" in the United States, and which has as its object the universal adoption of a flag, already designed and generally known, in order thereby to preserve in any time of danger all nationally and privately owned immovable monuments which form the cultural treasure of peoples', have resolved to conclude a Treaty with that end in view and to the effect that the treasures of culture be respected and protected in time of war and in peace, have agreed upon the following Articles:

Article 1. The historic monuments, museums, scientific, artistic, educational and cultural institutions shall be considered as neutral and as such respected and protected by belligerents.

The same respect and protection shall be due to the personnel of the institutions mentioned above.

The same respect and protection shall be accorded to the historic monuments, museums, scientific, artistic, educational and cultural institutions in time of peace as well as in war.

Article 2. The neutrality of, and protection and respect due to, the monuments and institutions mentioned in the preceding Article, shall be recognized in the entire expanse of territories subject to the sovereignty of each of the Signatory and Acceding States, without any discrimination as to the State allegiance of said monuments and institutions. The respective Governments agree to adopt the measures of internal legislation necessary to insure said protection and respect.

Article 3. In order to identify the monuments and institutions mentioned in Article 1, use may be made of a distinctive flag (red circle with a triple red sphere in the circle on a white background) in accordance with the model attached to this Treaty.

Article 4. The Signatory Governments and those which accede to this Treaty shall send to the Pan American Union, at the time of signature or accession, or at any time thereafter, a list of the monuments and institutions for which they desire the protection agreed to in this Treaty.

The Pan American Union, when notifying the Governments of signatures or accessions, shall also send the list of monuments and institutions mentioned in this Article, and shall inform the other Governments of any changes in said list.

Article 5. The monuments and institutions mentioned in Article 1 shall cease to enjoy the privileges recognized in the present Treaty in case they are made use of for military purposes.

Article 6. The States which do not sign the present Treaty on the date it is opened for signature may sign or adhere to it at any time.

Article 7. The instruments of accession, as well as those of ratification and denunciation of the present Treaty, shall be deposited with the Pan American Union, which shall communicate notice of the act of deposit to the other Signatory or Acceding States.

Article 8. The present Treaty may be denounced at any time by any of the Signatory or Acceding States, and the denunciation shall go into effect three months after notice of it has been given to the other Signatory or Acceding States.

In witness whereof the undersigned Plenipotentiaries, after having deposited their full powers, found to be in due and proper form, sign this Treaty on behalf of their respective Governments, and affix thereto their seals, on the dates appearing opposite their signatures.

(Here follow signatures)

Emblem of the 1935 Roerich Pact for the protection of cultural property

Annex II
Preliminary Draft International Convention for the Protection of Historic Buildings and Works of Art in Time of War, Proposed by the International Museums Office (October 1936)

The High Contracting Parties,

Whereas the preservation of artistic treasures is a concern of the community of States and it is important that such treasures should receive international protection;

Being convinced that the destruction of a masterpiece, whatever nation may have produced it, is a spiritual impoverishment for the entire international community;

Guided by the stipulations of the Hague Conventions of 1899 and 1907 concerning the protection of buildings dedicated to the arts;

Recognising that through the development of the technique of warfare monuments and works of art are in increasing danger of destruction, and that it is the duty of the High Contracting Parties to take steps to safeguard them from the destructive effects of war;

Being of opinion that such defensive action cannot be effectual unless it has already been prepared in time of peace organised both nationally and internationally;

Have appointed as their Plenipotentiaries:

Who, having exchanged their full powers, found in good and due form, have agreed upon the following provisions:

Article I.

The High Contracting Parties deem it to be incumbent upon every Government to organise the defence of historic buildings and works of art against the foreseeable effects of war, and undertake, each for his own part, to prepare that defence in time of peace.

Article 2.

1.   The High Contracting Parties agree to inform one another, whenever they see their way to do so, of the steps taken, prepared, or contemplated by their respective administrations in execution of Article 1 of the present Convention.

2.   The administrations of the Contracting States may, if they so desire, secure the technical collaboration of the International Museums Office in organising the protection of their artistic and historic treasures.

Article 3.

1.   The High Contracting Parties undertake to introduce into their military regulations and instructions such recommendations as may ensure that historic buildings and works of art are respected.

2.   Public authorities and military commands shall take steps to impress this conception of respect upon their troops, in order that the latter may co-operate in protecting historic buildings and works of art.

3.   The High Contracting Parties undertake to take steps to punish in time of war any person looting or damaging monuments and works of art.

4.   They will communicate to one another the texts of such laws or regulations as they may have enacted in application of this Article.

Article 4.

1.   The High Contracting Parties undertake to refrain from any act of hostility directed against any refuge that a High Contracting Party may have designated in his territory to shelter in time of war works of art or of historic interest that may be threatened by military operations.

2.   The number of such refuges shall be limited; they may take the form either of buildings erected for the purpose or of existing historic buildings or groups of buildings.

3.   To secure immunity, refuges must:

    (a)   be situated at a distance of not less than 20 kilometres from the most likely theatres of military operations, from any military objective, from any main line of communication, and from any large industrial centre (this distance may be reduced in certain cases in countries with a very dense population and small area);

    (b)   have already been notified in time of peace;
    (c)   not be used directly or indirectly for purposes of national defence;
    (d) be open to international inspection during hostilities.

4.   The military authorities shall have access to the refuges at any time for the purpose of satisfying themselves that they are not being used in any way contrary to the present Convention.

Article 5.

1.   The High Contracting Parties, acknowledging it to be their joint and several duty to respect and protect all monuments of artistic or historic interest in time of war, agree to take all possible precautions to spare such monuments during operations and to ensure that their use or situation shall not expose them to attack.

2.   Special protection shall be given to monuments or groups of monuments which:
    (a)   are isolated from any military objective within a radius of 500 metres;
    (b)   are not directly or indirectly used for purposes of national defence;
    (c)   have already been notified in time of peace;
    (d)   are open to international inspection during hostilities.

Article 6.

Any High Contracting Party may at any time declare that he is prepared to conclude with any other High Contracting Party, on a reciprocal basis, special agreements extending the immunity granted to refuges to certain monuments or groups of monuments the preservation of which, although they do not satisfy the conditions laid down in Article 4, is of fundamental importance to the international community.

Article 7.

1.   Refuges to which immunity has been granted and buildings enjoying the special protection provided for in Article 5, paragraph 2, shall be distinguished by a protective mark.

2.   This mark shall take the form of a light blue triangle inscribed in a white disc.

3.   The location and degree of visibility of protecting marks shall be left to the judgment of the authorities responsible for defence.

4.   The affixing of protecting marks in time of peace shall be optional.

5.   The High Contracting Parties undertake to guard against any misuse of protecting marks, and to punish the same should occasion arise.

6.   Monuments and museums shall be brought to the notice of the civil population, who shall be requested to protect them, and of the occupying troops, who shall be informed that they are dealing with buildings the preservation of which is the concern of the entire international community.

7.   The manner in which this shall be done is left to the judgment of national authorities. In the case, however, of buildings to which special protection cannot be granted, the marks provided must be different from that described in paragraph 2 of this Article.

Article 8.

The High Contracting Parties agree that historic buildings and works of art shall be immune from reprisals.

Article 9.

1.   Should a State which is at war with another State feel called upon to place under shelter in the territory of another country all or any of the works of art in its possession, the High Contracting Parties agree to grant immunity to the means of transport employed for that purpose, provided that the transfer is carried out under international supervision.

2.   A Belligerent State shall enjoy this immunity once only in respect of each work of art, and only in the direction of the country according hospitality.

3.   During transport and while stored abroad, works of art shall be exempt from confiscation and may not be disposed of either by the depositor or by the depositary.

Article 10.

The High Contracting Parties, recognising the necessity of extending the protection contemplated by this Convention to historic buildings and works of art threatened by disturbances or armed conflicts within a country, agree as follows:

1.   They may lend their friendly assistance to the contending parties for the purpose of safeguarding the threatened historic and artistic treasures.

2.   They may receive and shelter in their respective territories works of art coming from a country in which civil strife is prevalent, and endangered by acts arising out of such strife.

3.   Museums and collections of a public character may store works of art abroad during a period of civil strife.

So long as such works remain abroad, the museums which deposited them shall be deemed their owners.

Such deposits shall not be restored until the civil strife is at an end.

During transport and for the period of their deposit, such works of art shall be exempt from confiscation, and may not be disposed of either by the depositor or by the depositary.

4. Works of art in private ownership may receive protection in foreign territory, provided that they are there deposited on the responsibility and through the agency of a national museum or collection of a public character. The same rules concerning deposit and restoration shall apply, and restoration may be effected only through the agency of the depositing institution.

Article 11.

1. International Commissions of Inspection shall satisfy themselves while military operations are proceeding that no breach of the provisions of this Convention is committed.

2. Offences committed in breach of the provisions of this Convention shall be established by the International Commission of Inspection operating in the territory in which they were committed.

3. Details of the constitution and operation of these Commissions are laid down in the Regulations for the execution of this Convention.

Article 12.

1. The High Contracting Parties agree to meet from time to time in general conference to decide conjointly upon measures for ensuring the application of this Convention, and to review, if necessary, the Regulations for its execution.

2. The General Conference shall appoint its Standing Committee and Secretariat, whose powers in the intervals between sessions of the Conference shall be defined by the Regulations for the execution of this Convention.

Article 13.

In the event of disagreement between the belligerents as to the application of the provisions of this Convention, the Contracting States entrusted with the interests of the belligerents and the Standing Committee of the General Conference shall lend their good offices for the settlement of the dispute.

Final Provisions.

REGULATIONS FOR THE EXECUTION OF THE CONVENTION

Article 1.

As soon as the Convention comes into force, there shall be drawn up an international list of commissioners to whom missions arising out of the execution of the Convention may be entrusted during the period of hostilities. This list shall consist of persons of acknowledged impartiality, selected by the Standing Committee of the General Conference on the nomination of qualified institutions in the contracting countries (Courts of Justice, Government Departments, Academies, Universities and Museums).

Article 2.

1. As soon as the Convention has been ratified, each of the High Contracting Parties shall designate the refuges which are to enjoy in his territory the immunity provided for in Article 4 of the Convention, and the monuments which are to enjoy the special protection provided for in Article 5, paragraph 2.

2. Each High Contracting Party shall send to the Standing Committee of the Conference a list of the refuges and monuments designated, together with the written approval of the International Verification Commission referred to in Article 4 of these Regulations.

Article 3.

1. The International Verification Commission shall certify that the refuges and monuments designated satisfy the conditions laid down in Articles 4 and 5 of the Convention, respectively. It may also give an opinion on the number of refuges and the material conditions in which they are fitted up.

2. In the case of countries with a dense population and small area, it shall rest with the Commission to decide what minimum distance may be allowed between the refuges and the danger-points mentioned in Article 4, paragraph (a), of the Convention.

Article 4.

The International Verification Commissions shall consist of:

(a)   a representative of the State in whose territory the refuges and monuments have been designated;

(b)   a commissioner on the international list, appointed by the Standing Committee, who shall act as Chairman of the Commission;

(c)   a representative of each of such States as the Standing Committee may have named.

Article 5.

1. Applications for the appointment of a Verification Commission must be sent to the Standing Committee of the Conference, together with a list of the refuges and monuments designated. The Standing Committee shall immediately carry out the necessary consultations with a view to the definitive appointment of the Commis-

sion, which shall meet at the invitation of the Government concerned and at such place as the latter may appoint.

2.   The Commission's work of verification shall be conducted on the spot, and shall, if it thinks this necessary, deal separately with each of the refuges and monuments designated.

3.   The conclusions of the Verification Commission shall be delivered to the member of the Commission representing the Government concerned.

4.   The conclusions of the Verification Commission must be unanimously agreed by the members present.

Article 6.

1.   Each of the High Contracting Parties who has made the declaration referred to in Article 6 of the Convention shall forward to the Standing Committee of the General Conference, as soon as he thinks fit, a list of the monuments or groups of monuments for which he desires to secure immunity.

2.   The Standing Committee shall communicate this list to each of the High Contracting Parties, and shall lend them its good offices with a view to the conclusion, on a reciprocal basis, of the immunity agreements contemplated in Article 6 of the Convention.

Article 7.

1.   For each of the Contracting States involved in the Conflict, an International Commission of Inspection, as provided in Article 11 (eleven) of the Convention, shall be appointed by the Standing Commission immediately upon the outbreak of hostilities. It shall comprise: a commissioner from a neutral country, selected from the international list and appointed by the Standing Committee to act as Chairman of the Commission; a representative of the State in whose territory the inspection is to be carried out; and a representative (or his delegate) of the State to which the interests of the other belligerent in the same territory have been entrusted. This last-mentioned member may likewise be selected from among the commissioners on the international list belonging to neutral countries.

2.   The Chairmen of International Commissions of Inspection, or their delegates, may at any time inspect refuges and monuments enjoying the special protection provided for in Article 5 of the Convention.

3.   The Standing Committee may attach additional commissioners to the Chairman of the Commission, as the requirements of inspection may dictate.

4.   The Chairmen of International Commissions of Inspection may consult experts whose advice seems to them necessary in the performance of the missions entrusted to them.

5.   The conclusions of International Commissions of Inspection shall be adopted by majority vote. The representatives of the parties concerned shall have no vote.

6.   The conclusions of International Commissions of Inspection shall be submitted to the Standing Committee, which shall communicate them to each of the High Contracting Parties, and shall decide whether they shall also be made public.

7.   The Standing Committee shall decide upon the procedure to be followed for establishing breaches of or exceptions to the Convention for which no special provision has been made.

Article 8.

1.   Works of art may not be transferred from one refuge to another unless this is necessary for their safety.

2.   As soon as evacuation is completed the protecting mark must be removed.

3.   Exceptionally, should there be any obstacle to the transfer of works of art to a regular refuge, the responsible authorities shall decide what steps are to be taken to store them temporarily in a place of safety. Such temporary store may be shown by the protecting mark, which shall be affixed by the International Commission of Inspection, the latter having the sole right to affix it.

4.   In occupied territories, any other exceptional measures that may be dictated by unforeseeable circumstances and by the necessity of preserving monuments and works of art must be taken with the agreement of the International Commission of Inspection.

5.   In occupied territories, refuges and monuments enjoying *special protection* shall be under the supervision of the International Commission of Inspection of the occupying State.

6.   The International Commission of Inspection, jointly with the authorities of the occupying State, shall take all necessary steps for the preservation of any monuments which may be damaged. Such steps shall not, however, amount to more than temporary strengthening.

Article 9.

During military occupation, the national staff appointed to preserve and guard refuges, museums, or monuments must be retained in their employment, unless there is any legitimate military reason for this dismissal. They shall, however, be in the same position in relation to the military authorities of occupation as the civil population of the occupied territories.

Article 10.

In the event of the transfer of works of art to the territory of a foreign country as provided in Article 9 of the Convention, the following rules shall apply:

1.   Transport shall be carried out in collaboration with the International Commission of Inspection, to which an inventory of the works to be transferred shall be delivered.

2.   The International Commission of Inspection shall give notice of the proposed transfer to the Standing Committee of the General Conference, which shall inform the other belligerent or belligerents. Transport shall not take place until the latter have been so informed.

3.   The convoy shall be covered by the protecting mark, and accompanied by a delegate of the International Commission of Inspection, or by a neutral Commissioner appointed for the purpose by the Standing Committee.

4.   For transport otherwise than by land, the Standing Committee shall lay down additional rules as may be applicable in each particular case.

Article 11.

For the purposes of the application of Article 10 of the Convention, the Standing Committee of the Conference shall lend its good offices to the contending parties with a view to taking all necessary steps for the protection of monuments and works of art threatened by the operations.

Article 12.

1.   The General Conference provided for in Article 12 of the Convention shall consist of one representative of each of the Contracting States.

2.   The General Conference shall meet whenever necessary, but at least once in every five years. Any State may entrust its representation to another Contracting State, which shall in such case have as many votes as the number of States it represents.

3.   The first session of the General Conference shall be held in the year following the entry into force of the Convention.

4.   The Conference shall fix the number and the term of office of members of its Standing Committee, and shall designate the States from which they shall be drawn. Any State may entrust its representation to another State represented on the Standing Committee, and such State shall then have as many votes as the number of States it represents.

5.   The General Conference shall decide all matters connected with the application and proper operation of the Convention, and in gen-

eral all questions relating to the protection of the artistic and historic heritage of the international community in time of war.

6.   The Standing Committee shall perform the functions assigned to it by the Convention.

7.   In the intervals between sessions of the Conference, the Standing Committee shall settle all questions relating to the application of the Convention, except as the Conference may otherwise decide.

8.   The Standing Committee shall meet whenever necessary, but at least once in each year.

9.   The Standing Committee shall elect its Chairman and shall determine the powers to be vested in him and in the Secretariat of the Conference during the intervals between the Committee's sessions.

10.   The chairmanship may not be held in time of war by a national of a belligerent country.

11.   In time of war, any belligerent countries which are not represented on the Standing Committee shall appoint representatives, whose term of office come to an end as soon as their respective countries cease to be belligerents. If, however, it is impossible to balance the votes of the representatives of the belligerent countries on the Standing Committee, the voices of all of them shall become purely advisory. If the number of deliberative voices is thereby reduced to less than three, the Standing Committee may unanimously co-opt members belonging to neutral countries as substitutes for other Contracting States.

12.   The decisions of the Conference and of the Standing Committee shall be taken by a two-thirds majority of the members present; but unanimity must be secured for decisions of the Conference involving the special interests of Contracting States.

13.   Two-thirds of the members of the General Conference and of the Standing Committee shall form a quorum.

14.   The General Conference and the Standing Committee shall themselves determine the venue of their meetings. Any State may invite the General Conference and the Standing Committee to hold their sessions in its territory.

15.   In time of war, if the State in whose territory the Secretariat has its headquarters is a belligerent, the Standing Committee shall decide whether it shall be transferred to the territory of another State.

16.   Any High Contracting Party may at any time call the attention of the Standing Committee to any circumstance affecting the application or proper operation of the measures contemplated by the Convention.

17.   In the discharge of their duties under the Convention, members of International Commissions of Inspection, Commissioners en-

trusted with missions, and members of the Standing Committee and the Secretariat shall enjoy all the privileges and immunities belonging to international agents.

Annex III
Convention for the Protection of Cultural Property in the Event of Armed Conflict Signed at The Hague, 14 May 1954

The High Contracting Parties,

Recognizing that cultural property has suffered grave damage during recent armed conflicts and that, by reason of the developments in the technique of warfare, it is in increasing danger of destruction;

Being convinced that damage to cultural property belonging to any people whatsoever means damage to the cultural heritage of all mankind, since each people makes its contribution to the culture of the world;

Considering that the preservation of the cultural heritage is of great importance for all peoples of the world and that it is important that this heritage should receive international protection;

Guided by the principles concerning the protection of cultural property during armed conflict, as established in the Conventions of The Hague of 1899 and of 1907 and in the Washington Pact of 15 April 1935;

Being of the opinion that such protection cannot be effective unless both national and international measures have been taken to organize it in time of peace;

Being determined to take all possible steps to protect cultural property;

Have agreed upon the following provisions:

Chapter I:
General Provisions Regarding Protection

ARTICLE 1   DEFINITION OF CULTURAL PROPERTY

For the purposes of the present Convention, the term 'cultural property' shall cover, irrespective of origin or ownership:

(a)   movable or immovable property of great importance to the cultural heritage of every people, such as monuments of architecture, art or history, whether religious or secular; archaeological sites; groups of buildings which, as a whole, are of historical or artistic interest; works of art; manuscripts, books and other objects of artistic, historical or archaeological interest; as well as scientific collections and important collections of books or archives or of reproductions of the property defined above;

(b)   buildings whose main and effective purpose is to preserve or exhibit the movable cultural property defined in sub-paragraph (a) such as museums, large libraries and depositories of archives, and refuges intended to shelter, in the event of armed conflict, the movable cultural property defined in sub-paragraph (a);

(c)   centres containing a large amount of cultural property as defined in sub-paragraphs (a) and (b), to be known as 'centres containing monuments'.

ARTICLE 2   PROTECTION OF CULTURAL PROPERTY

For the purposes of the present Convention, the protection of cultural property shall comprise the safeguarding of and respect for such property.

ARTICLE 3   SAFEGUARDING OF CULTURAL PROPERTY

The High Contracting Parties undertake to prepare in time of peace for the safeguarding of cultural property situated within their own territory against the foreseeable effects of an armed conflict, by taking such measures as they consider appropriate.

ARTICLE 4   RESPECT FOR CULTURAL PROPERTY

1.   The High Contracting Parties undertake to respect cultural property situated within their own territory as well as within the territory of other High Contracting Parties by refraining from any use of the property and its immediate surroundings or of the appliances in use for its protection for purposes which are likely to expose it to destruction or damage in the event of armed conflict; and by refraining from any act of hostility directed against such property.

2.   The obligations mentioned in paragraph I of the present Article may be waived only in cases where military necessity imperatively requires such a waiver.

3.   The High Contracting Parties further undertake to prohibit, prevent and, if necessary, put a stop to any form of theft, pillage or misappropriation of, and any acts of vandalism directed against, cultural property. They shall refrain from requisitioning movable cultural property situated in the territory of another High Contracting Party.

4.   They shall refrain from any act directed by way of reprisals against cultural property.

5.   No High Contracting Party may evade the obligations incumbent upon it under the present Article, in respect of another High Contracting Party, by reason of the fact that the latter has not applied the measures of safeguard referred to in Article 3.

ARTICLE 5   OCCUPATION

1.   Any High Contracting Party in occupation of the whole or part of the territory of another High Contracting Party shall as far as possible support the competent national authorities of the occupied country in safeguarding and preserving its cultural property.

2.   Should it prove necessary to take measures to preserve cultural property situated in occupied territory and damaged by military operations, and should the competent national authorities be unable to take such measures, the Occupying Power shall, as far as possible, and in close co-operation with such authorities, take the most necessary measures of preservation.

3.   Any High Contracting Party whose government is considered their legitimate government by members of a resistance movement shall, if possible, draw their attention to the obligation to comply with those provisions of the Convention dealing with respect for cultural property.

ARTICLE 6   DISTINCTIVE MARKING OF CULTURAL PROPERTY

In accordance with the provisions of Article 16, cultural property may bear a distinctive emblem so as to facilitate its recognition.

ARTICLE 7   MILITARY MEASURES

1.   The High Contracting Parties undertake to introduce in time of peace into their military regulations or instructions such provisions as may ensure observance of the present Convention, and to foster in the members of their armed forces a spirit of respect for the culture and cultural property of all peoples.

2.   The High Contracting Parties undertake to plan or establish in peace-time, within their armed forces, services or specialist personnel whose purpose will be to secure respect for cultural property and to co-operate with the civilian authorities responsible for safeguarding it.

Chapter II: Special protection

ARTICLE 8   GRANTING OF SPECIAL PROTECTION

1.   There may be placed under special protection a limited number of refuges intended to shelter movable cultural property in the event of armed conflict, of centres containing monuments and other immovable cultural property of very great importance, provided that they:

(a)   are situated at an adequate distance from any large industrial centre or from any important military objective constituting a vulnerable point, such as, for example, an aerodrome, broadcasting station, establishment engaged upon work of national defence, a port or railway station of relative importance or a main line of communication;

(b)   are not used for military purposes.

2.   A refuge for movable cultural property may also be placed under special protection, whatever its location, if it is so constructed that, in all probability, it will not be damaged by bombs.

3.   A centre containing monuments shall be deemed to be used for military purposes whenever it is used for the movement of military

personnel or material, even in transit. The same shall apply whenever activities directly connected with military operations, the stationing of military personnel, or the production of war material are carried on within the centre.

4.   The guarding of cultural property mentioned in paragraph 1 above by armed custodians specially empowered to do so, or the presence, in the vicinity of such cultural property, of police forces normally responsible for the maintenance of public order shall not be deemed to be used for military purposes.

5.   If any cultural property mentioned in paragraph 1 of the present Article is situated near an important military objective as defined in the said paragraph, it may nevertheless be placed under special protection if the High Contracting Party asking for that protection undertakes, in the event of armed conflict, to make no use of the objective and particularly, in the case of a port, railway station or aerodrome, to divert all traffic therefrom. In that event, such diversion shall be prepared in time of peace.

6.   Special protection is granted to cultural property by its entry in the 'International Register of Cultural Property under Special Protection'. This entry shall only be made, in accordance with the provisions of the present Convention and under the conditions provided for in the Regulations for the execution of the Convention.

ARTICLE 9   IMMUNITY OF CULTURAL PROPERTY UNDER SPECIAL PROTECTION

The High Contracting Parties undertake to ensure the immunity of cultural property under special protection by refraining, from the time of entry in the International Register, from any act of hostility directed against such property and, except for the cases provided for in paragraph 5 of Article 8, from any use of such property or its surroundings for military purposes.

ARTICLE 10   IDENTIFICATION AND CONTROL

During an armed conflict, cultural property under special protection shall be marked with the distinctive emblem described in Article 16, and shall be open to international control as provided for in the Regulations for the execution of the Convention.

ARTICLE 11   WITHDRAWAL OF IMMUNITY

1.   If one of the High Contracting Parties commits, in respect of any item of cultural property under special protection a violation of the obligations under Article 9, the opposing Party shall, so long as this violation persists, be released from the obligation to ensure the immunity of the property concerned. Nevertheless, whenever possible, the latter Party shall first request the cessation of such violation within a reasonable time.

2.   Apart from the case provided for in paragraph 1 of the present Article, immunity shall be withdrawn from cultural property under special protection only in exceptional cases of unavoidable military necessity, and only for such time as that necessity continues. Such necessity can be established only by the officer commanding a force the equivalent of a division in size or larger. Whenever circumstances permit, the opposing Party shall be notified, a reasonable time in advance, of the decision to withdraw immunity.

3.   The Party withdrawing immunity shall, as soon as possible, so inform the Commissioner-General for cultural property provided for in the Regulations for the execution of the Convention, in writing, stating the reasons.

Chapter III:
Transport of Cultural Property

ARTICLE 12   TRANSPORT UNDER SPECIAL PROTECTION

1.   Transport exclusively engaged in the transfer of cultural property, whether within a territory or to another territory, may, at the request of the High Contracting Party concerned, take place under special protection in accordance with the conditions specified in the Regulations for the execution of the Convention.

2.   Transport under special protection shall take place under the international supervision provided for in the aforesaid Regulations and shall display the distinctive emblem described in Article 16.

3.   The High Contracting Parties shall refrain from any act of hostility directed against transport under special protection.

ARTICLE 13   TRANSPORT IN URGENT CASES

1.   If a High Contracting Party considers that the safety of certain cultural property requires its transfer and that the matter is of such

urgency that the procedure laid down in Article 12 cannot be followed, especially at the beginning of an armed conflict, the transport may display the distinctive emblem described in Article 16, provided that an application for immunity referred to in Article 12 has not already been made and refused. As far as possible, notification of transfer should be made to the opposing Parties. Nevertheless, transport conveying cultural property to the territory of another country may not display the distinctive emblem unless immunity has been expressly granted to it.

2. The High Contracting Parties shall take, so far as possible, the necessary precautions to avoid acts of hostility directed against the transport described in paragraph 1 of the present Article and displaying the distinctive emblem.

ARTICLE 14   IMMUNITY FROM SEIZURE, CAPTURE AND PRIZE

1. Immunity from seizure, placing in prize, or capture shall be granted to:

(a) cultural property enjoying the protection provided for in Article 12 or that provided for in Article 13;
(b) the means of transport exclusively engaged in the transfer of such cultural property.

2. Nothing in the present Article shall limit the right of visit and search.

Chapter IV: Personnel

ARTICLE 15   PERSONNEL

As far as consistent with the interests of security, personnel engaged in the protection of cultural property shall, in the interests of such property, be respected and, if they fall into the hands of the opposing Party, shall be allowed to continue to carry out their duties whenever the cultural property for which they are responsible has also fallen into the hands of the opposing Party.

Chapter V: The Distinctive Emblem

ARTICLE 16 EMBLEM OF THE CONVENTION

1. The distinctive emblem of the Convention shall take the form of a shield, pointed below, per saltire blue and white (a shield consisting of a royal-blue square, one of the angles of which forms the point of the shield, and of a royal-blue triangle above the square, the space on either side being taken up by a white triangle).
2. The emblem shall be used alone, or repeated three times in a triangular formation (one shield below), under the conditions provided for in Article 17.

ARTICLE 17 USE OF THE EMBLEM

1. The distinctive emblem repeated three times may be used only as a means of identification of:

   (a) immovable cultural property under special protection;
   (b) the transport of cultural property under the conditions provided for in Articles 12 and 13;
   (c) improvised refuges, under the conditions provided for in the Regulations for the execution of the Convention.

2. The distinctive emblem may be used alone only as a means of identification of:

   (a) cultural property not under special protection;
   (b) the persons responsible for the duties of control in accordance with the Regulations for the execution of the Convention;
   (c) the personnel engaged in the protection of cultural property;
   (d) the identity cards mentioned in the Regulations for the execution of the Convention.

3. During an armed conflict, the use of the distinctive emblem in any other cases than those mentioned in the preceding paragraphs of the present Article, and the use for any purpose whatever of a sign resembling the distinctive emblem, shall be forbidden.
4. The distinctive emblem may not be placed on any immovable cultural property unless at the same time there is displayed an authorization duly dated and signed by the competent authority of the High Contracting Party.

Chapter VI:
Scope of Application of the Convention

ARTICLE 18   APPLICATION OF THE CONVENTION

1.   Apart from the provisions which shall take effect in time of peace, the present Convention shall apply in the event of declared war or of any other armed conflict which may arise between two or more of the High Contracting Parties, even if the state of war is not recognized by one or more of them.

2.   The Convention shall also apply to all cases of partial or total occupation of the territory of a High Contracting Party, even if the said occupation meets with no armed resistance.

3.   If one of the Powers in conflict is not a Party to the present Convention, the Powers which are Parties thereto shall nevertheless remain bound by it in their mutual relations. They shall furthermore be bound by the Convention, in relation to the said Power, if the latter has declared that it accepts the provisions thereof and so long as it applies them.

ARTICLE 19   CONFLICTS NOT OF AN INTERNATIONAL CHARACTER

1.   In the event of an armed conflict not of an international character occurring within the territory of one of the High Contracting Parties, each party to the conflict shall be bound to apply, as a minimum, the provisions of the present Convention which relate to respect for cultural property.

2.   The parties to the conflict shall endeavour to bring into force, by means of special agreements, all or part of the other provisions of the present Convention.

3.   The United Nations Educational, Scientific and Cultural Organization may offer its services to the parties to the conflict.

4.   The application of the preceding provisions shall not affect the legal status of the parties to the conflict.

Chapter VII: Execution of the Convention

ARTICLE 20   REGULATIONS FOR THE EXECUTION OF THE CONVENTION

The procedure by which the present Convention is to be applied is defined in the Regulations for its execution, which constitute an integral part thereof.

ARTICLE 21   PROTECTING POWERS

The present Convention and the Regulations for its execution shall be applied with the co-operation of the Protecting Powers responsible for safeguarding the interests of the Parties to the conflict.

ARTICLE 22   CONCILIATION PROCEDURE

1.   The Protecting Powers shall lend their good offices in all cases where they may deem it useful in the interests of cultural property, particularly if there is disagreement between the Parties to the conflict as to the application or interpretation of the provisions of the present Convention or the Regulations for its execution.
2.   For this purpose, each of the Protecting Powers may, either at the invitation of one Party, of the Director-General of the United Nations Educational, Scientific and Cultural Organization, or on its own initiative, propose to the Parties to the conflict a meeting of their representatives, and in particular of the authorities responsible for the protection of cultural property, if considered appropriate on suitably chosen neutral territory. The Parties to the conflict shall be bound to give effect to the proposals for meeting made to them. The Protecting Powers shall propose for approval by the Parties to the conflict a person belonging to a neutral Power or a person presented by the Director-General of the United Nations Educational, Scientific and Cultural Organization, which person shall be invited to take part in such a meeting in the capacity of Chairman.

ARTICLE 23   ASSISTANCE OF UNESCO

1.   The High Contracting Parties may call upon the United Nations Educational, Scientific and Cultural Organization for technical assistance in organizing the protection of their cultural property, or in

connection with any other problem arising out of the application of the present Convention or the Regulations for its execution. The Organization shall accord such assistance within the limits fixed by its programme and by its resources.

2. The Organization is authorized to make, on its own initiative, proposals on this matter to the High Contracting Parties.

ARTICLE 24   SPECIAL AGREEMENTS

1. The High Contracting Parties may conclude special agreements for all matters concerning which they deem it suitable to make separate provision.

2. No special agreement may be concluded which would diminish the protection afforded by the present Convention to cultural property and to the personnel engaged in its protection.

ARTICLE 25   DISSEMINATION OF THE CONVENTION

The High Contracting Parties undertake, in time of peace as in time of armed conflict, to disseminate the text of the present Convention and the Regulations for its execution as widely as possible in their respective countries. They undertake, in particular, to include the study thereof in their programmes of military and, if possible, civilian training, so that its principles are made known to the whole population, especially the armed forces and personnel engaged in the protection of cultural property.

ARTICLE 26   TRANSLATIONS REPORTS

1. The High Contracting Parties shall communicate to one another, through the Director-General of the United Nations Educational, Scientific and Cultural Organization, the official translations of the present Convention and of the Regulations for its execution.

2. Furthermore, at least once every four years, they shall forward to the Director-General a report giving whatever information they think suitable concerning any measures being taken, prepared or contemplated by their respective administrations in fulfilment of the present Convention and of the Regulations for its execution.

ARTICLE 27   MEETINGS

1.   The Director-General of the United Nations Educational, Scientific and Cultural Organization may, with the approval of the Executive Board, convene meetings of representatives of the High Contracting Parties. He must convene such a meeting if at least one-fifth of the High Contracting Parties so request.
2.   Without prejudice to any other functions which have been conferred on it by the present Convention or the Regulations for its execution, the purpose of the meeting will be to study problems concerning the application of the Convention and of the Regulations for its execution, and to formulate recommendations in respect thereof.
3.   The meeting may further undertake a revision of the Convention or the Regulations for its execution if the majority of the High Contracting Parties are represented, and in accordance with the provisions of Article 39.

ARTICLE 28   SANCTIONS

The High Contracting Parties undertake to take, within the framework of their ordinary criminal jurisdiction, all necessary steps to prosecute and impose penal or disciplinary sanctions upon those persons, of whatever nationality, who commit or order to be committed a breach of the present Convention.

Final Provisions

ARTICLE 29   LANGUAGES

1.   The present Convention is drawn up in English, French, Russian and Spanish, the four texts being equally authoritative.
2.   The United Nations Educational, Scientific and Cultural Organization shall arrange for translations of the Convention into the other official languages of its General Conference.

ARTICLE 30   SIGNATURE

The present Convention shall bear the date of 14 May 1954 and, until the date of 31 December 1954, shall remain open for signature by all States invited to the Conference which met at The Hague from 21 April 1954 to 14 May 1954.

ARTICLE 31   RATIFICATION

1.   The present Convention shall be subject to ratification by signatory States in accordance with their respective constitutional procedures.
2.   The instruments of ratification shall be deposited with the Director-General of the United Nations Educational, Scientific and Cultural Organization.

ARTICLE 32   ACCESSION

From the date of its entry into force, the present Convention shall be open for accession by all States mentioned in Article 30 which have not signed it, as well as any other State invited to accede by the Executive Board of the United Nations Educational, Scientific and Cultural Organization. Accession shall be effected by the deposit of an instrument of accession with the Director-General of the United Nations Educational, Scientific and Cultural Organization.

ARTICLE 33   ENTRY INTO FORCE

1.   The present Convention shall enter into force three months after five instruments of ratification have been deposited.
2.   Thereafter, it shall enter into force, for each High Contracting Party, three months after the deposit of its instrument of ratification or accession.
3.   The situations referred to in Article 18 and 19 shall give immediate effect to ratifications or accessions deposited by the Parties to the conflict either before or after the beginning of hostilities or occupation. In such cases the Director-General of the United Nations Educational, Scientific and Cultural Organization shall transmit the communications referred to in Article 38 by the speediest method.

ARTICLE 34   EFFECTIVE APPLICATION

1.   Each State Party to the Convention on the date of its entry into force shall take all necessary measures to ensure its effective application within a period of six months after such entry into force.
2.   This period shall be six months from the date of deposit of the instruments of ratification or accession for any State which deposits its instrument of ratification or accession after the date of entry into force of the Convention.

ARTICLE 35   TERRITORIAL EXTENSION OF THE CONVENTION

Any High Contracting Party may, at the time of ratification or accession, or at any time thereafter, declare by notification addressed to the Director-General of the United Nations Educational, Scientific and Cultural Organization that the present Convention shall extend to all or any of the territories for whose international relations it is responsible. The said notification shall take effect three months after the date of its receipt.

ARTICLE 36   RELATION TO PREVIOUS CONVENTIONS

1.   In the relations between Powers which are bound by the Convention of The Hague concerning the Laws and Customs of War on Land (IV) and concerning Naval Bombardment in Time of War (IX), whether those of 29 July 1899 or those of 18 October 1907, and which are Parties to the present Convention, this last Convention shall be supplementary to the aforementioned Convention (IX) and to the Regulations annexed to the aforementioned Convention (IV) and shall substitute for the emblem described in Article 5 of the aforementioned Convention (IX) the emblem described in Article 16 of the present Convention in cases in which the present Convention and the Regulations for its execution provide for the use of this distinctive emblem.
2.   In the relations between Powers which are bound by the Washington Pact of 15 April 1935 for the Protection of Artistic and Scientific Institutions and of Historic Monuments (Roerich Pact) and which are Parties to the present Conventions, the latter Convention shall be supplementary to the Roerich Pact and shall substitute for the distinguishing flag described in Article III of the Pact the emblem defined in Article 16 of the present Convention, in cases in which the present Convention and the Regulations for its execution provide for the use of this distinctive emblem.

ARTICLE 37   DENUNCIATION

1.   Each High Contracting Party may denounce the present Convention, on its own behalf, or on behalf of any territory for whose international relations it is responsible.
2.   The denunciation shall be notified by an instrument in writing, deposited with the Director-General of the United Nations Educational, Scientific and Cultural Organization.

3. The denunciation shall take effect one year after the receipt of the instrument of denunciation. However, if, on the expiry of this period, the denouncing Party is involved in an armed conflict, the denunciation shall not take effect until the end of hostilities, or until the operations of repatriating cultural property are completed, whichever is the later.

ARTICLE 38   NOTIFICATIONS

The Director-General of the United Nations Educational, Scientific and Cultural Organization shall inform the States referred to in Articles 30 and 32, as well as the United Nations, of the deposit of all the instruments of ratification, accession or acceptance provided for in Articles 31, 32 and 39 and of the notifications and denunciations provided for respectively in Articles 35, 37 and 39.

ARTICLE 39   REVISION OF THE CONVENTION AND OF THE REGULATIONS FOR ITS EXECUTION

1. Any High Contracting Party may propose amendments to the present Convention or the Regulations for its execution. The text of any proposed amendment shall be communicated to the Director-General of the United Nations Educational, Scientific and Cultural Organization who shall transmit it to each High Contracting Party with the request that such Party reply within four months stating whether it:

(a) desires that a Conference be convened to consider the proposed amendment:

(b) favours the acceptance of the proposed amendment without a Conference; or

(c) favours the rejection of the proposed amendment without a Conference.

2. The Director-General shall transmit the replies, received under paragraph 1 of the present Article, to all High Contracting Parties.

3. If all the High Contracting Parties which have, within the prescribed time-limit, stated their views to the Director-General of the United Nations Educational, Scientific and Cultural Organization, pursuant to paragraph 1(b) of this Article, inform him that they favour acceptance of the amendment without a Conference, notification of their decision shall be made by the Director-General in accordance with Article 38. The amendment shall become effective for

all the High Contracting Parties on the expiry of ninety days from the date of such notification.

4.   The Director-General shall convene a Conference of the High Contracting Parties to consider the proposed amendment if requested to do so by more than one-third of the High Contracting Parties.

5.   Amendments to the Convention or to the Regulations for its execution, dealt with under the provisions of the preceding paragraph, shall enter into force only after they have been unanimously adopted by the High Contracting Parties represented at the Conference and accepted by each of the High Contracting Parties.

6.   Acceptance by the High Contracting Parties of amendments to the Convention or to the Regulations for its execution, which have been adopted by the Conference mentioned in paragraphs 4 and 5, shall be effected by the deposit of a formal instrument with the Director-General of the United Nations Educational, Scientific and Cultural Organization.

7.   After the entry into force of amendments to the present Convention or to the Regulations for its execution, only the text of the Convention or of the Regulations for its execution thus amended shall remain open for ratification or accession.

ARTICLE 40   REGISTRATION

In accordance with Article 102 of the Charter of the United Nations, the present Convention shall be registered with the Secretariat of the United Nations at the request of the Director-General of the United Nations Educational, Scientific and Cultural Organization.

IN FAITH WHEREOF the undersigned, duly authorized, have signed the present Convention.

Done at The Hague, this fourteenth day of May 1954, in a single copy which shall be deposited in the archives of the United Nations Educational, Scientific and Cultural Organization, and certified true copies of which shall be delivered to all the States referred to in Articles 30 and 32 as well as to the United Nations.

(Here follow signatures)

Regulations for the Execution of the Convention for the Protection of Cultural Property in the Event of Armed Conflict

CHAPTER I: CONTROL

Article 1   International List of Persons

On the entry into force of the Convention, the Director-General of the United Nations Educational, Scientific and Cultural Organization shall compile an international list consisting of all persons nominated by the High Contracting Parties as qualified to carry out the functions of Commissioner-General for Cultural Property. On the initiative of the Director-General of the United Nations Educational, Scientific and Cultural Organization, this list shall be periodically revised on the basis of requests formulated by the High Contracting Parties.

Article 2   Organization of Control

As soon as any High Contracting Party is engaged in an armed conflict to which Article 18 of the Convention applies:

(a) It shall appoint a representative for cultural property situated in its territory; if it is in occupation of another territory, it shall appoint a special representative for cultural property situated in that territory;

(b) The Protecting Power acting for each of the Parties in conflict with such High Contracting Party shall appoint delegates accredited to the latter in conformity with Article 3 below;

(c) A Commissioner-General for Cultural Property shall be appointed to such High Contracting Party in accordance with Article 4.

Article 3   Appointment of Delegates of Protecting Powers

The Protecting Power shall appoint its delegates from among the members of its diplomatic or consular staff or, with the approval of the Party to which they will be accredited, from among other persons.

Article 4   Appointment of Commissioner-General

1.   The Commissioner-General for Cultural Property shall be chosen from the international list of persons by joint agreement between the Party to which he will be accredited and the Protecting Powers acting on behalf of the opposing Parties.
2.   Should the Parties fail to reach agreement within three weeks from the beginning of their discussions on this point, they shall request the President of the International Court of Justice to appoint the Commissioner-General, who shall not take up his duties until the Party to which he is accredited has approved his appointment.

Article 5   Functions of Delegates

The delegates of the Protecting Powers shall take note of violations of the Convention, investigate, with the approval of the Party to which they are accredited, the circumstances in which they have occurred, make representations locally to secure their cessation and, if necessary, notify the Commissioner-General of such violations. They shall keep him informed of their activities.

Article 6   Functions of the Commissioner-General

1.   The Commissioner-General for Cultural Property shall deal with all matters referred to him in connection with the application of the Convention, in conjunction with the representative of the Party to which he is accredited and with the delegates concerned.
2.   He shall have powers of decision and appointment in the cases specified in the present Regulations.
3.   With the agreement of the Party to which he is accredited, he shall have the right to order an investigation or to conduct it himself.
4.   He shall make any representations to the Parties to the conflict or to their Protecting Powers which he deems useful for the application of the Convention.
5.   He shall draw up such reports as may be necessary on the application of the Convention and communicate them to the Parties concerned and to their Protecting Powers. He shall send copies to the Director-General of the United Nations Educational, Scientific and

Cultural Organization, who may make use only of their technical contents.

6. If there is no Protecting Power, the Commissioner-General shall exercise the functions of the Protecting Power as laid down in Articles 21 and 22 of the Convention.

Article 7   Inspectors and Experts

1. Whenever the Commissioner-General for Cultural Property considers it necessary, either at the request of the delegates concerned or after consultation with them, he shall propose, for the approval of the Party to which he is accredited, an inspector of cultural property to be charged with a specific mission. An inspector shall be responsible only to the Commissioner-General.

2. The Commissioner-General, delegates and inspectors may have recourse to the services of experts, who will also be proposed for the approval of the Party mentioned in the preceding paragraph.

Article 8   Discharge of the Mission of Control

The Commissioners-General for Cultural Property, delegates of the Protecting Powers, inspectors and experts shall in no case excccd their mandates. In particular, they shall take account of the security needs of the High Contracting Party to which they are accredited and shall in all circumstances act in accordance with the requirements of the military situation as communicated to them by that High Contracting Party.

Article 9   Substitutes for Protecting Powers

If a Party to the conflict does not benefit or ceases to benefit from the activities of a Protecting Power, a neutral State may be asked to undertake those functions of a Protecting Power which concern the appointment of a Commissioner-General for Cultural Property in accordance with the procedure laid down in Article 4 above. The Commissioner-General thus appointed shall, if need be, entrust to inspectors the functions of delegates of Protecting Powers as specified in the present Regulations.

Article 10   Expenses

The remuneration and expenses of the Commissioner-General for Cultural Property, inspectors and experts shall be met by the Party to which they are accredited. Remuneration and expenses of delegates of the Protecting Powers shall be subject to agreement between those Powers and the States whose interests they are safeguarding.

CHAPTER II: SPECIAL PROTECTION

Article 11   Improvised Refuges

1.   If during an armed conflict, a High Contracting Party is induced by unforeseen circumstances to set up an improvised refuge and desires that it should be placed under special protection, it shall communicate this fact to the Commissioner-General accredited to that Party.

2.   If the Commissioner-General considers that such a measure is justified by the circumstances and by the importance of the cultural property sheltered in this improvised refuge, he may authorize the High Contracting Party to display on such a refuge the distinctive emblem defined in Article 16 of the Convention. He shall communicate his decision without delay to the delegates of the Protecting Powers who are concerned, each of whom may, within a time-limit of thirty days, order the immediate withdrawal of the emblem.

3.   As soon as such delegates have signified their agreement or if the time-limit of thirty days has passed without any of the delegates concerned having made an objection, and if, in the view of the Commissioner-General, the refuge fulfils the conditions laid down in Article 8 of the Convention, the Commissioner-General shall request the Director-General of the United Nations Educational, Scientific and Cultural Organization to enter the refuge in the Register of Cultural Property under Special Protection.

Article 12   International Register of Cultural Property under Special Protection

1.   An 'International Register of Cultural Property under Special Protection' shall be prepared.

2.   The Director-General of the United Nations Educational, Scientific and Cultural Organization shall maintain this Register. He shall furnish copies to the Secretary-General of the United Nations and to the High Contracting Parties.

3.   The Register shall be divided into sections, each in the name of a High Contracting Party. Each section shall be subdivided into three paragraphs, headed: Refuges, Centres containing Monuments, Other Immovable Cultural Property. The Director-General shall determine what details each section shall contain.

Article 13   Requests for Registration

1.   Any High Contracting Party may submit to the Director-General of the United Nations Educational, Scientific and Cultural Organization an application for the entry in the Register of certain refuges, centres containing monuments or other immovable cultural property situated within its territory. Such application shall contain a description of the location of such property and shall certify that the property complies with the provisions of Article 8 of the Convention.
2.   In the event of occupation, the Occupying Power shall be competent to make such application.
3.   The Director-General of the United Nations Educational, Scientific and Cultural Organization shall, without delay, send copies of applications for registration to each of the High Contracting Parties.

Article 14   Objections

1.   Any High Contracting Party may, by letter addressed to the Director-General of the United Nations Educational, Scientific and Cultural Organization, lodge an objection to the registration of cultural property. This letter must be received by him within four months of the day on which he sent a copy of the application for registration.
2.   Such objection shall state the reasons giving rise to it, the only valid grounds being that:

(a)   the property is not cultural property;
(b)   the property does not comply with the conditions mentioned in Article 8 of the Convention.

3.   The Director-General shall send a copy of the letter of objection to the High Contracting Parties without delay. He shall, if necessary, seek the advice of the International Committee on Monuments, Artistic and Historical Sites and Archaeological Excavations and also, if he thinks fit, of any other competent organization or person.
4.   The Director-General, or the High Contracting Party requesting registration, may make whatever representations they deem neces-

sary to the High Contracting Parties which lodged the objection, with a view to causing the objection to be withdrawn.

5.   If High Contracting Party which has made an application for registration in time of peace becomes involved in an armed conflict before the entry has been made, the cultural property concerned shall at once be provisionally entered in the Register, by the Director-General, pending the confirmation, withdrawal or cancellation of any objection that may be, or may have been, made.

6.   If, within a period of six months from the date of receipt of the letter of objection, the Director-General has not received from the High Contracting Party lodging the objection a communication stating that it has been withdrawn, the High Contracting Party applying for registration may request arbitration in accordance with the procedure in the following paragraph.

7.   The request for arbitration shall not be made more than one year after the date of receipt by the Director-General of the letter of objection. Each of the two parties to the dispute shall appoint an arbitrator. When more than one objection has been lodged against an application for registration, the High Contracting Parties which have lodged the objections shall, by common consent, appoint a single arbitrator. These two arbitrators shall select a chief arbitrator from the international list mentioned in Article 1 of the present Regulations. If such arbitrators cannot agree upon their choice, they shall ask the President of the International Court of Justice to appoint a chief arbitrator who need not necessarily be chosen from the international list. The arbitral tribunal thus constituted shall fix its own procedure. There shall be no appeal from its decisions.

8.   Each of the High Contracting Parties may declare, whenever a dispute to which it is a Party arises, that it does not wish to apply the arbitration procedure provided for in the preceding paragraph. In such cases, the objection to an application for registration shall be submitted by the Director-General to the High Contracting Parties. The objection will be confirmed only if the High Contracting Parties so decide by a two-thirds majority of the High Contracting Parties voting. The vote shall be taken by correspondence, unless the Director-General of the United Nations Educational, Scientific and Cultural Organization deems it essential to convene a meeting under the powers conferred upon him by Article 27 of the Convention. If the Director-General decides to proceed with the vote by correspondence, he shall invite the High Contracting Parties to transmit their votes by sealed letter within six months from the day on which they were invited to do so.

Article 15   Registration

1.   The Director-General of the United Nations Educational, Scientific and Cultural Organization shall cause to be entered in the Register, under a serial number, each item of property for which application for registration is made, provided that he has not received an objection within the time-limit prescribed in paragraph 1 of Article 14.

2.   If an objection has been lodged, and without prejudice to the provision of paragraph 5 of Article 14, the Director-General shall enter property in the Register only if the objection has been withdrawn or has failed to be confirmed following the procedures laid down in either paragraph 7 or paragraph 8 of Article 14.

3.   Whenever paragraph 3 of Article 11 applies, the Director-General shall enter property in the Register if so requested by the Commissioner-General for Cultural Property.

4.   The Director-General shall send without delay to the Secretary-General of the United Nations, to the High Contracting Parties and, at the request of the Party applying for registration, to all other States referred to in Articles 30 and 32 of the Convention, a certified copy of each entry in the Register. Entries shall become effective thirty days after despatch of such copies.

Article 16   Cancellation

1.   The Director-General of the United Nations Educational Scientific and Cultural Organization shall cause the registration of any property to be cancelled:

(a)   at the request of the High Contracting Party within whose territory the cultural property is situated;

(b)   if the High Contracting Party which requested registration has denounced the Convention, and when that denunciation has taken effect;

(c)   in the special case provided for in Article 14, paragraph 5, when an objection has been confirmed following the procedures mentioned either in paragraph 7 or in paragraph 8 of Article 14.

2.   The Director-General shall send without delay, to the Secretary-General of the United Nations and to all States which received a copy of the entry in the Register, a certified copy of its cancellation. Cancellation shall take effect thirty days after the despatch of such copies.

CHAPTER III: TRANSPORT OF CULTURAL PROPERTY

Article 17   Procedure to Obtain Immunity

1.   The request mentioned in paragraph 1 of Article 12 of the Convention shall be addressed to the Commissioner-General for Cultural Property. It shall mention the reasons on which it is based and specify the approximate number and the importance of the objects to be transferred, their present location, the location now envisaged, the means of transport to be used, the route to be followed, the date proposed for the transfer, and any other relevant information.
2.   If the Commissioner-General, after taking such opinions as he deems fit, considers that such transfer is justified, he shall consult those delegates of the Protecting Powers who are concerned on the measures proposed for carrying it out. Following such consultation, he shall notify the Parties to the conflict concerned of the transfer, including in such notification all useful information.
3.   The Commissioner-General shall appoint one or more inspectors, who shall satisfy themselves that only the property stated in the request is to be transferred and that the transport is to be by the approved methods and bears the distinctive emblem. The inspector or inspectors shall accompany the property to its destination.

Article 18   Transport abroad

Where the transfer under special protection is to the territory of another country, it shall be governed not only by Article 12 of the Convention and by Article 17 of the present Regulations, but by the following further provisions:

(a)   while the cultural property remains on the territory of another State, that State shall be its depositary and shall extend to it as great a measure of care as that which it bestows upon its own cultural property of comparable importance;
(b)   the depositary State shall return the property only on the cessation of the conflict; such return shall be effected within six months from the date on which it was requested;
(c)   during the various transfer operations, and while it remains on the territory of another State, the cultural property shall be exempt from confiscation and may not be disposed of either by the depositor or by the depositary. Nevertheless, when the safety of the property requires it, the depositary may, with the assent of the depositor, have the property transported to the

territory of a third country, under the conditions laid down in the present article;

(d) the request for special protection shall indicate that the State to whose territory the property is to be transferred accepts the provisions of the present Article.

Article 19   Occupied Territory

Whenever a High Contracting Party occupying territory of another High Contracting Party transfers cultural property to a refuge situated elsewhere in that territory, without being able to follow the procedure provided for in Article 17 of the Regulations, the transfer in question shall not be regarded as misappropriation within the meaning of Article 4 of the Convention, provided that the Commissioner-General for Cultural Property certifies in writing, after having consulted the usual custodians, that such transfer was rendered necessary by circumstances.

CHAPTER IV: THE DISTINCTIVE EMBLEM

Article 20   Affixing of the emblem

1.   The placing of the distinctive emblem and its degree of visibility shall be left to the discretion of the competent authorities of each High Contracting Party. It may be displayed on flags or armlets; it may be painted on an object or represented in any other appropriate form.

2.   However, without prejudice to any possible fuller markings, the emblem shall, in the event of armed conflict and in the cases mentioned in Articles 12 and 13 of the Convention, be placed on the vehicles of transport so as to be clearly visible in daylight from the air as well as from the ground. The emblem shall be visible from the ground:

(a) at regular intervals sufficient to indicate clearly the perimeter of a centre containing monuments under special protection;

(b) at the entrance to other immovable cultural property under special protection.

Article 21   Identification of Persons

1.   The persons in Article 17, paragraph 2(b) and (c) of the Convention may wear an armlet bearing the distinctive emblem, issued and stamped by the competent authorities.

2.   Such persons shall carry a special identity card bearing the distinctive emblem. This card shall mention at least the surname and first names, the date of birth, the title or rank, and the function of the holder. The card shall bear the photograph of the holder as well as his signature or his fingerprints, or both. It shall bear the embossed stamp of the competent authorities.

3.   Each High Contracting Party shall make out its own type of identity card, guided by the model annexed, by way of example, to the present Regulations. The High Contracting Parties shall transmit to each other a specimen of the model they are using. Identity cards shall be made out, if possible, at least in duplicate, one copy being kept by the issuing Power.

4.   The said persons may not, without legitimate reason, be deprived of their identity card or of the right to wear the armlet.

Front

IDENTITY CARD

for personnel engaged in the
protection of cultural property

Surname
First names
Date of Birth
Title or Rank
Function

Is the bearer of this card under the terms of the
Convention of The Hague, dated 14 May, 1954, for
the Protection of Cultural Property in the event of
Armed Conflict.

Date of Issue   Number of Card

Reverse side

Signature of bearer or
fingerprints or both

Photo
of bearer

Embossed
stamp
of authority
issuing card

Height	Eyes	Hair

Other distinguishing marks

Annex IV
Protocol for the Protection of Cultural Property in the Event of Armed Conflict, Signed at The Hague, 14 May 1954

The High Contracting Parties are agreed as follows:

I

1.   Each High Contracting Party undertakes to prevent the exportation, from a territory occupied by it during an armed conflict, of cultural property as defined in Article 1 of the Convention for the Protection of Cultural Property in the Event of Armed Conflict, signed at The Hague on 14 May 1954.

2.   Each High Contracting Party undertakes to take into its custody cultural property imported into its territory either directly or indirectly from any occupied territory. This shall either be effected automatically upon the importation of the property or, failing this, at the request of the authorities of that territory.

3.   Each High Contracting Party undertakes to return, at the close of hostilities, to the competent authorities of the territory previously occupied, cultural property which is in its territory, if such property has been exported in contravention of the principle laid down in the first paragraph. Such property shall never be retained as war reparations.

4.   The High Contracting Party whose obligation it was to prevent the exportation of cultural property from the territory occupied by it shall pay an indemnity to the holders in good faith of any cultural property which has to be returned in accordance with the preceding paragraph.

II

5.   Cultural property coming from the territory of a High Contracting Party and deposited by it in the territory of another High Contracting Party for the purpose of protecting such property against the dangers of an armed conflict shall be returned by the latter, at the end of hostilities, to the competent authorities of the territory from which it came.

III

6.   The present Protocol shall bear the date of 14 May 1954 and, until the date of 31 December 1954, shall remain open for signature by all States invited to the Conference which met at The Hague from 21 April 1954 to 14 May 1954.

7.   (a)   The present Protocol shall be subject to ratification by signatory States in accordance with their respective constitutional procedures.

   (b)   The instruments of ratification shall be deposited with the Director-General of the United Nations Educational, Scientific and Cultural Organization.

8.   From the date of its entry into force, the present Protocol shall be open for accession by all States mentioned in paragraph 6 which have not signed it, as well as any other State invited to accede by the Executive Board of the United Nations Educational, Scientific and Cultural Organization. Accession shall be effected by the deposit of an instrument of accession with the Director-General of the United Nations Educational, Scientific and Cultural Organization.

9.   The States referred to in paragraphs 6 and 8 may declare, at the time of signature, ratification or accession, that they will not be bound by the provisions of Section 1 or by those of Section 11 of the present Protocol.

10.   (a)   The present Protocol shall enter into force three months after five instruments of ratification have been deposited.

   (b)   Thereafter, it shall enter into force, for each High Contracting Party, three months after the deposit of its instrument of ratification or accession.

   (c)   The situations referred to in Articles 18 and 19 of the Convention for the Protection of Cultural Property in the Event of Armed Conflict, signed at The Hague on 14 May 1954, shall give immediate effect to ratifications and accessions deposited by the Parties to the conflict either before or after the beginning of hostilities or occupation. In such cases, the Director-General of the United Nations Educational, Scientific and Cultural Organization shall transmit the communications referred to in paragraph 14 by the speediest method.

11. (a) Each State Party to the Protocol on the date of its entry into force shall take all necessary measures to ensure its effective application within a period of six months after such entry into force.

    (b) This period shall be six months from the date of deposit of the instruments of ratification or accession for any State which deposits its instrument of ratification or accession after the date of the entry into force of the Protocol.

12. Any High Contracting Party may, at the time of ratification or accession, or at any time thereafter, declare by notification addressed to the Director-General of the United Nations Educational, Scientific and Cultural Organization, that the present Protocol shall extend to all or any of the territories for whose international relations it is responsible. The said notification shall take effect three months after the date of its receipt.

13. (a) Each High Contracting Party may denounce the present Protocol on its own behalf, or on behalf of any territory for whose international relations it is responsible.

    (b) The denunciation shall be notified by an instrument in writing, deposited with the Director-General of the United Nations Educational, Scientific and Cultural Organization.

    (c) The denunciation shall take effect one year after receipt of the instrument of denunciation. However, if, on the expiry of this period, the denouncing Party is involved in an armed conflict, the denunciation shall not take effect until the end of hostilities, or until the operations of repatriating cultural property are completed, whichever is the later.

14. The Director-General of the United Nations Educational, Scientific and Cultural Organization shall inform the States referred to in paragraphs 6 and 8, as well as the United Nations, of the deposit of all the instruments of ratification, accession or acceptance provided for in paragraphs 7, 8 and 15 of the notifications and denunciations provided for respectively in paragraphs 12 and 13.

15. (a) The present Protocol may be revised if revision is requested by more than one-third of the High Contracting Parties.

    (b) The Director-General of the United Nations Educational, Scientific and Cultural Organization shall convene a Conference for this purpose.

    (c) Amendments to the present Protocol shall enter into force only after they have been unanimously adopted by the High Contracting Parties represented at the Conference and accepted by each of the High Contracting Parties.

(d) Acceptance by the High Contracting Parties of amendments to the present Protocol, which have been adopted by the Conference mentioned in subparagraphs (b) and (c), shall be effected by the deposit of a formal instrument with the Director-General of the United Nations Educational, Scientific and Cultural Organization.

(e) After the entry into force of amendments to the present Protocol, only the text of the said Protocol thus amended shall remain open for ratification or accession.

In accordance with Article 102 of the Charter of the United Nations, the present Protocol shall be registered with the Secretariat of the United Nations at the request of the Director-General of the United Nations Educational, Scientific and Cultural Organization.

IN FAITH WHEREOF the undersigned, duly authorized, have signed the present Protocol.

Done at The Hague, this fourteenth day of May 1954, in English, French, Russian and Spanish, the four texts being equally authoritative, in a single copy which shall be deposited in the archives of the United Nations Educational, Scientific and Cultural Organization, and certified true copies of which shall be delivered to all the States referred to in paragraphs 6 and 8 as well as to the United Nations.

(Here follow signatures)

Annex V
Resolutions Adopted by the Intergovernmental Conference on the Protection of Cultural Property in the Event of Armed Conflict (The Hague, 1954)

Resolution I

The Conference expresses the hope that the competent organs of the United Nations should decide, in the event of military action being taken in implementation of the Charter, to ensure application of the provisions of the Convention by the armed forces taking part in such action.

Resolution II

The Conference expresses the hope that each of the High Contracting Parties, on acceding to the Convention, should set up, within the framework of its constitutional and administrative system, a national advisory committee consisting of a small number of distinguished persons: for example, senior officials of archaeological services, museums, etc., a representative of the military general staff, a representative of the Ministry of Foreign Affairs, a specialist in international law and two or three other members whose official duties or specialized knowledge are related to the fields covered by the Convention. The Committee should be under the authority of the minister of State or senior official responsible for the national service chiefly concerned with the care of cultural property. Its chief functions would be:

(a) to advise the government concerning the measures required for the implementation of the Convention in its legislative, technical or military aspects, both in time of peace and during an armed conflict;

(b) to approach its government in the event of an armed conflict or when such a conflict appears imminent, with a view to ensuring that cultural property situated within its own territory or within that of other countries is known to, and respected and protected by the armed forces of the country, in accordance with the provisions of the Convention.

(c) to arrange, in agreement with its government, for liaison and co-operation with other similar national committees and with any competent international authority.

Resolution III

The Conference expresses the hope that the Director-General of the United Nations Educational, Scientific and Cultural Organization should convene, as soon as possible after the entry into force of the Convention for the Protection of Cultural Property in the Event of Armed Conflict, a meeting of the High Contracting Parties.

Annex VI
Convention and Protocol for the Protection of Cultural Property in the Event of Armed Conflict (The Hague, 14 May 1954); List of the 87 States Parties to the Convention (74 States Parties to the Protocol) at 5 July 1995

	Convention		Protocol	
States	Date of ratification (R) accession (A) succession (S)	Date of entry into force	Date of ratification (R) accession (A) succession (S)	Date of entry into force
Albania	20.12.1960 (A)	20.3.1961	20.12.1960 (A)	20.3.1961
Argentina	22.3.1989 (A)	22.6.1989		
Armenia (Rep. of)[1]	5.9.1993 (S)		5.9.1993 (S)	
Australia	19.9.1984 (R)	19.12.1984		
Austria	25.3.1964 (R)	25.6.1964	25.3.1964 (R)	25.6.1964
Azerbaijan (Rep. of)[1]	20.9.1993 (A)	20.12.1993	20.9.1993 (A)	20.12.1993
Belarus	7.5.1957 (R)	7.8.1957	7.5.1957 (R)	7.8.1957
Belgium	16.9.1960 (R)	16.12.1960	16.9.1960 (R)	16.12.1960
Bosnia and Herzegovina (Rep. of)[2]	12.7.1993 (S)		12.7.1993 (S)	

Brazil	12.9.1958 (R)	12.12.1958	12.9.1958 (R)	12.12.1958
Bulgaria	7.8.1956 (A)	7.11.1956	9.10.1958 (A)	9.1.1959
Burkina Faso	18.12.1969 (A)	18.3.1970	4.2.1987 (A)	4.5.1987
Cambodia	4.4.1962 (R)	4.7.1962	4.4.1962 (R)	4.7.1962
Cameroon	12.10.1961 (A)	12.1.1962	12.10.1961 (A)	12.1.1962
Côte d'Ivoire	24.1.1980 (A)	24.4.1980		
Croatia (Rep. of)[2]	6.7.1992 (S)		6.7.1992 (S)	
Cuba	26.11.1957 (R)	26.2.1958	26.11.1957 (R)	26.2.1958
Cyprus	9.9.1964 (A)	9.12.1964	9.9.1964 (A)	9.12.1964
Czech Republic[3]	26.3.1993 (S)		26.3.1993 (S)	
Dominican Republic	5.1.1960 (A)	5.4.1960		
Ecuador	2.10.1956 (R)	2.1.1957	8.2.1961 (R)	8.5.1961
Egypt[4]	17.8.1955 (R)	7.8.1956	17.8.1955 (R)	7.8.1956
Estonia	4.4.1995 (A)	4.7.1995		
Federal Republic of Yugoslavia (Serbia and Montenegro)[4,5]	13.2.1956 (R)	7.8.1956	13.2.1956 (R)	7.8.1956
Finland	16.9.1994 (A)	16.12.1994	16.9.1994 (A)	16.12.1994
France	7.6.1957 (R)	7.9.1957	7.6.1957 (R)	7.9.1957
Gabon	4.12.1961 (A)	4.3.1962	4.12.1961 (A)	4.3.1962
Georgia (Rep. of)[1]	4.11.1992 (S)		4.11.1992 (S)	
Germany[6]	11.8.1967 (R)	11.11.1967	11.8.1967 (R)	11.11.1967
Ghana	25.7.1960 (A)	25.10.1960	25.7.1960 (A)	25.10.1960
Greece	9.2.1981 (R)	9.5.1981	9.2.1981 (R)	9.5.1981
Guatemala	2.10.1985 (A)	2.1.1986	19.5.1994 (A)	19.8.1994
Guinea	20.9.1960 (A)	20.12.1960	11.12.1961 (A)	11.3.1962
Holy See	24.2.1958 (A)	24.5.1958	24.2.1958 (A)	24.5.1958
Hungary	17.5.1956 (R)	17.8.1956	16.8.1956 (A)	16.11.1956
India	16.6.1958 (R)	16.9.1958	16.6.1958 (R)	16.9.1958
Indonesia	10.1.1967 (R)	10.4.1967	26.7.1967 (R)	26.10.1967
Iran, Islamic Republic of	22.6.1959 (R)	22.9.1959	22.6.1959 (R)	22.9.1959
Iraq	21.12.1967 (R)	21.3.1968	21.12.1967 (R)	21.3.1968
Israel	3.10.1957 (R)	3.1.1958	1.4.1958 (A)	1.7.1958
Italy	9.5.1958 (R)	9.8.1958	9.5.1958 (R)	9.8.1958
Jordan	2.10.1957 (R)	2.1.1958	2.10.1957 (R)	2.1.1958
Kuwait	6.6.1969 (A)	6.9.1969	11.2.1970 (A)	11.5.1970
Kyrgyzstan (Rep. of)	3.7.1995 (A)	3.10.1995[7]		
Lebanon	1.6.1960 (R)	1.9.1960	1.6.1960 (R)	1.9.1960
Libyan Arab Jamahiriya	19.11.1957 (R)	19.2.1958	19.11.1957 (R)	19.2.1958
Liechtenstein	28.4.1960 (A)	28.7.1960	28.4.1960 (A)	28.7.1960
Luxembourg	29.9.1961 (R)	29.12.1961	29.9.1961 (R)	29.12.1961
Madagascar	3.11.1961 (A)	3.2.1962	3.11.1961 (A)	3.2.1962
Malaysia	12.12.1960 (A)	12.3.1961	12.12.1960 (A)	12.3.1961
Mali	18.5.1961 (A)	18.8.1961	18.5.1961 (A)	18.8.1961
Mexico	7.5.1956 (R)	7.8.1956	7.5.1956 (R)	7.8.1956
Monaco	10.12.1957 (R)	10.3.1958	10.12.1957 (R)	10.3.1958
Mongolia	4.11.1964 (A)	4.2.1965		
Morocco	3.8.1968 (A)	30.11.1968	30.8.1968 (A)	30.11.1968
Myanmar[4]	10.2.1956 (R)	7.8.1956	10.2.1956 (R)	7.8.1956

Netherlands	14.10.1958 (R)	14.1.1959	14.10.1958 (R)	14.1.1959
Nicaragua	25.11.1959 (R)	25.2.1960	25.11.1959 (R)	25.2.1960
Niger	6.12.1976 (A)	6.3.1977	6.12.1976 (A)	6.3.1977
Nigeria	5.6.1961 (A)	5.9.1961	5.6.1961 (A)	5.9.1961
Norway	19.9.1961 (R)	19.12.1961	19.9.1961 (R)	19.12.1961
Oman	26.10.1977 (A)	26.1.1978		
Pakistan	27.3.1959 (A)	27.6.1959	27.3.1959 (A)	27.6.1959
Panama	17.7.1962 (A)	17.10.1962		
Peru	21.7.1989 (A)	21.10.1989	21.7.1989 (A)	21.10.1989
Poland	6.8.1956 (R)	6.11.1956	5.8.1956 (R)	6.11.1956
Qatar	31.7.1973 (A)	31.10.1973		
Romania	21.3.1958 (R)	21.6.1958	21.3.1958 (R)	21.6.1958
Russian Federation[8]	4.1.1957 (R)	4.4.1957	4.1.1957 (R)	4.4.1957
San Marino[4]	9.2.1956 (R)	7.8.1956	9.2.1956 (R)	7.8.1956
Saudi Arabia	20.1.1971 (A)	20.4.1971		
Senegal	17.6.1987 (A)	17.9.1987	17.6.1987 (A)	17.9.1987
Slovak Republic[3]	31.3.1993 (S)		31.3.1993 (S)	
Slovenia (Rep. of)[2]	5.11.1992 (S)		5.11.1992 (S)	
Spain	7.7.1960 (R)	7.10.1960	26.6.1992 (A)	26.9.1992
Sudan	23.7.1970 (A)	23.10.1970		
Sweden	22.1.1985 (A)	22.4.1985	22.1.1985 (A)	22.4.1985
Switzerland	15.5.1962 (A)	15.8.1962	15.5.1962 (A)	15.8.1962
Syrian Arab Republic	6.3.1958 (R)	6.6.1958	6.3.1958 (R)	6.6.1958
Tajikistan (Rep. of)[1]	28.8.1992 (S)		28.8.1992 (S)	
Thailand	2.5.1958 (A)	2.8.1958	2.5.1958 (A)	2.8.1958
Tunisia	28.1.1981 (A)	28.4.1981	28.1.1981 (A)	28.4.1981
Turkey	15.12.1965 (A)	15.3.1966	15.12.1965 (A)	15.3.1966
Ukraine	6.2.1957 (R)	6.5.1957	6.2.1957 (R)	6.5.1957
United Republic of Tanzania	23.9.1971 (A)	23.12.1971		
Yemen (Rep. of)[9]	6.2.1970 (A)	6.5.1970	6.2.1970 (A)	6.5.1970
Zaire	18.4.1961 (A)	18.7.1961	18.4.1961 (A)	18.7.1961

NOTES

1. This State lodged a notification of succession at the mentioned date, by which it stated that it was bound by the Convention and its Protocol which the USSR ratified on 4 January 1957.
2. This State lodged a notification of succession at the mentioned date, by which it stated that it was bound by the Convention and its Protocol which Yugoslavia ratified on 13 February 1956.
3. This State lodged a notification of succession at the mentioned date, by which it stated that if was bound by the Convention and its Protocol which Czechoslovakia ratified on 6 December 1957.
4. In conformity with the procedure set forth in the Convention and the Protocol, both agreements enter into force, for the first States, three months after the deposit of instrument of ratification by the fifth State, Mexico.
5. The Federal Republic of Yugoslavia (Serbia and Montenegro) notified the Director-General on 27 April 1992 that it would strictly abide by all the interna-

tional obligations which the Socialist Federal Republic of Yugoslavia had assumed in the past.

6. The German Democratic Republic deposited an instrument of accession to the Convention and its Protocol on 16 January 1974. Through the accession of the German Democratic Republic to the Basic Law of the Federal Republic of Germany, with effect from 3 October 1990, the two German States have united to form one sovereign State.

7. Date foreseen for entry into force.

8. The instrument of ratification was deposited by the USSR, on 4 January 1957. The Director-General has been informed that the Russian Federation would continue the participation of the USSR in UNESCO conventions.

9. The People's Democratic Republic of Yemen deposited its instrument of accession on 6 February 1970. After the unification of the People's Democratic Republic of Yemen and the Yemen Arab Republic into a single sovereign State called 'the Republic of Yemen', the Ministers of Foreign Affairs of the Yemen Arab Republic and the People's Democratic Republic of Yemen informed the Secretary-General of the United Nations on 19 May 1990 that all treaties and agreements concluded between either the Yemen Arab Republic or the People's Democratic Republic of Yemen and other States and international organizations in accordance with international law which are in force on 22 May 1990 would remain in effect.

Annex VII
Convention on the Means of Prohibiting and Preventing the Illicit Import, Export and Transfer of Ownership of Cultural Property, Adopted by the General Conference at its Sixteenth Session, Paris, 14 November 1970

The General Conference of the United Nations Educational, Scientific and Cultural Organization, meeting in Paris from 12 October to 14 November 1970, at its Sixteenth Session,

Recalling the importance of the provisions contained in the Declaration of the Principles of International Cultural Co-operation, adopted by the General Conference at its fourteenth session,

Considering that the interchange of cultural property among nations for scientific, cultural and educational purposes increases the knowledge of the civilization of Man, enriches the cultural life of all peoples and inspires mutual respect and appreciation among nations,

Considering that cultural property constitutes one of the basic elements of civilisation and national culture, and that its true value can be appreciated only in relation to the fullest possible information regarding its origin, history and traditional setting,

Considering that it is incumbent upon every State to protect the cultural property existing within its territory against the dangers of theft, clandestine excavation and illicit export,

Considering that, to avert these dangers, it is essential for every State to become increasingly alive to the moral obligations to respect its own cultural heritage and that of all nations,

Considering that, as cultural institutions, museums, libraries and archives should ensure that their collections are built up in accordance with universally recognized moral principles,

Considering that the illicit import, export and transfer of ownership of cultural property is an obstacle to that understanding between nations which it is part of UNESCO's mission to promote by recommending to interested States, international conventions to this end,

Considering that the protection of cultural heritage can be effective only if organized both nationally and internationally among States working in close co-operation,

Considering that the UNESCO General Conference adopted a Recommendation to this effect in 1964,

Having before it further proposals on the means of prohibiting and preventing the illicit import, export and transfer of ownership of cultural property, a question which is on the agenda for the session as item 19,

Having decided, at its fifteenth session, that this question should be made the subject of an international convention,

Adopts this Convention on the fourteenth day of November 1970.

Article 1

For the purposes of this Convention, the term 'cultural property' means property which, on religious or secular grounds, is specifically designated by each State as being of importance for archaeology, prehistory, history, literature, art or science and which belongs to the following categories:

    (a)   rare collections and specimens of fauna, flora, minerals and anatomy, and objects of palaeontological interest;

    (b)   property relating to history, including the history of science and technology and military and social history, to the life of national leaders, thinkers, scientists and artists and to events of national importance;

    (c)   products of archaeological excavations (including regular and clandestine) or of archaeological discoveries;

    (d)   elements of artistic or historical monuments or archaeological sites which have been dismembered;

(e) antiquities more than one hundred years old, such as inscriptions, coins and engraved seals;
(f) objects of ethnological interest;
(g) property of artistic interest, such as:

    (i) pictures, paintings and drawings produced entirely by hand on any support and in any material (excluding industrial designs and manufactured articles decorated by hand);
    (ii) original works of statuary art and sculpture in any material;
    (iii) original engravings, prints and lithographs;
    (iv) original artistic assemblages and montages in any material;

(h) rare manuscripts and incunabula, old books, documents and publications of special interest (historical, artistic, scientific, literary, etc.) singly or in collections;
(i) postage, revenue and similar stamp, singly or in collections;
(j) archives, including sound, photographic and cinematographic archives;
(k) articles of furniture more than one hundred years old and old musical instruments.

Article 2

1. The States Parties to this Convention recognize that the illicit import, export and transfer of ownership of cultural property is one of the main causes of the impoverishment of the cultural heritage of the countries of origin of such property and that international co-operation constitutes one of the most efficient means of protecting each country's cultural property against all the dangers resulting therefrom.
2. To this end, the States Parties undertake to oppose such practices with the means at their disposal, and particularly by removing their causes, putting a stop to current practices, and by helping to make the necessary reparations.

Article 3

The import, export or transfer of ownership of cultural property effected contrary to the provisions adopted under this Convention by the States Parties thereto shall be illicit.

Article 4

The States Parties to this Convention recognize that for the purpose of the Convention property which belongs to the following categories forms part of the cultural heritage of each State:

(a) cultural property created by the individual or collective genius of nationals of the State concerned, and cultural property of importance to the State concerned created within the territory of that State by foreign nationals or stateless persons resident within such territory;

(b) cultural property found within the national territory;

(c) cultural property acquired by archaeological, ethnological or natural science missions, with the consent of the competent authorities of the country of origin of such property;

(d) cultural property which has been the subject of a freely agreed exchange;

(e) cultural property received as a gift or purchased legally with the consent of the competent authorities of the country of origin of such property.

Article 5

To ensure the protection of their cultural property against illicit import, export and transfer of ownership, the States Parties to this Convention undertake, as appropriate for each country, to set up within their territories one or more national services, where such services do not already exist, for the protection of the cultural heritage, with a qualified staff sufficient in number for the effective carrying out of the following functions:

(a) contributing to the formation of draft laws and regulations designed to secure the protection of the cultural heritage and particularly prevention of the illicit import, export and transfer of ownership of important cultural property;

(b) establishing and keeping up to date, on the basis of a national inventory of protected property, a list of important public and private cultural property whose export would constitute an appreciable impoverishment of the national cultural heritage;

(c) promoting the development or the establishment of scientific and technical institutions (museums, libraries, archives, laboratories, workshops ...) required to ensure the preservation and presentation of cultural property;

(d) organizing the supervision of archaeological excavations, ensuring the preservation 'in situ' of certain cultural property, and protecting certain areas reserved for future archaeological research;

(e) establishing, for the benefit of those concerned (curators, collectors, antique dealers, etc.) rules in conformity with the ethical principles set forth in this Convention; and taking steps to ensure the observance of those rules;

(f) taking educational measures to stimulate and develop respect for the cultural heritage of all States, and spreading knowledge of the provisions of this Convention;

(g) seeing that appropriate publicity is given to the disappearance of any items of cultural property.

Article 6

The States Parties to this Convention undertake:

(a) to introduce an appropriate certificate in which the exporting State would specify that the export of the cultural property in question is authorized. The certificate should accompany all items of cultural property exported in accordance with the regulations;

(b) to prohibit the exportation of cultural property from their territory unless accompanied by the above-mentioned export certificate;

(c) to publicize this prohibition by appropriate means, particularly among persons likely to export or import cultural property.

Article 7

The States Parties to this Convention undertake:

(a) to take the necessary measures, consistent with national legislation, to prevent museums and similar institutions within their territories from acquiring cultural property originating in another State Party which has been illegally exported after entry into force of this Convention, in the States concerned. Whenever possible, to inform a State of origin Party to this Convention of an offer of such cultural property illegally removed from that State after the entry into force of this Convention in both States;

(b) (i) to prohibit the import of cultural property stolen from a museum or a religious or secular public monument or similar institution in another State Party to this Convention after the entry into force of this Convention for the States concerned, provided that such property is documented as appertaining to the inventory of that institution;

(ii) at the request of the State Party of origin, to take appropriate steps to recover and return any such cultural property imported after the entry into force of this Convention in both States concerned, provided, however, that the requesting State shall pay just compensation to an innocent purchaser or to a person who has valid title to that property. Requests for recovery and return shall be made through diplomatic offices. The requesting party shall furnish, at its expense, the documentation and other evidence necessary to establish its claim for recovery and return. The Parties shall impose no customs duties or other charges upon cultural property returned pursuant to this Article. All expenses incident to the return and delivery of the cultural property shall be borne by the requesting Party.

Article 8

The States Parties to this Convention undertake to impose penalties or administrative sanctions on any person responsible for infringing the prohibitions referred to under Articles 6 (b) and 7 (b) above.

Article 9

Any State Party to this Convention whose cultural patrimony is in jeopardy from pillage of archaeological or ethnological materials may call upon other States Parties who are affected. The States Parties to this Convention undertake, in these circumstances, to participate in a concerted international effort to determine and to carry out the necessary concrete measures, including the control of exports and imports and international commerce in the specific materials concerned. Pending agreement, each State concerned shall take provisional measures to the extent feasible to prevent irremediable injury to the cultural heritage of the requesting State.

Article 10

The States Parties to this Convention undertake:

(a) to restrict by education, information and vigilance, movement of cultural property illegally removed from any State
Party to this Convention and, as appropriate for each country,
oblige antique dealers, subject to penal or administrative sanctions, to maintain a register recording the origin of each item
of cultural property, names and addresses of the supplier,
description and price of each item sold and to inform the
purchaser of the cultural property of the export prohibition to
which such property may be subject;

(b) to endeavour by educational means to create and develop in
the public mind a realization of the value of cultural property
and the threat to the cultural heritage created by theft, clandestine excavations and illicit exports.

Article 11

The export and transfer of ownership of cultural property under
compulsion arising directly or indirectly from the occupation of a
country by a foreign power shall be regarded as illicit.

Article 12

The States Parties to this Convention shall respect the cultural heritage within the territories for the international relations of which they
are responsible, and shall take all appropriate measures to prohibit
and prevent the illicit import, export and transfer of ownership of
cultural property in such territories.

Article 13

The States Parties to this Convention also undertake, consistent with
the laws of each State:

(a) to prevent by all appropriate means transfers of ownership of
cultural property likely to promote the illicit import or export
of such property;

(b) to ensure that their competent services co-operate in facilitating the earliest possible restitution of illicitly exported cultural property to its rightful owners;

(c)   to admit actions for recovery of lost or stolen items of cultural property brought by or on behalf of the rightful owners;

(d)   To recognize the indefeasible right of each State Party to this Convention to classify and declare certain cultural property as inalienable which should therefore *ipso facto* not be exported, and to facilitate recovery of such property by the State concerned in cases where it has been exported.

Article 14

In order to prevent illicit export and to meet the obligations arising from the implementation of this Convention, each State Party to the Convention should, as far as it is able, provide the national services responsible for the protection of its cultural heritage with an adequate budget and, if necessary, should set up a fund for this purpose.

Article 15

Nothing in this Convention shall prevent State Parties thereto from concluding special agreements among themselves or from continuing to implement agreements already concluded regarding the restitution of cultural property removed, whatever the reason, from its territory of origin, before the entry into force of this Convention for the States concerned.

Article 16

The States Parties to this Convention shall in their periodic reports submitted to the General Conference of the United Nations Educational, Scientific and Cultural Organization, on dates and in a manner to be determined by it, give information on the legislative and administrative provisions which they have adopted and other action which they have taken for the application of this Convention, together with details of the experience acquired in this field.

Article 17

1. The States Parties to this Convention may call on the technical assistance of the United Nations Educational, Scientific and Cultural Organization, particularly as regards:

(a) information and education;
(b) consultation and expert advice;
(c) co-ordination and good offices.

2. The United Nations Educational, Scientific and Cultural Organization may, on its own initiative, conduct research and publish studies on matters relevant to the illicit movement of cultural property.
3. To this end, the United Nations Educational, Scientific and Cultural Organization may also call on the co-operation of any competent non-governmental organization.
4. The United Nations Educational, Scientific and Cultural Organization may, on its own initiative, make proposals to States Parties to this Convention for its implementation.
5. At the request of at least two States Parties to this Convention which are engaged in a dispute over its implementation, UNESCO may extend its good offices to reach a settlement between them.

Article 18

This Convention is drawn up in English, French, Russian and Spanish, the four texts being equally authoritative.

Article 19

1. The Convention shall be subject to ratification or acceptance by States members of the United Nations Educational, Scientific and Cultural Organization in accordance with their respective constitutional procedures.
2. The instrument of ratification or acceptance shall be deposited with the Director-General of the United Nations Educational, Scientific and Cultural Organization.

Article 20

1. This Convention shall be open to accession by all States not members of the United Nations Educational, Scientific and Cultural

Organization which are invited to accede to it by the Executive Board of the Organization.

2.   Accession shall be effected by the deposit of an instrument of accession with the Director-General of the United Nations Educational, Scientific and Cultural organization.

Article 21

This Convention shall enter into force three months after the date of the deposit of the third instrument of ratification, acceptance or accession, but only with respect to those States which have deposited their respective instruments on or before that date. It shall enter into force with respect to any other State three months after the deposit of its instrument of ratification, acceptance or accession.

Article 22

The States Parties to this Convention recognize that the Convention is applicable not only to their metropolitan territories but also to all territories for the international relations of which they are responsible; they undertake to consult, if necessary, the governments or other competent authorities of these territories on or before ratification, acceptance or accession with a view to securing the application of the Convention to those territories, and to notify the Director-General of the United Nations Educational, Scientific and Cultural Organization of the territories to which it is applied, the notification to take effect three months after the date of its receipt.

Article 23

1.   Each State Party to this Convention may denounce the Convention on its own behalf or on behalf of any territory for whose international relations it is responsible.

2.   The denunciation shall be notified by an instrument in writing, deposited with the Director-General of the United Nations Educational, Scientific and Cultural Organization.

3.   The denunciation shall take effect twelve months after the receipt of the instrument of denunciation.

Article 24

The Director-General of the United Nations Educational, Scientific and Cultural Organization shall inform the States members of the Organization, the States not members of the Organization which are referred to in Article 20, as well as the United Nations, of the deposit of all the instruments of ratification, acceptance and accession provided for in Articles 19 and 20, and of the notifications and denunciations provided for in Articles 22 and 23, respectively.

Article 25

1. This Convention may be revised by the General Conference of the United Nations Educational, Scientific and Cultural Organization. Any such revision shall, however, bind only the States which shall become Parties to the revising convention.
2. If the General Conference should adopt a new convention revising this Convention in whole or in part, then, unless the new convention otherwise provides, this Convention shall cease to be open to ratification, acceptance or accession, as from the date on which the new revising convention enters into force.

Article 26

In conformity with Article 102 of the Charter of the United Nations, this Convention shall be registered with the Secretariat of the United Nations at the request of the Director-General of the United Nations Educational, Scientific and Cultural Organization.

Done in Paris this seventeenth day of November 1970, in two authentic copies bearing the signature of the President of the sixteenth session of the General Conference and of the Director-General of the United Nations Educational, Scientific and Cultural Organization, which shall be deposited in the archives of the United Nations Educational, Scientific and Cultural Organization, and certified true copies of which shall be delivered to all the States referred to in Articles 19 and 20 as well as to the United Nations.

The foregoing is the authentic text of the Convention duly adopted by the General Conference of the United Nations Educational, Scientific and Cultural Organization during its sixteenth session, which was held in Paris and declared closed the fourteenth day of November 1970.

IN FAITH WHEREOF we have appended our signatures this seventeenth day of November 1970.

The President of the General Conference
ATILIO DELL'ORO MAINI

The Director-General
RENE MAHEU

Annex VIII
Convention on the Means of Prohibiting and Preventing the Illicit Import, Export and Transfer of Ownership of Cultural Property (Paris, 14 November 1970); List of the 82 States Parties at 5 July 1995

States	Date of ratification (R) acceptance (Ac) accession (A) succession (S)	Date of entry into force
Algeria	24.6.1974 (R)	24.9.1974
Angola	7.11.1991 (R)	7.2.1992
Argentina	11.1.1973 (R)	11.4.1973
Armenia (Republic of)[1]	5.9.1993 (S)	
Australia	30.10.1989 (Ac)	30.1.1990
Bangladesh	9.12.1987 (R)	9.3.1988
Belarus	28.4.1988 (R)	28.7.1988
Belize	26.1.1990 (R)	26.4.1990
Bolivia	4.10.1976 (R)	4.1.1977
Bosnia-Herzegovina (Republic of)[2]	12.7.1993 (S)	
Brazil	16.2.1973 (R)	16.5.1973
Bulgaria[7]	15.9.1971 (R)	24.4.1972

Burkina Faso	7.4.1987 (R)	7.7.1987
Cambodia	26.9.1972 (R)	16.12.1972
Cameroon	24.5.1972 (R)	24.8.1972
Canada	28.3.1978 (Ac)	28.6.1978
Central African Republic	1.2.1972 (R)	1.5.1972
China (People's Republic of)	28.11.1989 (Ac)	28.2.1990
Colombia	24.5.1988 (Ac)	24.8.1988
Côte d'Ivoire	30.10.1990 (R)	30.1.1991
Croatia (Republic of)[2]	6.7.1992 (S)	
Cuba	30.1.1980 (R)	30.4.1980
Cyprus	19.10.1979 (R)	19.1.1980
Czech Republic[3]	26.3.1993 (S)	
Democratic People's Republic of Korea	13.5.1983 (R)	13.8.1983
Dominican Republic	7.3.1973 (R)	7.6.1973
Ecuador[7]	24.3.1971 (Ac)	24.4.1972
Egypt	5.4.1973 (Ac)	5.7.1973
El Salvador	20.2.1978 (R)	20.5.1978
Federal Republic of Yugoslavia (Serbia and Montenegro)[4]	3.10.1972 (R)	3.1.1973
Georgia (Republic of)[1]	4.11.1992 (S)	
Greece	5.6.1981 ()	5.9.1981
Grenada	10.9.1992 (Ac)	10.12.1992
Guatemala	14.1.1985 (R)	14.4.1985
Guinea	18.3.1979 (R)	18.6.1979
Honduras	19.3.1979 (R)	19.6.1979
Hungary	23.10.1978 (R)	23.1.1979
India	24.1.1977 (R)	24.4.1977
Ian (Islamic Republic of)	27.1.1975 (Ac)	27.4.1975
Iraq	12.2.1973 (Ac)	12.5.1973
Italy	2.10.1978	2.1.1979
Jordan	15.3.1974 (R)	15.6.1974
Kuwait	22.6.1972 (Ac)	22.9.1972
Kyrgyzstan (Republic of)[6]	3.7.1995 (A)	3.10.1995
Lebanon	25.8.1992 (R)	25.11.1992
Libyan Arab Jamahiriya	9.1.1973 (R)	9.4.1973
Madagascar	21.6.1989 (R)	21.9.1989
Mali	6.4.1987 (R)	6.7.1987
Mauritania	27.4.1977 (R)	27.7.1977
Mauritius	27.2.1978 (Ac)	27.5.1978
Mexico	4.10.1972 (Ac)	4.1.1973
Mongolia	23.5.1991 (Ac)	23.8.1991
Nepal	23.6.1976 (R)	23.9.1976
Nicaragua	19.4.1977 (R)	19.7.1977
Niger	16.10.1972 (R)	16.1.1973

Nigeria	24.1.1972 (R)	24.4.1972
Oman	2.6.1978 (Ac)	2.9.1978
Pakistan	30.4.1981 (R)	30.7.1981
Panama	13.8.1973 (Ac)	13.11.1973
Peru	24.10.1979 (Ac)	24.1.1980
Poland	31.1.1974 (R)	30.4.1974
Portugal	9.12.1985 (R)	9.3.1986
Qatar	20.4.1977 (Ac)	20.7.1977
Republic of Korea	14.2.1983 (Ac)	14.5.1983
Romania	6.12.1993 (R)	6.3.1994
Russian Federation[5]	28.4.1988 (R)	28.7.1988
Saudi Arabia	8.9.1976 (Ac)	8.12.1976
Senegal	9.12.1984 (R)	9.3.1985
Slovak Republic[3]	31.3.1993 (S)	
Slovenia (Republic of)[2]	5.11.1992 (S)	
Spain	10.1.1986 (R)	10.4.1986
Sri Lanka	7.4.1981 (Ac)	7.7.1981
Syrian Arab Republic	21.2.1975 (Ac)	21.5.1975
Tajikistan (Republic of)[1]	28.8.1992 (S)	
Tunisia	10.3.1975 (R)	10.6.1975
Turkey	21.4.1981 (R)	21.7.1981
Ukraine	28.4.1988 (R)	28.7.1988
United Republic of Tanzania	2.8.1977 (R)	2.11.1977
United States of America	2.9.1983 (Ac)	2.12.1983
Uruguay	9.8.1977 (R)	9.11.1977
Zaire	23.9.1974 (R)	23.12.1974
Zambia	21.6.1985 (R)	21.9.1985

NOTES

1. This State lodged a notification of succession at the mentioned date, by which it stated that it was bound by the Convention that the USSR ratified on 28 April 1988.
2. This State lodged a notification of succession at the mentioned date, by which it stated that it was bound by the Convention which Yugoslavia ratified on 3 October 1972.
3. This State lodged a notification of succession at the mentioned date, by which it stated that it was bound by the Convention which Czechoslovakia accepted on 14 February 1977.
4. The Federal Republic of Yugoslavia (Serbia and Montenegro) notified the Director-General on 27 April 1992 that it would strictly abide by all the international obligations which the Socialist Federal Republic of Yugoslovia had assumed in the past.
5. The instrument of ratification was deposited by the USSR on 28 April 1988. The Director-General has been informed that the Russian Federation would continue the participation of the USSR in UNESCO conventions.

6. Date foreseen for entry into force.
7. In conformity with the procedure set forth in the Convention, this agreement enters into force, for the first States, three months after the deposit of ratification by the third State, Nigeria.

Annex IX
Convention Concerning the Protection of the World Cultural and Natural Heritage, Adopted by the General Conference at its Seventeenth Session, Paris, 16 November 1972

The General Conference of the United Nations Educational, Scientific and Cultural Organization meeting in Paris from 17 October to 21 November 1972, at its seventeenth session,

Noting that the cultural heritage and the natural heritage are increasingly threatened with destruction not only by the traditional causes of decay, but also by changing social and economic conditions which aggravate the situation with even more formidable phenomena of damage or destruction,

Considering that deterioration or disappearance of any item of the cultural or natural heritage constitutes a harmful impoverishment of the heritage of all the nations of the world,

Considering that protection of this heritage at the national level often remains incomplete because of the scale of the resources which it requires and of the insufficient economic, scientific and technical resources of the country where the property to be protected is situated,

Recalling that the Constitution of the Organization provides that it will maintain, increase and diffuse knowledge, by assuring the conservation and protection of the world's heritage, and recommending to the nations concerned the necessary international conventions,

Considering that the existing international conventions, recommendations and resolutions concerning cultural and natural property demonstrate the importance, for all the peoples of the world, of safeguarding this unique and irreplaceable property, to whatever people it may belong,

Considering that parts of the cultural or natural heritage are of outstanding interest and therefore need to be preserved as part of the world heritage of mankind as a whole,

Considering that, in view of the magnitude and gravity of the new dangers threatening them, it is incumbent on the international community as a whole to participate in the protection of the cultural and natural heritage of outstanding universal value, by the granting of collective assistance which, although not taking the place of action by the State concerned, will serve as an effective complement thereto,

Considering that it is essential for this purpose to adopt new provisions in the form of a convention establishing an effective system of collective protection of the cultural and natural heritage of outstanding universal value, organized on a permanent basis and in accordance with modern scientific methods,

Having decided, at its sixteenth session, that this question should be made the subject of an international convention,

Adopts this sixteenth day of November 1972 this Convention.

I. DEFINITIONS OF THE CULTURAL AND THE NATURAL HERITAGE

Article 1

For the purposes of this Convention, the following shall be considered as 'cultural heritage':

monuments: architectural works, works of monumental sculpture and painting, elements or structures of an archaeological nature, inscriptions, cave dwellings and combinations of features, which are of outstanding universal value from the point of view of history, art or science;

groups of buildings: groups of separate or connected buildings which, because of their architecture, their homogeneity or their place in the landscape, are of outstanding universal value from the point of view of history, art or science;

sites: works of man or the combined works of nature and of man, and areas including archaeological sites which are of outstanding universal value from the historical, aesthetic, ethnological or anthropological points of view.

Article 2

For the purposes of this Convention, the following shall be considered as natural heritage:

natural features consisting of physical and biological formations or groups of such formation, which are of outstanding universal value from the aesthetic or scientific point of view;

geological and physiographical formations and precisely delineated areas which constitute the habitat of threatened species of animals and plants of outstanding universal value from the point of view of science or conservation;

natural sites or precisely delineated natural areas of outstanding universal value from the point of view of science, conservation or natural beauty.

Article 3

It is for each State Party to this Convention to identify and delineate the different properties situated on its territory mentioned in Articles 1 and 2 above.

II. NATIONAL PROTECTION AND INTERNATIONAL PROTECTION OF THE CULTURAL AND NATURAL HERITAGE

Article 4

Each State Party to this Convention recognizes that the duty of ensuring the identification, protection, conservation, presentation and transmission to future generations of the cultural and natural heritage referred to in Articles 1 and 2 and situated on its territory belongs primarily to that State. It will do all it can to this end, to the utmost of its own resources and, where appropriate, with any international assistance and co-operation, in particular, financial, artistic, scientific and technical, which it may be able to obtain.

Article 5

To ensure that effective and active measures are taken for the protection, conservation and presentation of the cultural and natural heritage situated on its territory, each State Party to this Convention shall endeavour, in so far as is possible, and as appropriate for each country:

(a) to adopt a general policy which aims to give the cultural and natural heritage a function in the life of the community and to integrate the protection of that heritage into comprehensive planning programmes;

(b) to set up within its territories, where such services do not exist, one or more services for the protection, conservation and presentation of the cultural and natural heritage with an appropriate staff and possessing the means to discharge their functions;

(c) to develop scientific and technical studies and research and to work out such operating methods as will make the State capable of counteracting the dangers that threaten its cultural or natural heritage;

(d) to take the appropriate legal, scientific, technical, administrative and financial measures necessary for the identification, protection, conservation, presentation and rehabilitation of this heritage; and

(e) to foster the establishment or development of national or regional centres for training in the protection, conservation and presentation of the cultural and natural heritage and to encourage scientific and research in this field.

Article 6

1. Whilst fully respecting the sovereignty of the States on whose territory the cultural and natural heritage mentioned in Articles 1 and 2 is situated, and without prejudice to property rights provided by national legislation, the States Parties to this Convention recognize that such heritage constitutes a world heritage for whose protection it is the duty of the international community as a whole to co-operate.

2. The States Parties undertake, in accordance with the provisions of this Convention, to give their help in the identification, protection, conservation and preservation of the cultural and natural heritage referred to in paragraphs 2 and 4 of Article 11 if the States on whose territory it is situated so request.

3. Each State Party to this Convention undertakes not to take any deliberate measures which might damage directly or indirectly the cultural and natural heritage referred to in Articles 1 and 2 situated on the territory of other States Parties to this Convention.

Article 7

For the purpose of this Convention, international protection of the world cultural and natural heritage shall be understood to mean the establishment of a system of international co-operation and assistance designed to support State Parties to the Convention in their efforts to conserve and identify that heritage.

III. INTERGOVERNMENTAL COMMITTEE FOR THE PROTECTION OF THE WORLD CULTURAL AND NATURAL HERITAGE

Article 8

1. An Intergovernmental Committee for the Protection of the Cultural and Natural Heritage of Outstanding Universal Value, called 'the World Heritage Committee', is hereby established within the United Nations Educational, Scientific and Cultural Organization. It shall be composed of 15 States Parties to the Convention, elected by States Parties to the Convention meeting in general assembly during the ordinary session of the General Conference of the United Nations, Educational, Scientific and Cultural Organization. The number of States members of the Committee shall be increased to 21 as from the date of the ordinary session of the General Conference following the entry into force of this Convention for at least 40 States.
2. Election of members of the Committee shall ensure an equitable representation of the different regions and cultures of the world.
3. A representative of the International Centre for the Study of the Preservation and Restoration of Cultural Property (Rome Centre), a representative of the International Council of Monuments and Sites (ICOMOS) and a representative of the International Union for Conservation of Nature and Natural Resources (IUCN), to whom may be added, at the request of States Parties to the Convention meeting in general assembly during the ordinary sessions of the General Conference of the United Nations Educational, Scientific and Cultural Organization, representatives of

other intergovernmental or non-governmental organizations, with similar objectives, may attend the meetings of the Committee in an advisory capacity.

Article 9

1. The term of office of States members of the World Heritage Committee shall extend from the end of the ordinary session of the General Conference during which they are elected until the end of its third subsequent ordinary session.
2. The term of office of one-third of the members designated at the time of the first election shall, however, cease at the end of the first ordinary session of the General Conference following that at which they were elected; and the term of office of a further third of the members designated at the same time shall cease at the end of the second ordinary session of the General Conference following that at which they were elected. The names of these members shall be chosen by lot by the President of the General Conference of the United Nations Educational, Scientific and Cultural Organization after the first election.
3. States members of the Committee shall choose as their representatives persons qualified in the field of the cultural or natural heritage.

Article 10

1. The World Heritage Committee shall adopt its Rules of Procedure.
2. The Committee may at any time invite public or private organizations or individuals to participate in its meetings for consultation on particular problems.
3. The Committee may create such consultative bodies as it deems necessary for the performance of its functions.

Article 11

1. Every State Party to this Convention shall, in so far as is possible, submit to the World Heritage Committee an inventory of property forming part of the cultural and natural heritage, situated in its territory and suitable for inclusion in the list provided for in paragraph 2 of this Article. This inventory, which shall not be considered exhaustive, shall include documentation about the location of the property in question and its significance.

2. On the basis of the inventories submitted by States in accordance with paragraph 1, the Committee shall establish, keep up to date and publish, under the title of 'World Heritage List', a list of properties forming part of the cultural heritage and natural heritage, as defined in Articles 1 and 2 of this Convention, which it considers as having outstanding universal value in terms of such criteria as it shall have established. An updated list shall be distributed at least every two years.

3. The inclusion of a property in the World Heritage List requires the consent of the State concerned. The inclusion of a property situated in a territory, sovereignty or jurisdiction over which is claimed by more than one State, shall in no way prejudice the rights of the parties to the dispute.

4. The Committee shall establish, keep up to date and publish, whenever circumstances shall so require, under the title 'List of World Heritage in Danger', a list of the property appearing in the World Heritage List for the conservation of which major operations are necessary and for which assistance has been requested under this Convention. This list shall contain an estimate of the cost of such operations. The list may include only such property forming part of the cultural and natural heritage as is threatened by serious and specific dangers, such as the threat of disappearance caused by accelerated deterioration, large-scale public or private projects or rapid urban or tourist development projects; destruction caused by changes in the use of ownership of the land; major alternations due to unknown causes; abandonment for any reason whatsoever; the outbreak or the threat of an armed conflict; calamities and cataclysms; serious fires, earthquakes, landslides; volcanic eruptions; changes in water level, floods and tidal waves. The Committee may at any time, in case of urgent need, make a new entry in the List of World Heritage in Danger and publicize such entry immediately.

5. The Committee shall define the criteria on the basis of which a property belonging to the cultural or natural heritage may be included in either of the lists mentioned in paragraphs 2 and 4 of this article.

6. Before refusing a request for inclusion in one of the two lists mentioned in paragraphs 2 and 4 of this article, the Committee shall consult the State Party in whose territory the cultural or natural property in question is situated.

7. The Committee shall, with the agreement of the States concerned, co-ordinate and encourage the studies and research needed for the drawing up of the lists referred to in paragraphs 2 and 4 of this article.

Article 12

The fact that a property belonging to the cultural or natural heritage has not been included in either of the two lists mentioned in paragraphs 2 and 4 of Article 11 shall in no way be construed to mean that it does not have an outstanding universal value for purposes other than those resulting from inclusion in these lists.

Article 13

1. The World Heritage Committee shall receive and study requests for international assistance formulated by States Parties to this Convention with respect to property forming part of the cultural or natural heritage, situated in their territories, and included or potentially suitable for inclusion in the lists referred to in paragraphs 2 and 4 of Article 11. The purpose of such requests may be to secure the protection, conservation, presentation or rehabilitation of such property.
2. Requests for international assistance under paragraph 1 of this article may also be concerned with identification of cultural or natural property defined in Articles 1 and 2, when preliminary investigations have shown that further inquiries would be justified.
3. The Committee shall decide on the action to be taken with regard to these requests, determine, where appropriate, the nature and extent of its assistance, and authorize the conclusion, on its behalf, of the necessary arrangements with the government concerned.
4. The Committee shall determine an order of priorities for its operations. It shall in so doing bear in mind the respective importance of the world cultural and natural heritage of the property requiring protection, the need to give international assistance to the property most representative of a natural environment or of the genius and the history of the peoples of the world, the urgency of the work to be done, the resources available to the States on whose territory the threatened property is situated and in particular the extent to which they are able to safeguard such property by their own means.
5. The Committee shall draw up, keep up to date and publicize a list of property for which international assistance has been granted.
6. The Committee shall decide on the use of the resources of the Fund established under Article 15 of this Convention. It shall seek ways of increasing these resources and shall take all useful steps to this end.

7. The Committee shall co-operate with international and national governmental and non-governmental organizations having objectives similar to those of this Convention. For the implementation of its programmes and projects, the Committee may call on such organizations, particularly the International Centre for the Study of the Preservation and Restoration of Cultural Property (the Rome Centre), the International Council of Monuments and Sites (ICMOS) and the International Union for Conservation of Nature and Natural Resources (IUCN), as well as on public and private bodies and individuals.
8. Decisions of the Committee shall be taken by a majority of two-thirds of its members present and voting. A majority of the members of the Committee shall constitute a quorum.

Article 14

1. The World Heritage Committee shall be assisted by a Secretariat appointed by the Director-General of the United Nations Educational, Scientific and Cultural Organization.
2. The Director-General of the United Nations Educational, Scientific and Cultural Organization, utilizing to the fullest extent possible the services of the International Centre for the Study of the Preservation and Restoration of Cultural Property (the Rome Centre), the International Council of Monuments and Sites (ICOMOS) and the International Union for Conservation of Nature and Natural Resources (IUCN) in their respective areas of competence and capability, shall prepare the Committee's documentation and the agenda of its meetings and shall have the responsibility for the implementation of its decisions.

IV. FUND FOR THE PROTECTION OF THE WORLD CULTURAL AND NATURAL HERITAGE

Article 15

1. The Fund for the Protection of the World Cultural and Natural Heritage of Outstanding Universal Value, called the 'World Heritage Fund', is hereby established.
2. The Fund shall constitute a trust fund, in conformity with the provisions of the Financial Regulations of the United Nations Educational, Scientific and Cultural Organization.
3. The resources of the Fund shall consist of:

(a)   compulsory and voluntary contributions made by the States Parties to this Convention.

(b)   contributions, gifts or bequests which may be made by:
   (i)   other States;
   (ii)   the United Nations Educational, Scientific and Cultural Organization, other organizations of the United Nations system, particularly the United Nations Development Programme or other intergovernmental organizations;
   (iii) public or private bodies or individuals;

(c)   any interest due on the resources of the Fund;

(d)   funds raised by collections and receipts from events organized for the benefit of the Fund; and

(e)   all other resources authorized by the Fund's regulations, as drawn up by the World Heritage Committee.

4.   Contributions to the Fund and other forms of assistance made available to the Committee may be used only for a certain programme or project, provided that the Committee shall have decided on the implementation of such programme or project. No political conditions may be attached to contributions made to the Fund.

Article 16

1.   Without prejudice to any supplementary voluntary contribution, the States Parties to this Convention undertake to pay regularly, every two years, to the World Heritage Fund, contributions, the amount of which, in the form of a uniform percentage applicable to all States, shall be determined by the General Assembly of States Parties to the Convention, meeting during the sessions of the General Conference of the United Nations Educational, Scientific and Cultural Organization. This decision of the General Assembly requires the majority of the States Parties present and voting, which have not made the declaration referred to in paragraph 2 of this Article. In no case shall the compulsory contribution of States Parties to the Convention exceed 1% of the contribution to the Regular Budget of the United Nations Educational, Scientific and Cultural Organization.

2.   However, each State referred to in Article 31 or in Article 32 of this Convention may declare, at the time of the deposit of its instruments of ratification, acceptance or accession, that it shall not be bound by the provisions of paragraph 1 of this Article.

3.   A State Party to the Convention which has made the declaration

referred to in paragraph 2 of this Article may at any time withdraw the said declaration by notifying the Director-General of the United Nations Educational, Scientific and Cultural Organization. However, the withdrawal of the declaration shall not take effect in regard to the compulsory contribution due by the State until the date of the subsequent General Assembly of States Parties to the Convention.

4.   In order that the Committee may be able to plan its operations effectively, the contributions of States Parties to this Convention which have made the declaration referred to in paragraph 2 of this Article shall be paid on a regular basis, at least every two years, and should not be less than the contributions which they should have paid if they had been bound by the provisions of paragraph 1 of this Article.

5.   Any State Party to the Convention which is in arrears with the payment of its compulsory or voluntary contribution for the current year and the calendar year immediately preceding it shall not be eligible as a Member of the World Heritage Committee, although this provision shall not apply to the first election.

The terms of office of any such State which is already a member of the Committee shall terminate at the time of the elections provided for in Article 8, paragraph 1 of this Convention.

Article 17

The States Parties to this Convention shall consider or encourage the establishment of national, public and private foundations or associations whose purpose is to invite donations for the protection of the cultural and natural heritage as defined in Articles 1 and 2 of this Convention.

Article 18

The States Parties to this Convention shall give their assistance to international fund-raising campaigns organized for the World Heritage Fund under the auspices of the United Nations Educational, Scientific and Cultural Organization. They shall facilitate collections made by the bodies mentioned in paragraph 3 of Article 15 for this purpose.

V.   CONDITIONS AND ARRANGEMENTS FOR INTERNATIONAL ASSISTANCE

Article 19

Any State Party to this Convention may request international assistance for property forming part of the cultural or natural heritage of outstanding universal value situated within its territory. It shall submit with its request such information and documentation provided for in Article 21 as it has in its possession and as will enable the Committee to come to a decision.

Article 20

Subject to the provisions of paragraph 2 of Article 13, sub-paragraph (c) of Article 22 and 23, international assistance provided for by this Convention may be granted only to property forming part of the cultural and natural heritage which the World Heritage Committee has decided, or may decide, to enter in one of the lists mentioned in paragraphs 2 and 4 of Article 11.

Article 21

1.   The World Heritage Committee shall define the procedure by which requests to it for international assistance shall be considered and shall specify the content of the request, which should define the operation contemplated, the work that is necessary, the expected cost thereof, the degree of urgency and the reasons why the resources of the State requesting assistance do not allow it to meet all the expenses. Such requests must be supported by experts' reports whenever possible.
2.   Requests based upon disasters or natural calamities should, by reason of the urgent work which they may involve, be given immediate, priority consideration by the Committee, which should have a reserve fund at its disposal against such contingencies.
3.   Before coming to a decision, the Committee shall carry out such studies and consultations as it deems necessary.

Article 22

Assistance granted by the World Heritage Committee may take the following forms:

(a) studies concerning the artistic, scientific and technical problems raised by the protection, conservation, presentation and rehabilitation of the cultural and natural heritage, as defined in paragraphs 2 and 4 of Article 11 of this Convention;

(b) provision of experts, technicians and skilled labour to ensure that the approved work is correctly carried out;

(c) training of staff and specialists at all levels in the field of identification, protection, conservation, presentation and rehabilitation of the cultural and natural heritage;

(d) supply of equipment which the State concerned does not possess or is not in a position to acquire;

(e) low-interest or interest-free loans which might be repayable on a long-term basis;

(f) the granting, in exceptional cases and for special reasons, of non-repayable subsidies.

Article 23

The World Heritage Committee may also provide international assistance to national or regional centres for the training of staff and specialists at all levels in the field of identification, protection, conservation, presentation and rehabilitation of the cultural and natural heritage.

Article 24

International assistance on a large scale shall be preceded by detailed scientific, economic and technical studies. These studies shall draw upon the most advanced techniques for the protection, conservation, presentation and rehabilitation of the natural and cultural heritage and shall be consistent with the objectives of this Convention. The studies shall also seek means of making rational use of the resources available in the State concerned.

Article 25

As a general rule, only part of the cost of work necessary shall be borne by the international community. The contribution of the State benefiting from international assistance shall constitute a substantial share of the resources devoted to each programme or project, unless its resources do not permit this.

Article 26

The World Heritage Committee and the recipient State shall define in the agreement they conclude the conditions in which a programme or project, for which international assistance under the terms of this Convention is provided, shall be carried out. It shall be the responsibility of the State receiving such international assistance to continue to protect, conserve and present the property so safeguarded, in observance of the conditions laid down by the agreement.

VI. EDUCATIONAL PROGRAMMES

Article 27

1. The States Parties to this Convention shall endeavour by all appropriate means, and in particular by educational and informed programmes, to strengthen appreciation and respect by their peoples of the cultural and natural heritage defined in Articles 1 and 2 of the Convention.
2. They shall undertake to keep the public broadly informed of the dangers threatening this heritage and of activities carried on in pursuance of this Convention.

Article 28

States Parties to this Convention which receive international assistance under the Convention shall take appropriate measures to make known the importance of the property for which assistance has been received and the role played by such assistance.

VII. REPORTS

Article 29

1. The States Parties to this Convention shall, in the reports which they submit to the General Conference of the United Nations Educational, Scientific and Cultural Organization on dates and in a manner to be determined by it, give information on the legislative and administrative provisions which they have adopted and other action which they have taken for the application of this Convention, together with details of the experience acquired in this field.

2. These reports shall be brought to the attention of the World Heritage Committee.
3. The Committee shall submit a report on its activities at each of the ordinary sessions of the General Conference of the United Nations Educational, Scientific and Cultural Organization.

VIII.   FINAL CLAUSES

Article 30

This Convention is drawn up in Arabic, English, French, Russian and Spanish, the five texts being equally authoritative.

Article 31

1. This Convention shall be subject to ratification or acceptance by States members of the United Nations Educational, Scientific and Cultural Organization in accordance with their respective constitutional procedures.
2. The instrument of ratification or acceptance shall be deposited with the Director-General of the United Nations Educational, Scientific and Cultural Organization.

Article 32

1. This Convention shall be open to accession by all States not members of the United Nations Educational, Scientific and Cultural Organization which are invited by the General Conference of the Organization to accede to it.
2. Accession shall be effected by the deposit of an instrument of accession with the Director-General of the United Nations Educational, Scientific and Cultural Organization.

Article 33

This Convention shall enter into force three months after the date of the deposit of the twentieth instrument of ratification, acceptance or accession, but only with respect to those States which have deposited their respective instruments of ratification, acceptance or accession on or before that date. It shall enter into force with respect to any other State three months after the deposit of its instrument of ratification, acceptance or accession.

Article 34

The following provisions shall apply to those States Parties to this Convention which have a federal or non-unitary constitutional system:

(a) with regard to the provisions of this Convention, the implementation of which comes under the legal jurisdiction of the federal or central legislative power, the obligations of the federal or central government shall be the same as for those States Parties which are not federal States;

(b) with regard to the provisions of this Convention, the implementation of which comes under the legal jurisdiction of individual constituent States, countries, provinces or cantons that are not obliged by the constitutional system of the federation to take legislative measures, the federal government shall inform the competent authorities of such States, countries, provinces or cantons of the said provisions, with its recommendation for their adoption.

Article 35

1. Each State Party to this Convention may denounce the Convention.
2. The denunciation shall be notified by an instrument in writing, deposited with the Director-General of the United Nations Educational, Scientific and Cultural Organization.
3. The denunciation shall take effect twelve months after the receipt of the instrument of denunciation. It shall not affect the financial obligations of the denouncing State until the date on which the withdrawal takes effect.

Article 36

The Director-General of the United Nations Educational, Scientific and Cultural Organization shall inform the States members of the Organization, the States not members of the Organization which are referred to in Article 32, as well as the United Nations, of the deposit of all the instruments of ratification, acceptance or accession provided for in Articles 31 and 32, and of the denunciation provided for in Article 35.

Article 37

1. This Convention may be revised by the General Conference of the United Nations Educational, Scientific and Cultural Organization. Any such revision shall, however, bind only the States which shall become Parties to the revising convention.
2. If the General Conference should adopt a new convention revising this Convention in whole or in part, then, unless the new convention otherwise provides, this Convention shall cease to be open to ratification, acceptance or accession, as from the date on which the new revising convention enters into force.

Article 38

In conformity with Article 102 of the Charter of the United Nations, this Convention shall be registered with the Secretariat of the United Nations at the request of the Director-General of the United Nations Educational, Scientific and Cultural Organization.

Done in Paris, this twenty-third day of November 1972, in two authentic copies bearing the signature of the President of the seventeenth session of the General Conference and of the Director-General of the United Nations Educational, Scientific and Cultural Organization, which shall be deposited in the archives of the United Nations Educational, Scientific and Cultural Organization, and certified true copies of which shall be delivered to all the States referred to in Articles 31 and 32 as well as to the United Nations.

The President of the General Conference   The Director-General of
UNESCO

Annex X
Convention Concerning the Protection of the World Cultural and Natural Heritage (Paris, 1972); List of the 145 States Parties at 27 January 1996

States	Date of ratification (R) acceptance (Ac) accession (A) succession (S)
Afghanistan	20.3.79 (R)
Albania (Republic of)	10.7.89 (R)
Algeria	24.6.74 (R)
Angola (People's Republic of)	7.11.91 (R)
Antigua and Barbuda	1.11.83 (Ac)
Argentina	22.8.74 (Ac)
Australia	23.8.78 (Ac)
Austria	18.12.92 (R)
Azerbaijan	16.3.94 (R)
Bangladesh	3.8.83 (Ac)
Bahrain (State of)	28.5.91 (R)
Belarus	12.10.88 (R)
Belize	6.11.90 (R)
Benin	14.6.82 (R)
Bolivia	4.10.76 (R)
Brazil	1.9.77 (Ac)

Bulgaria	7.3.74 (Ac)
Burkina Faso	2.4.87 (R)
Burundi	19.5.82 (R)
Cameroon	7.12.82 (R)
Cambodia	28.11.91 (Ac)
Canada	23.7.76 (Ac)
Cape Verde (Republic of)	28.4.88 (Ac)
Central African Republic	22.12.80 (R)
Chile	20.2.80 (R)
China (People's Republic of)	12.12.85 (R)
Colombia	24.5.83 (Ac)
Congo	10.12.87 (R)
Costa Rica	23.8.77 (R)
Côte d'Ivoire	9.1.81 (R)
Croatia (Republic of)[1*]	8.10.91 (S)
Cuba	24.3.81 (R)
Cyprus	14.8.75 (Ac)
Czech Republic[2*]	1.1.93 (S)
Denmark	25.7.79 (R)
Dominica	4.7.95 (R)
Dominican Republic	12.2.85 (R)
Ecuador	16.6.75 (Ac)
Egypt	7.2.74 (R)
El Salvador	8.10.91 (Ac)
Estonia	27.1.96 (R)
Ethiopia	6.7.77 (R)
Fiji	21.11.90 (R)
Finland	4.3.87 (R)
France	27.6.75 (Ac)
Gabon	30.12.86 (R)
Gambia	1.7.87 (R)
Georgia[3*]	9.4.91 (S)
Germany[4]	23.8.76 (R)
Ghana	4.7.75 (R)
Greece	17.7.81 (R)
Guatemala	16.1.79 (R)
Guinea	18.3.79 (R)
Guyana	20.6.77 (Ac)
Haiti	18.1.80 (R)
Holy See	7.10.82 (A)
Honduras	8.6.79 (R)
Hungary	15.7.85 (Ac)
India	14.11.77 (R)
Indonesia	6.7.89 (Ac)
Iran (Islamic Republic of)	26.2.75 (Ac)

Iraq	5.3.74 (Ac)
Ireland	16.9.91 (R)
Italy	23.6.78 (R)
Jamaica	14.6.83 (Ac)
Japan	30.6.92 (Ac)
Jordan	5.5.75 (R)
Kazakhstan	29.7.94 (Ac)
Kenya (Republic of)	5.6.91 (Ac)
Kyrgyzstan (Republic of)	3.10.95 (Ac)
Lao People's Democratic Republic	20.3.87 (R)
Latvia	10.4.95 (Ac)
Lebanon	3.2.83 (R)
Libyan Arab Jamahiriya	13.10.78 (R)
Luxembourg	28.9.83 (R)
Madagascar	19.7.83 (R)
Malawi	5.1.82 (R)
Malaysia	7.12.88 (R)
Maldives	22.5.85 (Ac)
Mali	5.4.77 (Ac)
Malta	14.11.78 (Ac)
Mauritania	2.3.81 (R)
Mauritius	7.12.95 (R)
Mexico	23.2.84 (Ac)
Monaco	7.11.78 (R)
Mongolia	2.2.90 (Ac)
Morocco	28.10.75 (R)
Mozambique	27.11.82 (R)
Myanmar (Union of)	29.7.94 (Ac)
Nepal	20.6.78 (Ac)
Netherlands[5]	26.8.92 (Ac)
New Zealand	22.11.84 (R)
Nicaragua	17.12.79 (Ac)
Niger	23.12.74 (Ac)
Nigeria	23.10.74 (R)
Norway	12.5.77 (R)
Oman	6.10.81 (Ac)
Pakistan	23.7.76 (R)
Panama	3.3.78 (R)
Paraguay	27.4.88 (R)
Peru	24.2.82 (R)
Philippines	19.9.85 (R)
Poland	29.6.76 (R)
Portugal	30.9.80 (R)
Qatar	12.9.84 (Ac)
Republic of Armenia[6]*	21.9.91 (S)

Republic of Bosnia and Herzegovina	6.3.92 (S)
Republic of Korea	14.9.88 (Ac)
Republic of Lithuania	31.3.92 (Ac)
Republic of San Marino	18.10.91 (R)
Romania	16.5.90 (Ac)
Russian Federation[8]	12.10.88 (R)
Saint Christopher and Nevis	10.7.86 (Ac)
Saint Lucia	14.10.91 (R)
Saudi Arabia	7.8.78 (Ac)
Senegal	13.2.76 (R)
Seychelles	9.4.80 (Ac)
Slovak Republic[2]*	1.1.93 (S)
Slovenia[9]*	25.6.91 (S)
Socialist Republic of Vietnam	19.10.87 (Ac)
Solomon Islands	10.6.92 (A)
Spain	4.5.82 (Ac)
Sri Lanka	6.6.80 (Ac)
Sudan	6.6.74 (R)
Sweden	22.1.85 (R)
Switzerland	17.9.75 (R)
Syrian Arab Republic	13.8.75 (Ac)
Tadjikistan[10]*	9.9.91 (S)
Thailand	17.9.87 (Ac)
Tunisia	10.3.75 (R)
Turkey	16.3.83 (R)
Turkmenistan[11]*	27.10.92 (S)
Uganda	20.11.87 (Ac)
Ukraine	12.10.88 (R)
United Kingdom of Great Britain and Northern Ireland	29.5.84 (R)
United Republic of Tanzania	2.8.77 (R)
United States of America	7.12.73 (R)
Uruguay	9.3.89 (Ac)
Uzbekistan[12]*	31.8.91 (S)
Venezuela	30.10.90 (Ac)
Yemen Republic[13]	7.10.80 (R)
Yugoslavia	26.5.75 (R)
Zaire	23.9.74 (R)
Zambia	4.6.84 (R)
Zimbabwe	16.8.82 (R)

NOTES

1 The Republic of Croatia made on 6 July 1992 a declaration of succession of States by which it considers itself committed to the Convention which Yugoslavia ratified on 26 May 1975.

2 This State deposited on 1 January 1993 a notification of succession of States by which it considers itself committed to the Convention. The Czech and Slovak Federal Republic accepted on 15 November 1990.

3 This State deposited on 4 November 1992 a notification of succession of States by which it considers itself committed to the Convention which the USSR. ratified on 12 October 1988.

4 Through the accession of the German Democratic Republic to the Basic Law of the Federal Republic of Germany, with effect from 3 October 1990, the two German States have united to form one Sovereign State. The Contracting Parties to the Unification Treaty 'have agreed that the treaties and agreements to which the Federal Republic of Germany is a contracting party ... remain in force and that their respective rights and obligations ... be applied' to the whole territory of Germany. The German Democratic Republic acceded to this Convention on 12 December 1988.

5 With an extension to the Netherlands Antilles.

6 This State deposited on 2 August 1993 a notification of succession of States by which it considers itself committed to the Convention which the USSR ratified on 12 October 1988.

7 This State deposited on 24 June 1993 a notification of succession of States by which it considers itself committed to the Convention which Yugoslavia ratified on 26 May 1975.

8 The instrument of ratification was deposited by the USSR on 12 October 1988.

9 This State deposited on 28 October 1992 a notification of succession of States by which it considers itself committed to the Convention which Yugoslavia ratified on 26 May 1975.

10 This State deposited on 28 August 1992 a notification of succession of States by which it considers itself committed to the Convention, which the USSR ratified on 12 October 1988.

11 This State deposited a notification of succession of States by which it considers itself committed to the Convention which the USSR ratified on 26 September 1994.

12 This State deposited a notification of succession of States by which it considers itself committed to the Convention which the USSR ratified on 12 October 1988.

13 The unification of the Yemen Arab Republic and the People's Democratic Republic of Yemen into a single Sovereign State, the Republic of Yemen, was proclaimed on 22 May 1990.

NB *The entry into force occurred on the date on which this State assumed responsibility for conducting international relations.

Annex XI
Resolution 20 of the Diplomatic Conference on the Reaffirmation and Development of International Humanitarian Law Applicable in Armed Conflicts, Geneva, 7 June 1977

PROTECTION OF CULTURAL PROPERTY

The Diplomatic Conference on the Reaffirmation and Development of International Humanitarian Law Applicable in Armed Conflicts, Geneva, 1974–1977,

Welcoming the adoption of Article 53 relating to the protection of cultural objects and places of worship as defined in the said Article, contained in the Protocol Additional to the Geneva Convention of 12 August 1949, and relating to the Protection of Victims of International Armed Conflicts (Protocol I),

Acknowledging that the Convention for the Protection of Cultural Property in the Event of Armed Conflict and its Additional Protocol, signed at The Hague on 14 May 1954, constitutes an instrument of paramount importance for the international protection of the cultural heritage of all mankind against the effects of armed conflict and that the application of this Convention will in no way be prejudiced by the adoption of the Article referred to in the preceding paragraph.

Urges States which have not yet done so to become Parties to the aforementioned Convention.

Fifty-fifth plenary meeting
7 June 1977

Select Bibliography[1]

ALEKSANDRO, E.A., *La protection du patrimoine culturel en droit international*, Sofia, Sofia Press, 1978, 184 pp.

——, *Le Pacte Roerich et la protection internationale des institutions et des valeurs culturelles*, Sofia, Sofia Press, 1978, 27 pp.

——, *International Legal Protection of Cultural Property*, Sofia, Sofia Press, 1979, 164 pp.

ALOISI, U., 'Protezione internazionale delle cose di pregio storico o artistico', *Guistizia penale* (Rome), Vol. 41, August 1935, pp.577–600.

ALTTUNOV, I., 'Problemata za zashtita na kulturnite tsennosti v sluchai na voina', *Izvestiia na Instituta za Pravni Nauki* (Sofia), Vol. 12, No. 2, 1962, pp.31–70.

ARCIONI, G., 'La protection des biens culturels – l'un des buts de notre défense générale', *Le mois economique et financier* (Basle), No. 9, 1981, pp.23–5.

——, 'Protezione dei beni culturali: uno degli scopi della nostra difesa generale', *Rivista militare della svizzera italiana* (Locarno), No. 5, 1984, pp.365–74.

ARNOUX DE FLEURY DE L'HERMITE, H. d', *Objets et monuments d'art devant le droit des gens*, Paris, L. Clercx, 1934, 189 pp.

Art et archéologie: recueil de législation comparée et de droit international, No. 1, *La protection des collections nationales d'art et d'histoire: essai de réglementation internationale*, Paris, International Museums Office, 1939, 118 pp.

Association internationale pour la protection des populations civiles et des monuments historiques, 'Les Lieux de Genève', *La guerre moderne et la protection des civils: vers la solution de cet angoissant problème*, Geneva, 1943, 107 pp.

AUER, E.M., 'Schutz der Kulturgüter bei bewaffneten Konflikten', IV. 'Erfahrungen mit Bergeräumen im zweiten Weltkrieg', *Mitteilungsblatt der Museen Osterreichs* (Vienna), Vol. 16, No.9/10, October 1967, pp.159–62.

——, 'Schutz der Kulturgüter bei bewaffneten Konflikten', V. 'Technische Richtlinie für Grundschutz in Gebäuden', *Mitteilungsblatt der Museen Osterreichs* (Vienna), Vol. 16, No. 11/12, December 1967, pp.191–2.

BASSIOUNI, C., 'Reflections on criminal jurisdiction in international protection of cultural property', *Syracuse Journal of International Law and Commerce* (Syracuse, New York), Vol. 10, No. 2, 1983, pp.218–322.

BATOUNCOV, G., 'La protection des biens culturels, monuments historiques et œuvres d'art en cas de conflit', Doctoral thesis, Paris, 1955, 250 pp.

BEREZOWSKI, C., *Ochrona prawnomiedzynarodowa zabytkow i dziel sztuki w czasie wojny* (International Legal Protection of Monuments and Works of Art during Conflicts), Warsaw, 1948.

BERTI, Antonio, 'La convenzione per la protezione dei beni culturali in caso di conflitto armato', *Rassegna dell'arma dei carabinieri* (Rome), No. 2, March–April 1963, pp.310–10.

BOLLA, G., 'Protection of cultural property during armed conflicts', in International Institute of Human Rights, *Résumé des Cours*, 5e session d'enseignement, Strasbourg, 1974, pp.GB/1–14.

——, 'Extension territoriale et application pratique de la Convention de 1954', in *Da Antonio Canova alla convenzione dell'aja. La protezione della opera d'arte in caso di conflitto armatto*, A cura di Stetano Rosso Mazzinghi Sansoni editore, 1975.

BOSLY, H., 'La responsabilité des Etats et des individus quant à l'application de la Convention de La Haye sur la protection des biens culturels en cas de conflit armé, in Istituto internazionale di diritto umanitario, *La protezione internazionale dei beni culturali/The international protection of cultural property/La protection internationale des biens culturels*, Rome, Dragan European Foundation, 1986, pp.81–6.

BOYLAN, P.J., *Réexamen de la Convention pour la protection des liens culturels en cas de conflit armé (Convention de La Haye de 1954)*, Paris, UNESCO, 1993, 179 pp.

——, *Review of the Convention for the Protection of Cultural Property in the Event of Armed Conflict (The Hague Convention of 1954)*, Paris, UNESCO, 1993, 248 pp.

BREDDELS, J., 'The dissemination of The Hague Convention: in armed forces, the civilian population and the academic circles', in Istituto internazionale di diritto umanitario, *La protezione internazionale dei beni culturali/The international protection of cultural property/La protection internationale des biens culturels*, Rome, Dragan European Foundation, 1986, pp.101–5.

BREUCKER, J., de, 'La réserve des nécessités militaires dans la Convention de La Haye du 14 mai 1954 sur la protection des biens culturels', *Revue de droit pénal militaire et de droit de la guerre* (Brussels), XIV–3–4, 1975, pp.255–69.

——, 'Pour les vingt ans de la Convention de La Haye du 14 mai

1954 pour la protection des biens culturels', *Revue belge de droit international* (Brussels), Vol. XI, No. 2, 1975, pp.525–47.

BRÜDERLIN, P., *Kulturgüterschutz in der Schweiz: gemäss internationalem Abkommen on Den Haag (1954) über 'Kulturgüterschutz bei bewaffneten Konflikten'*, Zurich, P. Brüderlin, 1978, 117 pp.

BUHSE, K.-H., *Der Schutz von Kulturgut im Krieg: Unter besonderer Berücksichtigung der Konvention zum Schutz des Kulturguts im Falle eines bewaffneten Konflikts vom 14. Mai 1954*, Hamburg, Hansischer Gildenverlag, 1959, 150 pp.

BURR, N.R., *Safeguarding Our Cultural Heritage. A bibliography on the protection of museums, works of art, monuments, archives and libraries in time of war*, Washington, DC, The Library of Congress, 1952, 117 pp.

BYSTRICKY, R., *Mezinarodni kulturni dohody a organizace* (International Cultural Agreements and Organizations), Prague, Orbis, 1962, pp.178–84.

CALZADA, M. de la, 'La protección jurídica internacional del patrimonio cultural en caso de guerra', *Revista de estudios políticos* (Madrid), Vol. 43, May–June 1952, pp.141–82.

CARDINI, F., *La culture de la guerre*, Paris, Gallimard, 1992.

CASSOU, J. (ed.), *Pillage par les Allemands des œuvres d'art et des bibliothèques appartenant à des Juifs en France*, Paris, Editions du Centre, 1947, 268 pp.

CAVALLI, F., 'La Santa Sede e la Convenzione dell'Aja per la proteztione dei beni culturali in caso di conflitto armato', *Revista di studi politici internazionali* (Florence), Vol. 27, 1960, pp.126–37.

CHKLAVER, G., 'Projet d'une Convention pour la protection des institutions et monuments consacrés aux arts et aux sciences', *Revue de droit international* (Paris), 1930, pp.589–92.

——, 'Le mouvement en faveur du Pacte Roerich', *Revue de droit international* (Paris), 1933, pp.460–62.

——, 'The Roerich Pact', *Biosophical Review* (New York), 1933.

——, 'La protection des monuments historiques et des œuvres d'art en temps de guerre', in *Premier congrès d'études internationales organisé par l'Association des études internationales*, Paris, Institut de hautes études internationales de l'Université de Paris, 1938, pp.64–7.

CLEMEN, P. de, *Der Zustand der Kunstdenkmäler auf dem westlichen Kriegschauplatz*, Leipzig, E.A. Seemann, 1916, 48 pp.

——, *Kunstschutz im Kriege*, Leipzig, E.A. Seemann, 1919, 2 vols.

CLEMENT, E., 'Le concept de responsabilité collective de la communauté internationale pour la protection des biens culturels dans le conventions et recommandations de l'UNESCO', *Revue belge de droit international* (Brussels), No. 2, 1993, pp.534–51.

——, 'Some Recent Practical Experience in the Implementation of the

1954 Hague Convention', *International Journal of Cultural Property*, (Berlin, New York), Vol. 3, No. 1, 1994, pp.11–25.

CLOSCA, I., 'New code for the protection of civilian population and property during armed conflict', *International Review of The Red Cross* (Geneva), twentieth year, No. 219, November–December 1980, pp.287–315.

Colloque d'experts européens sur la Convention de La Haye du 14 mai 1954 pour la protection des biens culturels en cas de conflit armé. Zurich, les 29, 30 et 31 octobre 1969, Zurich, Société suisse des biens culturels (Final report), 1969, 61 pp.

Colloque d'experts internationaux sur l'adaptation du droit international relatif à la protection de la propriété culturelle au développement technique des moyens de guerre, Institut international de droit humanitaire (San Remo), Florence, 31 October 1986.

'Conventions internationales en vigueur et autres déclarations de gouvernements concernant la protection des monuments et œuvres d'art au cours des conflits armés', *Mouseion* (Paris), monthly supplement, September–October 1939, pp.5–12.

COREMANS, P.B., *La protection scientifique des œuvres d'art en temps de guerre; l'expérience européenne pendant les années 1939–1945*, Brussels, Laboratoire central des musées, 1946, 30 pp.

CRABB, J., 'International Humanitarian Law and the Protection of Cultural Property', *Yearbook, International Institute of Humanitarian Law* (San Remo), 1986–7, pp.267–9.

CZIGLER, S.V., *Schutz der Kunstwerke im Krieg*, Budapest, 1938, 2 pp.

DANSE, M., 'Communication relative à la formation culturelle dans l'armée aérienne au regard des dispositions de l'article 7, al. 1 de la Convention du 14 mai 1954', in *Congrès de Florence 1961. Recueil de la Société internationale de droit pénal militaire et de droit de la guerre*, Vol. 2, Strasbourg, 1963, pp.147–51.

DIENG, A., 'Réflexions sur la protection de l'homme et du patrimoine culturel', in Istituto internazionale di diritto umanitario, *La protezione internazionale dei beni culturali/The international protection of cultural property/La protection internationale des biens culturels*, Rome, Dragan European Foundation, 1986, pp.69–75.

'Dokumente zum Schutz der Kulturgüter bei bewaffneten Konflikten (1874, 1899, 1907, 1935, 1954)', *Zeitschrift für ausländisches öffentliches recht und völherrecht* (Stuttgart), Vol. 16, No. 1, 1955, pp.76–102.

DOLZER, R. 'Der Kulturgüter im Friedensvölkerrecht', in R. DOLZER, E. JAYME and R. MUSSGNUG, *Rechtsfragen des internationalen Kulturgüterschutzes*, Symposium vom 22/23 Juni 1990 im Internationalen Wissenschaftsforum Heidelberg, Heidelberg, C.F. Müller Juristischer Verlag, 1994, pp.149–59.

DOLZER, R., E. JAYME and R. MUSSGNUG, *Rechtsfragen des internationalen*

Kulturgüterschutzes, Symposium vom 22/23 Juni 1990 im Heidelberg, C.F. Müller Juristischer Verlag, 1994, 238 pp.

DORMANN, K. 'The Protection of Cultural Property as laid down in the Roerich Pact of 15 April 1935', *Humanitäres Völkerrecht* (Bonn, Bochum), No. 4, 1993, pp.230–31.

DUBOFF, L.D. (ed.), *Art Law: Domestic and International*, South Hackensack, NJ, F.B. Rothman, 1975, 627 pp.

ELBINGER, L.K. 'The neutraliry of art. The Roerich Pact's quest to protect art from the ignorance of man', *Foreign Service Journal*, April 1992, pp.16–20.

ENGSTLER, L., *Die territoriale Bindung von Kulturgütern im Rhamen des Völkerrechts*, Cologne/Berlin, C. Heymann, 1964, 301 pp.

——, 'Die Kennzeichnung von Kulturgut nach der Haager Konvention von 1954 zum Schutz von Kulturgut bei bewaffneten Konflikten', *Neue Juristische Wochenschrift* (Munich), Vol. 22, No. 35, August 1969, pp.1514–18.

ESTREICHER, K. (ed.), *Cultural Losses of Poland. Index of Polish cultural losses during the German occupation, 1939–1944*, London (n.p.), 1944, pp.XVII, 497.

EUSTATHIADES, C.T., 'La protection des biens culturels en cas de conflit armé et la Convention de La Haye du 14 mai 1954', *Etudes de droit international, 1929–1959*, Volume III, Athens, Klissiounis publishers, 1959, pp.393–524.

——, 'La réserve des nécessités militaires et la Convention de La Haye pour la protection des biens culturels en cas de conflit armé', in *Hommage d'une génération de juristes au président Basdevant*, Paris, A. Pédone, 1960, pp.183–209.

FABJAN, K., 'Kulturgüterschutz unter besonderer Berücksichtigung des Nahostkonfliktes', *Jahrbuch der Diplomatischen Akademie Wien* (Vienna), 1971–2, pp.90–99.

FERNANDEZ-QUINTANILLA, R., 'Un nuevo convenio de El Haya', *Politica internacional* (Madrid), 18, April–June 1954, pp.63–5.

Final Act, Convention, and Protocol adopted by the United Nations Conference on the Protection of Cultural Property in the Event of Armed Conflict, together with Regulations for the Execution of the Convention and Resolutions attached to the Final Act. The Hague, 14 May 1954, London, H.M. Stationery Office, 1956, 49 pp.

Final Act of the Intergovernmental Conference on the Protection of Cultural Property in the Event of Armed Conflict. The Hague, 1954, Paris, UNESCO, 1954, 83 pp.

FISCHER, H., 'The Protection of Cultural Property in Armed Conflicts: After the Hague Meeting of Experts', *Humanitäres Völkerrecht* (Bonn, Bochum), No. 4, 1993, pp.188–90.

FLANNER, J. *Men and Monuments*, London, Hamish Hamilton, 1957, 316 pp.

FLEURY, A. de, *Objets et monuments devant le droit des gens*, Paris, 1934.

Fonti bibliografiche del patto internazionale Roerich, Bologna, Comitato del Patto Internazionale Roerich, 1950, 33 pp.

FORAMITTI, H., 'Schutz der Kulturgüter bei bewaffneten Konflikten', III. 'Der Fragebogen über Grundschutzbergungsräume', *Mitteilungsblatt der Museen Osterreichs* (Vienna), Vol. 17, No. 3/4, April 1968, pp.46–50.

——, 'Schutz der Kulturgüter bei bewaffneten Konflikten', II. 'Rückstellungsmöglichkeit on widerrechtlich entferntem Kulturgut nach bewaffneten Konflikten', *Mitteilungsblatt der Museen Osterreichs* (Vienna), Vol. 18, No. 3/4, April 1969, pp.53–9.

___ 'Schutz der Kulturgüter bei bewaffneten Konflikten', VIII. 'Teil A. und B. Expertentagung Zürich', *Mitteilungsblatt der Museen Osterreichs* (Vienna), Vol. 19, No. 1/2, February 1970, pp.9–13; No. 3/4, April 1970, pp.41–52.

——, 'Schutz der Kulturgüter bei bewaffneten Konflikten', XI. 'Teil 1 und 2. Einige Gesichtspunkte der Durchsetzbarkeit in modernen Kriegen', *Mitteilungsblatt der Museen Osterreichs* (Vienna), Vol. 20, No. 5/6, June 1971, pp.71–7; No. 7/8, August 1970, pp.107–14.

FORSDYKE, J., 'The museum in war-time', *The British Museum Quarterly* (London), Vol. 15, 1952, pp.1–9.

FOUNDOUKIDES, E., 'L'Office international des musées et la protection des monuments et œuvres d'art en temps de guerre', *Mouseion* (Paris), Vol. 35–6, 1936, pp.187–200.

——, *La reconstruction sur le plan culturel*, Paris, International Museums Office, 1947.

FRANCIONI, F., 'World Cultural Heritage List and National Sovereignty', *Humanitäres Völkerrecht* (Bonn, Bochum), No. 4, 1993, pp.195–8.

FURR, N.R., *Safeguarding Our Cultural Heritage. A bibliography on the protection of museums, works of art, monuments, archives and libraries in time of war*, Washington, DC, The Library of Congress, 1952, 117 pp.

Gaagskaya Konventsiya 1954 goda o zashchite kulturnykh tsennostei v sluchae vooruzhennogo konflikta (The 1954 Hague Convention on the Protection of Cultural Property in the Event of Armed Conflict), Moscow, Yurizdat, 1957, 44 pp.

GALENSKAYA, L., 'International co-operation in cultural affairs', *The Hague Academy of International Law – Collected Courses*, Vol. 198, The Hague, 1986, pp.265–331.

——, *Muzy i pravo. Pravovye voprosy mezhdunarodnogo sotrudnichestva v oblasti kul'tury* (The muses and the law. Legal questions involved in international co-operation in the field of culture), Leningrad, Izdatel'stvo Leningradskogo universiteta, 1987, 220 pp.

GHAZALI, E., 'Contribution à l'étude des accords culturels vers un droit international de la culture', doctoral thesis, Paris, 1977.

GLASER, S., 'La protection internationale des valeurs humaines', *Revue générale de droit international public* (Paris), No. 2, 1957, pp.211 *et seq.*

GOY, R., 'Le retour et la restitution des biens culturels à leur pays d'origine en cas d'appropriatiojn illégale', *Revue générale de droit international public* (Paris), 1979, pp.962–85.

GRAHAM, G.M., 'Protection and revision of cultural property: issues of definition and justification', *The International Lawyer* (Chicago), Vol. 21, 1987, pp.755–93.

GRIFFO, P., *La difesa del patrimonio archeologico agrigentino contro i pericoli della recente guerra*, Agrigente, Soprintendenza alle antichità di Agrigento, 1946, 28 pp.

GRIGORE, C., I. CLOSCA and G. BADESCU, *La protection des biens culturels en Roumanie*, Bucharest, Association roumaine de droit humanitaire, 1994, 131 pp.

GRISOLIA, M., *La tutela delle cose d'arte*, Rome, Soc. Ed. del 'Foro Italiano', 1952, 546 pp.

GUENTHER-HORNIG, M., *Kunstschutz in den von Deutschland besetzten Gebieten 1939–1945*, Tübingen, Institut dür Besatzungsfragen, 1958, 144 pp.

'Guerre terrestre et aérienne. La protection des monuments et œuvres d'art au cours des conflits armés: projet de convention internationale et exposé des motifs', *Revue de droit international et de législation comparée* (Paris), Vol. XX, No. 3, 1939, pp.608–24.

'Haager Abkommen (Das) zum Schutze on Kulturgütern im Falle bewaffenter Zusammenstösse vom 14. Mai 1954', in H. KRAUS, *Internazionale Gegenwartsfragen*, Würzburg 1963, pp.445–56.

HALL, A.R., 'The recovery of cultural objects dispersed during World War II', *The Department of State Bulletin*, (Washington, DC), Vol. XXV, No. 635, 1951, pp.337–44.

——, 'U.S. program for return of historic objects to countries of origin, 1944–1954', *The Department of State Bulletin* (Washington, DC), Vol. XXXI, No. 797, 1954, pp.493–8.

HARTWIG, B., 'Der Schutz von Kulturgut im Kriege', *Bundeswehrwaltung* (Bonn), Vol. 5, 1961, pp.33–6.

——, 'Welche militärisch bedeutsamen Aenderungen bringt das Abkommen zum Schutz von Kulturgut bei bewaffneten Konflikten vom 14. mai 1954', *Revue de droit pénal militaire et de droit de la guerre* (Brussels), I-1, 1962, pp.85–96.

——, 'Die Konvention zum Schutz von Kulturgut bei bewaffneten Konflikten', *Neue Zeitschrift für Wehrrecht* (Berlin), Vol. 9, No.3/4, 1967, pp.97–102.

HAUNTON, M., 'Peacekeeping, Occupation and Cultural Property', *Humanitäres Völkerrecht* (Bonn, Bochum), No. 4, 1993, pp.199–203.

HERDEGEN, M., 'Der Kulturgüterschutz im Kriegsvölkerrecht', in R. DOLZER, E. JAYME and R. MUSSENGNUG *Rechtsfragen des internationalen*

Kulturgüterschutzes, Symposium vom 22/23 Juni 1990 im Internationalen Wissenschaftsforum Heidelberg, Heidelberg, C.F. Müller Juristischer Verlag, 1994, pp.161–73.

HOLLANDER, B., *The International Law of Art, for Lawyers, Collectors and Artists*, London, Bowes & Bowes, 1959, pp.17–55.

HOUDEK, F.G., *Protection of Cultural Property and Archaeological Resources*, New York, Oceana Publications, 1988.

HUPPERT, H.-H., *Die Vorbehaltsklausen der militärischen Notwendigkeit in den kriegsrechtlichen Konventionen – dargestellt am Kulturschutzabkommen om 14. Mai 1954*, Würzburg, Schmitt & Mayer, 1968, 132 pp.

'Information as an Instrument for Protection against War Damages to the Cultural Heritage', report from a seminar, June 1994, Stockholm, ICOMOS Sweden, The Central Board of National Antiquities, Swedish National Commission for UNESCO, 1994, 119 pp.

Istituto internazionale di diritto umanitario, *La protezione internazionale dei beni culturali/The international protection of cultural property/La protection internationale des biens culturels*, Rome, Dragan European Foundation, 1986, 246 pp.

JEVTICH, M., 'Zastita muzejskih sbirki u slucaju rata' (Protection of museum collections in the event of war), in Referenti VIII kongresu Saveza muzejskego drustava Jugoslavije. Pula, 26–28/5/1975, pt. 1, *Muzeologija* (Zagreb), Vol. 17, 1975, pp.38–50.

KAMENSKI, A., 'La Croix-Rouge des valeurs culturelles', *Journal de Genève* (Geneva), 23 March 1939.

KAMINSKI, T., 'Ochrona dobr kultury – najwyzsym moralnym nakazem i obowieszkem' (The protection of cultural property – an overriding moral obligation), *Biuletyn informacyjny Zarzadu muzéow i ochrony zabytkow* (Warsaw), No. 132, JanuaryMarch 1979, pp.115–19.

KILIAN, M., 'Kriegsvölkerrecht und Kulturgut: Die Bemühungen um den Schutz der Kulturgüter bei bewaffneten Auseinandersetzungen', *Neue Zeitschrift für Wehrrecht* (Berlin), Vol. 25, No. 2, 1983, pp.41–57.

KISS, A.-C., 'La notion de patrimoine commun de l'humanité', *The Hague Academy of International Law – Collected Courses*, The Hague, Vol. 175, II, 1982, pp.103–256.

KRAUS, H., 'Das Haager Abkommen zum Schutz von Kulturgütern im Falle bewaffneter Zusammenstösse vom 14. Mai 1954, in W. SCHÄTZEL and H.-J. SCHLOCHAUER, (eds), *Rechtsfragen der internationalen Organization: Festschrift für Hans Wehberg zu seinem 70. Geburtstag*, Frankfurt-am-Main, Klostermann, 1956, 408 pp.

——, 'Das Haager Abkommen zum Schutz von Kulturgütern im Falle bewaffneter Zusammenstösse vom 14. Mai 1954', in *Internationale Gegenwartsfragen: Völkerrecht: Staatenethik, Internationalpolitik: Ausgewählte kleine Schriften von Herbert Kraus*, Würzburg, Holzner-Verlag, 1963, pp.445–6.

'Kriegsvölkerrecht: Der Schutz von Kulturgut bei bewaffneten Konflikten', *Unterrichstblätter für die Bundeswehrverwaltung* (Hamburg), Vol. 3, 1964, pp.174–6.

Kulturelle Erbe (Das) im Risiko der, Modernität, Salzburger Symposium 1992 unter dem Ehrenschutz des Landeshauptmannes von Salzburg und des Bürgermeisters der Stadt Salzburg. Gerhard, SLADEK (ed.), Wien, 'Sicherheit & Demokratie', 1993, 279 pp.

(Der) Kulturgüterschutz bei bewaffneten Konflikten: Vorträge des 122. Kurses der Schweizerischen Verwaltungskurse an der Handelshochschule St. Gallen vom 10–11.4.1967, St. Gall, Handelshochschule St. Gall, 1967, 159 pp.

Kulturgüterschutz: Ein aufruf zu Transnationaler Aktion. Private Initiativen zwischen Interessen und Verantwortung, Wien, Osterreichische Gesellschaft für Kulturgüterschutz, 1995, 137 pp.

Kunstdenkmäler (Zerstörte) an der Westfront. Das Schonungslose Vorgehen der Engländer und Franzosen, 2, Auflage zusammengstellt im Amtlichen Auftrage, abgeschlossen im August 1917, Weimar, Kiepenheuer, 1917, 34 pp.

'La protection des biens culturels en cas de conflit armé' (mimeo), 126th course organized in agreement with the Département fédéral de l'intérieur and the Société suisse de cours administratifs at the École des hautes études économiques et sociales, St. Gall, on 25 and 26 January 1968 at Montreux, St. Gall, 1968, ix, 111 pp.

La protection des monuments et des œuvres d'art en temps de guerre, Paris, International Institute of Intellectual Co-operation, International Museums Office, 1939, 232 pp.

'La protection des monuments et objets historiques et artistiques contre les destructions de la guerre. Proposition de la Société néerlandaise d'archéologie', *Mouseion* (Paris), Vol. 39–40, 1937, pp.81–9.

LAPRADELLE, A. de, 'Le Pacte Roerich', *Nouvelles littéraires* (Paris), June 1937.

LAPUENTE Y GARCIA, A., *Appel aux intellectuels*, Buenos Aires, 1941, 14 pp.

LATTMANN, E., *Schutz der Kulturgüter bei bewaffneten Konflikten: Die schweizerische Gesetzgebung und Praxis aufgrund des Haager Abkommen vom 14. Mai 1954 für den Schutz von Kulturgut bei bewaffneten Konflikten*, Zurich, Schulthess, 1974, 210 pp.

LAVACHERY, H., *Les techniques de protection des biens culturels en cas de conflit armé*, Paris, UNESCO, 1954.

'Les mesures de protection prises dans différents pays contre les dangers de la guerre', *Mouseion* (Paris), suppl., September–October 1939, pp.13–22.

LORENTZ, S., 'Muzeum narodowe podozas powstania Warszawskiego' (The National Museum during the Warsaw insurrection of 1944 –

extracts from memoirs), *Muzeanictwo* (Poznan), No. 13, 1966, pp.7–10, 205.

MAGGIORE, R., 'Jus in bello: il problema della protezione dei beni culturali nei conflitti armati', *Ressegna dell'arma dei carabinieri* (Rome), No. 5, September–October 1975, pp.879–908.

MAKAGIANSAR, M., 'The thirtieth anniversary of the Convention for the Protection of Cultural Property in the Event of Armed Conflict (The Hague, 1954): Results and Prospects', in Istituto internazionale di diritto umanitario, *La protezione internazionale dei beni culturali/ The international protection of cultural property/La protection internationale des biens culturels*, Rome, Dragan European Foundation, 1986, pp.27–40.

MALINTROPPI, A., 'La protezione "speciale" della Città del Vaticano in caso di conflitto armato', *Revista di diritto internazionale* (Milan), Vol. 43, 1960, pp.607–29.

——, *La protezione dei beni culturali in caso di conflitto armato*, Milan, Giuffrè, 1966, 54 pp.

MARGUILLIER, A., *La destruction des monuments sur le front occidental. Réponse aux plaidoyers allemands*, Paris/Brussels, Van Oest & Ciel, 1919, 81 pp.

MATTEUCCI, M., 'Su la Convenzione per la protezione dei beni culturali in caso di conflitto armato', *Rivista di diritto internazionale* (Milan), Vol. 41, No. 4, 1958, pp.670–76.

'Meeting of Experts on the Application and Effectiveness of the Convention for the Protection of Cultural Property in the Event of Armed Conflict (The Hague, 14 May 1954), Final Report, The Hague, 5–7 July 1993', *Humanitäres Völkerrecht* (Bonn, Bochum), No. 4, 1993, pp.232–4.

'Meeting of Legal Experts on the Convention for the Protection of Cultural Property in the Event of Armed Conflict (The Hague, 1954), Vienna, 17–19 October 1983. Final Report', Paris, UNESCO (CLT-83/CONF.641/1), 14 pp.

MERANGHINI, U., 'La protezione dei beni culturali nella guerra moderna', *Archivio di ricerche giuridiche* (Modena), Vol. 16, 1962, pp.35–52.

——, 'La difesa dei beni culturali dall'offesa bellica', *Revue de droit pénal militaire et de droit de la guerre* (Brussels), VII-1, 1968, pp.133–46.

MERRIMAN, J.H., 'Two ways of thinking about cultural property', *American Journal of International Law*,Vol. 80, No. 4, pp.831–53.

MIHAN, G., *Looted Treasure: Germany's Raid on Art*, London, Alliance Press, 1943, 93 pp.

MONDEN, A., 'Art objects as common heritage of mankind', *Belgian Review of International Law* (Brussels), Vol. 19, 1986, 327–38.

MULINEN, F. de, 'A propos de l'application en Suisse de la Convention de La Haye pour la protection des biens culturels', *Revue militaire suisse* (Lausanne), No. 4, April 1965, pp.181–8.

NAFZIGER, J.A.R., 'UNESCO-centred management of international conflict over cultural property', *The Hastings Law Journal* (San Francisco), Vol. 27, No. 5, 1976, pp.1051–67.

——, International penal aspects of protecting cultural property', *International Lawyer* (Chicago), Vol. 19, No. 3, Summer 1985, pp.835–52.

——, 'International penal aspects of crimes against cultural property and the protection of cultural property', in BASSIOUNI, M. CHERIF (ed.), *International Criminal Law, Vol. I: Crimes*, Dobbs Ferry, NY, Transnational Publishers, Inc., 1986, pp.525–39.

NAHLIK, S.-E., *Grabiez Dziel sztuki: Prodowod zbrodni miedzynarodowej* (The pillage of works of art: a geneology of international crime), Wroclaw, Cracow, 1958, 482 pp.

——, 'Des crimes contre les biens culturels', *Newsletter of the Association of Attenders and Alumni of the Hague Academy of International Law* (The Hague), Vol. 29, 1959, pp.14–27.

——, 'Le cas des collections polonaises au Canada: considérations juridiques', *Annuaire polonais des affaires internationales* (Warsaw), 1959–1960, pp.172–90.

___, *Miedzynarodowa ochrona dobr kulturalnych: ochrona prawna w razie konfliktow zbrojnych* (The international protection of cultural property: legal protection in the event of armed conflict), Warsaw, 1962, 170 pp.

——, 'Sprawa ochrony dobr kulturalnych w razie konfliktu zbrojnego' (The protection of cultural property in the event of armed conflict), *Newsletter of the Polish National Commission for UNESCO* (Warsaw), No. 9, 1962, pp.19–21.

——, 'La protection internationale des biens culturels en cas de conflit armé', *Recueil des cours de l'Académie de droit international* (The Hague), Vol. 120, II, 1967, pp.61–163.

——, 'On some deficiencies of The Hague Convention of 1954 on the Protection of Cultural Property in the Event of Armed Conflict', *Newsletter of the Association of Attenders and Alumni of the Hague Academy of International Law* (The Hague), Vol. 44, 1974, pp.100–108.

——, 'International law and the protection of cultural property in armed conflicts', *The Hastings Law Journal* (San Francisco), Vol. 27, No. 5, 1976, pp.1069–87.

——, 'Convention for the Protection of Cultural Property in the Event of Armed Conflict, The Hague 1954: general and special protection', in Istituto internazionale di diritto umanitario, *La protezione internazionale dei beni culturali/The international protection of cultural property/La protection internationale des biens culturels*, Rome, Dragan European Foundation, 1986, pp.87–1000.

——, 'Protection des biens culturels', in *Les dimensions internationales du droit humanitaire*, Geneva/Paris, Editions Pedone/Institut Henry-Dunant/UNESCO, 1986, pp.237–49.

——, 'Protection of cultural property', in *International Dimensions of Humanitarian Law*, Geneva/Henry Dunant Institute/Paris/ UNESCO, 1988, pp.203–15.

——, 'Protección de los bienes culturales', in *Las dimensiones internacionales del derecho humanitario*, Madrid, Tecnos, Istituto Henry Dunant/UNESCO, 1990, pp.203–13.

——, 'Zashchita kul'turnykh tsennostei', in *Mezhdunarodnoe gumanitarnoe pravo*, Moskva, Institut problem gumanizma i meloserdiya, 1993, pp.277–92.

NICHOLAS, L.H., *The Rope of Europa. The Fate of Europe's Treasures in the Third Reich and the Second World War*, New York, Alfred A. Knopf, 1994, 500 pp. (Includes an extensive bibliography.)

NIEC, H. 'The "Human Dimension" of the protection of Cultural Property in the Event of Armed Conflict', *Humanitäres Völkerrecht* (Bonn, Bochum), No. 4, 1993, pp.204–12.

NIECIOWNA, H., 'Sovereign rights to cultural property', *Polish Yearbook of International Law* (Warsaw), No. 4, 1971, pp.239–53.

NOBLECOURT, A., *Protection of Cultural Property in the Event of Armed Conflicts*. Paris, UNESCO, 1958, 346 pp.

NOWLAN, J., 'Cultural Property and the Nuremberg War Crimes Trial', *Humanitäres Völkerrecht* (Bonn, Bochum), No. 4, 1993, pp.221–3.

NUNES Y DOMINGUEZ, J. de J., 'La protection des monuments historiques et artistiques en temps de guerre et le droit international', in *Premier Congrès d'études internationales organisé par l'Association des études internationales. Publication de l'Institut de hautes études internationales de l'Université de Paris*, Paris, Les Editions Internationales, 1938, pp.68–83.

O'KEEFE, P.J. and L.V. PROTT, 'Cultural Property', in R. BERNHARDT (ed.), *Encyclopedia of Public International Law*, Vol. 9, Amsterdam, North-Holland Publishing Company, 1985, pp.62–4.

ORYSLAK, S., 'Ochrona zabytkow – obowiazkem panstwa i powinnoscia jego obywateli' (The protection of historic monuments: the duty of the State and of its citizens), *Biuletyn informacyjny Zarzadu muzéow i ochrony zabytkow* (Warsaw), No. 115, March–April 1975, pp.142–8.

PENNA, L. Rao, 'State and individual responsibility for application of The Hague Convention', in Istituto internazionale di diritto umanitario, *La protezione internazionale dei beni culturali/The international protection of cultural property/La protection internationale des biens culturels*, Rome, Dragan European Foundation, 1986, pp.77–80.

PEROW, A., *Roerich and his Banner of Peace*, Chicago, Rassvet, 1936.

PREDOME, G., 'Per une migliore protezione del patrimonio artistico monumentale in caso di guerra', *Rivista di studi politici internazionalia* (Florence), Vol. 17, 1950, pp.646–50.

PREUX, J. de, 'La Convention de La Haye et le récent développement du droit des conflits armés', in Istituto internazionale di dirritto umanitario, *La protezione internazionale dei beni culturali/The international protection of cultural property/La protection internationale des biens culturels*, Rome, Dragan European Foundation, 1986, pp.107–17.

Protection des biens culturels en cas de conflit armé: Convention de La Haye du 14 mai 1954, Règlement d'exécution de la Convention, Protocole de La Haye du 14 mai 1954, Berne, Federal Department of the Interior, 1963, 36 pp.

PROTT, L.V., 'Commentary: 1954 Hague Convention for the Protection of Cultural Property in the Event of Armed Conflict', in N. RONZITTI (ed.), *The Law of Naval Warfare*, Dordrecht, Martinus Nijhoff Publishers, 1988, pp.582–93.

——, 'The Protocol to the Convention for the Protection of Cultural Property in the Event of Armed Conflict (The Hague Convention), 1954', *Humanitäres Völkerrecht* (Bonn, Bochum), No. 4, 1993, pp.191–4.

PROTT, L.V. and P.J. O'KEEFE, *Law and the Cultural Heritage*, Vol. I, *Discovery and Excavation*, Abingdon, Professional Books Ltd., 1984, 434 pp.

QUYNN, D.M. 'The art confiscation of the Napoleonic wars', *American Historical Review* (Washington, DC), No. 3, 1945.

——, 'Legal expert meeting on the Convention on the Protection of Cultural Property in the Event of Armed Conflict (The Hague, 1954), Vienna, 17–19 October 1983. Final Report', Paris, UNESCO, (Doc. CLT–83/CONF.641/I.), 14 pp.

RENAN, J., 'L'organisation de la défense du patrimoine artistique et historique espagnol pendant la guerre civile', *Mousaion*, No. 39/40, 1937, pp.7–66.

RONARD, O., 'Le danger aérien et la sauvegarde des objets d'art aux Pays-Bas', *Revue générale de droit aérien* (Paris), Vol. 8, 1939, pp.68–75.

ROUSSEAU, C., *Le droit des conflits armés*, Paris, Editions A. Pédone, 1983, pp.132–3.

SAINT-PAUL, G., *Le lieu de Genève*, Strasbourg, Les éditions universitaires de Strasbourg, 1936, 24 pp.

SARHOLZ, H., 'Der Schutz des Kulturguts im Kriege Eine völkerrechtliche und sittliche Verpflichtung im Frieden. Ein Rückblick und seine Folgerungen', *Ziviler Luftschutz* (Coblenz), No. 12, 1959, pp.343–9.

SAUNIER, C., *Les conqêtes artistiques de la Révolution et de l'Empire*, Paris, H. Laurens, 1902.

SCHEER, B.D., *Schutz von Kulturgut bei bewaffneten Konflikten*, Bonn/ Bad Godesberg, Bundesamt für zivilen Bevölkerungsschutz, 1973, 39 pp.

SCHNEIDER, J.T., *Report to the Secretary of the Interior on the Preservation of Historic Sites and Buildings*, Washington DC, US Department of the Interior, 1935.

Schutz (Der) von Kulturgütern bei bewaffneten Konflikten: Haager Konvention vom 14. Mai 1954 für den Schutz on Kulturgütern bei bewaffneten Konflikten, Bonn/Bad Godesberg, Bundesamt für zivilen Bevölkerungsschutz, 1966, 31 pp.

Schutz (Der) on Kulturgut bei bewaffneten Konflikten in Bild und Wort, Bonn, Bundesministerium der Verteidigung, 1972, 47 pp.

'Schutz (Der) von Kulturgut in bewaffneten Konflikten', *Zivilschutz* (Berne), Vol. 25, No. 9, 1978, pp.277–81.

Schweizerische Verwaltungskurse an der Hochschule St. Gallen: 122. Kurs, St. Gallen, 10–11 April 1967. Der Kulturgüterschutz bei bewaffneten Konflikten, St. Gall, Institut für Verwaltungskurse, 1967.

Schweizerische Verwaltungskurse an der Hochschule St Gallen: 126. Kurs, Montreux, 25.–26. Januar 1968. La protection des biens culturels en cas de conflit armé, St. Gall, Institut für Verwaltungskurse, 1968.

SVENSMA, T.P., 'The intergovernmental conference and convention for the protection of cultural property', *Library Review*, (Copenhagen), Ejnar Munksgaard, 1954, pp.76–83.

SHIBAYEW, Vl, *Roerich Pact signed by United States and all Latin American Governments*, Lahore, Lion Press, 1935.

SIEGRIEST, M. *Nicholas Roerich, Apostle of World Unity*, reprint from World Unity by Society of Friends, New York, Roerich Museum, 1928.

SIEROSZEWSKI, W., 'Konwencja haska z 1954 r. a konflikt na Bliskim Wschodzie' (The Hague Convention of 1954 and the Middle-East conflict), *Ochrana zabytkow* (Warsaw), Vol. 26, No. 3, 1973, pp.170–5'.

——, *Ochrona prawna dobr kultury na forum miedzynarodowym w swietle legislacji UNESCO* (The legal protection of cultural goods in the international forum in the light of UNESCO legislation), Warsaw, Biblioteka muzealnictwa i ochrony zbytkow, B. series, 1974, 246 pp.

SMIRNOFF, S., *Historische Baudenkmaler und deren Rechtschutz in Kriegszeiten*, Zurich, Fretz und Wasmuth, 1941, 14 pp.

SOLF, W.A., 'Cultural property, protection in armed conflict, in R. BERNHARDT (ed.), *Encyclopedia of Public International Law*, Amsterdam, North-Holland Publishing Company, Vol. 9, 1985, pp.64–8.

Sonderausstellung Kulturgüterschutz-Vorsorge zum Schutz des Kulturellen Erbes in Zeiten on Not und Gefahr, UNESCO Convention of the

Hague, 1954. Vienna, Österreichische Gesellschaft für Kulturgüterschutz, 1983, 73 pp.

STAVRAKI, E., 'La Convention pour la protection des biens culturels en cas de conflit armé: une Convention du droit international humanitaire', Thesis for a doctorate in law, mimeo, Paris, University of Paris I–Panthéon-Sorbonne, 1987–8, 482 pp.

STRAHL, R., 'The retention and retrieval of art and antiquities through international and national means: the tug of war over cultural property', *Brooklyn Journal of International Law* (New York), Vol. 5, No. 1, 1979, pp.103–28.

STREBEL, H., 'Die Haager Konvention zum Schutze der Kulturgüter im Fall eines bewaffneten Konflikts vom 14. Mai 1954', *Zeitschrift für ausländisches öffentliches Recht und Völkerrecht* (Stuttgart), Vol. 16, No. 1, 1955, pp.33–75.

STREIFF, S., 'Kulturgüterschutz als nationale Aufgabe und Völkerrechtliche Verpflichtung', *Zivilschutz* (Berne), Vol. 12, No. 3, 1965, pp.1–7.

——, 'Der Kulturgüterschild: Das Kennzeichen das Haager Abkommens für den Schutz von Kulturgut bei bewaffneten Konflikten, *Zivilschutz* (Berne), Vol. 17, No. 6, 1970, pp.161–4.

——, 'L'écusson des biens culturels. Le signe distinctif de la Convention de La Haye pour la protection des biens culturels en cas de conflit armé, *Protection civile* (Berne), No. 9, 1970, 4 pp.

——, 'Das Personal des Kulturgüterschutzes. Ein Sonderfall des Kriegsvölkerrechtes', *Der Bund* (Berne), No. 261, 8 November 1971.

SUJANOVA, O., 'Ochrana pamiatok v pripade mimoriadnych okolnosti', *Muzeum* (Bratislava), Vol. 18, No. 4, 1973, pp.212–19.

'Symposium organized on the occasion of the 30th Anniversary of the Hague Convention on the Protection of Cultural Property in the Event of Armed Conflict, in co-operation with UNESCO, ICRC, Faculta di scienze politiche, C. Alfieri, Centro studi turistici di Firenze under the auspices of the Italian Ministries of Cultural Property and Tourism, Florence, 22–24 November 1984', in Istituto internazionale di diritto umanitario, *La protezione internazionale dei beni culturali/The international protection of cultural property/La protection internationale des biens culturels*, Rome, Dragan European Foundation, 1986.

TAUDON, R.C., 'Roerich Pact Movement', *Allahbad Leader*, 17 October 1936.

TAYLOR, F.H. *The Taste of Angels. A history of art collecting from Rameses to Napoleon*, Boston, Little Brown, 1948.

——, 'The international protection of cultural property', *Proceedings of the American Society of International Law* (Washington, DC), 1977, pp.196–207.

'The international protection of works of art and historic monuments', in *Documents and State Papers*, Washington, DC, US Government Printing Office, June 1949. pp.821–71.

TOMAN, J., *UNESCO's Mandate for Implementation of the Hague Convention for the Protection of Cultural Property in the Event of Armed Conflict*, Geneva, 1983, 109 pp.

——, 'La protection des biens culturels dans les conflits armés internationaux: cadre juridique et institutionnel', in SWINIARSKI, C. (ed.), *Studies and Essays on International Humanitarian Law and Red Cross Principles, in Honour of Jean Pictet*, Geneva/The Hague, ICRC, Martinus Nijhoff Publishers, 1984, pp.559–80.

——, *La protection des biens culturels en cas de conflit armé: projet d'un programme d'action. Étude et commentaire*, Paris, UNESCO, 1984.

TREUE, W., *Kunstraub: Über die Schicksale von Kunstwerken in Krieg, Revolution und Frieden*, Düsseldorf, Droste Verlag, 1957, 358 pp; English translation: Art Plunder. The fate of works of art in war, revolution and peace, London/New York, J. Day, 1960, 264 pp.

TULPINCK, C. 'Les œuvres de l'intelligence devant la guerre', *Revue de l'art ancien et moderne*, (Paris), Vol. 68, November 1935, pp.326–30.

UNESCO, *Textes ayant servi de précédents au projet de Convention pour la protection des biens culturels en cas de conflit armé* (UNESCO/ODG/2, 18 August 1952).

——, *La protection des biens culturels en cas de conflit armé: informations sur la mise en œuvre de la Convention pour la protection des biens culturels en cas de conflit armé, La Haye, 1954*, Paris, UNESCO/SHC/MD/1, 1967, 42 pp.

——, *Protection of cultural property in case of armed conflict: Information on the implementation of the Convention for the Protection of Cultural Property in the Event of Armed Conflict, The Hague, 1954*, Paris, UNESCO/SHC/MD/1, 1967, 42 pp.

——, *Information on the Implementation of the Convention for the Protection of Cultural Property in the Event of Armed Conflict, The Hague, 1954*, Paris, UNESCO/SHC/MD/6, 1970, 31 pp.

——, *La protection des biens culturels en cas de conflit armé: informations sur la mise en œuvre de la Convention pour la protection des biens culturels en cas de conflit armé, La Haye, 1954*, Paris, UNESCO/SHC/MD/6, 1970, 31 pp.

UNVERHAU, K. 'Der Schutz on Kulturgut bei bewaffneten Konflikten', doctoral thesis, Göttingen, 1955, 113 pp.

US Committee on Conservation of Cultural Resources, *The Protection of Cultural Resources Against the Hazards of War. A Preliminary Handbook*, Washington, DC, 1942, 46 pp.

VEDOVATO, G., 'La protezione internazionale dei monumenti storici contro le offense aeree, con une postilla su iniziative svizzere per la tutela di Firenze', *Rivista di studi politici internazionali* (Florence), 1944, 39 pp.

——, 'La protezione internazionale dei monumenti storici contro le offense aeree', in VEDOVATO, G. *Diritto internazionale bellico: tre studi*, Florence, G.C. Sansoni, 1946, pp.175–217.

——, *Il patrimonio storico-artistico-culturale e la guerra aerea*, Prolusione inaugurale dell'Anno academico 1953–1954, Florence, Scuola di guerra aerea, 1954, 95 pp.

——, 'La protezione del patrimonio artistico, storico e culturale nella guerra moderna', in Congrès de Florence 1961, *Recueil de la Société internationale de droit pénal militaire et de droit de la guerre*, Strasbourg, Vol. 2, 1963, pp.117–39.

VERGIER-BOIMOND, J. *Villes sanitaires et cités d'asile. Contribution à l'étude des moyens de protection des formations sanitaires de l'armée et des populations civiles dans la guerre moderne*, Paris, Editions internationales, 1938, 368 pp.

VERRI, P. 'La suerte de los bienes culturales en los conflictos armados', *Revista internacional de la Cruz Roja* (Geneva), 10th year, No. 68, March–April 1985, pp.67–85; No. 69, May–June 1985, pp.127–39.

——, 'Le destin des biens culturels dans les conflits armés', *Revue internationale de la Croix-Rouge* (Geneva), No. 752, March–April 1985, pp.67–85; No. 753, May–June 1985, pp.127–39.

——, 'The condition of cultural property in armed conflict', *International Review of the Red Cross* (Geneva), 25th year, No. 245, March–April 1985, pp.67–85; No. 246, May–June 1985, pp.127–39.

——, 'Le condizioni dei beni culturali nei conflitti armati dall'antichità alla vigilia della Seconda Guerra mondiale', in Istituto internazionale di diritto umanitario, *La protezione internazionale dei beni culturali/The international protection of cultural property/La protection internationale des biens culturels*, Rome, Dragan European Foundation, 1986, pp.41–68.

VISSCHER, C. de, 'La protection internationale des objets d'art et des monuments historiques', part 1: 'La conservation du patrimoine artistique et historique en temps de paix', *Revue de droit international et de législation comparée* (Paris), 1935, pp.32–74; Part 2: 'Les monuments historiques et les œuvres d'art en temps de guerre et dans les traités de paix', *Revue de droit international et de législation comparée*, 1935, pp.246–88.

——, 'International protection of works of art and historic monuments', *International Information and Cultural Series*, (Washington, DC), No. 8, 1949, pp.821–71.

WACHTER, O., *Restaurierung und Erhaltung von Büchern, Archivalien und Graphiken: mit Berücksichtigung des Kulturgüterschutzes laut Haager Konvention von 1954*, Vienna, H. Böhlau, 1975, 281 pp.

WEHBERG, H., 'Der Schutz der Kunstwerke im Kriege', *Museumskunde Zeitschrift für Verwaltung und Technik öffentlicher und privater Sammlungen*, Vol. XI, No. 2, pp.49–68.

WILHELM, R.-J., 'La Croix-Rouge des monuments', *Revue internationale de la Croix-Rouge* (Geneva), No. 430, October 1954, pp.793–815.

——, 'Das "Rote Kreuz der Denkmäler": Chronik', *Revue internationale de la Croix-Rouge – Deutsche Beilage* (Geneva), Vol. VI, May 1955, pp.76–88, and July 1955, pp.122–8.

——, 'La "Cruz Roja de los monumentos". Crónica', *Review internationale de la Croix-Rouge– Suplemento Español* (Geneva), Vol. VII, May–July 1955, pp.77–88 and 118–23.

——, 'The "Red Cross of monuments". Chronicle', *Revue internationale de la Croix-Rouge – English Supplement*, (Geneva), Vol. VIII, May 1955, pp.76–87, and July 1955, pp.118–23.

WILLIAMS, S., *The International and National Protection of Movable Cultural Property: a comparative study*, Dobbs Ferry, NY, Oceana Publications, 1978.

WYSS, M.P, *Kultur als eine Dimension des Völkerrechtsordnung. Vom Kulturgüterschutz zur internationalen kulturelle Kooperation*, Zurich, Schulthess Polygraphischer Verlag, 1992, 353 pp.

ZIETELMAN, E., 'Der Krieg und die Denkmalpflege', *Zeitschrift für Völkerrecht*, (Wroclaw), Vol. 10, 1917–18, pp.1–19.

NOTE

1   For further bibliographical information, particularly on international humanitarian law, we recommend the *Bibliography of International Humanitarian Law Applicable in Armed Conflicts*, 2nd revised and enlarged edition, Geneva, ICRC/ Henry Dunant Institute, 1987, 606pp.

Index

accommodation, military 102–3
acts of hostility 138, 139, 152, 154, 165, 175, 297, 388
adequate distance 97, 100, 104, 117, 286
  definition 101, 109
aerial warfare 178–9, 256
  see also Hague Rules concerning the control of radio in time of war and air warfare (1922)
aerodromes 97, 100, 101, 102, 106, 124, 140
aircraft 30, 153–4, 168, 170, 178
Allied High Command 20, 338
American Commission for the Protection and Salvation of Artistic and Historic Monuments in War Areas 20
Angkor 80, 218, 225
archaeological services 355
archaeological sites 41, 45, 49, 51, 53, 64, 87–8, 265, 344, 359, 360
  control of 363
  in occupied territory 87–8
  see also International Council on Monuments and Sites (ICOMOS)
architectural monuments *see* monuments
archives 5, 45, 47, 49, 52, 53, 60, 294, 336, 360
armed conflict 3, 195, 196–7, 259, 322, 355–6, 361, 369–70, 371, 372, 373
  immediate entry into Register on outbreak of 129, 134
  international 25, 26, 203, 215, 369, 379–80, 386, 390
  protection of victims of 379–81
  see also internal conflicts
armed forces 47, 60, 74, 76, 91–3, 104, 167, 294, 361, 386
  legal advisers to 94, 276

regulations and instructions 19, 91, 92, 93, 139, 300
specialist personnel within 91, 93–4, 174, 175
training 19, 91, 92–3, 147, 273–6, 300
of United Nations 29, 93, 203–5, 355
see also land forces; naval forces
Armistice Agreements 20–1
armlets 176, 187, 189, 191, 192, 194
arms reduction 14, 289
art
  buildings dedicated to 7, 9, 10, 11, 12, 18, 45, 46, 47, 177, 178, 295, 296, 297, 298, 299
  definition 51
  monuments of 41, 45, 50–1
  works of 5, 6, 7–8, 9, 11, 19, 20, 21, 25, 29, 40, 45, 46, 51, 52–3, 59, 71, 83, 91, 95, 99, 151, 208, 292, 294, 295, 296, 297, 298, 299, 336–7, 379, 380, 382, 387, 391, 392
Athens Conference (1931) 18
attacks 103–4, 139, 297, 384, 391–2, 393
authorities
  civilian 80, 91, 93–4, 166, 175, 210, 341
  military 79, 91, 93–4, 146–7, 166
  national 61–2, 83, 84, 85, 86, 94, 107, 146, 147, 344, 345

banditry 210
Bluntschli, Jean-Gaspar 7–8, 151, 152
Bolan, P.J. 46
bombardment 7, 9, 10, 46, 62, 90, 98, 99, 101, 261, 297
  aerial 13, 103, 179
  land 13
  naval 11–13, 47, 53, 177–8, 318, 319
booby-traps 28–9
books 25, 40, 45, 49, 51, 52, 93, 360
  see also libraries
booty 4, 7, 170